The Regulation of Intelligence Activities under International Law

ELGAR INTERNATIONAL LAW

Editorial Board: Fausto Pocar, *University of Milan, Italy and ICTY, The Hague, the Netherlands*, Christian Tams, *University of Glasgow, UK*, Nigel D. White, *University of Nottingham, UK*, Jacob Katz Cogan, *University of Cincinnati, USA* and Hilary Charlesworth, *Australian National University*

This important series will present high quality monographs that analyse current thinking and research across the field of international law, rigorously examining key concepts as well as provoking debate and questions for further research. Some volumes will draw on insights from disciplines other than law, such as economics and politics, in an attempt to arrive at a genuinely inter-disciplinary perspective. Seeking to attract original thinking and new, challenging research, proposals are encouraged that primarily engage with new and previously under-developed themes in the field, or alternatively offer an innovative analysis of areas of uncertainty in the existing law.

For a full list of Edward Elgar published titles, including the titles in this series, visit our website at www.e-elgar.com.

The Regulation of Intelligence Activities under International Law

Sophie Duroy

Fellow, KFG Berlin-Potsdam Research Group 'The International Rule of Law: Rise or Decline?', Berlin, Germany

ELGAR INTERNATIONAL LAW

Cheltenham, UK • Northampton, MA, USA

© Sophie Duroy 2023

All rights reserved. No part of this publication may be reproduced, stored in a retrieval system or transmitted in any form or by any means, electronic, mechanical or photocopying, recording, or otherwise without the prior permission of the publisher.

Published by
Edward Elgar Publishing Limited
The Lypiatts
15 Lansdown Road
Cheltenham
Glos GL50 2JA
UK

Edward Elgar Publishing, Inc.
William Pratt House
9 Dewey Court
Northampton
Massachusetts 01060
USA

A catalogue record for this book
is available from the British Library

Library of Congress Control Number: 2023934059

This book is available electronically in the Elgaronline
Law subject collection
http://dx.doi.org/10.4337/9781803927084

ISBN 978 1 80392 707 7 (cased)
ISBN 978 1 80392 708 4 (eBook)

Printed and bound by CPI Group (UK) Ltd, Croydon, CR0 4YY

Contents

List of figures	vi
List of tables	vii
Acknowledgements	viii
List of abbreviations	x

1 Introduction to *The Regulation of Intelligence Activities under International Law* 1

PART I LEGALITY

2 Intelligence activities and international law 32

3 Mapping state responsibility in the CIA war on terror 70

PART II ACCOUNTABILITY

4 International legal accountability for an internationally wrongful act resulting from intelligence activities 122

5 Effective accountability 154

6 International legal accountability in the CIA war on terror 184

PART III COMPLIANCE

7 State compliance with international law in intelligence matters: a behavioural approach 250

8 Epilogue: comprehensive regulation in the twenty-first-century security landscape 289

Index 300

Figures

1.1	The regulation of intelligence activities under international law	4
5.1	Pyramids of supports and sanctions	172
6.1	The United States' accountability network	188
6.2	Djibouti's accountability network	209
6.3	Poland's accountability network	218
6.4	The Gambia's accountability network	227
6.5	The United Kingdom's accountability network	238

Tables

3.1	CIA secret detention sites	77
3.2	Public knowledge timeline concerning the CIA programme	96
4.1	Forms of international legal accountability	130
5.1	Evaluation factors	177
6.1	Evaluation of the United States' accountability network	189
6.2	Evaluation of Djibouti's accountability network	211
6.3	Evaluation of Poland's accountability network	220
6.4	Evaluation of the Gambia's accountability network	228
6.5	Evaluation of the United Kingdom's accountability network	239
6A.1	Competent institutional accountability mechanisms regarding the CIA war on terror	247
7.1	Decision-making model	267
7.2	Factors	268
7.3	Case-study design	270
7.4	France	274
7.5	The United States	277
7A.1	Scoring table	284

Acknowledgements

First and foremost I am grateful to Martin Scheinin for his boundless support and confidence in my ability to write this book. I am indebted to his work as UN Special Rapporteur on the Promotion and Protection of Human Rights and Fundamental Freedoms while Countering Terrorism and I consider myself privileged to have benefited from his insights and support throughout. I would also like to thank Anne van Aaken, whose work has been inspirational for a substantial part of this book and whose comments have greatly improved its content. I am further indebted to Sarah Nouwen and Asaf Lubin for taking the time to thoroughly read and comment on an earlier version of the manuscript.

This book has benefited from many friendly conversations in the gardens of Villa Salviati, on the Badia Fiesolana terrace, and in (virtual) meeting rooms. For these, I am particularly grateful to Giovanna Gilleri, Arpitha Kodiveri, Kerttuli Lingenfelter, Matilda Merenmies, Rebecca Munro, Jasmine Sommardal, Aurélie Villanueva, and Rebecca Williams. Separate thanks are due to Hannah Adzakpa and Nastazja Potocka-Sionek for their patient comments on many drafts as part of our writers' group. I hope they won't resent me for revealing here that we named it the Justice League.

The book also benefited from the support of the residents and neighbours of the KFG villa, from the proposal stage to the submission of the manuscript. Particular thanks go to Helmut Aust, Tomer Broude, James Devaney, Prisca Feihle, Rishi Gulati, Liliya Khasanova, Liesbeth Lijnzaad, Nina Reiners, Hallvard Sandven, Sophie Schuberth, Praggya Surana, and Nathanael van der Beek. I am further grateful to all my KFG colleagues for their support and intellectual wit, and for always pushing me further in my thinking. Additional thanks are due to Tamara Kübler, student assistant at the KFG, whose help with designing several of the book's figures has been invaluable.

Ce livre est dédié à mon père, qui m'a enseigné le pouvoir des mots écrits et la nécessité de se préoccuper des personnes au cœur des événements historiques.

FUNDING

The research leading to this book was carried out thanks to funding from the French Ministry of Research, Higher Education and Innovation and the European University Institute. I finalised the manuscript during a fellowship at the Kolleg-Forschungsgruppe (KFG) 'The International Rule of Law: Rise or Decline?', funded by the Deutsche Forschungsgemeinschaft.

PREVIOUS PUBLICATION

Short excerpts of Chapter 1 have been published in: S. Duroy (2020) 'Remedying Violations of Human Dignity and Security: State Accountability for Counterterrorism Intelligence Cooperation'. In: Christophe Paulussen and Martin Scheinin (eds) *Human Dignity and Human Security in Times of Terrorism*. T.M.C. Asser Press, The Hague.

Short excerpts of Chapter 3 (including Table 3.1) have been published in my contribution, entitled 'Black Sites', to the *Elgar Encyclopedia on Human Rights*, edited by Christina Binder, Manfred Nowak, Jane A. Hofbauer, and Philipp Janig (Edward Elgar Publishing, 2022).

A version of Chapter 7 'State Compliance with International Law in Intelligence Matters: A Behavioural Approach' has appeared in the *Journal of International Dispute Settlement*, Volume 13 Issue 2 (June 2022) (Oxford University Press).

Sophie Duroy
Berlin, September 2022

Abbreviations

9/11	11 September 2001
ACHPR	African Charter on Human and Peoples' Rights
ACHR	American Convention on Human Rights
ACommHPR	African Commission on Human and Peoples' Rights
ACtHPR	African Court on Human and Peoples' Rights
ASR	International Law Association, Draft Articles on the Responsibility of States for Internationally Wrongful Acts
CAT	United Nations Convention against Torture and Other Cruel, Inhuman or Degrading Treatment or Punishment
CCPR	United Nations Human Rights Committee
CED	United Nations Committee on Enforced Disappearance
CIA	United States Central Intelligence Agency
CIDT	Cruel, inhuman, and degrading treatment
CIL	Customary international law
CoE	Council of Europe
CPED	International Convention for the Protection of All Persons from Enforced Disappearance
DoD	United States Department of Defense
ECCJ	ECOWAS Community Court of Justice
ECHR	European Convention on Human Rights
ECOWAS	Economic Community of West African States
ECPT	European Committee for the Prevention of Torture
ECtHR	European Court of Human Rights
EEZ	Exclusive economic zone
EIT	Enhanced interrogation techniques
EU	European Union
HRC	UN Human Rights Council
HVD	High-value detainee

IAC	International armed conflict
IACHR	Inter-American Commission on Human Rights
IACtHR	Inter-American Court of Human Rights
ICAO	International Civil Aviation Organization
ICC	International Criminal Court
ICCPR	International Covenant on Civil and Political Rights
ICJ	International Court of Justice
ICRC	International Committee of the Red Cross
ICTY	International Criminal Tribunal for the former Yugoslavia
IHL	International humanitarian law
IHRL	International human rights law
ILC	International Law Commission
MoN	Memorandum of Notification
NATO	North Atlantic Treaty Organization
NIAC	Non-international armed conflict
NSA	United States National Security Agency
OAS	Organization of American States
OLC	Office of Legal Counsel (United States Government, Department of Justice)
OSCE	Organization for Security and Co-operation in Europe
OTP	ICC Office of the Prosecutor
PCIJ	Permanent Court of International Justice
PTC	ICC Pre-Trial Chamber
SOFA	Statute of Forces Agreement
SSCI	United States Senate Select Committee on Intelligence
UN	United Nations
UNCAT	United Nations Committee against Torture
UNCLOS	United Nations Convention on the Law of the Sea
UNGA	United Nations General Assembly
UNSC	United Nations Security Council
UPR	Universal periodic review
VCCR	Vienna Convention on Consular Relations
VCDR	Vienna Convention on Diplomatic Relations

WGAD United Nations Working Group on Arbitrary Detentions
WHO   World Health Organization

1. Introduction to *The Regulation of Intelligence Activities under International Law*

This book starts with 9/11.[1] It also starts with a personal disclosure: 9/11 is the first world event I remember. I grew up in a time when, in matters of counter-terrorism, the end justified all the means. It took me years to start perceiving this reality, which older generations called the 'new normal', as contingent. While I was learning to question the only normality I had ever known, this post-9/11 'new normal' was slowly leading to a paradigm shift in the regulation of intelligence activities under international law. This book theorises the new regulatory paradigm.

As should be clear, 9/11 itself did not change the law. Nor did the attacks damage Western values, laws, or institutions. States did this through their responses to the attacks. States' values, laws, and institutions could very well still be the same today as they were on 10 September 2001 had their responses been compliant with the rule of law. As we all know, this is not what happened. Yet, as states' intelligence practice changed in response to 9/11, the international legal framework governing intelligence stayed the same. If anything, it became clearer. The legality (or lack thereof) of specific intelligence activities remained identical before and after 9/11: what was unlawful on 10 September did not become lawful on 12 September.

However, the US-led 'global war on terror' launched in response to 9/11 had an unintended consequence, namely state accountability for violations of international law resulting from intelligence activities. These accountability proceedings before international forums constituted the first ever affirmation of international law's *ratione materiae* application to intelligence activities, i.e., state activities that had so far been widely considered as outside international law's realm. Notwithstanding, the impact of state accountability goes much further than the mere clarification of what constitutes legally acceptable state conduct. Accountability proceedings also affect state behaviour and compliance, especially when part of a broader regulatory strategy. By ignoring and

---

[1] '9/11' is the commonly accepted way to refer to the attacks of 11 September 2001 carried out by al Qaeda against the United States.

distorting applicable legal norms, the US-led war on terror inadvertently led to the reaffirmation and stronger enforcement of these norms, influencing states' compliance with international law in intelligence matters. In other words, the attempt to evade all legal constraints upon intelligence after 9/11 indirectly backfired, resulting in the emergence of a comprehensive model of regulation.

In this book, I theorise the regulation of intelligence activities building on these three layers: legality (Part I); accountability (Part II); and compliance (Part III). On the eve of 9/11, only the first layer (legality) existed, though both this affirmation and the content of the applicable legal framework were highly disputed. Today, more than twenty years after 9/11, international practice has made it possible to identify a comprehensive and integrated model of regulation. Further, drawing on the lessons from the past two decades of intelligence practice allows me to make a normative claim, namely that compliance with international law in their intelligence activities serves states' national security interests.

In this chapter, I present the book's argument, first in the abstract and then within the historical and legal context of the twenty-first-century security landscape, identifying the main gaps that this book fills (section 1.1). I then define the key terms of the research, namely 'intelligence activities' and 'regulation under international law' (section 1.2). In section 1.3, I present and justify my methodological approach and choices. Finally, I outline the structure of the book (section 1.4).

1.1 THE ARGUMENT

The argument I present in this book is that intelligence activities are comprehensively regulated in the international legal order. In this argument, regulation refers to more than legal regulation. On top of international law itself, regulation also encompasses the social, cognitive, and political forms of constraints upon states that aim to ensure compliance with international law. My argument follows four incremental steps, corresponding to layers of regulation.

The first step of the argument is based upon ethics, as a ground layer of regulation. Until the role of international law in regulating intelligence activities was recognised, moral principles were considered the sole general framework to determine the permissibility of intelligence activities.[2] Although this book's engagement with ethics is minimal, the historical and social role of ethics still informs the regulation of intelligence activities under international law, both

---

[2] Whereas international law scholarship on intelligence is recent and still minimal, the extensive scholarly literature in intelligence ethics is a testament to the role of ethics in regulating intelligence.

through law itself, which sometimes reflects ethical principles, and through its independent influence on states' and individuals' behaviour. The role of ethics is strongest regarding intelligence activities that are, in the Kantian terminology, 'radical evils'. Intelligence involving the use of torture or enforced disappearance, among other violations of non-derogable rights, constitutes a *malum in se* and can never be justified ethically. Ideally, the moral stain attached to these methods should be enough to deter all states from using them, without the need for a legal norm repeating the prohibition. Other intelligence activities may, on the contrary, present complex ethical questions. This is the case with surveillance, for instance. Neither essentially wrong nor morally right, these activities may only be assessed by taking the broader context into account. This is normally where the role of the law becomes most important.

The next step of the argument is thus based upon legality and corresponds to the first layer of regulation. When it comes to radical evils, or *mala in se*, legal prohibitions simply express in positive law the moral wrongfulness of the act. Still, the inscription of a *malum in se* in the law makes the prohibition administrable and amenable to the rule of law. Other intelligence activities may be considered *mala prohibita*, in the sense that they only become wrongful because the law prohibits them. Legal norms thus govern intelligence activities, prohibiting some and allowing others, usually within strict parameters. In an ideal world, virtuous states would therefore abstain from engaging in internationally wrongful intelligence activities out of respect for the rule of law. Were that the case, the argument would stop there and the present book would be restricted to its first substantive chapter, setting the legal framework for intelligence activities. However, the world order has never been composed of solely virtuous actors.

Hence, the next step of the argument is based upon the enforcement of state responsibility for internationally wrongful acts. I call this process international legal accountability, and it constitutes the second layer of regulation. The underlying rationale is that, if the weight of moral wrongfulness and unlawfulness is not enough to deter states from employing prohibited intelligence activities or methods, then surely the prospect of being held to account would be able to convince them. At this point, the argument faces the main weakness of international law, namely its lack of a centralised enforcement mechanism. In this book, I address this weakness by theorising the functioning of the international legal order. I conceive of the international legal order as a network of states and supra-national bodies unique to each state. Thus conceived of, the international legal order is capable of holding a state to account in a decentralised manner through the individual and cumulative capacities and strengths of the actors of the network. In practice, I find that, through the imposition of direct or reputational sanctions, but also through supporting activities and rewards, instances of state accountability do happen in the international legal order. Further, they can deter non-virtuous states from engaging in unlawful intelligence activities when the sanctions or rewards outweigh the benefits to be gained by engaging in the unlawful activity. In such a case, accountability is effective in inducing compliance.

However, the international legal order cannot always impose strong enough sanctions, and the least virtuous states may simply see their interests better protected in pursuing unlawful activities despite the sanctions. The regulation of intelligence activities under international law is cemented in the final step of the argument: compliance. The theoretical and empirical analysis I conduct in this book shows that the likelihood of effective accountability has become the determinant factor for compliance in intelligence matters. Achieving compliance thus requires that the international legal order be able to administer 'effective accountability'. This third layer of regulation therefore relies on the previous two as indispensable elements, but also encompasses the extra-legal social and cognitive factors that help make accountability effective in inducing compliance. In this sense, the third layer can be conceived of as an effective regulatory strategy, the aim of which is compliance with international law.

Figure 1.1 visually presents the model of regulation.

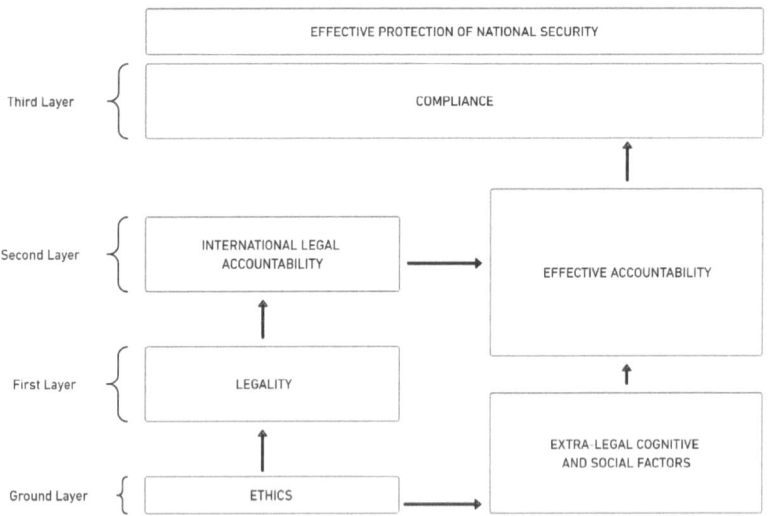

Figure 1.1   *The regulation of intelligence activities under international law*

Let me now briefly address my normative claim, presented as the uppermost part of the model: compliance with international law in intelligence matters leads to the effective protection of national security. I write this book neither with the intent to justify past or current intelligence practices, nor to claim that they should all be prohibited. Although it might surprise some readers when presented with the above argument, I write this book with the intent to improve security, for individuals and nations alike. My interdisciplinary approach and the temporal distance from some of the events analysed allow me to critically assess the effects of modern intelligence practices on states' national security. This book thus breaks away from the majority of existing scholarship on intelligence and international law by not taking for granted claims as to the necessity of non-compliance to advance national security interests. Instead, I evaluate these claims critically and rely on empirical evidence to disprove them.

Doing so requires looking beyond short-term intelligence successes and pressures, extracting ourselves from our biases and fears, and going back to the rationale for intelligence. We value intelligence not as an end in itself, but because it is sometimes necessary to ensure our security.[3] Here, I am not only referring to national security. National security, like intelligence, can only be valued as a means to people's security, not in itself.[4] If the rationale for the existence of intelligence agencies and practices is our security (rather than agencies' or the government's security), then we should do all we can to ensure that it fulfils its existential aim as much as possible with the fewest possible negative externalities. In consequence, the final claim I make in this book is that the effective protection of national security requires compliance with international law in intelligence matters. I defend this claim in the final chapter of this book, drawing the lessons from intelligence practice in the twenty-first-century security landscape.

1.1.1 The Argument in Context

Often spoken about as the world's second oldest profession, espionage constitutes a transhistorical phenomenon, of which intelligence represents the modern form.[5] Yet, even though 'intelligence activities are now accepted as a common, even inherent, attribute of the modern state',[6] states have always

---

[3] Ross W Bellaby, 'Redefining the Security Paradigm to Create an Intelligence Ethic' [2022] Intelligence and National Security 1.

[4] Jeremy Waldron, *Torture, Terror, and Trade-Offs: Philosophy for the White House* (Oxford University Press 2010) 116.

[5] Olivier Chopin and Benjamin Oudet, *Renseignement et sécurité* (2nd edn, Armand Colin 2019) 31.

[6] Geoffrey B Demarest, 'Espionage in International Law' (1995) 24 Denv. J. Int'l L. & Pol'y 321, 330.

abstained from explicitly regulating them in the international order. Until the end of the Cold War, and maybe even until 9/11, both states and academic commentators appeared to agree that intelligence activities were justified by a realist vision of the world, supported by the 'artful ambiguity'[7] of international law. However, the absence of any international treaty or customary law specifically addressing intelligence activities does not mean that they are 'neither legal nor illegal',[8] nor that international law has 'little impact on the practice of intelligence gathering'.[9]

The regulatory paradigm shift I identify in this book originates in two distinct historical events. First, the end of the Cold War brought down the principle of reciprocity as the leading legal principle regulating intelligence activities. After the Cold War, rather than the other block's intelligence agencies, intelligence communities mainly faced non-state actors. The end of the carefully attained-Cold War equilibrium was made salient by a second event: 9/11. On that day, the one remaining superpower, the US, was attacked on its own territory by a non-state actor, al Qaeda. The aftermath of 9/11 entrenched the demise of the principle of reciprocity as the sole means of regulation. The shift induced by the end of the Cold War and 9/11 became permanent: the twenty-first-century security landscape. Within this new landscape and security paradigm, a new paradigm of regulation emerged, prompted by the need for adequate regulation of intelligence activities. In this section, after describing the twenty-first-century security landscape and its underlying ethical fallacies and contradictions (ground layer), I identify the gaps that the three main layers of regulation (legality, accountability, compliance) fill within this landscape.

As will become clear, I consider 9/11 as the founding act of the twenty-first century security landscape. Naturally, this landscape evolved and developed after 9/11. However, we remain in the same paradigm, even following Russia's aggression against Ukraine in February 2022. Indeed, even as other security threats complement and surpass that of transnational terrorism, the approaches, tools, and techniques developed in response to 9/11 are still used today. Modern intelligence powers and practices were shaped by the war on terror. In consequence, defining and critically assessing the twenty-first century security landscape as it emerged in the aftermath of 9/11 remains of utmost relevance today.

---

[7] Craig Forcese, 'Spies Without Borders: International Law and Intelligence Collection' (2011) 5 J. Nat'l Sec. L. & Pol'y 179, 205.

[8] A Radsan, 'The Unresolved Equation of Espionage and International Law' (2007) 28 Michigan Journal of International Law 595, 596.

[9] Glenn Sulmasy and John Yoo, 'Counterintuitive: Intelligence Operations and International Law' (2007) 28 Mich. J. Int'l L. 625, 625.

1.1.1.1 The twenty-first-century security landscape

It has become common for both security and human rights scholars to state that 'everything changed' on 9/11. But what changed, exactly? The 'old' security landscape is our point of reference here. The pre-9/11 security landscape was characterised by an emphasis on national security. It was focused on sovereignty and territorial integrity, and extremely state-centred. As the Cold War starkly illustrates, security was conceived of as a zero-sum game between states.

In contrast, the post-9/11 security landscape united virtually all states against a common enemy: terrorism. Terrorism constitutes both the root and the rationale of the twenty-first-century security landscape. The enemy is an undefined non-state actor. It is pervasive and global, dangerous, inhumane, and the threat it poses justifies extraordinary measures to prevent it from materialising. To protect themselves against terrorism, states, governments and populations united against the terrorists beyond usual divisions. This security landscape is thus characterised by an 'us versus them' mentality, and by the perceived need for new and greater powers to face the terrorist threat.

The underlying theory of this new landscape is the liberty–security conundrum, that is, the assumption that security and liberty are balanced against each other, so that the protection of security might require the sacrifice of the rule of law and human rights. This trade-offs discourse had its heyday in the aftermath of 9/11. Its main argument is that, to be as safe as we were on 10 September 2001, we now need to sacrifice some of our liberties. The pre-existing balance is no longer satisfying – or maybe it never was.

On the international scene, the trade-offs mentality was embedded in the international framework for combating terrorism, drafted through a series of post-9/11 UN Security Council (UNSC) Chapter VII resolutions. This framework effectively made intelligence cooperation to fight terrorism a legal obligation of states. It thereby provided an extremely powerful justification for increasingly intrusive intelligence practices.

Prior to 9/11, it would have been unconscionable for Chapter VII resolutions to require that states introduce specified counterterrorism legislation in their domestic legal orders.[10] 9/11 took place at a time characterised by increasing international cooperation in institutional settings. This context probably explains how the post-9/11 Security Council could adopt a 'dominant super-legislative role',[11] using binding resolutions to regulate states' responses

---

[10] Fionnuala Ní Aoláin, 'The Ever-Expanding Legislative Supremacy of the Security Council in Counterterrorism' in Arianna Vedaschi and Kim Lane Scheppele (eds), *9/11 and the Rise of Global Anti-Terrorism Law: How the UN Security Council Rules the World* (Cambridge University Press 2021) 34.

[11] Ní Aoláin (n 10) 36.

to terrorism. Resolution 1373,[12] adopted in the immediate aftermath of 9/11, thus required all states to change their domestic laws to create a separate crime of terrorism and made international intelligence cooperation a legal obligation. The template established in Resolution 1373 was followed and elaborated upon in a series of further Chapter VII resolutions aiming to combat terrorism.[13]

In these Chapter VII resolutions – which are both binding and superior to other sources of law[14] – all states were addressed, and all were required to prepare themselves to combat terrorism in the manner outlined in the resolutions. States were not only permitted, but often 'required to respond to the threat of international terrorism by expanding the scope of executive power, loosening restraints on surveillance, deploying the military in unconventional ways, engaging in deepening transnational cooperation among security services, and more'.[15] Despite the sensitive area (national security) and the extremely demanding changes required of states, compliance was swift and quasi-universal.[16] While governments' self-interest in implementing resolutions increasing the executive power should not be discounted to explain compliance, it bears noting that these domestic changes were mandated by the Security Council. In other words, they were made in order to comply with international law, hence providing them with the strongest form of legitimacy before all audiences and facilitating their implementation.[17]

---

[12] S.C. Res. 1373 (28 September 2001).

[13] See especially, S.C. Res. 1611 (7 July 2005); S.C. Res. 1618 (4 August 2005); S.C. Res. 2133 (27 January 2014); S.C. Res. 2170 (15 August 2014).

[14] The ICJ held that Article 103 UN Charter requires that UN Charter obligations of Member States prevail over any other international treaty, and that Member States' obligations under Chapter VII Security Council resolutions are the same as under the Charter itself. See Military and Paramilitary Activities in and against Nicaragua (Nicaragua v. United States of America), ICJ Reports 1984, 392 para 107; Questions of Interpretation and Application of the 1971 Montreal Convention Arising from the Aerial Incident at Lockerbie (Libyan Arab Jamahiriya v. United States of America and Libyan Arab Jamahiriya v. United Kingdom), ICJ Reports 1992, vol. 1, 16 para 42; and 113 para 39.

[15] Kim Lane Scheppele and Arianna Vedaschi, 'Conclusion: The Afterlife of 9/11' in Arianna Vedaschi and Kim Lane Scheppele (eds), *9/11 and the Rise of Global Anti-Terrorism Law: How the UN Security Council Rules the World* (Cambridge University Press 2021) 247.

[16] UN Secretary-General Kofi Annan even stated in January 2002 that 'the cooperation it has received from Member States [has] been unprecedented and exemplary'. United Nations, Secretary-General, Addressing Council Meeting on Counter-Terrorism, Says United Nations 'Stands Four-Square' against Scourge. Press Release SG/SM/8105; SC/7277, 18 January 2002.

[17] Scheppele and Vedaschi (n 15) 247–248.

Still, the tools established in the UNSC's global counterterrorism framework lacked meaningful safeguards. This regulatory framework allowed states, including authoritarian ones, to address their own domestic 'threats' through the language of counterterrorism. It thereby legitimated a crackdown on human rights and the rule of law in the name of preventing and fighting terrorism – now a legal obligation of states. The Security Council's far-reaching global legislative measures have displaced and rendered almost meaningless many constitutional and international human rights protections.[18] Intelligence communities worldwide suddenly saw some of their most controversial practices made lawful, and even become obligatory, as long as the fight against terrorism – a term that the UNSC did not bother to define – could be invoked. The rule of law became a secondary concern, if at all, in intelligence cooperation, while the counterterrorism powers of intelligence communities became virtually unlimited. In other words, in the name of security against terrorism, human rights were sacrificed without a second thought. The justification for this new state of affairs was compelling: not only were these changes and activities lawful, but they were also necessary to *comply* with international law. The liberty–security conundrum thus became binding international law.

The exceptional measures enacted at domestic and international level in the immediate aftermath of 9/11 have become permanent.[19] There is a strong lock-in effect of security-enhancing measures, regardless of whether they achieve their stated purpose. Put simply, no one wants to be blamed for the next attack or failure; hence, no one takes the responsibility to discontinue emergency security measures. Yet, the balancing mentality underlying these measures remains as fallacious today as it was two decades ago.

The main flaw of the counterterrorism discourse is the implication that the threat from terrorist attacks is balanced against the threat that the state poses to individuals' rights, so that when one raises, the other diminishes. On the contrary, the terrorist threat to security complements and may even enhance state threats to individual security when, as is the case in many countries since 9/11, the government is granted additional powers to deal with the terrorist threat. As emphasized by Locke already in 1689, the very means given to the state to combat our common enemies (the terrorists) may very well be used by the government to combat its own enemies (political opposition, minorities,

---

[18] Martin Scheinin, 'Impact of Post-9/11 Counter-Terrorism Measures on All Human Rights' in Manfred Nowak and Anne Charbord (eds), *Using Human Rights to Counter Terrorism* (Edward Elgar Publishing 2018).

[19] On the structure and effects of the transnational counterterrorist order that emerged after 9/11, see Fiona de Londras, *The Practice and Problems of Transnational Counter-Terrorism* (Cambridge University Press 2022).

etc.).²⁰ This means that the state is not recognised as an impartial guardian of individuals' security, as the counterterrorism security discourse seeks to imply, but as a subjective party that forms an integral part of the security threat.²¹ This assumption is at the core of IHRL, the main purpose of which is the protection of the individual against negative interference with her rights by the state.

The increased exercise of state power to enhance national security therefore does not do much in favour of individuals' security, but has the potential to (and in fact does) infringe greatly on (at least some) individuals' security. Of course, the positive obligations of the state to secure the human rights of individuals within its jurisdiction against interference by private parties (e.g., terrorists) have been recognised generally in respect of many rights.²² Yet, it would be absurd to infer from the existence of such positive obligations that, to realise them, the negative obligations of the state not to violate those rights should themselves be diminished. Therefore, counterterrorism policies, i.e., enhanced state powers to combat the terrorist threat, cannot legitimately have as their aim or effect reducing the security of the individual against state power and other threats. Hence, from the perspective of individuals' security, national security cannot legitimately take precedence.

On paper, the balancing exercise is easy to grasp. A reduction in liberty is achieved by enhancing the power of the state, so that the accrued power capacity can be used to combat terrorism and make the population, or more likely the nation, more secure – but its people less free. Proponents of a balancing approach between security and liberty therefore emphasize the 'social good' aspect of security: 'we' accept to be a little less free for 'us' to be a little more secure. This balancing discourse has been at the core of the counterterrorism approach after 9/11. However, it fails to take into account that what is at stake is an interpersonal trade-off, that 'we' and 'us' often are not the same subjects. Hence, what is happening really is 'a trade-off of the liberty of a few for the sake of the enhanced security of some and the diminished security of others'.²³

The sense of aspirational security justifying such talk about trade-offs is security against violent attacks, as well as freedom from care, anxiety or

---

[20] John Locke, *Two Treatises of Government* (1689) II chapter 6 section 93.

[21] Piet Hein van Kempen, 'Four Concepts of Security – A Human Rights Perspective' (2013) 13 Human Rights Law Review 1, 11.

[22] E.g., ECtHR *Osman v. United Kingdom*, Application No 23452/94, Grand Chamber Judgment 28 October 1998 (*Osman*) para 116; IACtHR *Velasquez Rodriguez v. Honduras* (Judgment) IACtHR Series C No 4 (29 July 1988) paras 172–175.

[23] Waldron (n 4) 146; see also David Luban, *Torture, Power, and Law* (Cambridge University Press 2014); David Cole, 'Their Liberties, Our Security: Democracy and Double Standards' [2003] 31 Int'l J. Legal Info. 290–311.

apprehension of such attacks.[24] When in fear of an attack, citizens expect their government to act and respond to the threat. The more unusual or drastic the response, the stronger its psychological reassurance on the population.[25] This phenomenon is called action bias. The risk of a violent attack from a terrorist organisation could well still be the same,[26] but the position of governmental institutions is now more secure and governmental powers have increased. However, this does not mean that individuals' security has benefited in any way from this governmental exercise of power. Quite the opposite, for the benefit of such psychological reassurance, civil liberties may have been traded-off, the rule of law undermined, and security as a social good damaged.[27] If we assume that liberty is the ultimate goal of individual security – in that individuals are only free to enjoy their rights when they are secure that the state will not arbitrarily and unnecessarily interfere with them – then any talk about trade-offs can only have at its core a narrow conception of national security, i.e., the security of governmental institutions.

Intelligence practices epitomise the liberty–security conundrum. Take surveillance, for instance. Surveillance notoriously infringes on individuals' right to privacy. The rationale for surveillance practices is that a phenomenon (terrorism; organised crime) represents a threat to a legitimate interest, such as national security or public order. This threat's existence necessitates a response to prevent it from materialising: surveillance. Hence, to protect national security against terrorism or organised crime, citizens need to accept that they will have less privacy.[28] This trade-off seems intuitive and is presented as unavoidable. However, it is subject to the same fallacies as other counterterrorism practices relying on a balancing between security and liberty. As the Pegasus scandal demonstrated, providing the state with the means to fight our common enemies also (and often mostly) allows it to fight its own enemies.[29] The Snowden leaks showed that, in this respect, mass surveillance is subject to

---

[24] See the Oxford English Dictionary's definition of security: '1. The state or condition of being or feeling secure'; '1.a. Freedom from care, anxiety or apprehension; absence of worry or anxiety; confidence in one's safety or well-being'; '2. Freedom from danger or threat', https://www.oed.com/view/Entry/174661 (accessed 9 September 2022).

[25] Waldron (n 4) 45.

[26] As Waldron puts it, 'an enhanced ability to combat terrorism is not the same as an actual diminution of the terrorist threat' Waldron (n 4) 44.

[27] Waldron (n 4) 45.

[28] Notwithstanding that non-citizens and/or non-residents generally have no choice but to accept this trade-off in which their security is often not part of the deal.

[29] Pegasus is spyware developed and commercialised to states by the Israeli company NSO. Pegasus can be covertly installed on most mobile devices, and has been used by many governments against opposition figures, journalists, and human rights

the same deviances as targeted surveillance.³⁰ Further, as the multidisciplinary SURVEILLE project highlighted, electronic mass surveillance produces at best medium-level usability scores, while triggering extremely high intrusion on the right to privacy.³¹ This means that the price to be paid in terms of the reduction in rights is grossly disproportionate to the potential security gains. Moreover, with mass surveillance, it becomes clear that the sacrifice in terms of both privacy rights and the rule of law affects everyone – not just the terrorists, criminals, or those we consider 'others'. Yet, lest one condone the underlying ideological justification that human beings are not all entitled to the same amount of dignity and rights, the obvious risk of the government also using its powers on *us* should only be an ancillary objection to such practices.

Intelligence practices are thus rationalised by the alleged necessity of balancing liberty and security. However, human rights are on both sides of the equation. Security is not an abstract value. When we speak of security, whether national or individual, we speak of the security of our rights. We value national security not in its own right but because, and only because, it is a necessary part of protecting individual rights. In turn, as Ross Bellaby argues, the ethical value of intelligence comes from its role in protecting the individual and the political community.³² This role informs when 'intelligence is justified as a means of protection, as well as when it is prohibited as an unjustified violation'.³³ To create a practical model allowing states to face security challenges effectively while also abiding by the ethical and moral standards of the societies they serve, one would thus need to take into account the necessity for flexibility and moral reasoning. Law filled this role. International law, including IHRL, encompasses both the state's security goals and the morale and values of the international community of states.³⁴ While it often reflects and builds upon ethical principles, law can draw a hard line between permissible and impermissible policies where ethics might not. In its current form, the international legal framework is thus flexible enough to provide states with all

---

activists, among others. See, e.g., the Guardian's Pegasus homepage for news and explainers: https://www.theguardian.com/news/series/pegasus-project

³⁰ For a catalogue of the various revelations by Edward Snowden regarding the United States' surveillance activities, see Lawfare, 'Snowden Revelations': https://www.lawfareblog.com/snowden-revelations

³¹ SURVEILLE 'Surveillance: Ethical issues, legal limitations, and efficiency' FP7-SEC-2011-284725. See Deliverable D2.8: SURVEILLE Paper Assessing Surveillance in the Context of Preventing a Terrorist Act; SURVEILLE Paper on Mass Surveillance by the National Security Agency (NSA) of the United States of America.

³² Bellaby (n 3) 4.

³³ ibid 6.

³⁴ Mary Ellen O'Connell, *The Art of Law in the International Community* (Cambridge University Press 2019).

the necessary means and methods to protect their political communities and individuals while respecting states' common values (as reflected in international law), including and especially in times of acute crisis.

In consequence, because human rights are on both sides of the liberty–security equation, the permissibility of intelligence activities infringing on human rights should be assessed from a human rights perspective. International human rights law comprises rules and procedures to assess whether an infringement on a right constitutes a violation thereof or is instead justified by competing interests. Indeed, permissible exceptions to the norm, restrictions upon rights, and circumstances precluding wrongfulness are provided by the legal framework itself. Legal norms are not to be balanced against extra-legal considerations, and especially less so when individual rights are concerned. Human rights are 'supposed to *restrict* trade-offs of some people's liberty and well-being for the sake of others' [liberty and well-being]. They are not supposed to be traded off themselves'.[35] Hence, it is doubtful that restrictions, derogations or balancing exercises beyond those already provided for by the legal texts themselves would be considered necessary or acceptable to protect individuals and political communities, whether from an ethical or legal standpoint.[36] In addition, as will become clear throughout this book, if the nation's security is the aim, most measures in breach of international law will actually be useless at best, and counter-productive at worst. As summarised by Paul Lauritzen in the counterterrorism context, 'in the fight against terrorism, the choice is not between national security and human rights. It is between national security with an appropriate respect for human rights and tyranny without either'.[37] Within this new security landscape, the need for a clear legal framework governing intelligence activities thus became acute.

1.1.1.2 The need for a clear legal framework
After the Cold War, non-state actors started constituting the main threat to states' security. With different agendas to Cold War-superpowers' intelligence agencies, these non-state actors could not be expected to abide by the same rules, nor use the same means and methods. Against this background, 9/11, perceived as a massive failure in intelligence gathering and coordination, triggered claims for increased executive powers to face the 'new' transnational and globalised terrorist threat. As a result, intelligence agencies worldwide

---

[35] Waldron (n 4) 13 (original italics).
[36] On the 'protective' narrative giving rise to these trade-offs, see Iris Marion Young, 'The Logic of Masculinist Protection: Reflections on the Current Security State' (2003) 29 Signs: Journal of Women in Culture and Society 1.
[37] Paul Lauritzen, 'Counterterrorism, Dignity, and the Rule of Law' (2012) 95 Soundings: An Interdisciplinary Journal 452, 465.

have gained, de facto and/or de jure, more powers and missions than ever before in democracies (e.g., law enforcement, interrogation, detention, use of force). In parallel, intelligence cooperation has been encouraged and even made binding by UN Security Council Resolution 1373,[38] and operations and exchanges of information with foreign partners have increased exponentially. National security has thus been invoked as a blanket justification for enhanced executive power, alongside limited oversight and review by other state organs.

Indeed, in the meantime, formal accountability and/or oversight mechanisms of executive acts, and particularly of intelligence activities, have stayed tied to the domestic level and have rarely seen their competence evolve to match this executive power increase. It bears mentioning that, had domestic oversight effectively prevented intelligence communities from engaging in blatantly internationally wrongful conduct in the war on terror, the international legal order's role in regulating intelligence would have been more limited. Effective domestic oversight constitutes the best means of ensuring both the legality and effectiveness of intelligence without compromising on secrecy needs. The regulation of intelligence activities under international law should, therefore, be considered a second-best form of regulation, the aim of which is to induce states to establish effective oversight and accountability mechanisms at the domestic level. In consequence, regulation in the international legal order will have fully succeeded once states have all implemented effective mechanisms of oversight at the domestic level, thereby ensuring compliance with international law without the need for regulatory interventions in the international legal order.

Alongside intelligence communities' increased power in the aftermath of 9/11, the development and expanding use of modern technologies by intelligence communities started to pose new legal issues. Human targets became the norm, triggering questions as to the applicability of IHRL. Furthermore, intelligence leaks and scandals multiplied. It slowly became untenable to keep pretending that intelligence activities remained unregulated by international law and obeyed only a realist reciprocity principle between superpowers. In other words, when confronted with states' intelligence responses to 9/11, it could no longer be argued that international law authorised states to respond to national security threats in any way and manner they deemed necessary. A paradigm shift from realism to formalism thus became ineluctable after the attacks of 9/11. Yet, the lack of a clear and comprehensive framework through which to assess the status of intelligence activities under international law remains acute. It constitutes the first gap that this book purports to remedy.

---

[38] S.C. Res. 1373 (28 September 2001), paras 2(b), 2(e), and 3.

1.1.1.3 The need for international legal accountability

It is a relatively undisputed reality that states must collect and exchange intelligence to protect their populations against transnational terrorism and other credible threats to their national security.[39] Yet, the necessity of both intelligence and cooperation does not erase the fact that some of the means and methods adopted by intelligence agencies in recent decades, and particularly since 9/11, are highly problematic from a legal (not to mention ethical) perspective. For preventative and intelligence-gathering purposes, intelligence activities have given rise to gross human rights violations, including violations of the prohibitions of torture, arbitrary detention and enforced disappearance, routine extra-judicial killings, overwhelming privacy violations, and many other wrongful acts.

Domestic bodies in charge of overseeing and holding intelligence agencies to account have been confronted with doctrines of state secrecy and national security, immunities, statutes of limitation, and the general lack of transparency surrounding intelligence activities. They have consequently proven highly ineffective in preventing and remedying abuses of power and breaches of international law. International intelligence cooperation is posing further challenges to national oversight mechanisms. Indeed, oversight bodies lack the capacity to oversee the actions of foreign intelligence agencies. Further, in most jurisdictions, the extensive use of the third-party (or 'operator control') rule prevents the disclosure of foreign intelligence to oversight bodies.

The binding effect of states' international obligations on their intelligence services is self-evident. As organs of the state, intelligence agencies and other state actors performing intelligence activities must behave in accordance with the international obligations binding the state, whatever their origin and character.[40] Since their acts will normally be attributed to the state, any breach of an international obligation by a state's intelligence community will trigger the state's responsibility for an internationally wrongful act. Yet, the mere engagement of international responsibility cannot produce effects by itself, nor can it provide redress to victims: the state needs to be held to account for the violations of victims' rights.

However, approaching accountability (i.e., the enforcement of state responsibility) according to the horizontal interstate perspective featured in the law of state responsibility, as codified in the ILC Articles on State Responsibility

---

[39] Whether this is effective is yet another issue, partially addressed later in the book.
[40] International Law Commission, Draft Articles on Responsibility of States for Internationally Wrongful Acts 2001 (Supplement No 10 (A/56/10), chpIVE1) 76, Articles 4 and 12.

(ASR),[41] is of little use in human rights law, and even less so when intelligence cooperation is concerned. Indeed, states have no (political, economic, or other) interest in holding their intelligence partners to account for wrongs that did not directly injure them and which they believe enhanced their national security. In practice, and particularly when the primary norms infringed protect non-state actors, the ASR regime of invocation of state responsibility 'provides accountability only to the extent that states are entitled to invoke [these primary norms]'.[42]

A broader and more flexible conceptualisation of accountability is therefore required to effectively address and remedy states' wrongful acts stemming from intelligence activities and cooperation, taking into consideration the crucial role played by non-state actors in holding states to account. To fill this second gap, I conceptualise the enforcement of state responsibility as 'international legal accountability', which can be considered the missing part of the ASR regime. The concept of international legal accountability then allows me to analyse and evaluate international practice accurately, identifying remaining accountability gaps and the reasons underlying them.

1.1.1.4 The need to understand compliance

In order to regulate effectively, a regulator must be responsive to the subjects it regulates. Responsiveness implies understanding the reasons driving a subject to behave in a certain way and the factors influencing their beliefs, preferences, interests, and motives. In other words, regulation is not a one-size-fits-all endeavour. Law is, to a certain extent, a uniform instrument of regulation. Accountability, in contrast, allows subjects to explain themselves and takes into account their circumstances and justifications. To be effective at inducing compliance, accountability needs to not only rely upon the normative strength of law, but also make use of all the other extra-legal factors influencing the regulated state's behaviour within a responsive regulatory strategy. Regulation is thus is a deeply individualised process. Hence, to regulate states' intelligence activities effectively, we must identify the factors influencing states' (non-)compliance with international law in their intelligence activities. This constitutes the third gap that this book fills.

To understand international law's influence on states' intelligence activities, I model state decision-making in intelligence matters using a modified rational choice equation. This decision-making model accounts for relevant mecha-

---

[41] International Law Commission, Draft Articles on Responsibility of States for Internationally Wrongful Acts, Part Three.
[42] Jutta Brunnée, 'International Legal Accountability through the Lens of the Law of State Responsibility' (2005) 36 Netherlands Yearbook of International Law 21, 30.

nisms of influence, their interactions, and the conditions under which one or another mechanism is most likely either to effectuate change or to enhance the prospect that another mechanism will do so. The decision-making model furthers our understanding of state behaviour and highlights available paths to enhance compliance with international law in intelligence matters.

Indeed, regulation has little value in itself: we regulate to improve compliance. In turn, we value compliance not because rule following would be intrinsically good but because, in intelligence matters, compliance with international law enhances national security. Effective regulation therefore does not constitute a hindrance to the practice of intelligence. Rather, it is a call to make intelligence more effective at its task, namely protecting national security. In consequence, the overarching research question addressed by this book reads as follows: how are intelligence activities regulated under international law?

1.2　KEY DEFINITIONS

My research agenda is determined by the terms of the research question addressed: how are intelligence activities regulated under international law? In the following subsections, I provide the definitions relied on for 'intelligence activities' and 'regulation under international law' in the rest of the book.

1.2.1　Intelligence Activities

In its simplest definition, by former in-house historian for the CIA Michael Warner, 'intelligence is secret, state activity to understand or influence foreign entities'.[43] Warner's definition is the one that best matches the perspective I adopt in this book. It does not unduly differentiate between the product (information); the activities (collection and/or action, and the underlying conduct to operationalise them); and their aims (understanding or influencing foreign entities).[44] As I show in this book, distinctions between these notions are often purely theoretical and rarely match the reality of practice. Legal regulation is not abstract, but attaches to the conduct and its aims. Therefore, we need to consider intelligence comprehensively, rather than through its distinctive parts. This also implies that the material scope of this book (intelligence

---

[43] Michael Warner, 'Wanted: A Definition of "Intelligence"' (2002) 46 Studies in Intelligence 9.

[44] In contrast, e.g., the United States Department of Defence's Dictionary of military and associated terms distinguishes between the product, the activities, and the organisations under its definition of intelligence. Office of the Chairman of the Joint Chiefs of Staff, DOD Dictionary of Military and Associated Terms (Washington DC: The Joint Staff, November 2021), 107.

activities) is broader than what is sometimes considered 'pure' intelligence, namely intelligence collection activities.[45] My choice not to restrict the material scope of this research to intelligence collection activities only is likely to be criticised but, as I explain below, it is justified.

Legal scholars often distinguish between intelligence collection activities and active operations, with some arguing that the latter (whether referred to as covert action, active measures, or by any other appellation)[46] do not constitute intelligence activities. I will refer to active operations as covert actions hereafter, without prejudice to what these actions involve or the state performing them. Covert action thus understood includes propaganda, political and economic action, paramilitary operations, and lethal action. It also includes covert operations on a state's own territory,[47] as well as clandestine diplomacy with other states and non-state actors.[48] In practice, composite operations involving collection and action are frequent and frequently performed by the same actors. Further, many states have used, and continue to use their intelligence agencies for highly violent activities abroad. One could of course retort that all the activities performed by intelligence agencies are not necessarily intelligence activities, and that defining intelligence activities by reference to the actors performing them is tautological. Still, when most of the world's agencies in charge of intelligence collection are also in charge of secret activities aiming to influence foreign (or domestic non-state) entities, the burden of proof should fall upon those trying to narrow the scope of what we consider intelligence. As Len Scott argues, 'to exclude such activities from discussion about intelligence and intelligence services raises questions about the political agendas of those seeking to delineate and circumscribe the focus of enquiry'.[49] From an international law perspective, there is a clear motive for drawing the distinction: when

---

[45] For the purpose of simplicity, intelligence collection activities can be understood as those forming the 'intelligence cycle'. Stages of the cycle include planning; collection; processing; analysis; and dissemination.

[46] On the various appellations and their implications, see Len Scott, 'Secret Intelligence, Covert Action and Clandestine Diplomacy' (2004) 19 Intelligence and National Security 322. On the affinities between covert action and diplomacy in US foreign policy after 9/11, see Magda Long, 'American Covert Action and Diplomacy after 9/11' (2022) 33 Diplomacy & Statecraft 379.

[47] On the existence of covert action at home, see Scott (n 46) 324 and 335–337.

[48] Clandestine diplomacy refers to situations 'where intelligence services are used to engage in secret and deniable discussions with adversaries' Scott (n 46) 330–332; On this aspect and the differences with secret diplomacy, see also Huw Dylan, 'Secret Interventions and Clandestine Diplomacy' in Robert Dover, Huw Dylan and Michael S Goodman (eds), *The Palgrave Handbook of Security, Risk and Intelligence* (Palgrave Macmillan UK 2017).

[49] Scott (n 46) 323.

performed abroad, covert action generally constitutes an unambiguous breach of the core principles of international law.[50] Should we include covert action in the definition of intelligence, it would become harder to argue, as many legal scholars have done, that intelligence would be either internationally lawful or unregulated under international law.[51]

Further, intelligence scholarship overwhelmingly focuses on the Anglosphere and on foreign (rather than domestic) intelligence and targeting.[52] This narrow focus creates distorted perceptions of what intelligence is and how it is performed.[53] 'Intelligence elsewhere'[54] is not necessarily structured according to the same divisions and principles as in the US and UK. Rather, distinct intelligence cultures arise from states' specific historical and social characteristics.[55] We should therefore be wary of generalising what intelligence would be *by nature* from the highly biased perceptions that Anglo-American-focused scholarship has created.[56] The taxonomy and organisational division between types of activities, types of threats, or supervising ministries is contingent and variable. It does not obey any kind of universal truth about the nature of intelligence itself. The same is true of states' security priorities and the types of activities performed by states' intelligence communities. As explained by Richard Aldrich and John Kasuku, in the Global South, intelligence 'is more focused on regime security and covert action'.[57] Excluding domestic intelligence and covert action from this book's material focus, as most of international law and intelligence scholarship does, would therefore only perpetuate these biased perceptions.

Regardless of the perspective and country one writes from and about,[58] there is an additional, practical reason for which I deem it artificial to consider that

---

[50] See Chapter 2, section 2.4.1.

[51] See Chapter 2, section 2.2.

[52] Damien Van Puyvelde and Sean Curtis, '"Standing on the Shoulders of Giants": Diversity and Scholarship in Intelligence Studies' (2016) 31 Intelligence and National Security 1040. In this study, 70% of all articles focused on the US's and UK's intelligence agencies, while the remaining 30% were primarily focused on Russia or the Soviet Union, Germany, and Israel.

[53] Richard J Aldrich and John Kasuku, 'Escaping from American Intelligence: Culture, Ethnocentrism and the Anglosphere' (2012) 88 International Affairs 1009.

[54] Philip HJ Davies and Kristian C Gustafson, *Intelligence Elsewhere: Spies and Espionage Outside the Anglosphere* (Georgetown University Press 2013).

[55] Aldrich and Kasuku (n 53).

[56] Sophia Hoffmann, 'Why Is There No IR Scholarship on Intelligence Agencies? Some Ideas for a New Approach' (2019) 23 ZMO Working Papers 14; Aldrich and Kasuku (n 53); Van Puyvelde and Curtis (n 52).

[57] Aldrich and Kasuku (n 53) 1013.

[58] Should the reader wish that I position myself, my perspective is that of a Western European scholar, with the privilege and biases this status carries.

'intelligence activities' only include intelligence collection and analysis activities. Indeed, where does one draw the line between intelligence collection and the operationalisation of the information collected? In other words, at which point does an operation relying on intelligence collection, means, personnel, and funding cease to be an intelligence activity? Let me first illustrate this issue with an example from the domestic sphere: when does domestic surveillance cease to be an intelligence activity? Is it when the information is collected; when it is analysed; when it is used to identify a suspect or unlawful conduct; when it is used to arrest someone; when it is used in support of interrogation; or maybe at some later point? I doubt that anyone knows precisely where to draw this definitional line, and I doubt a consensus would be readily available should we draw such a line.

A similar argument applies to the foreign realm. Operation 'Neptune Spear', culminating in the killing of Osama bin Laden in Pakistan in 2011, is generally considered a successful US covert action. The operation first involved tracking bin Laden down through intelligence collection and analysis, performed by the CIA and the NSA. This was followed by a paramilitary hit, planned under the leadership of the CIA but fielded by the military's Joint Special Operations Command (JSOC). As Loch Johnson concludes, 'the result was neither caterpillar nor butterfly—a complicated and lethal blend of JSOC military and Agency intelligence capabilities'.[59] In most fields of law, we would call the operation a composite act and assess its overall legality rather than look at the legality of its different components. When looking at it from a definitional perspective, it would be similarly absurd to draw an artificial line between the intelligence collection and analysis part designed to locate bin Laden, and the operative part designed to kill or capture him. The first part exists only to allow the second part to take place. In other words, locating bin Laden was never the end goal, and discovering his whereabouts was only valuable because this knowledge could be operationalised. Concluding that locating bin Laden was intelligence but the paramilitary hit was not creates an artificial distinction between a set of activities that are not only factually linked but also interdependent.

Some lawyers might feel justified in distinguishing the collection part from the operationalisation part, if only to assess and defend the legality of intelligence collection. For certain purposes, such as establishing the legal framework governing intelligence, looking at intelligence activities individually is indispensable. Separation between constituent acts might similarly be justified when performed by courts and tribunals seeking to establish responsibility for

---

[59] Loch K Johnson, *The Third Option: Covert Action and American Foreign Policy* (Oxford University Press 2022) 150.

wrongful acts, but all parts of the operation would still be considered. Yet, what use is there in legal scholarship considering only some of the constituent parts of a single operation? The paramilitary hit would not be made less unlawful (should it be so) by the potential lawfulness of the intelligence collection. In other words, such an operation would not become lawful just because part of it, considered in isolation, might have been. The analysis resulting from such a partial view would, in addition, be incomplete and, as such, present little utility.

In my view, it would be dishonest to write a book on the regulation of intelligence activities under international law while excluding a significant part of agencies' activities and operations from the book's material scope. This is especially so as, particularly in the West, covert actions have increased exponentially in the period following 9/11.[60]

In consequence, drawing heavily on Warner, I define intelligence as follows: intelligence is secret, state activity to understand or influence foreign *and domestic* entities. Intelligence thus defined is a state activity, which can be performed by any state organ or delegated by one to another state or non-state entity.[61] I refer to the 'intelligence community' as encompassing the variety of state actors performing intelligence activities or responsible for them in case of delegation. A terminological clarification remains however needed with regard to the activities themselves. 'Intelligence activities' logically encompass all secret state activities performed to understand or influence foreign and domestic entities, thus including covert action. In contrast, the term 'espionage', as often used in the literature, is to be understood as referring only to foreign intelligence collection activities, unless stated otherwise.

1.2.2 Regulation under International Law

In this book, I am concerned with the regulation of intelligence activities under international law. International law is understood first by reference to its substantive sources and content. These are commonly recognised as the sources enumerated in Article 38 of the ICJ Statute:

a. international conventions, whether general or particular, establishing rules expressly recognized by the contesting states;
b. international custom, as evidence of a general practice accepted as law;

---

[60] For US figures and analysis, see Johnson (n 59) 143–163; and Long (n 46).
[61] Intelligence can indeed be delegated by a state organ to another entity, with attribution of the former's acts to the latter under Article 5 (non-state actor) or Article 8 (other state) ASR. This scenario is not considered specifically in the book but similar conclusions would apply.

c. the general principles of law recognized by civilized nations;
  d. subject to the provisions of Article 59, judicial decisions and the teachings of the most highly qualified publicists of the various nations, as subsidiary means for the determination of rules of law.[62]

International law also provides the procedures for international legal accountability. In this regard, international law first provides the rules for the establishment of state responsibility for an internationally wrongful act, whether under customary law as reflected in the ASR[63] or under treaty-based rules. International law also grounds the process for the enforcement of international responsibility, which I call international legal accountability. Such rules of procedure can be found in Part Three of the ASR or under specific treaties, especially regarding the enforcement of responsibility before human rights courts and bodies.

Regulation refers here to the process of limitation, stemming from international law, of states' freedom in intelligence matters. This process includes and rests upon positive international law itself (legality) and its aim is to ensure compliance with applicable law. However, when I speak of regulation throughout this book, I refer to a lot more than simply legality. The regulatory process also includes the conduct and decisions of other states and actors of the international legal order (particularly international organisations and supra-national courts and bodies) that participate in defining and clarifying the law and in enforcing international legality, i.e., holding states to account for their intelligence activities in breach of international law. International legal accountability is thus a major constitutive element of the regulatory process, and effective regulation requires accounting for a large number of extra-legal factors influencing state behaviour.

1.3 METHODS

Asking how intelligence activities are regulated under international law is not a question that can be answered using only doctrinal legal methods. Rather, I employ a range of theoretical approaches and methods in order to provide a comprehensive answer to this question. In consequence, this book is divided into three parts, corresponding to the three main layers of regulation. Each part answers a sub-question, using apposite methods, theories, and combinations thereof.

---

[62] United Nations, Statute of the International Court of Justice, 18 April 1946, Article 38.
[63] International Law Commission, Draft Articles on Responsibility of States for Internationally Wrongful Acts.

1.3.1 Legality: Doctrinal Legal Methods

Part I focuses on the first layer of regulation: legality. It answers the book's first research question: how does international law govern intelligence activities? In Part I, I identify the international legal framework governing intelligence activities. To do so, I use doctrinal research methods. The 'doctrinal method' consists of a 'close analysis of authoritative texts intrinsic to the discipline of law'.[64] It is sometimes referred to as 'classical legal analysis' and it relies on legal positivism as the underlying theoretical approach to international law. Normative concerns (what the law *should* be) do not enter the analysis. Rather, the analysis aims to identify applicable positive law, i.e., what the law *is*.

The case study in Part I (Chapter 3) also represents an example of traditional legal methods, identifying the applicable legal norms and applying them to the facts of the case study. In this instance, the case study focuses on the CIA-led war on terror as an intelligence gathering programme epitomising the liberty–security conundrum at the core of intelligence activities. I rely on available facts and material to assess whether state responsibility is engaged for all forms of participation in the CIA-led rendition, detention, and interrogation programme. In this case study, I use doctrinal legal methods to demonstrate that international law, including the law on state responsibility, applies to a variety of intelligence activities and cooperation therein. Further justification regarding case selection is provided in Chapter 3.

1.3.2 Accountability: Social Science Approaches to International Law

Part II focuses on the second layer of regulation: accountability. It answers the book's second research question: under which conditions does international legal accountability become an effective tool to regulate intelligence activities? This is not a legal question. In consequence, non-legal theoretical approaches and methods are needed to answer it.

The question first requires a conceptualisation effort. As a method, conceptualisation involves writing out clear, concise definitions for a key concept. In conceptualising 'international legal accountability', my aim is to define the concept to be reflective of actual practice and to operationalise it so that it can be evaluated. I define the process of international legal accountability, building on legal and non-legal sources. To ensure that my conceptualisation reflects international practice, I identify several dimensions of international legal

---

[64] Suzanne Egan, 'The Doctrinal Approach in International Human Rights Scholarship' in Lee McConnell and Rhona KM Smith (eds), *Research Methods in Human Rights* (Routledge 2018) 25.

accountability that can be used to classify its various forms. My conceptualisation efforts thus culminate in an original taxonomy of forms of international legal accountability. Through this conceptualisation endeavour, I thus theorise international legal accountability practice and specify its different elements, forms, and objectives for further operationalisation and evaluation.

Then, to theorise effective accountability, I turn to social science theories and insights. I first use theoretical applications[65] of behavioural experiments, carefully transferring their findings to states as units of analysis. Behavioural approaches to international law rely on experimental findings from behavioural economics and cognitive psychology to explain various aspects of international law's functioning.[66] Theoretical applications of behavioural findings allow me to analyse how states' preferences and behaviour are influenced by exogenous social forces, including legal norms and accountability processes. I then theorise the functioning of the international legal order. For this purpose, I apply theories of regulation, originally developed for private law regulatory issues,[67] to the international legal order as a social order. Indeed, states may be usefully analysed as formal organisations embedded in, and structured by, a wider institutional environment that functions as a networked, nodal regulator: the international legal order. I subsequently interpret behavioural findings through the lens of regulatory theory to develop a theory of effective accountability as nodal, networked responsive regulation by the international legal order. This theory of effective accountability allows me to answer the second research question, identifying the factors making accountability effective as a regulatory tool.

Finally, to fully operationalise international legal accountability as a concept, I develop a framework to evaluate the potential of a network of accountability mechanisms (i.e., the international legal order as a regulator unique to each state) to provide accountability in practice. The evaluative framework comprises groups of indicators selected to represent the potential that a given

---

[65] As explained by Tomer Broude, 'theoretical applications take research scenarios in which a divergence from perfect rationality is noted on the basis of general empirical evidence, and then apply the ramifications to a legal rule or institution. The application is theoretical in the sense that although it is empirically valid in one area, it is being applied in a different legal field and set of circumstances; hence, empirical authority is reduced. ... In international legal research, theoretical application could also include cases in which insights from behavioural economics in other areas of law are applied to international law, or instances in which non-legal [international relations] research on behaviour of states and other actors has international legal implications', Tomer Broude, 'Behavioral International Law' [2015] 163 U. Pa. L. Rev. 1099 1132.

[66] Anne van Aaken, 'Behavioral International Law and Economics' (2014) 55 Harvard International Law Journal 62; Broude (n 65).

[67] Peter Drahos (ed), *Regulatory Theory* (1st edn, ANU Press 2017).

network of accountability mechanisms will be able to provide accountability for wrongful acts resulting from intelligence activities. The case study in Part II (Chapter 6) constitutes an empirical evaluation of accountability as a second layer of regulation, aiming to identify its potential and limits. Building on Part I's case study, Chapter 6 focuses on accountability in the CIA-led war on terror. In this case study, I test the extent to which the potential of states' networks of accountability mechanisms explains these states' actual accountability, applying the evaluative framework thus developed to a set of states selected as typical cases on a dual comparative scale.[68] Further justification for the case selection is provided in Chapter 6.

1.3.3 Compliance: Social Science and Legal Methods

Part III focuses on the third and final layer of regulation: compliance. It answers the book's last research question: how does international law influence state behaviour in intelligence matters? This is, again, a social science question. To answer it, I first employ a behavioural approach to intelligence decision-making, i.e., identifying and analysing the effects of the biases and heuristics present at all levels of intelligence decision-making. This aspect of the analysis employs theoretical applications of cognitive psychology and behavioural game theoretics insights. I then draw regulatory implications using a law-in-context approach[69] informed by behavioural insights.

Second, I model state decision-making in intelligence matters. For this purpose, I develop a modified rational-choice equation integrating behavioural insights. The aim is for the model to accurately represent states' intelligence decision-making in practice. Then, I trace the influence of international law and effective accountability in state compliance and test my hypothesis as to the determinant role of the likelihood of effective accountability. To this end, I use a most-similar cases case-study design,[70] taking France and the United States as most-similar cases and applying the decision-making model to the

---

[68] Under this case selection method, the selected cases (one or more) are typical examples of some cross-case relationship. John Gerring, 'Case Selection for Case-Study Analysis: Qualitative and Quantitative Techniques' in Janet M Box-Steffensmeier, Henry E Brady and David Collier (eds), *The Oxford Handbook of Political Methodology* (Oxford University Press 2008).

[69] According to the editors of the Law in Context series at Cambridge University Press, 'a contextual approach involves treating legal subjects broadly, using materials from other humanities and social sciences, and from any other discipline that helps to explain the operation in practice of the particular legal field or legal phenomena under investigation'.

[70] Under this case selection method, the selected cases (often two) are similar in all respects except the variable(s) of interest. Gerring (n 68) 668.

factual situations under scrutiny. I evaluate the expectation of compliance of both states regarding a specific covert action, allowing me to identify the determinant role of the likelihood of effective accountability in the decision-making process and final outcome.

In the book's final chapter, I draw the normative implications from the full model of regulation and make explicit the link between compliance and the effective protection of national security. I draw historical, legal, and political lessons from the practice of intelligence in the twenty-first-century security landscape, providing empirical support to the normative claim that compliance with international law in their intelligence activities serves states' national security. In other words, the effective regulation of intelligence activities under international law enhances states' national security.

1.4 STRUCTURE OF THE BOOK

As indicated earlier, this book is divided into three parts, corresponding to the three main layers of regulation: legality (Part I); accountability (Part II); and compliance (Part III).

Part I. Legality

Chapter 2. Intelligence activities and international law
Chapter 2 addresses the relationship between international law and intelligence activities. It demonstrates, through doctrinal analysis, that international law comprehensively addresses intelligence activities. The chapter begins with a literature review showing the lack of a comprehensive framework through which to apprehend the interactions between international law and intelligence. Then, I identify a paradigm shift in the interactions between international law and intelligence after the Cold War. This multifactorial shift towards the twenty-first-century security landscape led to the need and possibility to identify a clear international legal framework governing intelligence activities based on their objectives, means, and methods. I sketch this legal framework, distinguishing between three types of intelligence activities: first, intelligence activities inherently prohibited by international law due to their objectives, in direct contradiction with core principles of international law; second, intelligence activities explicitly allowed by international law, within strict parameters; and third, intelligence activities regulated according to their means and methods only. This three-tiered taxonomy includes all intelligence activities and is flexible enough to incorporate new technological developments and activities as they emerge.

Chapter 3. Mapping state responsibility in the CIA war on terror

Chapter 3 focuses on state responsibility for wrongful acts resulting from intelligence activities in the CIA-led rendition, detention, and interrogation programme. The programme constituted the trigger for the first-ever international accountability processes, all around the world, for wrongful acts resulting from intelligence activities. In consequence, it constitutes an ideal case study to analyse the functioning of the first layer of regulation (legality). I analyse the programme and the various forms of state cooperation therein from the perspective of state responsibility, empirically demonstrating how the first layer of regulation applies to all sorts of intelligence activities and forms of state conduct. Following a summary of the most relevant factual, legal, and political elements of the CIA programme, I identify the applicable legal framework underlying US responsibility and I map foreign states' responsibility for cooperation in the programme. This systematic analysis of state responsibility in the CIA-led global war on terror is the first of its kind in the literature. The case study confirms that the first layer of regulation (legality) encompasses and applies to all forms of intelligence activities. Indeed, even in such a wide-reaching and complex web of intelligence activities as the CIA war on terror, one can apply the primary and secondary rules of international law systematically to determine whether a wrongful act has been committed and state responsibility is engaged.

Part II. Accountability

Chapter 4. International legal accountability for an internationally wrongful act resulting from intelligence activities

Chapter 4 focuses on state accountability (i.e., the enforcement of state responsibility) for an internationally wrongful act resulting from intelligence activities. For various reasons, interstate forms of accountability remain unused in intelligence matters. Yet, states are still held to account through other mechanisms such as international courts and bodies. To theorise and analyse this international practice, I conceptualise international legal accountability, accounting for non-state actors' role in the enforcement of state responsibility. In this regard, the concept constitutes the missing part of the regime of invocation of responsibility established in Part Three of the ILC Articles on State Responsibility, which addresses only interstate forms of accountability. The original and multidimensional taxonomy of forms of international legal accountability that I propose in this chapter is of general applicability. However, I justify the specific necessity of the concept of international legal accountability in intelligence matters, and I define its objectives in this context.

Chapter 5. Effective accountability
Chapter 5 theorises effective accountability. Drawing on behavioural insights and regulatory theory, I identify the conditions through which international legal accountability constitutes an effective regulatory tool. I first conceive of the international legal order as a social order, as the regulator of states' actions. Conceptualised as a network of accountability mechanisms unique to each state, the international legal order conforms to a networked, nodal mode of governance. I then analyse international legal accountability as a form of responsive regulation by the international legal order, regulating states' actions through supporting activities, rewards, and escalating sanctions. Then, combining behavioural insights and regulatory theory, I put forward a theory of effective accountability. Accountability is effective when it embeds the principles of networked, nodal responsive regulation and leads to state compliance. Finally, operationalising the concept of international legal accountability, I present an evaluative framework to assess the potential of the international legal order to hold states effectively accountable for their wrongful acts resulting from intelligence activities.

Chapter 6. International legal accountability in the CIA war on terror
Chapter 6 focuses on state accountability for wrongful acts resulting from intelligence activities in the CIA-led rendition, detention, and interrogation programme. The case study aims to identify the factors determining whether a state will be held accountable for wrongful acts resulting from intelligence activities. Focusing on the second layer of regulation (accountability), I critically assess whether a strong network of accountability mechanisms necessarily correlates with higher rates of accountability. For this purpose, I analyse the accountability of five states selected as typical cases on a dual comparative scale: the United States; Djibouti; Poland; the Gambia; and the United Kingdom. The case study highlights that the mere possibility of accountability is often insufficient to achieve accountability in practice, and there is no guarantee that such accountability will be effective in inducing compliance. Further, while a correlation exists between the theoretical potential of a network and actual accountability, the theoretical potential of the network represents the upper limit of what regulation can achieve through accountability. A strong network of accountability mechanisms thus represents an advantage in achieving accountability, but extra-legal factors influencing state behaviour must also be taken into account for accountability to be effective in inducing compliance.

Part III. Compliance

Chapter 7. State compliance with international law in intelligence matters: a behavioural approach

Chapter 7 addresses the reasons underlying states' compliance or non-compliance with international law in their intelligence activities. It aims to trace the influence of international law on state behaviour in intelligence matters. Through a behavioural analysis of state conduct in intelligence matters and the modelling of intelligence decision-making, I demonstrate that state behaviour in intelligence matters can be explained and predicted by the likelihood of effective accountability. I test this claim with a comparative case study using France and the United States as most-similar cases. The case study illustrates the functioning of the decision-making model and the decisive role of the likelihood of effective accountability in intelligence decision-making. The comparative analysis also highlights the importance of extra-legal factors and behavioural insights in understanding and explaining (non-)compliance. Finally, I identify compliance-enhancing paths and underline the necessity of a comprehensive model of regulation integrating all three layers to achieve compliance.

Epilogue: comprehensive regulation in the twenty-first-century security landscape

Chapter 8 concludes the book and addresses the normative claim I introduced at the outset: compliance with international law in their intelligence activities serves states' national security. I first summarise the main findings and contributions of the book, and answer each of the research questions presented in this Introduction. I then integrate my model of regulation within the twenty-first-century security landscape, drawing the lessons from the past twenty years of counterterrorism and security practices and assessing the consequences for the effective protection of national security. I conclude that the effective protection of national security requires state compliance with international law in their intelligence activities. Because it leads to compliance, effective regulation therefore serves states' national security.

* * *

As I finish writing this book, the world is facing a heightened number of security challenges, including a lengthy pandemic, a war of aggression in Europe, the dire effects of climate change, widespread disinformation, and an increasing backlash against democratic values and human rights. Many of states' responses to these global challenges are similar to those adopted twenty years earlier to face the threat of transnational terrorism. These responses are evidence that the expansion of executive and emergency powers and purported 'trade-offs' between security and liberty remain the preferred means of addressing security challenges. The twenty-first-century security landscape, born with 9/11 and characterised by the constant balancing of security and liberty, has become our new normal. Yet, as states face a growing number of challenges deemed to be national security threats, the rule of law should not be, once again, a mere afterthought. If the global war on terror has taught us anything, it is that extra-legal measures are counter-productive to the achievement of (lasting) peace and security. Only through respect for human rights and the international rule of law can we really achieve greater security, for individuals and nations alike. The need for a clear international legal framework and for the effective regulation of intelligence activities is still as acute today as it was on 9/11. My hope is that this book can bring us one step closer.

PART I

Legality

2. Intelligence activities and international law

2.1 INTRODUCTION

For as long as intelligence activities and international law have coexisted, it has been written and believed that there was 'something almost oxymoronic about addressing the legality of espionage under international law'.[1] According to this view, both would have developed side by side without ever (meaningfully) interacting. This 'realpolitik' vision of international law has prevailed in scholarly writings and international practice up until the end of the Cold War. Until then, scholars and policy-makers alike considered that national security objectives trumped legal and ethical concerns or, to put it simply, that the end justified the means. This view was reinforced by the strikingly underdeveloped domestic legal status of intelligence communities and the almost complete absence of arrangements for overseeing intelligence activities.

Yet, although peacetime espionage is never explicitly addressed by international law, since the birth of international law itself,[2] a small but constant stream of scholarly articles has examined the international legality of espionage. The focus on intelligence activities more generally is rather recent. It can be considered a consequence of the appearance of new threats, new responses, and overall a new legal paradigm for the work of intelligence communities. For the purposes of simplicity, one could date the beginning of this new 'intelligence era' to 9/11, but most of its components can be traced back to the end of the Cold War. Indeed, the collapse of the USSR marked the downfall of the equilibrium established between the West and East blocks, according to which the principle of reciprocity was the crucial means of regulating intelligence activities.

---

[1] Daniel B Silver, 'Intelligence and Counterintelligence' in John Norton Moore and Robert F Turner (eds), *National Security Law* (2nd edn, Carolina Academic Press 2005) (updated and revised by Frederick P Hitz and JE Shreve Ariail) 935, 965.

[2] Grotius, 'On the Law of War and Peace', Book III, Ch. IV xviii 655 (1695: F. Kelsey translation, Clarendon Press 1925).

As defined in the Introduction, intelligence is secret, state activity to understand or influence foreign and domestic entities.[3] A review of the existing international law literature clearly evidences the lack of a framework that comprehensively addresses all intelligence activities and makes sense of the various interactions identified between intelligence activities and international law. The present chapter seeks to fill this gap by providing a comprehensive account and analysis of these interactions. I start by reviewing the main scholarly positions on the status of intelligence activities in international law (section 2.2), a review necessary to understand the (legal) paradigm shift witnessed in the past decades (section 2.3). I then build upon these foundations to sketch the international legal framework governing intelligence activities today (section 2.4). Finally, I highlight how this legal framework, together with the automatic engagement of state responsibility for its violation, represents the first layer of the regulation of intelligence activities under international law (section 2.5).

2.2 THE SCHOLARLY DIVIDE: REALPOLITIK vs FORMALISM

Scholars writing about the relationship between international law and intelligence often endorse one of either side of an unresolved debate: the realist view or the formalist view. The realist view maintains that intelligence protects the very existence of states, so that states have not and will not allow any international legal constraint on it. In contrast, formalists consider that international law naturally applies to intelligence services and oversight bodies as organs of the state, and thus intelligence activities are subject to the same international legal constraints as other state activities.

An important part of the academic literature focuses on the age-old question of the legality of peacetime espionage – it indeed seems to be universally accepted that spying is legally permissible during armed conflicts.[4] A few authors go further and attempt to list and analyse the various ways in which international law and intelligence activities interact. From their work emerges a set of disparate rules that indirectly constrain the conduct of intelligence communities worldwide. What also becomes evident when reviewing this literature, however, is that scholars are lacking a common framework through which to assess the status of intelligence activities under international law. This lacuna is apparent in the differing approaches taken by the authors, as well as in the various models they use to present the results of their analyses.

---

[3] Chapter 1, section 1.2.1.
[4] See below section 2.4.2.2 for a more nuanced analysis of this issue.

2.2.1 The Formalist Account

Cold War era intelligence regulation was almost exclusively state-centric and reliant on the principle of reciprocity. Focusing on Cold War era espionage, Simon Chesterman thus identifies three corpuses of international rules restricting the freedom of the intelligence community in peacetime.[5] First, the principle of non-intervention, as formulated by the PCIJ in the *Lotus* case,[6] prohibits unauthorised entry into a foreign state's territory as well as unauthorised use of such territory. Second, treaty law governing diplomatic and consular relations implicitly tolerates limited intelligence gathering as forming a necessary part of diplomacy. However, it also grants states an absolute discretion to terminate consular or diplomatic relationships, or the presence of any such personnel.[7] The final area of interaction concerns arms control treaties. Chesterman regards the various agreements on strategic arms limitations between the US and the USSR (and later in multilateral settings) concluded in the 1960s and 1970s as explicitly providing for a right to collect intelligence in order to assess compliance with the treaties' obligations.[8] The treaties protect this right by providing for a corresponding duty of the state under surveillance not to interfere with the collection of information.

Hinting at a paradigm shift, Chesterman highlights that the end of the Cold War destabilised the existing equilibrium,[9] whereas 9/11 put an end to reciprocity as the rationale for limiting intelligence activities. Indeed, the post-9/11 terrorist threat was not counterbalanced by fears of state-imposed consequences for violating the law.[10] Although the remainder of Chesterman's book focuses on surveillance, other authors have attempted to list the current sources of regulation for intelligence activities generally in the twenty-first-century security landscape.

Dieter Fleck, adopting a different approach, starts by questioning the generally accepted premise that all intelligence activities would inherently be

---

[5] Simon Chesterman, *One Nation Under Surveillance: A New Social Contract to Defend Freedom Without Sacrificing Liberty* (Oxford University Press 2011) Chapter 1 'The Spy Who Came In from the Cold War'.
[6] S.S. Lotus (France v. Turkey), Judgment, 1927 P.C.I.J. (ser. A) No. 10 (Sept. 7), para 18: 'The first and foremost restriction imposed by international law upon a State is that—failing the existence of a permissive rule to the contrary— it may not exercise its power in any form in the territory of another State. In this sense jurisdiction is certainly territorial; it cannot be exercised by a State outside its territory except by virtue of a permissive rule derived from international custom or from a convention.'
[7] Chesterman (n 5) 32.
[8] ibid 33–34.
[9] ibid 36–37.
[10] ibid 38.

tolerated by international law.[11] According to this premise, when examined in isolation from the means used to achieve their objectives, intelligence activities do not constitute an internationally wrongful act. Hence, the reasoning goes, intelligence objectives themselves are permissible, if not lawful, and only the underlying conduct can be questioned.[12] Yet, looking at covert action in particular, Fleck observes that international law contains a corpus of rules prohibiting subversive action in peacetime, as reflected in the UN General Assembly 'Friendly Relations Declaration'.[13] The principles of sovereignty and of non-intervention, as defined in the Declaration, thus prohibit intervention in the political independence of another state; unauthorised entry into a foreign state's airspace or territory; illegal exercise of jurisdiction on foreign territory; and attempts to destabilise the government of another state.[14] Hence, covert action, the aims of which usually conflict with at least one of these principles, would be prohibited due its objective and not (only) the underlying conduct.[15]

For this reason, Fleck emphasises that intelligence activities in breach of these principles can never be justified under customary international law.[16] In addition, he argues, the fact that states commit these acts clandestinely shows the absence of *opinio juris* in favour of recognising the legality of covert action.[17] This argument, whether it applies to covert action only or to intelligence activities more generally, has been highly debated in the literature. Realist authors have attempted to rebuke it by arguing that 'several states' now claim responsibility for their intelligence acts.[18] Consequently, because

---

[11] Dieter Fleck, 'Individual and State Responsibility for Intelligence Gathering Symposium: State Intelligence Gathering and International Law' (2006) 28 Michigan Journal of International Law 687, 688–694.

[12] This is the position defended by the most nuanced realist scholars and the majority of the formalist side.

[13] Declaration on Principles of International Law concerning Friendly Relations and Co-operation among States in Accordance with the Charter of the United Nations, adopted by UN General Assembly Resolution 2625 (XXV), 24 October 1970.

[14] Fleck (n 11) 692–693.

[15] Fleck nevertheless mentions that the underlying conduct, if it constitutes 'a crime', can also be the cause of illegality. ibid 693.

[16] ibid 693.

[17] ibid 693.

[18] As far as the present author is aware, only the US has ever formally acknowledged its involvement in espionage over foreign states, and only on three occasions: the U-2 incident in 1960; the 1982 incident involving US reconnaissance flights over Nicaragua; and the Snowden revelations in 2014. See, respectively: Secretary Herter, 'United States Plane Downed in Soviet Union: Statement by Secretary Herter', 42 DEP'T ST. BULL. 816, 816 (1960); US Ambassador to the UN, Jean Kirkpatrick, 'Declaration before the UN Security Council', U.N. SCOR, 37th Sess., 2335th meeting,

espionage is admitted by states and 'a majority of scholarly literature', states practicing it would demonstrate the required *opinio juris* of believing they are acting lawfully.[19] Yet, in order to agree with these authors,[20] one would have to consider that (mostly secret and patchy) state practice makes the law. Such a position cannot be sustained without discarding the well-established process of the formation of customary international law (CIL), which necessarily comprises public, general, and uniform state practice, together with *opinio juris*.[21]

Responding to this scholarly claim that the illegality of some intelligence activities would be nullified by CIL developments, Iñaki Navarrete and Russell Buchan thoroughly debunk the 'mainstream view' by providing a comprehensive analysis of the formation of customary exceptions in matters of peacetime espionage.[22] Regarding state practice, they first explain that physical acts of espionage committed in secret on the ground do not qualify as state practice for the purpose of CIL formation.[23] In addition, they note that the sole form of available public state practice, coming through domestic legislation providing a legal basis for the functions of intelligence agencies and delineating the extent of their powers, merely represents a trend that can be found in a few Western liberal democracies. It is therefore neither general nor representative.[24]

Then, regarding *opinio juris*, Navarrete and Buchan carefully examine states' statements on peacetime espionage. They are forced to conclude with the absence of any *opinio juris* in favour of customary exceptions to international law for any form of espionage.[25] Indeed, while states have not shied away from supporting the permissibility of espionage from international spaces, they have been extremely careful never to express themselves about the existence of a customary rule authorising other forms of espionage. States

---

para 132, U.N. Doc. S/PV.2335 (25 March 1982); and Barack Obama, 'Remarks by the President on Review of Signal Intelligence' (17 January 2014), para 139.

[19] For an express rebuttal of Fleck's argument, see Fabien Lafouasse, *L'espionnage Dans Le Droit International* (Nouveau monde 2012) 26–27. Quotes translated from French.

[20] See Iñaki Navarrete and Russell Buchan, 'Out of the Legal Wilderness: Peacetime Espionage, International Law and the Existence of Customary Exceptions' (2019) 51 897 footnote 12 for an extended list of scholars supporting this view and arguing for customary exceptions to international law regarding peacetime espionage.

[21] See ILC, 'Draft conclusions on identification of customary international law', Adopted by the International Law Commission at its seventieth session, in 2018, and submitted to the General Assembly as a part of the Commission's report covering the work of that session (A/73/10, para 65).

[22] Navarrete and Buchan (n 20).

[23] ibid 920.

[24] ibid 923–926.

[25] ibid 927–934.

have thus either used legal euphemisms[26] to ensure that conventional developments did not spill over into CIL, or adopted a plausible deniability attitude preventing any development of a legal norm.[27] In conclusion, despite frequent practice, the different forms of peacetime espionage used by states have never given rise to any customary exception because the practice is accompanied by a 'sense of wrong'.[28] Strikingly, no claim as to the existence of a customary exception to international law has ever been made by a state.

Dieter Fleck further looks at the corpuses of law that intelligence activities, whether inherently lawful or not, might be breaching when operationalised. Breaking with the interstate focus adopted by the rest of the literature, Fleck highlights that most modern intelligence activities may be in breach of international human rights law due to the methods used.[29] He also stresses that intelligence objectives do not justify derogating from human rights regimes, a welcome clarification in the midst of talks about trade-offs between liberty and security. Then, as was also argued by Chesterman, Fleck notes that special treaty regimes may contain specific restrictions to intelligence-gathering methods. He concludes, expectedly, that international law prohibits intelligence gathering if and when coupled with additional elements of illegality. Yet, he is the first one to consider objectives, and not only conduct, as susceptible of constituting an element of illegality.[30]

2.2.2 Formalism and Pragmatism

Taking account of the post-9/11 paradigm shift in the interactions between international law and intelligence communities, Ashley Deeks adopts yet a different approach to the issue.[31] Starting from the premise that we are facing a necessary momentum towards a more formalist view of the relationship between intelligence and international law, Deeks advocates moving from

---

[26] ibid 928 on the 'Policy of Silence'.

[27] ibid 934–941. See also Alexandra H Perina, 'Black Holes and Open Secrets: The Impact of Covert Action on International Law' (2014) 53 Colum. J. Transnat'l L. 507.

[28] Navarrete and Buchan (n 20), quoting Quincy Wright, 'Espionage and the Doctrine of Non-Intervention in Internal Affairs' in Roland J Stanger, Richard A Falk and Quincy Wright (eds), *Essays on Espionage and International Law* (Ohio State University Press 1962) writing that peacetime espionage 'appears to be a case in which frequent practice has not established a rule of law because the practice is accompanied not by a sense of right but by a sense of wrong'.

[29] Fleck (n 11) 693.

[30] See also Craig Forcese, 'Pragmatism and Principle: Intelligence Agencies and International Law' (2016) 102 19, 80.

[31] Ashley Deeks, 'Confronting and Adapting: Intelligence Agencies and International Law' (2016) 102 Virginia Law Review 599.

a state-centric paradigm of intelligence regulation to one that takes into account and protects individual rights. Accordingly, she identifies three sources of law governing peacetime intelligence activities: customary international law related to sovereignty, non-intervention, and territorial integrity; treaties governing diplomatic and consular relations; and IHRL. Deeks adopts a pragmatic middle ground in the realism/formalism debate, proposing a framework that would 'strike a sustainable balance between the national security equities of states and core rights-related values'.[32] Such a framework would achieve this aim thanks to a sliding-scale interpretive approach to the international law/intelligence relationship. Hence, when the target of an activity is an individual, states should interpret their international obligations strictly in order to minimise the risk of harm. In contrast, when states undertake more traditional intelligence activities that primarily implicate the equities of other states, they should be permitted greater flexibility in interpreting relevant international law. Deeks justifies this approach primarily on the basis that states have tacitly consented to it. However, by so doing, she invokes one of the customary exceptions later debunked by Navarrete and Buchan.[33]

In his response to Deeks, Craig Forcese presents an original three-tier analysis of the interactions between intelligence activities and international law.[34] He first distinguishes intelligence collection, which he argues is not regulated per se by international law, from covert action. He deems the latter regulated by international law 'to the extent that it amounts to coercive interference into the affairs of another state or the non-consensual exercise of state powers on the territory of another state'.[35] Forcese then nuances this duality with a third layer. He thus points out that both intelligence collection and covert action are regulated by more specific international rules or regimes (such as IHRL) governing the underlying conduct of the activity at stake.[36]

Forcese then moves on to assessing Deeks' sliding-scale model. While recognising some virtue to the pragmatism of the approach, which incorporates international law into the decision-making process of intelligence agencies,[37] he warns against the resulting weakening of international legal norms that would inevitably follow the adoption of this realist policy as representing the *content* of the law.[38] Concluding, Forcese underlines that 'it is better to protect law, and accept that questions of expediency may deprioritize legality in the

---

[32] ibid 606.
[33] ibid 605.
[34] Forcese (n 30).
[35] ibid 80.
[36] ibid 68; 80.
[37] ibid 82.
[38] ibid 83–85.

calculus conducted by states, than to "collapse ... any distinction between law and politics, between breach and compliance".'[39]

A similar attempt at pragmatism can be observed in Asaf Lubin's endeavour to theorise a 'liberty right to spy' on the model of just war theories.[40] Lubin starts from the assumption that intelligence collection is necessary in all domains of international relations, but also that it actually advances international peace and security. This flawed realist premise leads to an attempt to justify, using a kind of backward inductive reasoning,[41] a right to spy belonging to states. Yet, this is done without sufficient legal grounding or justification. On the contrary, this conflation of international politics, state practice, and the law demonstrates a misunderstanding of the function and workings of international law. Further, damaging the integrity of the law through a pragmatic attempt to align it with state practice has the perverse consequence of granting states a legal right to advance their national security, no matter how they define it, through whatever means they deem fit. Lubin's approach also confuses issues of legality and compliance: non-compliance should be addressed by appropriate support activities and enforcement interventions, not by changing the law to make the problem disappear.[42] As Lauterpacht emphasised in a different context, the failure of existing enforcement strategies is 'a failure of political will, not of legal right'.[43]

The realist belief in military force and unfettered intelligence activities forming the premise of Lubin's argument has failed to create the national (or indeed international) security it promised. Rather, it has aggravated the secu-

---

[39] ibid 84, quoting Nigel D White, *Advanced Introduction to International Conflict and Security Law* (Edward Elgar Publishing 2014) 70.

[40] Asaf Lubin, 'The Liberty to Spy' (2020) 61 Harv. Int'l LJ 185.

[41] In game theory, backward induction is the process of reasoning backwards in time, from the end of a problem or situation, to determine a sequence of optimal actions. Here, the solution to the problem (non-compliance) would however be found by creating a right removing (rather than solving) the problem: states' right to spy.

[42] The danger of such an approach was highlighted by the US Supreme Court in a case concerning Native American land, in which the Court stated that: 'Unlawful acts, performed long enough and with sufficient rigor, are never enough to amend the law. To hold otherwise would be to elevate the most brazen and longstanding injustices over the law, both rewarding wrong and failing those in the right'. *McGirt v. Oklahoma*, 591 U.S. 18-9526, 9 July 2020, 42.

[43] Records of the International Military Tribunal, Volume 19, 461 (26 July 1946), Statement by British prosecutor Shawcross, partially authored by Hecht Lauterpacht.

rity dilemma.⁴⁴ It has also been repeatedly disproved by empirical evidence⁴⁵ and one could easily argue that realist theories have made the world manifestly less secure. Yet, these theories constitute the sole rationale justifying why international law should apply differently to intelligence activities compared with other state activities in peace and security matters. Damaging the integrity and normative strength of general norms of international law on the basis of such realist assumptions should, therefore, not appear wise nor promising to anyone concerned about improving security. This conclusion stands even if one assumes, as Lubin does, that 'the law on espionage is filled with a myriad of legal gaps'⁴⁶ and 'blind spots'.⁴⁷

2.2.3 Stuck in Another Era? The Realist Account

Other scholars, on the contrary, stick to the realpolitik view and refuse to acknowledge that international law could possibly, let alone meaningfully, regulate intelligence activities.⁴⁸ John Radsan thus advises the academic community that, 'accepting that espionage is beyond the law, we should move on to other projects – with grace'.⁴⁹ Others also consider that regulation would be detrimental to peace and security.⁵⁰ Yet, because of their strictly interstate perspective and their focus on establishing either the legality of intelligence activities per se or their lack of regulation by international law (and thus

---

⁴⁴ The security dilemma is a situation whereby 'the means by which a state tries to increase its security decrease the security of others'. Robert Jervis, 'Cooperation under the Security Dilemma' (1978) 30 World Politics 167, 169.

⁴⁵ For an analysis of damages inflicted to international peace and security by political espionage justified on the basis of realist theory, with multiple historical and recent examples, see Russell Buchan, *Cyber Espionage and International Law* (Hart Publishing 2019) Chapter 2.

⁴⁶ Lubin (n 40) 231.

⁴⁷ ibid 242.

⁴⁸ See e.g., Matteo Tondini, 'Espionage and International Law in the Age of Permanent Competition' (2018) 57 Military Law and Law of War Review 17; Catherine Lotrionte, 'Countering State-Sponsored Cyber Economic Espionage under International Law' (2015) 40 North Carolina Journal of International Law 443; Lafouasse (n 19); Glenn Sulmasy and John Yoo, 'Counterintuitive: Intelligence Operations and International Law' (2007) 28 Mich. J. Int'l L. 625; Roger D Scott, 'Territorially Intrusive Intelligence Collection and International Law' (1999) 46 AFL Rev. 217; Geoffrey B Demarest, 'Espionage in International Law' (1995) 24 Denv. J. Int'l L. & Pol'y 321. To a lesser extent, see A Radsan, 'The Unresolved Equation of Espionage and International Law' (2007) 28 Michigan Journal of International Law 595 arguing not that espionage is lawful but that it simply is 'beyond the law' (597) and that 'international law does not change the reality of espionage' (623).

⁴⁹ Radsan (n 48) 597.

⁵⁰ Sulmasy and Yoo (n 48).

their non-illegality), the positions embraced by realist authors are necessarily incomplete and outdated.

First, by failing to account for the increasing importance of human targets in modern intelligence activities (bulk data collection, surveillance, counterterrorism, rendition, lethal drone strikes, etc.), realist authors negate the relevance of IHRL in assessing the legality of such activities. The abstract object of 'espionage' thus conceived by realist authors is a fiction, separated from its objectives and underlying conducts. And there seems to be very little value in asserting that espionage is unregulated if one cannot operationalise it lawfully. As a result, the realist assessment is necessarily incomplete, if not artificial.

In addition, because realist authors simultaneously misunderstand the formation of customary international law,[51] their argument on customary exceptions would result in an absurd conclusion if we applied it to modern intelligence activities. The fact that all states are violating IHRL through their intelligence activities and consider it 'right' to do so for national security reasons would make it lawful for states to violate IHRL and demonstrate the required *opinio juris* at the same time. The realpolitik argument therefore appears fallacious. It is also outdated, belonging more to the Cold War era than to the post-9/11 context, and it increasingly moves away from the practice of intelligence communities themselves, which dedicate growing resources to ensuring the international legality of their actions.[52] Paradoxically, therefore, realists appear disconnected from the very reality of today's intelligence activities.

Further, the focus of many of these authors on showing the legality of intelligence activities *in abstracto* is redundant: the legality of intelligence activities cannot be dissociated from the legality of the underlying conduct and from the legality of their objectives. Hence, and without purporting to solve the age-old debate over legality,[53] it appears from the literature review conducted in this section that the inherent legality (or non-prohibition) of certain or all intelligence activities is a moot question. What matters is whether the means and objectives of the intelligence activity under scrutiny are of such a nature as to constitute an internationally wrongful act. Intelligence activities triggering

---

[51] See Navarrete and Buchan (n 20).

[52] E.g., the number of legal officers within the CIA grew from ten in the mid-1970s to approximately 150 in 2010. See Jack Goldsmith, *Power and Constraint: The Accountable Presidency after 9/11* (W W Norton & Company 2012) 87. Reasons for this pervading legalism are explained in the next section.

[53] Over which the ICJ declined to pronounce itself, despite several opportunities to do so. *United States Diplomatic and Consular Staff in Tehran (United States v. Iran)* [1980] ICJ Reports 1980 3 (ICJ) [40]; *Military and Paramilitary Activities in and against Nicaragua (Nicaragua v. United States)* [1986] ICJ Reports 1986 14 (ICJ) [123, 136–140].

the application of international law either involve an unlawful underlying conduct and/or objective, and they constitute an internationally wrongful act; or the underlying conduct *and* objective do not breach any principle or rule of international law, and the activity is permissible.

2.3 THE PARADIGM SHIFT

Intelligence historian Christopher Andrew thoroughly documented the difficulties that Western intelligence communities experienced in adapting to the changes resulting from the end of the Cold War.[54] The breakdown of the equilibrium induced by the opposition of the West and East blocks meant that intelligence agencies could no longer accurately predict threats.[55] However, Andrew also highlights that both the West and the East had experienced important intelligence failures already before the 1990s.[56] Such failures, he explains, can be attributed to intelligence services' lack of attention to the Middle East and their insufficient knowledge about theology and non-Western cultures.[57] Surprisingly, however, the end of the Cold War did not result in a redirection of resources to those so-called 'emerging' threats. Quite the opposite, until 9/11, most intelligence communities in the West were blind to the threat posed by al Qaeda. Exacerbating this blissful ignorance were institutional blockages and an embedded short-term historical perspective,[58] both of which made it 'impossible to understand adequately the threat from Islamist terrorism'.[59] As Dick Heuer famously explained, 'major intelligence failures are usually caused by failures of analysis, not failures of collection. Relevant information is discounted, misinterpreted, ignored, rejected, or overlooked because it fails to fit a prevailing mental model or mind-set'.[60] The dramatic intelligence failures of 9/11 and Operation Iraqi Freedom are evidence that the transition to a post-Cold-War world was arduous.

---

[54] Christopher Andrew, *The Secret World: A History of Intelligence* (1st edn, Allen Lane 2018).
[55] ibid 701–730 Chapter 30 'Holy Terror'.
[56] To cite only one, the Iranian Revolution caught the US completely unprepared and unaware. Andrew (n 54) 701–703.
[57] Andrew quotes Sir Mark Allen, the 'leading Arabist in SIS', who concluded after 9/11: 'We were just looking the wrong way … the failure to appreciate the significance of radical Islam since the Second World War was largely a consequence of our mindset that Arab nationalism was the key issue.' Andrew (n 54) 737.
[58] Andrew (n 54) 720–723, 728, 737.
[59] ibid 730.
[60] Richards J Heuer, *Psychology of Intelligence Analysis* (Center for the Study of Intelligence, Central Intelligence Agency 1999) 65.

The end of the equilibrium made necessary by the Cold War also brought down the principle of reciprocity as the leading legal principle regulating intelligence activities. Instead, intelligence communities now faced non-state actors. With different agendas to Cold War superpowers' intelligence agencies, these non-state actors could not be expected to abide by the same rules nor use the same means and methods. As old threats became less significant and new challenges arose, intelligence communities started reacting to their repeated failures in sometimes extreme ways.[61] They thus experimented with 'new' types of responses or, more accurately, reverted to extra-legal means and methods where deemed 'necessary'. This was particularly visible in the US-led response to 9/11, the 'global war on terror', aptly labelled as both 'a moral failure and a lamentable fiasco'.[62] At the same time, the development and increasing use of modern technologies by intelligence communities started to pose new legal issues. Human targets became the norm, triggering questions as to the applicability of IHRL, and intelligence leaks and scandals multiplied. It became untenable to continue to pretend that intelligence activities remained unregulated by international law and obeyed only a realist reciprocity principle between superpowers. In other words, it could no longer be argued that international law authorised states to respond to security threats in any way and manner they deemed necessary.

The literature review conducted in the previous section evidenced a real paradigm shift between the regulation of intelligence activities during the Cold War era and the modern post-9/11 regulation. While a more realist vision of the issue, in which the principle of reciprocity governed intelligence activities in a purely interstate paradigm, prevailed during the Cold War, we have now moved to a more formalist vision of the interactions between intelligence activities and international law. This is due to a number of factors, some of which were identified in preceding paragraphs.

Ashley Deeks justifies the necessary shift towards a formalist vision of the interactions between intelligence activities and international law by reference to four interlocking domains of change,[63] providing a sensible framework to apprehend the rationale underlying the modern paradigm. First, she explains, the general public has acquired a new breadth of knowledge about, and is

---

[61] This has been referred to as 'accountability ping-pong', i.e., reactive measures that overcorrect the last politicised and sensationalised intelligence failure, thus paving the way for flipside errors. Philip E Tetlock and Barbara A Mellers, 'Intelligent Management of Intelligence Agencies: Beyond Accountability Ping-Pong' (2011) 66 American Psychologist 542.

[62] Hugues Moutouh and Jérôme Poirot, *Dictionnaire du renseignement* (Perrin 2018) 193. Translated from French.

[63] Deeks (n 31) 600–629.

increasingly attentive to intelligence activities undertaken by states. This is both due to and reinforced by the stream of intelligence leaks (facilitated by electronic means), but also by somewhat voluntary efforts to demonstrate transparency from intelligence communities,[64] as well as by the increased physical detectability of some intelligence activities (e.g., rendition flights, targeted killings, cyber malware, etc.). The consequence of this 'near-real time' provision of information is that the public reacts to the information and can exert pressure on its government (which may in turn exert pressure on a foreign government) through its reactions.

Second, in the wake of what was perceived as a massive failure in intelligence gathering (9/11) and following claims for increased executive powers to face the 'new' transnational and globalised terrorist threat, intelligence agencies worldwide have gained, de facto or de jure, more powers and missions than ever before in democracies (e.g., law enforcement, interrogation, detention, use of force, and virtually unlimited surveillance powers). As Deeks highlights, 'these new missions implicate non-state actors as never before'[65] and trigger interactions with individuals who are not associated with any foreign government. This renders moot any reliance on the principle of reciprocity to govern such interactions.

Third, Deeks emphasises the increasingly legalised culture of intelligence communities. This phenomenon, termed 'intelligence legalism',[66] began when states gave legal status to their intelligence agencies. It was exacerbated in recent decades due to increasing domestic regulations[67] (which include international rules and standards) and agencies' growing understanding of the relevance of legal compliance for their perceived legitimacy and the necessity of cooperation.[68] In other words, because the public is more aware of their activities, intelligence agencies are increasingly governed by law. This leads them to pay increasing attention to the law and to include it as a relevant factor in their decision-making processes.[69] In addition, intelligence activities are increasingly the subject of litigation, causing intelligence communities to adapt as decisions on their legal compliance are made. Deeks predicts that, as disclosures about intelligence activities become more frequent, litigation will

---

[64] On public disclosures and their motives, see Ofek Riemer, 'Politics Is Not Everything: New Perspectives on the Public Disclosure of Intelligence by States' (2021) 42 Contemporary Security Policy 554.
[65] Deeks (n 31) 622.
[66] Margo Schlanger, 'Intelligence Legalism and the National Security Agency's Civil Liberties Gap' (2015) 6 Harv. Nat'l Sec. J. 112.
[67] Deeks (n 31) 624.
[68] Deeks (n 31) 628.
[69] See Chapter 7 for the modelling of these decision-making processes.

increase exponentially and plaintiffs' chances of being successful will follow suit.[70]

Finally, as a link to the three preceding changes, Deeks highlights the 'humanisation' of international law, or the move away from a pure Westphalian vision of international law. Indeed, the protection of individuals by international law can be observed in diverse areas beyond human rights law, including investment, intellectual property, the conduct of hostilities, and the environment. This is on par with individuals' increased access to international forums. Hence, the argument could be summarised as follows: because individuals are subject to legal protection and have more information about intelligence activities and avenues to obtain redress if their rights are breached, intelligence communities must take the law into account in their activities. In consequence, placing human rights at the centre of security intelligence is right not only in principle but also at the pragmatic level.[71]

Furthermore, both the nature of modern security threats, emanating as much from non-state actors as from states themselves, and the development of new technologies and methods of intelligence collection have shifted the focus from the principle of reciprocity to a wider corpus of rules. As I explained earlier in this section, this shift has rendered moot the carefully attained interstate equilibrium of the Cold War.[72] While the rules developed during the Cold War era remain applicable to interstate relations, new intelligence activities have triggered the applicability of a number of 'new' rules. These rules of international law have a territorial and extraterritorial reach, they apply to activities targeting both states and individuals and, as demonstrated in the next section, they apply to *all* intelligence activities. There is no 'legal limbo' or ambiguity about the applicability of international law to intelligence activities in the post-9/11 paradigm. With this new paradigm has come an era of increased state accountability for intelligence activities constituting internationally wrongful acts. Accountability processes have clarified the principles and legal framework governing intelligence activities, and affirmed their applicability to intelligence activities. As a result, a legal framework can now be unambiguously identified.

---

[70] Deeks (n 31) 625–628.
[71] Peter Gill and Mark Phythian, *Intelligence in an Insecure World* (Polity Press 2018) 213.
[72] Chesterman (n 5) 38.

2.4 INTERNATIONAL LAW AND INTELLIGENCE ACTIVITIES: THE LEGAL FRAMEWORK

Having established that addressing the international legality of intelligence activities is not as oxymoronic as it may seem from a Cold War era mind-set, I now move to sketching the international legal framework governing intelligence activities. It is common practice to consider that the interaction of disparate rules of international law with intelligence matters simply 'constrain' intelligence communities' range of action. However, this section shows that it is no less correct to claim that international law actually *governs* intelligence activities.

The areas of interaction between international law and intelligence activities are usually presented according to different models: wartime/peacetime; geographical; conduct-based; rule-based; etc. I propose to abandon these distinctions, focusing instead on examining intelligence activities and categories of constituent acts according to whether they inherently constitute an internationally wrongful act; are explicitly allowed by international law; or are regulated through their underlying conduct only.

2.4.1 Intelligence Activities Inherently Prohibited by International Law

The permissibility of many wartime intelligence activities can be justified on the basis that the obligation to respect the territory or government of enemy belligerents is lifted by the necessities of war.[73] Outside armed conflicts, however, the principles of sovereignty, non-intervention, territorial integrity, self-determination, and the prohibition of the use of force form the foundations of the post-World-War-II international legal order. Affirmed in Article 2 of the UN Charter,[74] the precise content of these principles has been developed first in UNGA Resolution 2625 (XXV) ('Friendly Relations Declarations'),[75] widely

---

[73] See below section 2.4.2.2.
[74] United Nations Charter, Article 2:
   The Organization and its Members, in pursuit of the Purposes stated in Article 1, shall act in accordance with the following Principles.
   (1) The Organization is based on the principle of the sovereign equality of all its Members. ...
   (4) All Members shall refrain in their international relations from the threat or use of force against the territorial integrity or political independence of any state, or in any other manner inconsistent with the Purposes of the United Nations.
[75] Friendly Relations Declaration (n 13).

considered to represent customary international law.[76] The Friendly Relations Declaration defined non-intervention and listed conducts in breach of state sovereignty. A decade later, UNGA Resolution 36/103 – the status of which as representing positive law is more contested due to having been adopted through a vote[77] – further specified the content of states' rights and obligations with regard to Articles 2(1) and 2(4).[78] Two types of intelligence activities are identified as inherently contravening the principles of non-intervention and territorial sovereignty as defined in those instruments: covert action and territorially intrusive acts. They are examined and analysed separately in the following subsections.

2.4.1.1 Covert action

Covert action is the US term of choice to refer to what other states might call 'special operations', 'special political action', 'disruptive operations', 'active measures', 'event-shaping', and many other things. I use the term 'covert action' to refer to these types of active measures generally, without prejudice to the state conducting them. The literature generally adopts the definition provided by the US National Security Act Sec. 503(e). It defines covert action as an 'activity or activities of the United States Government to influence political, economic, or military conditions abroad, where it is intended that the role of the United States Government will not be apparent or acknowledged publicly'.[79] While we should also account for the existence of covert action on a state's own territory (for instance by the British intelligence community in Northern Ireland), a generalised (non-US-specific) version of this definition constitutes a good starting point. However, it should be clear that covert action is not exclusive of intelligence collection. Covert action not relying on previous and concomitant intelligence collection and analysis would likely be doomed and, in practice, composite operations involving both collection and action are legion.

The core of any covert action is its objective, namely to 'influence political, economic, or military conditions abroad' through all means deemed necessary. Secrecy and/or plausible deniability are the two other constitutive elements. The various official and unofficial definitions focus on the objective (influencing foreign states' internal affairs) and the nature of the action (secret),

---

[76] See *Nicaragua* v. *US* (n 53) paras 99–111.

[77] The results of the vote: 120 in favour, 22 against, six abstentions, with most Western states voting against.

[78] UN General Assembly, Resolution 36/103, 'Declaration on the Inadmissibility of Intervention and Interference in the Internal Affairs of States', U.N. Doc A/36/761 (1981).

[79] National Security Act of 1947 (50 U.S.C. 3093), Section 503 (e).

but do not mention the means used to do so. The term 'covert action' and its non-US synonyms thus cover a broad spectrum of activities. They include in particular propaganda, clandestine diplomacy, political and economic action, paramilitary operations, and lethal action. Cyber operations aiming at secretly influencing political, economic, or military conditions abroad would also be covered by existing definitions.[80]

Covert action, which implies secretly influencing foreign political, economic or military situations, inherently contravenes core principles of international law. Indeed, both the prohibition on the use of force, either amounting to an armed attack[81] or constituting 'less grave' forms of the use of force,[82] and the principle of non-intervention, which involves 'the right of every sovereign state to conduct its affairs without outside interference',[83] form part of customary international law[84] and constitute 'an essential foundation of international relations'[85] as expressed by Articles 2(1) and (4) of the UN Charter.

Regarding coercive (covert) action under the principles of non-use of force and of non-intervention, the ICJ explained in *Nicaragua* v. *US* that

> The element of coercion, which defines, and indeed forms the very essence of, prohibited intervention, is particularly obvious in the case of an intervention which uses force, either in the direct form of military action, or in the indirect form of support for subversive or terrorist armed activities within another State. As noted above (paragraph 191), General Assembly resolution 2625 (XXV) equates assistance of this kind with the use of force by the assisting State when the acts committed in another State 'involve a threat or use of force'. These forms of action are therefore wrongful in the light of both the principle of non-use of force, and that of non-intervention.[86]

Covert action falling short of the use of force would still be in breach of the principle of non-intervention provided it includes an element of coercion. In practice, the means and techniques used by a state to coerce another state in

---

[80] See Michael N Schmitt (ed), *Tallinn Manual 2.0 on the International Law Applicable to Cyber Operations: Prepared by the International Groups of Experts at the Invitation of the NATO Cooperative Cyber Defence Centre of Excellence* (2nd ed, Cambridge University Press 2017) (hereinafter: 'Tallinn Manual 2.0') rule 66: 'A State may not intervene, including by cyber means, in the internal or external affairs of another State'.
[81] UN Charter, Article 2(4).
[82] Friendly Relations Declaration (n 13) and *Nicaragua* v. *US* (n 53) para 191.
[83] *Nicaragua* v. *US* (n 53) para 202.
[84] ibid para 191.
[85] *Corfu Channel Case (United Kingdom v Albania) (Merits)* [1949] ICJ Reports 1949 35 (ICJ).
[86] *Nicaragua* v. *US* (n 53) para 205.

relation to the exercise of the latter's state powers can be varied and nuanced. The Friendly Relations Declaration defines the principle of non-intervention as including the following prohibition:

> No State or group of States has the right to intervene, directly or indirectly, for any reason whatever, in the internal or external affairs of any other State. Consequently, armed intervention and *all other forms of interference* or attempted threats against the personality of the State or against its political, economic and cultural elements, are in violation of international law. (Emphasis added)

Resolution 36/103, though having a more contested status,[87] added the phrase 'in any form or for any reason whatsoever' to that statement, and further defined which rights of states were covered by the principle of non-intervention:

(a) Sovereignty, political independence, territorial integrity, national unity and security of all States, as well as national identity and cultural heritage of their peoples;

(b) The sovereign and inalienable right of a State freely to determine its own political, economic, cultural and social system, to develop its international relations and to exercise permanent sovereignty over its natural resources, in accordance with the will of its people, without outside intervention, interference, subversion, coercion or threat in any form whatsoever;

(c) The right of States and peoples to have free access to information and to develop fully, without interference, their system of information and mass media and to use their information media in order to promote their political, social, economic and cultural interests and aspirations, based, inter alia, on the relevant articles of the Universal Declaration of Human Rights and the principles of the new international information order.[88]

Hence, covert action aimed at coercively influencing in any way, in any form and for any reason whatsoever, the internal (political, economic, cultural, social) affairs of another state by definition violates the principle of non-intervention because such action interferes with a sovereign state's right to control its own internal affairs and to function effectively.[89] It is therefore difficult to envisage a way in which covert action, the very purpose of which is to intervene in the domestic affairs of another state, could ever be interna-

---

[87] See footnote 77.
[88] UN General Assembly, Resolution 36/103 (n 78). The Declaration was adopted by a vote and, due to the number of oppositions to it, is less representative of customary law than the Friendly Relations Declarations. Nevertheless, it provides additional precisions regarding the content of the principles.
[89] *Nicaragua* v. *US* (n 53) para 202.

tionally lawful.⁹⁰ In fact, research shows that states resort to covert action when they lack a legal exemption from the non-intervention principle.⁹¹ This leads to the unavoidable conclusion that covert action targeting a foreign state is inherently prohibited by international law.

Cyber covert action deserves specific attention. Indeed, while cyber espionage does not, as a matter of positive law and by itself, trigger a breach of the principle of non-intervention,⁹² other cyber activities can constitute covert action. Thus, cyberattacks and operations coming short of the prohibition on the use of force will fall under the principle of non-intervention, as will composite acts involving cyber espionage followed by a coercive use, by the same state, of the information thus collected.⁹³

In addition, and as noted by Dieter Fleck, covert action can also be prohibited due to the methods used to achieve the stated interventionist objective.⁹⁴ However, this is simply an additional ground of illegality, as the activity itself is already inherently unlawful. Thus, regulation on the basis of the underlying conduct is secondary to regulation of the objectives, or ends, of this specific type of intelligence activity. Yet, it is worth mentioning – if only because it opens additional avenues to seek redress – that, as individuals are increasingly the direct targets of covert action (e.g., extraordinary rendition or lethal drone strikes), IHRL is applicable. IHRL thus governs the underlying conduct when individuals are targeted, directly or indirectly, by state action abroad and end up under the extraterritorial jurisdiction of the directing state.

2.4.1.2 Territorially intrusive acts

Territorially intrusive acts form a category of intelligence activities comprising any non-consensual or unauthorised intrusion into a foreign state's territory. They include covert action but also various forms of intelligence collection, and thus deserve to be analysed separately from covert action. The legality of territorially intrusive acts should be assessed with regard to the principles of non-intervention and territorial sovereignty, which form the foundation of the sovereignty of states. While the principle of non-intervention will be

---

⁹⁰ Covert action on the state's own territory, for instance targeting non-state domestic entities, would be subjected to a different corpus of rules. International human rights law and, in the case of a non-international armed conflict, international humanitarian law would constitute the applicable legal framework to assess its legality.

⁹¹ Michael Poznansky, 'Feigning Compliance: Covert Action and International Law' (2019) 63 International Studies Quarterly 72.

⁹² Buchan (n 45) 65.

⁹³ François Delerue, *Cyber Operations and International Law* (Cambridge University Press 2020) 241–257.

⁹⁴ Fleck (n 11) 693.

triggered by coercive action on the part of a foreign state, likely leading to the characterisation of the activity as a covert action, the principle of territorial sovereignty follows a doctrine closer to that of strict liability. Indeed, central to territorial sovereignty is every state's right to determine entry and egress from its own territory, which includes its land area, internal waters,[95] territorial sea,[96] national airspace,[97] and cyber infrastructure physically located within its borders,[98] as well as the right to perform governmental functions, to the exclusion of any other state, within its territory.[99]

Territorially intrusive acts therefore violate international law notably because they are inherently in breach of the principle of territorial sovereignty. The principle requires respect for the territorial integrity of other states and prohibits the exercise of sovereign power over the territory of another state. While simultaneously a regulation of the nature of the underlying conduct (territorially intrusive), the principle of territorial sovereignty excludes from lawfulness whole categories of intelligence activities regardless of how the territorial intrusion is performed, and therefore irrespective of whether the underlying conduct is also prohibited by international law under a specific rule or treaty regime. In that sense, the principle of territorial sovereignty relates to the nature of territorially intrusive acts and only leaves few, precisely defined, intelligence activities in the realm of intrinsic non-illegality or permissibility based on the lawfulness of their underlying conduct.

Hence, notwithstanding the permissibility of specific forms of territorially intrusive acts under *lex specialis* or through consent,[100] the following taxonomy can be drafted:

---

[95] UN General Assembly, Convention on the Law of the Sea (UNCLOS) 1982, Article 8.
[96] UN General Assembly, Convention on the Law of the Sea (UNCLOS), Article 3.
[97] International Civil Aviation Organization, Convention on Civil Aviation (Chicago Convention) 1944 (15 UNTS 295) Article 1.
[98] Tallinn Manual 2.0 (n 80) Rule 2: 'A State enjoys sovereign authority with regard to the cyber infrastructure, persons, and cyber activities located within its territory, subject to its international legal obligations.'
[99] See Judge Max Huber's statement in *Island of Palmas*, 2 RIAA (Perm Ct Arb 1928) 829, 838: 'Sovereignty in the relations between States signifies independence. Independence in regard to a portion of the globe is the right to exercise therein, to the exclusion of any other State, the functions of a State.'
[100] The International Law Commission, Draft Articles on Responsibility of States for Internationally Wrongful Acts, UN Doc. A/56/10 ('ASR'), Article 20 provides that: 'Valid consent by a State to the commission of a given act by another State precludes the wrongfulness of that act in relation to the former State to the extent that the act remains within the limits of the consent'. There are several crucial elements in that provision. First, the consent must be valid, i.e., it may not be presumed but it can be implicit; it must be given by a person authorised to consent on behalf of the state; and

(1) Intelligence activities involving a physical intrusion on the target state's territory, apart from those by diplomatic and consular staff,[101] violate the target state's territorial sovereignty. These encompass undercover agents without diplomatic or consular status, and thus what is commonly referred to as 'spying' or human intelligence.

(2) Intelligence activities involving an intrusion into the target state's national airspace, except when authorised or consensual, violate the target state's territorial sovereignty[102] as well as the Chicago Convention (Article 3bis).[103]

(3) Intelligence activities involving an intrusion into the target state's territorial waters (internal waters or territorial sea), except when authorised or consensual, violate the target state's territorial sovereignty as well as the UNCLOS (Article 19(2)(c)).[104]

(4) Intelligence activities involving an electronic intrusion into cyber infrastructure physically located within the target state's borders violate its territorial sovereignty. This is the case irrespective of whether targeted computer networks and systems are operated by state organs or private actors, and of whether they produce damage to the infrastructure or involve an interference or usurpation of inherently governmental functions.[105] Such factors are only relevant to the proportionality of the response by the injured state, and not to the breach itself, which is characterised as soon as there is intrusion.[106]

---

it may not conflict with a peremptory norm. Second, the act only becomes lawful in relation to the state that gave consent, and may therefore remain wrongful in relation to other states. This also means that the primary obligation remains in force between all parties: it is only dispensed with for that specific act. Third, the act only becomes lawful in so far as it remains within the limits of the consent: consent to a given act only precludes the wrongfulness of that very act, for the duration and within the conditions attached to the consent. Unforeseeable consequences will thus not be covered by consent to the act from which they derive. Fourth, consent must be given in advance or at the time of commission of the act.

[101] For these, see below Section 2.4.3.1.

[102] *Nicaragua* v. *US* (n 53) para 205.

[103] International Civil Aviation Organization, Convention on Civil Aviation (Chicago Convention).

[104] UN General Assembly, Convention on the Law of the Sea (UNCLOS).

[105] UN General Assembly (2015), *Report of the Group of Government Experts on Developments in the Field of Information and Telecommunications in the Context of International Security*, A/70/174, 22 July 2015, para 27.

[106] Buchan (n 45) 54: 'My view is that states exercise territorial sovereignty over the cyber infrastructure that is physically located within their territory on the same basis and to the same extent that they exercise territorial sovereignty over their physical territory'. Menno Kamminga 'Extraterritoriality' (2012) *Max Planck Encyclopedia*

Regarding remote access cyber espionage, Craig Forcese raises another potential ground of illegality. According to him, remote intrusion onto the territory of another state through cyber means constitutes an exercise of extraterritorial enforcement jurisdiction, or extraterritorial state power, which in most cases would be in breach of the principle of sovereignty.[107] Forcese justifies this claim on the basis that remote access cyber operations involve 'the transmission of electrical impulses in a manner that changes (and does not simply observe) the status quo in a foreign state'.[108] While the justification may appear stretched, it provides further support to the position that any intrusion, whether it produces effects or not, constitutes a violation of territorial sovereignty.

This is however not the position adopted by the International Group of Experts in charge of drafting the Tallinn Manual 2.0. According to them, remote access cyber intelligence activities breach the principle of territorial sovereignty only to the extent that they involve an intrusion into cyber infrastructure physically located within the target state's borders *and* that they produce physical damage and/or affect the functionality of the infrastructure or involve an interference with or usurpation of inherently governmental functions.[109] Territorially intrusive cyber activities falling short of these additional criteria would most likely involve intelligence collection (exfiltration of data) or observation[110] and be construed as 'cyber espionage'. They would be regulated under Rule 32, which provides that 'Although peacetime cyber espionage by States does not per se violate international law, the method by which it is carried out might do so'. In other words, the Tallinn Manual 2.0 proposes that cyber espionage activities be regulated according to their underlying conduct only, and that their lawfulness 'depends on whether the way in which the

---

of Public International Law, para 22: 'The legal regime applicable to extraterritorial enforcement is quite straightforward. Without the consent of the host State such conduct is absolutely unlawful because it violates that State's right to respect for its territorial integrity'. Forcese (n 30) 80: 'I am not aware of any authority demonstrating that the legality of enforcement jurisdiction depends on the scale of the physical presence'. States' reactions to the Snowden revelations also invoked the principle of sovereignty to condemn US cyber espionage. For a recent example and an argument in favour of recognising a breach of sovereignty in the absence of physical effects, see Talita Dias, Antonio Coco and Tsvetelina J van Benthem, 'Illegal: The SolarWinds Hack under International Law' (2022) 33 European Journal of International Law 4.

[107] Forcese (n 30) 78–80.
[108] ibid 80.
[109] Tallinn Manual 2.0 (n 80) Rule 4.
[110] To the extent that observation could be performed without exfiltrating data, which is doubtful in most cases.

operation is carried out violates any international law obligations that bind the State'.¹¹¹

The discussion under Rule 66 further clarifies that:

> Cyber espionage per se, as distinct from the underlying acts that enable the espionage ... does not qualify as intervention because it lacks a coercive element. In the view of the International Group of Experts, this holds true even where intrusion into cyber infrastructure in order to conduct espionage requires the remote breaching of protective virtual barriers (e.g., the breaching of firewalls or the cracking of passwords).¹¹²

Hence, if a cyber operation does not breach sovereignty as defined by Rule 4 and does not constitute a prohibited intervention under Rule 66, its legality could only be assessed based upon the lawfulness of the method employed. This would be so irrespective of the severity of the damages, such as the exfiltration of data (including, e.g., nuclear codes), inflicted on the receiving state by such an intrusive but non-destructive cyber operation.

Yet, it bears noting that the Experts did not provide any legal justification for their position that the principle of sovereignty provides less protection to a state's cyber infrastructure than to a state's physical territory.¹¹³ Hence, it appears preferable to follow the well-established standards of customary international law on the principle of territorial sovereignty¹¹⁴ to analyse the legality of cyber activities involving an intrusion into the cyber infrastructure of a state.

Activities in breach of the principle of territorial sovereignty may also be unlawful on the ground that they violate the prohibition on the use of force, or constitute a prohibited intervention or an armed attack. They may further be unlawful because their underlying conduct violates applicable treaty regimes or rules, such as the Chicago Convention; the UNCLOS; international telecommunications regulations; diplomatic and consular law; rules on immunities; IHRL; international humanitarian law (IHL); or other applicable bilateral and multilateral agreements.

---

¹¹¹ Tallinn Manual 2.0 (n 80) Rule 32, discussion para 6.
¹¹² ibid Rule 66, para 33.
¹¹³ See footnote 106 for critics of the Tallinn Manual's approach, and support for following the standards established by customary international law.
¹¹⁴ The ASR (n 100), Article 37, commentary para 4 recalls that 'State practice also provides many instances of claims for satisfaction in circumstances where the internationally wrongful act of a State causes non-material injury to another State. Examples include ... violations of sovereignty or territorial integrity'.

2.4.2 Intelligence Activities Explicitly Allowed by International Law

In contrast, international law sometimes provides authorisation and legitimation for specific intelligence activities through the regulation of their effects, means or limits, or by using 'legal euphemisms'.[115] Hence, while intelligence activities are never explicitly declared lawful, some must nevertheless be considered legally permissible. In such cases, the specific treaty regime authorising the activity (under a designation that never mentions 'intelligence' or 'espionage') functions as a *lex specialis* to more general principles of international law. Therefore, provided the activity at stake respects the limitations and conditions imposed by treaty, such activity must be considered lawful even if, in the absence of a treaty provision, it would violate the principle of non-intervention or of territorial sovereignty. Activities fitting this description include specific forms of reconnaissance and of wartime intelligence.

2.4.2.1 Reconnaissance

Reconnaissance has been 'authorised' from international spaces, namely outer space, the high seas, and international airspace, through various treaty provisions. The Outer Space Treaty of 1967 provides that

> States Parties to the Treaty shall carry on activities in the exploration and use of outer space, including the Moon and other celestial bodies, in accordance with international law, including the Charter of the United Nations, in the interest of maintaining international peace and security and promoting international cooperation and understanding.[116]

The treaty further clarifies that 'The moon and other celestial bodies shall be used by all State Parties to the Treaty exclusively for peaceful purposes'.[117] Although the language was purposefully left ambiguous and the 'peaceful purposes' provision should theoretically only concern the moon and other celestial bodies, it has been interpreted as authorising the use of reconnaissance satellites from outer space.[118]

In very similar language, the UNCLOS proclaims in Article 87 the freedom of the high seas, and clarifies in Article 88 that 'The high seas shall be reserved

---

[115] Navarrete and Buchan (n 20) 928.

[116] Treaty on Principles Governing the Activities of States in the Exploration and Use of Outer Space, including the Moon and Other Celestial Bodies, Article III.

[117] Article IV.

[118] Jinyuan Su, 'Use of Outer Space for Peaceful Purposes: Non-Militarization, Non-Aggression and Prevention of Weaponization' (2010) 36 J. Space L. 253, 258. See also ECtHR, *Weber and Saravia* v. *Germany*, 29 June 2006, Application No. 54934/00, para 88.

for peaceful purposes'.[119] Comparable interpretation of the peaceful purpose provision has led to considering reconnaissance from the high seas as generally permissible.[120] Finally, parallel to the freedom of the high seas exists a freedom of international airspace,[121] which includes airspace over the high seas but also over the more recently created exclusive economic zone (EEZ) of states.[122] States' freedom of flight in international airspace, including for reconnaissance purposes, is commonly recognised.[123]

It is now generally accepted, in the form of state practice and matching *opinio juris*, that surveillance and reconnaissance activities conducted from outer space, the high seas, and international airspace are lawful in that they do not infringe on the sovereignty of any state and do not violate any rule of international law.[124] This is the result of a permissive interpretation of an otherwise ambiguous norm in all three situations, whereby the rule's ambiguity has been exploited to provide substantive authorisation to act. By agreeing to this expansive interpretation of a norm purposefully silent about reconnaissance,[125] state practice and *opinio juris* have consolidated the permissive power of international law in these situations. In all likelihood, due to the legitimation provided by law, actions undertaken following this authorisation have been bolder and more overt than they would have been without it.

As regard the EEZ, reconnaissance from the international airspace *over* the EEZ should be distinguished from reconnaissance from *within* the EEZ itself. International air law recognises each state's full and absolute sovereignty over the airspace above its territory and territorial waters, including the right to impose its jurisdiction over such airspace.[126] Airspace above the EEZ is thus excluded from the scope of state sovereignty,[127] and justifiably so since

---

[119] UN General Assembly, Convention on the Law of the Sea (UNCLOS).

[120] Oliver J Lissitzyn, 'Electronic Reconnaissance from the High Seas and International Law' (1980) 61 International Law Studies 563, 569.

[121] International Civil Aviation Organization, Convention on Civil Aviation (Chicago Convention) Article 12.

[122] Chicago Convention, Articles 1 and 2. Reconnaissance from *within* the EEZ is a more contested matter, as I explain below.

[123] Raul Pedrozo, 'Military Activities in the Exclusive Economic Zone: East Asia Focus' (2014) 90 International Law Studies 240: 'Long-standing state practice supports the position that surveillance and reconnaissance operations conducted in international airspace beyond the 12-nm territorial sea are lawful activities. Since the end of World War II, surveillance and reconnaissance operations in international airspace have become a matter of routine'.

[124] Navarrete and Buchan (n 20) 943–944.

[125] Navarrete and Buchan (n 20) 929–934.

[126] Chicago Convention, Articles 1 and 2.

[127] Pedrozo (n 123) 519–520; Joshua L Cornthwaite, 'Can We Shoot Down That Drone?' (2019) 52 Cornell International Law Journal 475, 506.

the coastal state does not enjoy territorial sovereignty in its EEZ but only sovereign rights over economic resources within the EEZ.[128] Hence, it would be hard to justify why the coastal state should enjoy any kind of sovereignty or regulatory power regarding the airspace over the EEZ. The UNCLOS instead preserves third states' full freedoms of overflight, including for military uses.[129] Consequently, in so far as it does not interfere with the coastal state's economic rights, reconnaissance from the airspace over the EEZ cannot be considered unlawful under the UNCLOS. Some confusion in the literature and state practice has however muddied the distinction,[130] and reconnaissance from within/over the EEZ is less unanimously considered lawful than from the high seas/international airspace.

Reconnaissance has also been authorised from the territorial airspace of states in more limited ways through arms control treaties. Simon Chesterman identifies the verification regime of the Anti-Ballistic Missile Treaty and SALT I Agreement[131] as providing for a right to collect intelligence, protected by corresponding obligations of the territorial state.[132] This verification regime model, reproduced or extended in later arms control agreements between the US and USSR and in multilateral settings,[133] effectively establishes a claim-right to reconnaissance from the territorial airspace of other parties with respect to assessing compliance with arms control obligations.[134] This represents a pragmatic solution to evident issues of trust between parties to arms reduction agreements. This narrowly regulated right to intelligence collection constitutes a well-defined exception to states' exclusive sovereignty

---

[128] UNCLOS, Article 56; Kay Hailbronner, 'Freedom of the Air and the Convention on the Law of the Sea' (1983) 77 The American Journal of International Law 490, 506; Efthymios Papastavridis, 'Intelligence Gathering in the Exclusive Economic Zone' (2017) 93 International Law Studies 31, 453–454.

[129] UNCLOS Article 58(1); Hailbronner (n 128) 506

[130] Asaf Lubin, 'The Dragon-Kings Restraint: Proposing a Compromise for the EEZ Surveillance Conundrum' (2018) 57 Washburn Law Journal 17.

[131] Anti-Ballistic Missile Systems Treaty (ABM), done at Moscow, 26 May 1972, in force 3 October 1972 (United States announced its withdrawal on 13 December 2001), Article XII; SALT I Agreement, done at Moscow, 26 May 1972, in force 3 October 1972, Article V.

[132] Chesterman (n 5) 34 referencing ABM Treaty, Article XII paras 2 and 3; and SALT I Agreement Article V, paras 2 and 3.

[133] See: Intermediate-Range Nuclear Forces (INF) Treaty, done at Washington, DC, 8 December 1987, in force 1 June 1988, Article XII; Strategic Arms Reduction Treaty Text (START I), done at Moscow, 31 July 1991, in force December 1994, Article X; and Treaty on Open Skies, done at Helsinki, 24 March 1992, in force 1 January 2002, Articles I(1), II(4), III–VI, and IX.

[134] Chesterman (n 5) 34.

over their territorial airspace, which does not spill over to create any such right outside specific treaty regimes.

2.4.2.2 Wartime intelligence

Wartime intelligence represents another example of expansive interpretation leading to authorisation. Indeed, the laws of war only address the prisoner status of spies. They thus legitimate but do not explicitly declare the legality of spying, although the 1899 and 1907 Hague Regulations, unique in this respect, permit the employment of 'methods necessary for obtaining information about the enemy and the country'.[135] Various conventions regulate the treatment of enemy spies by belligerent states[136] and determine who can be considered a spy.[137] In this sense, while a spy can be harshly punished by the injured party, they are not a war criminal and their actions do not engage the international responsibility of the sending state because wartime espionage is not an internationally wrongful act. Despite – or maybe thanks to – this superficial regulation, wartime human espionage is thus made legitimate and, in consequence, permissible.

Covert action and territorially intrusive means of intelligence collection during wartime are legitimated on a similar basis as human intelligence because they can be repressed by the territorial state, as when a state shoots a reconnaissance aircraft in its territorial airspace. In contrast, non-intrusive means of intelligence collection cannot result in the punishment of any 'spy' caught in the act by the injured party. However, as Quincy Wright explained,

---

[135] Convention (II) with Respect to the Laws and Customs of War on Land and its annex: Regulations concerning the Laws and Customs of War on Land. The Hague, 29 July 1899, Article 24. According to the United Kingdom's *Joint Service Manual of the Law of Armed Conflict*, this can include 'the employment of informers or agents in enemy-held territory'. Although, as the United States' *Law of War Manual* rightly states, 'Information gathering measures ... may not violate specific law of war rules'. Further, IHL emphasises that neither prisoners of war nor protected persons under the Fourth Geneva Convention may be ill-treated in the search for intelligence (Article 31, Convention (IV) relative to the Protection of Civilian Persons in Time of War. Geneva, 12 August 1949).

[136] 1899 Hague Regulations (n 135), Article 30: 'A spy taken in the act cannot be punished without previous trial.' and Article 31: 'A spy who, after rejoining the army to which he belongs, is subsequently captured by the enemy, is treated as a prisoner of war, and incurs no responsibility for his previous acts of espionage.' See also Geneva Convention IV (n 135), Article 5; Protocol Additional to the Geneva Conventions of 12 August 1949, and relating to the Protection of Victims of International Armed Conflicts (Protocol I), 8 June 1977, Articles 45(3) and 46(1); and Rule 107, ICRC Study on the Codification of International Humanitarian Law.

[137] 1899 Hague Regulations (n 135), Article 29; 1977 Additional Protocol I (n 136), Article 46(2).

'the legitimacy of espionage in time of war arises from the absence of any general obligation of belligerents to respect the territory or government of the enemy State, and from the lack of any specific convention against it'.[138] This justification covers all types of wartime intelligence activities. Hence, non-intrusive means of intelligence collection must also be considered legitimate and permissible during wartime because the principle of sovereignty is lifted by the necessities of war. In consequence, despite how very little treaty law has to say about them, all forms of wartime intelligence activities can be legitimated on its basis.

However, there is a caveat to this seemingly general authorisation. The prohibition of certain acts, or means and methods, also applies in wartime. Because international humanitarian law (IHL) functions as a *lex specialis* to some of the international law applicable during peacetime, wartime intelligence is lawful only in so far as it does not violate IHL, or any other rule of international law that is not displaced by the applicability of IHL. The latter includes norms of international human rights law (IHRL) and general international law that become or remain applicable during armed conflicts.[139] Therefore, as an agent of the sending state, the spy may engage the responsibility of the state for an internationally wrongful act if, during the course of their mission, they commit an act in violation of applicable rules of international law. In this sense, wartime espionage is also regulated according to the underlying conduct.

The status of cyber intelligence during armed conflict deserves special consideration, especially considering that IHL explicitly regulates only the prisoner status of spies.[140] The Tallinn Manual 2.0 emphasises that the rules governing the conduct of hostilities are directly applicable to cyberattacks and operations.[141] Thus, during armed conflicts, cyber operations may not be indiscriminate[142] (they must be capable of being aimed and be aimed at a military objective, and their effects must be controllable) and they must be

---

[138] Wright (n 28) 12.

[139] E.g., regarding the inviolability of diplomatic premises during armed conflict, Vienna Convention on Diplomatic Relations (VCDR) 1961 (500 UNTS 95) Article 45(1); Vienna Convention on Consular Relations (VCCR) 1963 (596 UNTS 261) Article 27(1)(a).

[140] Tallinn Manual 2.0 (n 80) Rule 89 reproduces for cyber espionage the IHL rule on the treatment of spies but, due to a geographical criterion, de facto excludes remote access cyber espionage.

[141] Tallinn Manual 2.0 (n 80) Rule 80. See also, for a summary of the applicability of IHL to cyber activities, J Horowitz, 'Cyber Operations under International Humanitarian Law: Perspectives from the ICRC' (2020) 24 ASIL Insights.

[142] Additional Protocol I, Article 51(4). See also Tallinn Manual 2.0 (n 80) Rules 105 and 111.

proportionate.[143] While dual use cyber targets (i.e., cyber infrastructure used for both military and civilian purposes) are military objectives, IHL requires that all feasible measures be taken to identify the targeted cyber infrastructure as a military objective.[144] Further, some property is especially protected from cyberattack and parties to the conflict have a duty to take 'passive precautions' to protect the civilian population against the dangers that might result from cyber operations.[145] In addition, data necessary for the delivery of protected services is protected pursuant to the principle of distinction.[146] This includes civil (governmental) data, banking data, and medical data, although the latter would be protected in any event. Indeed, irrespective of whether a cyber operation rises to the level of an attack under IHL, certain cyber infrastructure, such as medical systems, may not be made the object of a cyber operation.[147] Existing state practice and *opinio juris* overwhelmingly supports this interpretation of the law.[148] Hence, while some cyberattacks and operations may become lawful under IHL, limits remain as to what parties to the conflict may lawfully achieve through cyber means and methods during armed conflicts. Any cyber operation going beyond what is authorised by IHL would engage the responsibility of the state for a breach of the relevant IHL rule, as well as of any other applicable rule of international law. In particular, cyber operations targeting civilians or civilian infrastructure do not become lawful during armed conflicts.

---

[143] Additional Protocol I, Articles 51(5)(b) and 57(2)(a). See also Tallinn Manual 2.0 (n 80) Rules 113 and 117.
[144] Additional Protocol I, Articles 48 and 52(2). See also Tallinn Manual 2.0 (n 80) Rules 99–102 and Rule 115.
[145] Additional Protocol I, Article 58(c). See also Tallinn Manual 2.0 (n 80) Rules 114 and 121.
[146] Additional Protocol I, Article 52(1), Article 12 and Geneva Convention I Article 19 and Geneva Convention IV Article 18 for medical units. See also Tallinn Manual 2.0 (n 80). Rules 93–97.
[147] Additional Protocol I, Article 57(1).
[148] See the Paris Call for Trust and Security in Cyberspace, 12 November 2018, supported by 78 states; and several public governmental views on the applicability of international law (including IHL) to cyber operations: https://cyberlaw.ccdcoe.org/wiki/List_of_articles#National_positions. Note, however, the surprising British interpretation of the principle of territorial sovereignty, denying it the status of a 'rule' with regard to cyber activities.

2.4.3 Intelligence Activities Regulated According to their Underlying Conduct

Intelligence activities that are not explicitly allowed by international law, nor inherently prohibited because they constitute covert action or territorially intrusive acts in violation of the principle of territorial sovereignty, are neither inherently lawful nor unlawful. Rather, their legality must be determined by examining the underlying conduct. The relevant question is whether the underlying conduct constitutes an internationally wrongful act. Activities falling into this category are as follows: diplomatic and consular intelligence collection; remote access non-intrusive cyber intelligence activities; and domestic intelligence.

2.4.3.1 Diplomatic and consular intelligence collection

The practice of intelligence collection by diplomatic and consular staff posted abroad is implicitly acknowledged by the 1961 Vienna Convention on Diplomatic Relations (VCDR), which includes among the functions of a diplomatic mission that of 'ascertaining *by all lawful means* conditions and developments in the receiving State, and reporting thereon to the government of the sending State'.[149] This provision implies that intelligence collection (including through cyber means)[150] by members of the diplomatic mission is authorised in so far as the underlying conduct does not breach any applicable legal norm. The caveat refers to the obligation of diplomatic and consular staff to respect the rules and regulations of the receiving state,[151] in addition to applicable rules of international law regulating intelligence collection more generally. In that respect, the ICJ clearly stated that acts of 'espionage' by diplomatic (and presumably consular) officials constitute 'abuses of their functions' and cannot be regarded as a lawful means through which information may be collected.[152]

This interpretation is reinforced by Article 41 of the VCDR, which provides that the premises of the mission shall not be used 'in any manner incompatible with the functions of the mission as laid down in the present Convention or

---

[149] VCDR Article 3(d) (emphasis added); see also VCCR Article 5(c). And see Tallinn Manual 2.0 (n 80) Rule 43 with regard to cyber activities.

[150] See Buchan (n 45) 70–94 for the applicability of the VCDR and VCCR to cyber espionage, and 89–94 for the use of diplomatic missions and consular posts for cyber espionage.

[151] But see Craig Forcese, 'Spies Without Borders: International Law and Intelligence Collection' (2011) 5 J. Nat'l Sec. L. & Pol'y 179, 200, arguing that if the receiving state were to expressly preclude such information collection by law, thereby rendering all such activities unlawful, the local law could not be reconciled with the Convention because it would preclude the very exercise of the diplomatic function.

[152] *Tehran Hostages* (n 53) para 84.

by other rules of general international law or by any special agreements in force between the sending and the receiving State'.[153] This provision makes it unlawful to, for instance, use diplomatic premises as cyber data collection centres or as a base to engage in cyber espionage against the receiving state or a third state.[154]

If the Convention implicitly admits some intelligence collection as part of the functions of diplomatic missions,[155] it also grants the receiving state powers to prevent, limit, and end it. Hence, the receiving state can limit a mission's size and composition, and its consent is required to install a wireless transmitter or establish regional offices. In addition, diplomats' freedom of movement may be restricted for reasons of national security.[156] The Convention also provides for receiving state approval of military attachés, presumably in order to ascertain their intelligence function.[157] More generally, diplomats have a duty to respect the laws and regulations of the receiving state and not to interfere in its internal affairs.[158] With regard to these last two provisions, state practice regards espionage as well as cyber espionage as constituting an unlawful interference and almost all domestic jurisdictions criminally prohibit espionage. In consequence, diplomatic or consular (cyber) espionage does not appear to ever be construed as lawful under the VCDR and VCCR.[159] In addition, acts of cyber espionage against the receiving state would constitute a violation of the principle of territorial sovereignty.[160]

As agents of the sending state, the breach of international rules by diplomatic staff engages the responsibility of the sending state. Yet, it would not be engaged for an unlawful act of intelligence collection (which is per se permitted by the Vienna Conventions, although with stringent limitations), but for the breach of rules violated by the underlying conduct: the use of unlawful means

---

[153] For consular staff, see VCCR Article 55.
[154] Buchan (n 45) 92. See also Tallinn Manual 2.0 (n 80) Rules 41 and 43, paras 3 and 5.
[155] But see Delupis' interpretation of *what* can be collected: 'I believe that diplomats commit acts contrary to international law if they gather *secret* information. Their task may be to collect information from various sources in the host state, but they have a duty not to overstep a certain mark beyond which their activities become treacherous and hostile to the host state. Once they attempt to amass "secret" information i.e., information not commonly available or classified as secret by authorities in the host state, diplomats overstep the line of legality in international law'; Ingrid Delupis, 'Foreign Warships and Immunity for Espionage' (1984) 78 American Journal of International Law 53, 69.
[156] VCDR Articles 11, 27(1), 12, and 26; VCCR Articles 20, 35(1), 6, and 34.
[157] VCDR Article 7.
[158] VCDR Article 41(1); VCCR Article 55(1).
[159] Buchan (n 45) 90–91.
[160] ibid 92.

to collect intelligence. Because the procedural immunity granted to diplomatic staff is absolute,[161] it protects those engaged in intelligence collection through *unlawful means*. Therefore, the traditional remedy for overstepping the explicit and implicit boundaries of diplomacy is to declare a diplomat 'persona non grata', normally prompting a swift recall of the person to the sending state.[162] Strikingly, no state has ever explicitly invoked the responsibility of the sending state for acts of espionage. Rather, the formula often used to justify declaring a diplomat persona non grata or to break off diplomatic relations (in extreme cases) is that a diplomat has engaged in 'activities incompatible with his or her diplomatic status', without mention of state responsibility. Yet, this practice, based on the principle of reciprocity, does not erase the underlying legal issue: although no criminal pursuits against the diplomat can be instituted by the receiving state, their actions still engage the responsibility of the sending state if the means used to operationalise the collection of intelligence were in breach of international law. Applicable international rules governing the underlying conduct are numerous and include, in addition to diplomatic and consular law, the principle of non-intervention; IHRL; international telecommunications law; and the immunity of heads of states.

2.4.3.2 Remote access non-intrusive cyber intelligence activities

Cyber activities involving an intrusion into cyber infrastructure located on the territory of another state constitute a violation of the territorial sovereignty of that state.[163] However, states may store their data on another state's territory, and some cyber operations may be non-intrusive. These remote access non-intrusive cyber intelligence activities are not governed, prima facie, by the principle of territorial sovereignty. They are not necessarily lawful either, but an analysis of the underlying conduct is necessary to determine their legality.

The first situation is that of cyber espionage targeting a state's data while it is located on foreign cyber infrastructure. This could be regarded, in certain circumstances, as an interference with that state's right to perform governmental functions. The Tallinn Manual 2.0 Experts concluded that a computer operation that changes or deletes data related to the delivery of a governmental

---

[161] Note however the more limited immunity granted to consular staff (VCCR, Art. 41) and that honorary consular officers do not enjoy immunity from criminal proceedings (VCCR, Art. 63). In particular, consular staff only enjoy immunity for acts performed in the exercise of their consular functions, which espionage is not. Thus, and despite a qualified procedural immunity (Art. 41(1)), since espionage constitutes a grave crime in most jurisdictions, consular staff can be arrested and tried for such acts under the VCCR.

[162] VCDR Article 9(1); VCCR Article 23(1).

[163] See section 2.4.1.2 above.

function amounts to an unlawful interference.[164] While the Experts did not specifically address the example of cyber espionage in this paragraph, the implication is nevertheless clear: the Experts did not regard the observation and/or exfiltration (as opposed to the 'changing or deleting') of data as constituting an interference with the performance of governmental functions.[165] This view is not shared by all authors, but state practice and the current state of international law do not permit departing from it as a matter of positive law.[166] Hence, to the extent that they do not change or delete data related to the performance of a governmental function, and thus do not constitute an unlawful exercise of jurisdictional power, remote access non-intrusive cyber intelligence activities are regulated according to their underlying conduct only.

A second situation concerns the production of effects on cyber infrastructure located on the territory of the target state without intrusion. Such a situation is often the result of a remote operation involving a distributed denial of service (DDoS),[167] alone or in combination with another cyber or physical act. This kind of operation could be construed as a breach of sovereignty on the ground that it constitutes an interference with the target state's exercise of governmental functions. Such a view is not widespread,[168] but it is grounded in customary international law. Indeed, the production of effects abroad,[169] such as when an upstream state pollutes a watercourse, producing effects in a downstream state, engages the responsibility of the state from which the effects are produced.[170]

---

[164] Tallinn Manual 2.0 (n 80) Rule 4, discussion para 16.

[165] This is confirmed by Rule 32 of the Manual.

[166] See Buchan (n 45) 56–61 for a comprehensive discussion.

[167] According to Newton's Telecom Dictionary, a denial of service (DoS) attack 'prevents a website from being responsive by overwhelming it with thousands of requests (pings). Often these requests originate from a robotic network, more commonly referred to as a botnet. "Bots" are malware-infected computers belonging to unwitting individuals. The bots become part of a botnet—a grouping of bots—which is controlled by the unfriendly actor. Bots may be used to perform a variety of unsavory acts, such as sending spam and collecting data for identity theft. Botnets are usually composed of computers from many geographic locations, so the action is called a distributed DoS, or DDoS.'

[168] But see some support from the French and Japanese governmental views (n 148).

[169] See the 'no-harm' principle, best articulated in the ILC 2001 Draft Articles on the Prevention of Transboundary Harm. The principle requires states to exercise due diligence in preventing, stopping or redressing foreseeable and significant transboundary harm, including where it results from lawful activity carried out by non-state actors.

[170] In the *Trail Smelter* arbitration, the US made a claim for violation of its sovereignty in respect of the damage caused by a smelter located on Canadian territory. The Tribunal did not refer explicitly to sovereignty in its judgment but stated that, 'under the principles of international law ... no State has the right to use or permit the use of its territory in such a manner as to cause injury by fumes in or to the territory of another or the properties of persons therein, when the case is of serious consequence and the injury

The same should normally hold true for all state-sponsored cyber operations producing effects, irrespective of whether there has been any penetration or intrusion in cyber infrastructure located on the territory of the target state. However, it remains a reflection *de lege ferenda*. Notwithstanding, when such state-sponsored non-intrusive cyber operations result in the temporary loss of functioning of governmental services, as was the case in the DDoS operation conducted against Estonia in 2007, then it can reasonably be argued that, because such operations constitute an interference with the state's performance of governmental functions, they constitute a breach of that state's sovereignty.[171] Absent such a breach of sovereignty, other non-intrusive cyber operations will be regulated according to their underlying conduct only.

Few rules of international law are applicable to the underlying conduct of non-intrusive remote access cyber operations. Indeed, if the remote access activity does not violate either the principle of sovereignty or the principle of non-intervention, then the only constraints on the activity stem from a reduced number of rules, including diplomatic immunities, privacy protections[172] (to the extent that their applicability does not depend upon the jurisdiction of the state directing the operation),[173] and rules governing international spaces if the operation is conducted from these spaces.

2.4.3.3 Domestic intelligence

Intelligence collection conducted by a state on its own territory is lawful in so far as the state does not breach any applicable rule of international law. Indeed, their sovereign status provides states with the freedom to collect intelligence over places, persons, and things situated under their jurisdiction. This freedom is only limited by the specific rules of international law the state has consented to, among which we find diplomatic immunities and international human rights law, though other rules can potentially become applicable depending on the underlying conduct.

---

established by clear and convincing evidence'. Trail Smelter Arbitration (*United States v. Canada*), Arbitral Trib., 3 U.N. Rep. Int'l Arb Awards 1905 (1941).

[171] The very definition of state sovereignty includes the state's right to perform governmental functions, to the exclusion of any other state, within its territory. See above footnote 99.

[172] A violation of the right to privacy of a human person is an internationally wrongful act. However, obtaining 'information' as such is not if (hypothetically) nobody's privacy was violated.

[173] See Buchan (n 45) 95–122 for an assessment of the extra-territorial application of the ICCPR and the ECHR in cyber espionage; and Marko Milanovic, 'Human Rights Treaties and Foreign Surveillance: Privacy in the Digital Age' (2015) 56 Harvard International Law Journal 66, 111 suggesting a new ground of jurisdiction in surveillance cases: 'virtual control of data'.

First, a state cannot breach the inviolability of diplomatic and consular staff, premises, communications, and bags in order to collect intelligence.[174] As a consequence, states that intercept communications occurring in diplomatic missions or in the personal premises of diplomats violate international law. Likewise, a state that opens official diplomatic correspondence acts unlawfully, even when such correspondence is stored electronically on servers located abroad.[175] Further, all states are under an obligation of due diligence to protect the premises of diplomatic missions and consular posts. This obligation requires them, among other things, to protect cyber infrastructure and computer devices located on the premises against cyber threats, regardless of the source of the threat.[176] Taken together, the inviolability provisions of the VCDR and the VCCR provide an extensive legal protection to physical and electronic information related to the performance of the functions of diplomatic missions and consular posts against intelligence collection by the receiving state[177] and, to a lesser extent, by third states.[178]

In addition, following the ICJ order of 3 March 2014 in the case of Timor-Leste against Australia,[179] it can be argued that, when states are engaged in the peaceful settlement of a dispute with another state under Article 2(3) of the UN Charter, they are under an obligation to respect the confidentiality of the other state's communications with their judicial counsel. Such an obligation applies even if the documents, data, or communications are stationed or take place on their territory. Hence, the prohibition of intervention in the domestic affairs of another state, deduced from the sovereign equality of states, extends to cover the communications between states and their counsel in international dispute settlement – irrespective of where they take place.[180] In that sense, this prohibition constitutes another limit on domestic intelligence collection.

---

[174] VCDR Articles 22, 24, 27, 29, 30, and 31; VCCR Articles 31, 33, 35, 41, and 43. With regard to cyber operations and cyber infrastructure located in a sending state's diplomatic or consular premises, see Buchan (n 45) 73–89 and Tallinn Manual 2.0 (n 80) Rules 39, 40 and 41.

[175] Buchan (n 45) 89.

[176] VCDR Article 22; VCCR Article 31; Buchan (n 45) 78–82.

[177] Buchan (n 45) 89.

[178] In addition to the duty of the receiving state to protect the premises, property and means of transportation of the mission (VCDR Art. 22, VCCR Art. 31), third states must respect the inviolability of official correspondence when in transit, which includes transit through their electronic servers (VCDR Art. 40(3) and VCCR Art. 54(3). Buchan (n 45) 89.

[179] *Questions relating to the Seizure and Detention of Certain Documents and Data (Timor-Leste v. Australia)*, Provisional Measures, Order of 3 March 2014, ICJ Reports 2014, 147.

[180] For further analysis of this 'new' right to non-interference with a state's communications with its counsel, see Iñaki Navarrete, 'L'espionnage en temps de paix en droit

Further, the means used to collect intelligence domestically may not be in breach of international human rights norms, such as the right to privacy and the prohibition of torture and cruel, inhuman and degrading treatment. The evolving case-law of regional and international human rights courts and bodies regarding the permissibility (and conditions thereof) of surveillance measures and interrogation methods constitutes the legal framework of reference. There are thus regional variations depending on the competent body's case-law. Generally, however, interference with the right to privacy is considered arbitrary and therefore impermissible if it is not prescribed by law, legitimate, necessary, and proportionate.[181] In addition, in cases where a state accesses the electronic data of an individual located within its territory, privacy guarantees apply even if the data collected resides on cyber infrastructure located outside its territory.[182] Regarding interrogation methods, it is commonly accepted that 'human intelligence cannot be extracted through abusive interrogation',[183] though the standards of what is considered abusive might differ slightly.

There also exists a 'duty to warn' in international law, read under IHRL provisions and applicable to both territorial and extraterritorial intelligence collection, but restricted to persons under the jurisdiction of the state. Hence, states have an obligation, arising from their duty to protect under human rights law, to 'warn individuals subject to their jurisdiction of any real and immediate risk to their life, bodily integrity, or liberty and security of person, posed by foreign intelligence services'.[184] Whereas domestic law may impose a duty to warn also in relation to persons not subject to the jurisdiction of the state,[185] in

---

international public' (2016) 53 Canadian Yearbook of International Law/Annuaire canadien de droit international 1, 51–62.

[181] Surveillance and Human Rights: Report of the Special Rapporteur on the promotion and protection of the right to freedom of opinion and expression, UN Doc. A/HRC/41/35, 28 May 2019, para. 24; The right to privacy in the digital age: Report of the Office of the United Nations High Commissioner for Human Rights, UN Doc. A/HRC/27/37, 30 June 2014, paras 21–30.

[182] Buchan (n 45) 97; Tallinn Manual 2.0 (n 80) Rule 34.

[183] Forcese (n 151) 196.

[184] Marko Milanovic, 'More on the Duty to Warn Persons Threatened by Foreign Intelligence Services' (*EJIL Talk!*, 10 June 2019). See also, with regard to the murder of Jamal Khashoggi, the report by the UN Special Rapporteur on extrajudicial, summary or arbitrary killings Agnes Callamard, A/HRC/41/CRP.1, stating in particular: 'If the United States (or any other party to the ICCPR) knew, or should have known, of a foreseeable threat to Khashoggi's life and failed to warn him, while he was in Turkey (or elsewhere), and under circumstances with respect to which it could be argued that he was under their functional jurisdiction, then the United States or any other State would have violated their obligations to protect Mr. Khashoggi's life.'

[185] E.g., US Intelligence Community Directive 191. For an account of recent US practice towards persons not under its jurisdictions, see Edwin Djabatey, 'Duty to

international law the duty is subject to a jurisdictional threshold[186] and is only triggered if a specific unlawful threat to the life of an individual was reasonably foreseeable to the state. It is an obligation of due diligence, meaning that the state can take a number of relevant considerations into account in deciding on how to fulfil it.[187]

Finally, domestic intelligence operations matching the definition of covert action 'at home' are also subject to IHRL. Relevant rights notably include the rights to life, to liberty and security of the person, to privacy, and the prohibitions of torture, cruel, inhumane and degrading treatments and of enforced disappearance. If hostilities between the government and non-state entities rise to the level of a non-international armed conflict,[188] relevant IHL provisions would also become applicable and govern the permissibility of intelligence operations within the conflict.

2.5 CONCLUSIONS: LEGALITY AS THE FIRST LAYER OF REGULATION

The present chapter demonstrated that intelligence activities and international law are not as foreign as parts of the literature portray them. Following the paradigm shift induced by the end of the Cold War equilibrium and confirmed by states' responses to the modern terrorist threat, the move away from the realpolitik view of the relationship between international law and intelligence activities became ineluctable. In consequence, I adopted a more formalist stance to make sense of the interactions between international law and intelligence activities in the twenty-first-century security landscape. This approach is supported by an analysis of the scholarly literature and by modern intelligence activities and practices.

The most important purpose served by this chapter was to establish that international law comprehensively addresses intelligence activities, so that there is no 'grey zone' or 'legal limbo' in which states would be free to act fully unconstrained. The chapter also disproved claims that 'espionage' would be either internationally lawful or unlawful as constituting misunderstandings

---

Warn: Has the Trump Administration Learned from the Khashoggi Failure?', *Just Security*, 6 November 2019.

[186] However, note the differing approaches to jurisdiction – the Human Rights Committee adopting a looser conception than regional human rights bodies. Milanovic emphasises that 'the key point here . . . is that a state lacking the capacity to fulfil the duty to warn will never be expected to have to do so'. Milanovic (n 184).

[187] Milanovic (n 184).

[188] ICTY, *Prosecutor* v. *Dusko Tadic*, Decision on the Defence Motion for Interlocutory Appeal on Jurisdiction, IT-94-1-A, 2 October 1995, para 70.

of public international law and of the formation of customary international law. Rather than address this moot issue in detail, I looked instead at the international legality of the objectives and means of all types and categories of intelligence activities. This approach allowed for a comprehensive sketch of the international legal framework governing intelligence activities. Using a novel taxonomy, I divided intelligence activities between three categories: those inherently prohibited by international law; those explicitly allowed by international law; and intelligence activities that belong to neither of the first two categories and are therefore regulated according to their underlying conduct only. This three-tiered taxonomy is particularly valuable because it includes all intelligence activities and is flexible enough to incorporate new activities and technological developments as they emerge.

The issue of legality, dealt with in this chapter, constitutes the key part of the first layer of regulation of intelligence activities under international law. This first layer also comprises the engagement of state responsibility as a direct and immediate consequence of the breach of legality.[189] Chapter 3 provides an illustration of this process, addressing complex issues of state responsibility and complicity in intelligence matters through a case-study on the CIA-led 'global war on terror'. Nevertheless, legality itself should not be confused with the separate issues of state responsibility and of states' choices and motives for complying with or ignoring international law in their intelligence decision-making. Indeed, this chapter focused exclusively on clarifying the framework of primary norms applicable to intelligence activities. It is then left to the law of state responsibility, subsequently and through a separate analysis involving the application of secondary norms, to determine whether a prima facie breach of an applicable primary norm constitutes an internationally wrongful act engaging the responsibility of the state, and what consequences should follow. This chapter thus established the foundations necessary to pursue, in the following chapters, an analysis of issues of responsibility and accountability for internationally wrongful acts resulting from intelligence activities.

---

[189] See generally International Law Commission, Draft Articles on Responsibility of States for Internationally Wrongful Acts 2001 (Supplement No 10 (A/56/10), chpIVE1) 76; James Crawford, *State Responsibility: The General Part* (Cambridge University Press 2013).

3. Mapping state responsibility in the CIA war on terror

3.1 INTRODUCTION

The United States' Central Intelligence Agency's (CIA) rendition, detention, and interrogation programme provides an emblematic case-study to analyse state responsibility in the modern intelligence context. The programme itself, led by an intelligence agency and comprising many modern forms of intelligence, constitutes an example of counterterrorism intelligence cooperation pushed to its furthest, highlighting the 'systemic inadequacies of the accountability structure over intelligence agencies'.[1] Indeed, the CIA-led 'global war on terror' epitomises the liberty–security conundrum at the core of intelligence activities and of states' justifications for them. The balancing act's extreme bias in favour of security (however defined) after 9/11 made it impossible for the international community to ignore further the pressing need to start holding states to account for their intelligence operations.[2] In fact, the programme constituted the trigger for the first-ever international accountability processes for wrongful acts resulting from non-domestic intelligence activities all around the world.

The CIA-led programme thus plays a crucial role in defining intelligence in the twenty-first-century security landscape and in highlighting both the challenges of international regulation and the potential for effective accountability. The worldwide reach of the programme, the increasing publicity surrounding it, the never-ending challenges and disputes it triggers, and the variety of legal issues it raises all participate in the programme's significance in shaping our

---

[1] Gerald Staberock, 'Intelligence and Counter-Terrorism: Towards a Human Rights and Accountability Framework?' in Ana Salinas de Frías (ed), *Counter-Terrorism: International Law and Practice* (Oxford University Press 2011) 352.

[2] The renewed interest for the issue of democratic oversight and accountability of intelligence services, observable through the high number of reports and research articles on the topic since 2002, is possibly one of the most significant policy changes stemming from the publicity of the CIA-led programme.

understanding of modern intelligence activities and of their regulation.[3] In consequence, it constitutes an ideal case-study to analyse the functioning of the first two layers of the regulation of states' intelligence activities, respectively here (legality) and in Chapter 6 (accountability).

The present chapter analyses the programme and the various forms of state cooperation from the perspective of state responsibility. It thus aims at empirically demonstrating how the first layer of regulation (legality) applies to all sorts of intelligence activities and forms of state conduct. Following a summary of the most relevant factual, legal, and political elements of the CIA programme (section 3.2), the chapter turns to the applicable legal framework underlying the United States' responsibility (section 3.3) and the mapping of cooperating states' responsibility (section 3.4). Concluding remarks regarding the applicability of international law to intelligence activities are provided in section 3.5.

3.2 THE CIA-LED RENDITION, DETENTION, AND INTERROGATION PROGRAMME

The CIA programme was highly classified, held outside the United States (US), and designed to place detainee interrogations beyond the reach of the law. It entailed the abduction and disappearance of detainees and their extra-legal transfer on secret flights to undisclosed locations, followed by their incommunicado detention, interrogation, torture, and abuse at the hands of the CIA or other states' intelligence services. Victims who survived torture[4] were eventually transferred into US military custody at Guantánamo Bay or into another state's custody, or released.

The current most comprehensive source of factual information about the programme is the declassified executive summary of the US Senate Select Committee on Intelligence's 'Committee Study of the CIA's Detention and Interrogation Program' (SSCI Study).[5] The Committee, chaired by Senator Dianne Feinstein, began reviewing the programme in March 2009 and

---

[3] Any claim to representativeness would necessarily be hindered by the high level of secrecy surrounding the majority of intelligence activities. Given the subject-matter, this choice of case-study can therefore only be made on rather pragmatic criteria, one of which is the publicity of the facts. I nevertheless hope that the case-study is representative enough of modern intelligence activities for empirical findings to have high external validity.

[4] At least one detainee (Gul Rahman) died in CIA custody as a result of torture.

[5] United States Senate Select Committee on Intelligence, *Torture Report: Committee Study of Central Intelligence Agency's Detention and Interrogation Program: Executive Summary* (2014).

approved the study in December 2012 by a vote of nine to six. The Study's executive summary was approved for public disclosure on 11 December 2014. The full SSCI Study, which exceeds 6700 pages and is based on more than six million pages of CIA materials, remains classified. Nevertheless, its 524-page executive summary provides a wealth of details about the inner workings of the CIA and its rendition, detention, and interrogation programme, together with the names of 119 CIA detainees.[6] When read together with the dataset[7] and reading keys[8] developed by the Bureau of Investigative Journalism and the Rendition Project, it constitutes the most comprehensive and reliable source of information about the programme to this day.

The main findings of the Study can be broadly classified into five categories:

1. The CIA's 'enhanced interrogation techniques' were not effective.[9]
2. The CIA provided misleading information about the operation of the programme and its effectiveness to policy-makers and the public.[10]
3. The CIA programme was far more brutal than the CIA represented to policy-makers and the American public.[11]
4. The CIA's management of the programme was inadequate and deeply flawed.[12]
5. The CIA programme harmed US diplomacy and national security.[13]

The priority given to torture's (lack of) effectiveness in the Study is hardly surprising against the background of the US's change of policy following the attacks of 9/11. Whether torture was considered good or bad suddenly stopped depending on legal or moral considerations. Rather, the debate turned to whether it 'worked', i.e., produced life-saving intelligence. This general acceptance by the US population of torture as a lesser evil in relation to the greater evil of terrorism is, in part, what distinguishes the US war on terror from

---

[6] Appendix 2 to the Study, declassified.
[7] The current published version of this dataset, compiled by the Rendition Project, is available at: http://www.therenditionproject.org.uk/prisoners/data.html.
[8] Sam Raphael, Crofton Black and Ruth Blakeley, 'CIA Torture Unredacted' (2019), https://www.therenditionproject.org.uk/unredacted/the-report.html.
[9] Finding 1.
[10] Findings 2, 5, 6, 9, 10. Although this is outside the scope of the SSCI Study, the CIA also provided misleading information about the operation of the programme and its effectiveness to foreign intelligence agencies and governments. See Intelligence and Security Committee, 'Detainee Mistreatment and Rendition: 2001–2010' (2018).
[11] Findings 3, 4, 14.
[12] Findings 11, 12, 13, 15, 16, 17, 18.
[13] Findings 7, 8, 19, 20.

other instances of state torture or counterterror wars.[14] The balancing act was embodied in the two infamous Bybee-Yoo 'Torture Memos' of 1 August 2002. The first authorised the use of 'enhanced interrogation techniques' amounting to torture by the CIA against suspected terrorists.[15] The other complemented it by dismantling, through dubious legal interpretation, the prohibition of torture in US and international law, and finding a novel use of the necessity defence under US law 'to avoid prosecution of US officials who tortured to obtain information that saved many lives'.[16] Torture was thus redefined in such a way as to invite its use with impunity. Later memoranda from the Office of Legal Counsel reinforced this mentality by determining that the enhanced interrogation techniques were legal in part because they produced 'specific, actionable intelligence' and 'substantial quantities of otherwise unavailable intelligence' that saved lives.[17]

That the CIA programme was ineffective and counter-productive to American counterterrorism policies therefore did not come as a shock to most outside the US. However, it finally defeated from the inside the very reasoning according to which the programme was authorised and conducted. What *should* have been shocking, instead, is that the effectiveness mentality resulted in findings of torture and abuse being relegated to third position in the Study. It is primarily on those that the next sections will focus, with the intention of mapping conduct engaging state responsibility for participation in the programme.

---

[14] According to a 2007 Pew Research Center survey, only 29% of Americans believed torture was never justified, with 43% saying that the use of torture can be justified against suspected terrorists to gain key information sometimes (31%) or often (12%). Dataset available at: http://www.pewresearch.org/fact-tank/2008/06/13/torture-justified/.

[15] August 1, 2002, Memorandum for John A. Rizzo from Jay S. Bybee, re: Interrogation of al Qaeda Operative.

[16] August 1, 2002, Memorandum for Alberto S. Gonzalez from Jay S. Bybee, Re: Standards of Conduct for Interrogation Under 18 U.S.C. §§ 2340–2340A.

[17] May 30, 2005, Memorandum for John A. Rizzo from Steven G. Bradbury, re: Application of United States Obligations Under Article 16 of the Convention Against Torture to Certain Techniques that May Be Used in the Interrogation of High Value al Qaeda Detainees; July 20, 2007, Memorandum for John A. Rizzo from Steven G. Bradbury, re: Application of War Crimes Act, the Detainee Treatment Act, and Common Article 3 of the Geneva Conventions to Certain Techniques that May be Used by the CIA in the Interrogation of High Value al Qaeda Detainees.

3.2.1 Factual and Policy Background

On 17 September 2001, US President George W Bush signed a covert action Memorandum of Notification (MoN) granting the CIA unprecedented counter-terrorism powers, including the authority to covertly capture and detain individuals 'posing a continuing, serious threat of violence or death to U.S. persons and interests or planning terrorist activities'.[18] The MoN made no reference to interrogations or coercive interrogation techniques but became the founding act of the CIA's secret detention scheme.

On 4 October 2001, following the invocation of the principle of collective self-defence under Article 5 of the North Atlantic Treaty,[19] a secret agreement was made by NATO allies. In this unpublished text, NATO members adopted, inter alia, a set of eight measures affording the CIA a mandate to pursue its war on terror, thereby mimicking the effects of the MoN at the international level.[20] These measures notably included undertakings to:

1. Enhance intelligence-sharing and cooperation, both bilaterally and in the appropriate NATO bodies, relating to the threats posed by terrorism and the actions to be taken against it;
2. Provide increased security for the United States' and other allies' facilities on NATO territory;
3. Provide blanket overflight clearances for the United States' and other allies' aircrafts for military flights related to operations against terrorism; and
4. Provide access to ports and airfields on NATO territory, including for refuelling, for the United States and other allies for operations against terrorism.[21]

These measures would later prove essential to the existence of the CIA's extraordinary rendition scheme. Indeed, a total of 40 states formally agreed

---

[18] United States Senate Select Committee on Intelligence (n 5) 11.
[19] The principle was invoked by NATO on 12 September and activated on 2 October after it was determined with certainty that the attacks of 11 September had been directed against the US from abroad.
[20] Dick Marty, 'Secret Detentions and Illegal Transfers of Detainees Involving Council of Europe Member States' (Parliamentary Assembly of the Council of Europe 2007) PACE Doc. 11302 rev. para 93.
[21] See NATO, 'Statement to the Press by NATO Secretary General, Lord Robertson, on the North Atlantic Council Decision on Implementation of Article 5 of the Washington Treaty following the 11 September 2001 attacks against the United States', Brussels, 4 October 2001, available at: http://www.nato.int/docu/speech/2001/s011004b.htm; and Marty (n 20) para 91.

to provide some or all of these broad permissions and protections, well beyond NATO membership of 18 at the time.[22] NATO's crucial role for the programme did not stop there though. Within the framework of the multilateral NATO-SOFA (Statute of Forces Agreement) and NATO's secrecy and security of information regime, the US later concluded secret bilateral agreements with NATO members and 'NATO aspirants' to set up secret detention facilities and conduct ad hoc operations on their territories.[23]

The SSCI Study highlights that, despite obtaining broad authorisations and protections at national and international levels, the CIA was not prepared to take custody of its first detainee.[24] Following the MoN, the CIA explored the possibility of establishing clandestine detention facilities in several countries but ultimately concluded that US military bases were the best option for the CIA to detain individuals. In late March 2002, however, the imminent capture of Abu Zubaydah prompted the CIA to again consider various detention options. To avoid declaring Abu Zubaydah to the International Committee of the Red Cross (ICRC), the CIA decided to seek authorisation to clandestinely detain him at a facility in Thailand. According to the SSCI Study, President Bush approved the CIA's proposal despite 'certain gaps in [CIA] planning/ preparations'. In fact, the CIA also lacked a plan for the eventual disposition of its detainees so that, after taking custody of Abu Zubaydah, CIA officers concluded that he 'should remain incommunicado for the remainder of his life'.[25]

According to the SSCI Study, the CIA also did not review its past experience with coercive interrogations nor its previous statement to Congress that 'inhumane physical or psychological techniques are counterproductive because they do not produce intelligence and will probably result in false answers'.[26] In addition, the CIA made no attempt to contact government officials with interrogation expertise. Instead, in July 2002, on the basis of consultations with contract psychologists and with very limited internal deliberation, the CIA requested approval from the Department of Justice to use a set of coercive interrogation techniques. The techniques were adapted from the training of US military personnel at the US Air Force Survival, Evasion, Resistance and Escape school, designed to prepare US military personnel for the conditions and treatment to which they might be subjected if taken prisoner by countries that do not adhere to the Geneva Conventions.[27]

---

[22] Marty (n 20) para 105.
[23] See below section 3.4.2 and Marty (n 20) paras 112–166.
[24] United States Senate Select Committee on Intelligence (n 5) Finding 11.
[25] ibid Finding 11.
[26] ibid Finding 11.
[27] The fact that using these techniques would mean that the US itself was in breach of the Geneva Conventions was not entirely lost on the US Government, which

On 1 August 2002, the Office of Legal Counsel (OLC) of the Department of Justice issued a memorandum authorising the use of ten of these techniques, and provided 'guidelines' for determining the legality of additional enhanced interrogation techniques (EITs).[28] The ten techniques approved, used and abused were the following: 'attention grasp, walling, facial hold, facial slap (insult slap), cramped confinement, wall standing, stress positions, sleep deprivation, insects placed in a confinement box, and waterboarding'.[29] The memorandum formed part of a series of OLC memoranda attempting to dismantle the prohibition of torture together with the basic protections afforded to CIA detainees everywhere in the world. As a result, the legal obligations of the US were redefined so narrowly that there were hardly any to comply with anymore, and US officials could therefore almost truthfully proclaim that they complied with them.[30] To quote George Orwell, 'nothing was illegal since there were no longer any laws'.[31]

As it began detention and interrogation operations, the CIA deployed untrained and inexperienced personnel. Interrogation training was only implemented seven months after the CIA took custody of Abu Zubaydah, and more than three months after the CIA began using its enhanced interrogation techniques on him and other detainees. CIA Director George Tenet only issued formal guidelines for interrogations and conditions of confinement at detention sites in January 2003, by which time 40 of the 119 documented CIA detainees had already been detained and interrogated by the CIA.[32] Yet, this institutionalisation of torture is at least as disturbing as the ill-preparation of the CIA.

---

attempted to ensure through dubious legal interpretation that the Geneva Conventions would not apply to its war on terror against al Qaeda, nor to CIA detainees as 'unlawful combatants'. Memorandum from the President on the humane treatment of Taliban and al Qaeda detainees, 7 February 2002, available at: https://en.wikisource.org/wiki/Humane_Treatment_of_al_Qaeda_and_Taliban_Detainees.

[28] August 1, 2002, Memorandum for John A. Rizzo from Jay S. Bybee, re: Interrogation of al Qaeda Operative.

[29] ibid.

[30] See e.g., White House Fact Sheet on the Status of Detainees at Guantanamo Bay, 7 February 2002, available at: https://georgewbush-whitehouse.archives.gov/news/releases/2002/02/20020207-13.html; Statement by the President, United Nations International Day in Support of Victims of Torture, 26 June 2003, available at: https://georgewbush-whitehouse.archives.gov/news/releases/2003/06/20030626-3.html; Speech by President Bush, 6 September 2006: 'And so the CIA used an alternative set of procedures. These procedures were designed to be safe, to comply with our laws, our Constitution, and our treaty obligations. The Department of Justice reviewed the authorized methods extensively and determined them to be lawful', transcript available at: https://www.npr.org/templates/story/story.php?storyId=5777480.

[31] George Orwell, *Nineteen Eighty-Four* (Secker & Warburg 1949).

[32] United States Senate Select Committee on Intelligence (n 5) Finding 11.

Table 3.1   *CIA secret detention sites*

From	To	Location	SSCI Study Codename
March 2002	December 2002	Thailand	Green
September 2002	April 2004	Afghanistan	Cobalt
December 2002	September 2003	Poland	Blue
January 2003	December 2003	Afghanistan	Gray
September 2003	April 2004	Guantánamo Bay, Cuba	Indigo/Maroon
September 2003	November 2005	Romania	Black
April 2004	September 2006	Afghanistan	Orange
February 2005	March 2006	Lithuania	Violet
March 2006	March 2008	Afghanistan	Brown

Torture became a professional skill,[33] with a method inspired by efficiency, authorised techniques and corresponding training, allowing its practitioners to evade guilt without claiming innocence: they were 'just doing their job', as approved by the highest levels of government.

3.2.2   Secret Detention and Extraordinary Rendition

Evidence retrieved from various sources converges to show that the CIA operated detention sites abroad according to the timeline provided in Table 3.1.[34]

The CIA programme was clouded in an unprecedented level of secrecy designed to nullify the effects and protections of the law, rendering its victims helpless and permitting no prospect for accountability. CIA detainees were often shuffled between detention sites – CIA black sites and proxy detention sites[35] – sometimes up to ten times, according to a modus operandi known as extraordinary rendition. As defined by the British Intelligence and Security Committee, the phrase describes 'the extra-legal transfer of persons from one jurisdiction or state to another, for the purposes of detention and interrogation

---

[33] On the fallacies of the rhetoric of professionalism in the exercise of torture, see Darius M Rejali, *Torture and Democracy* (Princeton University Press 2007) 454–458.

[34] Raphael, Black and Blakeley (n 8); United States Senate Select Committee on Intelligence (n 5).

[35] The CIA made extensive use of 'proxy detention', i.e., transferring people to other states for the purpose of interrogation or detention without charge. Some detainees were then rendered back into CIA custody while others remained in third states' custody. See below section 3.4.1.

outside the normal legal system, where there was a real risk of torture or cruel, inhuman or degrading treatment'.[36]

Victims were rendered from one secret detention place to another using a standardised transfer procedure, which involved a 'security check' by masked CIA personnel. This check consisted of victims having their clothes cut into pieces; being subjected to full cavity searches and to the insertion of anal suppositories; being dressed in diapers and overalls; hooded; handcuffed; and strapped to a mattress on the aircraft.[37] The CIA ensured secrecy over rendition flights by using front companies, operating in unmarked planes, filing false flight plans or flying without any flight plan.[38]

Detainees were held outside any legal system, in what has been termed a 'legal black hole'[39] or 'limbo of rightlessness'.[40] They were brutally interrogated using methods amounting to torture, including techniques not approved by the Department of Justice.[41] Torture was, in most cases, ordered by CIA Headquarters not because of a strong presumption of guilt, but because of a presumption of knowledge of information.

Within the rendition, detention, and interrogation programme, the CIA operated what could be described as a core programme: the rendition, detention, and interrogation of 'high-value detainees' (HVDs). Seventeen of the 119 detainees in the CIA programme have been classified as HVDs by the CIA.[42] These men are those whom the US considered to be of the highest *intelligence* value. As such, the HVD scheme embodies the dehumanisation of individu-

---

[36] This definition was adopted by the ECtHR in *Babar Ahmad and Others* v. *The United Kingdom*, App. Nos. 24027/07, 11949/08 and 36742/08, 6 July 2012, para 113.

[37] ICRC, 'ICRC Report on the Treatment of Fourteen "High Value Detainees" in CIA Custody' (2007) 28–31. For other detainees (not HVDs), see statements by Ahmed Agiza and Mohammed Alzery reported in UNCAT, *Agiza* v. *Sweden*, CAT/C/34/D/233/2003 and CCPR, *Alzery* v. *Sweden*, CCPR/C/88/D/1416/2005; or by Khalid El-Masri, reported in ECtHR, *El-Masri* v. *The Former Yugoslav Republic of Macedonia*, App. No. 39639/09, 13 December 2012.

[38] See Helsinki Foundation for Human Rights, 'Explanation of Rendition Flight Records Released by the Polish Air Navigation Services Agency' 22 February 2010; Human Rights Council, 'Joint Study on Global Practices in Relation to Secret Detention in the Context of Countering Terrorism of the Special Rapporteur on the Promotion and Protection of Human Rights and Fundamental Freedoms While Countering Terrorism' (UN General Assembly 2010) A/HRC/13/42 paras 116–117; Marty (n 20) paras 180–190.

[39] Johan Steyn, 'Guantanamo Bay: The Legal Black Hole' (2004) 53 The International and Comparative Law Quarterly 1.

[40] David Luban, 'The War on Terrorism and the End of Human Rights' (2002) 22 Phil. & Pub. Pol'y Q. 10.

[41] United States Senate Select Committee on Intelligence (n 5) Finding 14.

[42] The list is available on the Rendition Project database (n 7).

als, reducing them to mere means with regard to the 'all-consuming end of intelligence gathering'.[43] A leaked ICRC report documents the conditions of detention of 14 HVDs in CIA custody. They had

> no knowledge of where they were being held, no contact with persons other than their interrogators or guards. Even their guards were usually masked and, other than the absolute minimum, did not communicate in any way with the detainees. None had real – let alone regular – contact with other persons detained ... None had any contact with legal representation... None of the fourteen had any contact with their families ... As such, the fourteen had become missing persons. ... This regime was clearly designed to undermine human dignity and to create a sense of futility by inducing, in many cases, severe physical and mental pain and suffering, with the aim of obtaining compliance and extracting information, resulting in exhaustion, depersonalization and dehumanization.[44]

The enhanced interrogation techniques were developed primarily with HVDs in mind, and specifically the CIA's first detainee, Abu Zubaydah.[45] The HVDs were subjected to extreme levels of torture through the intensive and combined use of various EITs, occasioning important lasting physical and mental sequelae.[46] The absurdity of the CIA's use of torture, which we can attribute to a systemic problem of imputed knowledge, is well documented in the Study: CIA officers assumed that HVDs knew something, but they did not know what. They tortured them, but the detainees did not provide any ground-breaking information. CIA officers then assumed that detainees were withholding information and tortured them further. This vicious reasoning led several detainees to fabricate intelligence[47] while many others simply did not provide what new information they were wrongly alleged to be holding.[48] Hence, despite the

---

[43] Helen Duffy, *The 'War on Terror' and the Framework of International Law* (2nd ed, Cambridge University Press 2015) 779.

[44] ICRC (n 37) 28–31.

[45] According to the SSCI Study, EITs were used on 39 detainees, including the 17 high-value detainees.

[46] The SSCI Study documents in detail the torture of Abu Zubaydah, Al-Nashiri, Ramzi Bin al-Shibh and Khaled Seikh Mohammed and the lasting consequences on their physical and mental health.

[47] E.g., Khaled Seikh Mohammed admitted to having fabricated intelligence on several occasions while being waterboarded 'at least 183 times' within a few weeks. After being rendered to Egypt by the CIA, Ibn Sheikh al-Libi claimed under torture that 'Iraq was supporting al-Qaida and providing assistance with chemical and biological weapons'. He later retracted this claim, but not before it was cited by US Secretary of State Colin Powell in his February 2003 speech to the United Nations designed to build support for the invasion of Iraq. United States Senate Select Committee on Intelligence (n 5) 85–93, 141 (footnote 857).

[48] United States Senate Select Committee on Intelligence (n 5) Findings 1 and 2.

length of the SSCI Study, one cannot find a single documented instance of actual intelligence obtained through the CIA programme.

As of August 2022, sixteen HVDs were still being held in US military custody at Guantánamo Bay – the seventeenth, Ibn Sheikh al-Libi, died in Libyan custody after having been held and tortured by the CIA and Egyptian services. Five of those still in Guantánamo Bay – Ammar al-Baluchi, Khaled Sheikh Mohammed, Mustafa al-Hawsawi, Ramzi bin al-Shibh, and Walid bin Attash – have been charged with conspiracy and other crimes relating to the 9/11 attacks. In addition, Abd al-Rahim al-Nashiri has been charged for crimes related to the USS Cole bombing. All six are set to stand trial in a DoD-run military commission but the cases have remained mired in pre-trial proceedings since 2012.[49] In addition, Encep Nurjaman, Mohammed Farik Bin Amin, and Mohammed Nazir Bin Lep were charged in August 2021 with crimes related to the 2002 and 2003 bombings at a JW Marriott in Jakarta, Indonesia.[50] Finally, in June 2022, Abd al-Hadi al-Iraqi pleaded guilty to commanding insurgents who committed lethal attacks on US allied forces in 2003 and 2004 in Afghanistan. He is awaiting sentencing.[51] Among non-HVD detainees, only one, Majid Khan, has been convicted.[52] The others are detained without charges.[53]

---

[49] Despite charges having been sworn for sometimes more than ten years, the proceedings in all six cases still remain in the pre-trial phase. More recently, all statements made by the five detainees charged with crimes relating to the 9/11 attacks have been judged inadmissible because of the detainees' treatment during previous interrogations; and the US Court of Appeals for the DC Circuit threw out every single pre-trial order and ruling on appeal of those orders by the US Court of Military Commission Review issued over the preceding three and a half years in the case of Al-Nashiri. Re: Abd Al-Rahim Hussein Muhammed Al-Nashiri, No. 18-1279 (D.C. Cir. 2019).

[50] All documents related to the military proceedings against them can be accessed on the Office of Military Commissions website: https://www.mc.mil/Cases.aspx?caseType=omc&status=1&id=55.

[51] All documents related to the military proceedings against al-Iraqi can be accessed on the Office of Military Commissions website: https://www.mc.mil/Cases.aspx?caseType=omc&status=1&id=47.

[52] All documents related to the military proceedings against Majid Khan can be accessed on the Office of Military Commissions website: https://www.mc.mil/Cases.aspx?caseType=omc&status=1&id=45.

[53] Some detainees have been charged and then seen those charged withdrawn – usually because they had been tortured – but remain detained. Others have never been charged. See Human Rights Watch, 'Guantanamo Trials': https://www.hrw.org/guantanamo-trials and *The New York Times*, 'The Guantánamo Docket', available at: https://www.nytimes.com/interactive/projects/guantanamo/detainees/current.

As of August 2022, nine of the 131 total CIA detainees[54] had deceased,[55] 23 were still in detention, 62 had been released, and the status of the other 38 was unknown. The SSCI Study also highlights that more than one fifth (26) of the 119 listed CIA detainees did not, according to the CIA itself, meet the CIA's own standard for detention under the MoN of 17 September 2001.[56] In other words, the CIA did not believe that they posed 'a continuing, serious threat of violence or death to US persons and interests or [were] planning terrorist activities'.

3.3 APPLICABLE LEGAL FRAMEWORK

This section maps the international legal norms applicable to the CIA-led war on terror with the aim of establishing state responsibility for the breach of these norms. To this end, I identify the applicable legal framework and analyse the details of affected rights and obligations. Before proceeding further, however, some preliminary remarks are in order. First, whilst US responsibility is addressed throughout as that of the principal wrongdoer, it is only considered *in abstracto*, and findings of responsibility are without prejudice to the justiciability of the matter and the possibility of invoking such responsibility, both of which depend on other factors. The same applies to the responsibility of cooperating states, examined in section 3.4. Second, except where stated otherwise, issues of attribution and applicable law are taken to be resolved. This is especially so regarding the opposability clause of Article 16(b) ASR,[57] as all human rights and humanitarian law obligations for which state complicity can be established are binding, in substance, on all states involved.

Finally, except where stated otherwise, circumstances precluding wrongfulness are not applicable to the situations under scrutiny. The attacks of 11

---

[54] The SSCI Study only took into account prisoners who were at some point held in a CIA-run prison. Yet, there is strong evidence that for at least 12 additional detainees held in US military detention or by another state, the CIA was involved in their rendition, detention and/or torture. The present case-study includes those 12 individuals in its materials, and the phrase 'CIA detainees' will be taken as covering them except where indicated otherwise.

[55] According to the current state of knowledge, only one detainee (Gul Rahman) was killed in CIA custody. Ibn Sheikh al-Libi was killed in Libyan custody, and the other seven were killed after escaping (three) or after release (four). The list does not include the nine detainees who died in US custody but were never held by the CIA, as they are beyond the scope of this case-study.

[56] United States Senate Select Committee on Intelligence (n 5) Finding 15.

[57] International Law Commission, Draft Articles on Responsibility of States for Internationally Wrongful Acts 2001 (Supplement No 10 (A/56/10), chpIVE1) 76 ('ASR').

September 2001 were not of such a nature as to give rise to 'an irreconcilable conflict between an essential interest ... and an obligation of the state invoking necessity',[58] triggering a state of necessity under Article 25 ASR. Yet, even if they were, the state of necessity would not extend *ratione temporis* to cover the operation of the CIA programme over six years. Rather, it would be limited to the prevention of an objectively established, grave and imminent peril, such as a certain and inevitable upcoming attack of the same scale.[59] There is no information showing that such a peril was ever objectively established. Further, it hardly needs stressing that the CIA programme was not the 'only way' to prevent such an attack, despite assertions to the contrary by the CIA and the Bush administration.[60] In any case, the state of necessity could never preclude the wrongfulness of breaches of peremptory norms,[61] including the prohibition of torture[62] and enforced disappearance,[63] nor could it preclude the wrongfulness of breaches of non-derogable human rights obligations.[64]

3.3.1 International Human Rights Law

The CIA programme was self-evidently a violation of many human rights. Yet, the applicability of IHRL was often contested, due mostly to the (purposeful) extraterritorial nature of the acts.[65] It is now generally accepted that states' obligations under human rights treaties arise when individuals are within the

---

[58] ASR, commentary to Article 25, para 2.
[59] ASR Article 25(1) and commentary paras 14–18; *Gabčikovo-Nagymaros Project (Hungary v Slovakia)* [1997] ICJ Reports 1997 7 (International Court of Justice) [54].
[60] United States Senate Select Committee on Intelligence (n 5) Finding 2.
[61] ASR Article 26.
[62] ASR Article 26 and commentary, para 5.
[63] IACtHR, *Goiburú et al. v. Paraguay*, Series C No. 153. Merits, Reparations and Costs (2006), para 84.
[64] ASR Article 25(2)(a) provides that: 'In any case, necessity may not be invoked by a State as a ground for precluding wrongfulness if: (a) the international obligation in question excludes the possibility of invoking necessity'.
[65] See 'Consideration of Reports Submitted by States Parties under Article 40 of the Covenant, United States of America, Addendum, Comments by the Government of the United States of America on the Concluding Observations of the Human Rights Committee', HRC, UN Doc. CCPR/C/USA/CO/3/Rev.1/Add.I, 1 November 2007, in which the US responded to the Human Rights Committee that it considered the ICCPR not to apply extraterritorially, and that it was not bound by it in its war on terror. By simultaneously arguing that IHL did not apply either to CIA detainees because they were 'unlawful combatants', the US administration sought to create a 'legal black hole', in which no international or national law applied.

state's territory or when they are subject to its jurisdiction abroad.[66] The notion of jurisdiction has been developed exclusively within the field of international human rights law, and has been interpreted and applied in a sometimes confusing and incoherent manner.[67] In contrast, and despite serving partially the same function, the rules on attribution codified in the ASR are a wealth of clarity. On that basis, Martin Scheinin puts forward a compelling argument, according to which, jurisdiction represents no more than the requirement of a factual link between the state and the wrongful act suffered by the complainant – a requirement that can be assessed by reference to the rules on admissibility (for complaints under human rights treaties) or on attribution (under the regime of state responsibility).[68]

In practice, however, and with the notable exception of the Human Rights Committee's case-law and General Comment No 36,[69] international courts and bodies have developed two models of extraterritorial applicability of human rights obligations by reference to jurisdiction, and seem to require that one at least be met in addition to formal admissibility criteria.[70] Accordingly,

---

[66] UN Human Rights Committee, 'General Comment No. 31, The Nature of the General Legal Obligation Imposed on States Parties to the Covenant' (2004) CCPR/C/21/Rev.1/Add.13 31.

[67] Martin Scheinin, 'Just Another Word? Jurisdiction in the Roadmaps of State Responsibility and Human Rights' in Malcolm Langford and others (eds), *Global Justice, State Duties* (Cambridge University Press 2012); Marko Milanovic, 'Extraterritoriality and Human Rights: Prospects and Challenges', *Human Rights and the Dark Side of Globalisation* (Routledge 2016).

[68] Scheinin (n 67). A similar approach has been adopted by the Human Rights Committee in assessing individual complaints, deciding on the (extraterritorial) applicability of the ICCPR based on the existence of a factual link between the state and the violation: see, e.g., *Munaf v. Romania*, CCPR/C/96/D/1539/2006, 21 August 2009, para 14.2: 'The Committee recalls its jurisprudence that a State party may be responsible for extra-territorial violations of the Covenant, if it is a link in the causal chain that would make possible violations in another jurisdiction. Thus, the risk of an extra-territorial violation must be a necessary and foreseeable consequence and must be judged on the knowledge the State party had at the time.'

[69] See *Munaf* (n 68). With respect to the right to life, the Committee adopts a 'control over rights' approach: 'In light of article 2, paragraph 1, of the Covenant, a State party has an obligation to respect and to ensure the rights under article 6 of all persons who are within its territory and all persons subject to its jurisdiction, that is, all persons over whose enjoyment of the right to life it exercises power or effective control. This includes persons located outside any territory effectively controlled by the State, whose right to life is nonetheless impacted by its military or other activities in a direct and reasonably foreseeable manner.' UN Human Rights Committee, 'General Comment No. 36, Article 6 (Right to Life)' (2019) CCPR/C/GC/36 para 63.

[70] Although references to jurisdiction could in most cases also be formulated under actual admissibility criteria. See Scheinin (n 67) 224–225.

extraterritorial jurisdiction arises either when the state exercises de facto effective control over part of a territory abroad (spatial model)[71] or when the state exercises authority and control over an individual (personal model).[72] If this jurisdictional test is satisfied and the complaint is otherwise admissible, then the state's obligations under the treaty become applicable, and the criteria for attribution, as a *ratione personae* admissibility condition, should in theory be satisfied too. In this sense, human rights jurisdiction is grounding: it constitutes the necessary relationship between the state and the individual giving rise to rights and obligations.[73]

However, and this is where the concept of jurisdiction becomes particularly confusing, there is no consensus on the range of state obligations that apply extraterritorially.[74] Whereas all obligations would be applicable under the spatial model,[75] under the personal model, it would seem from recent case-law that this could be dependent upon the degree of control exercised by the state in a particular situation, at least in respect of the ECHR:

> It is clear that, whenever the State through its agents exercises control and authority over an individual, and thus jurisdiction, the State is under an obligation under Article 1 to secure to that individual the rights and freedoms under Section 1 of the Convention that are relevant to the situation of that individual. In this sense, therefore, the Convention rights can be 'divided and tailored'.[76]

---

[71] *Legal Consequences of the Construction of a Wall in the Occupied Palestinian Territory, Advisory Opinion* [2004] ICJ Reports 2004 136 (International Court of Justice), paras 109–11; *Armed Activities on the Territory of the Congo* (*Democratic Republic of the Congo* v. *Uganda*), Judgment, ICJ Reports 2005, 168, paras 179 and 216–217; ECtHR *Loizidou* v. *Turkey* (preliminary objections), App. No. 15318/89, 23 February 1995, para 62; UNCAT, 'Conclusions and recommendations: United Kingdom of Great Britain and Northern Ireland', UN Doc. CAT/C/CR/33/3, 10 December 2004, para 4(b).

[72] ECtHR, *Cyprus* v. *Turkey*, App. Nos. 6780/74 and 6950/75, 26 May 1975, para 8; *Al-Skeini and Others* v. *The United Kingdom*, App. No. 55721/07, 7 July 2011, para 136; CCPR, *Lopez-Burgos* v. *Uruguay*, CCPR/C/13/D52/1979, 29 July 1981, paras 12.2–12.3; UNCAT, 'Consideration of Reports Submitted by States Parties under Article 19 of the Convention, United States of America', UN Doc. CAT/C/ USA/CO/2, 25 July 2006, para 20.

[73] See Lea Raible, *Human Rights Unbound: A Theory of Extraterritoriality* (Oxford University Press 2020).

[74] See Milanovic (n 67) 58–59, arguing in favour of a third and more predictable model that would see negative obligations apply without territorial limits while positive obligations would be linked to jurisdiction.

[75] See footnote 71 and *Bankovic and Others* v. *Belgium and 16 Other Contracting States*, App. No. 52207/99, ECtHR, 2 December 2001, para 75.

[76] *Al-Skeini* (n 72), para 137. Compare however with *Bankovic* (n 75), para 75, holding the exact opposite. The uncertainty that crept into ECtHR jurisprudence with the inadmissibility decision in *Bankovic* was about jurisdiction as effective control over

This approach is controversial and leads to unpredictable results.[77] However, for present purposes it is sufficient to note that, according to the case-law of competent courts and bodies, situations of detention, in which physical power and control over the individual is complete, will trigger the extraterritorial application of all relevant human rights treaties. Moreover, even where obligations can be 'divided and tailored', it is arguable that the state's obligations towards an individual in its custody would be extensive, if not cover the full range of rights and obligations guaranteed by applicable treaties.[78]

3.3.2 International Humanitarian Law

International humanitarian law (IHL) is applicable to the CIA programme only in so far as the acts at stake are carried out in the context of and in association with a genuine armed conflict. A generally accepted definition has been put forward by the ICTY in *Tadic*: 'an armed conflict exists whenever there is a resort to armed force between States or protracted armed violence between governmental authorities and organized armed groups or between such groups within a State'.[79]

Such genuine armed conflicts are limited in time and space. With regard to the operation of the CIA programme, they are characterised solely in relation to Afghanistan and Iraq.[80] In respect of Afghanistan, the initial US-led coalition military operation against the Taliban government (Operation Enduring Freedom – OEF), beginning on 7 October 2001, qualified as an international armed conflict (IAC) because the Taliban were the de facto government of Afghanistan and, as such, represented the state. After the fall of the Taliban regime in November 2001, and with the establishment of the Karzai government on 18 June 2002, the IAC ended. In its place an 'internationalised' non-international armed conflict (NIAC) began, in which Afghan forces, sup-

---

territory (spatial model) so that there is in theory no uncertainty related to detentions abroad, for which governments have accepted that IHRL obligations apply under the personal model of jurisdiction. Yet, *Bankovic* had a much broader impact, as the complexities and contradictions of the reasoning in *Al-Skeini* show.

[77] Milanovic (n 67) 57–58.

[78] ECtHR, *Öcalan v. Turkey*, App. No. 46221/99, 12 March 2003, para 91; *Al-Saadoon and Mufdhi v. United Kingdom*, App. No. 61498/08, 2 March 2010, paras 86–89.

[79] ICTY, *Prosecutor v. Dusko Tadic*, Decision on the Defence Motion for Interlocutory Appeal on Jurisdiction, IT-94-1-A, 2 October 1995, para 70.

[80] On the applicability of IHL to the global war on terror, see also Duffy (n 43) Chapters 6B.1 and 10.4.2.

ported by OEF and ISAF[81] forces, fought anti-government forces on Afghan territory. The armed conflict remained a NIAC for the rest of the period in which the CIA programme operated.

The initial US-led attack on Iraq, beginning on 20 March 2003, also qualified as an IAC. With the fall of the Saddam Hussein government in April 2003, the US and the UK became occupying powers, a situation still governed by the laws applicable to IACs. When the Coalition Provisional Authority transferred all governmental authority to the Iraqi interim government on 28 June 2004, the occupation was considered to have ended under the Geneva Conventions.[82] Thereafter and during the rest of the period in which the CIA programme operated, hostilities in Iraq were considered a NIAC.

Conversely, there are several issues preventing the categorisation of the 'global war on terror' as a legal concept, despite assertions to the contrary by successive US administrations.[83] As al Qaeda is not a state, the conflict could only be of a non-international character. A situation is susceptible of being classified as a NIAC if (1) hostilities are protracted beyond mere internal disturbances or sporadic riots; (2) parties can be defined and identified; (3) the territorial scope of the conflict can be defined and identified; and (4) the beginning and the end of the conflict can be defined and identified. The application of these criteria to the alleged global armed conflict against al Qaeda does not support the US's position:

(1) The concept of 'protracted armed violence' supposes hostilities of a certain level of intensity, often over a certain period of time. It is hard to see where, apart from Afghanistan and Iraq, such a level of fighting has been attained during the operation of the CIA programme.
(2) Whereas the US is a clearly identifiable party, 'al Qaeda and its associates' is much harder to define.
(3) There are no territorial boundaries to the war on terror: it is 'global' because it occurs everywhere an (alleged) al Qaeda operative can be found.
(4) The temporal limits of this 'war' are unclear; it might allegedly end only when the US will no longer be a target for terrorism, or never.[84]

---

[81] International Security Assistance Force: a NATO-led security mission in Afghanistan, established by UNSC Res. 1386 of December 2001.
[82] Knut Dörmann and Laurent Colassis, 'International Humanitarian Law in the Iraq Conflict' (2004) 47 German Yearbook of International Law 293.
[83] See UN Doc. CCPR/C/USA/CO/3/Rev.1/Add.I (n 65).
[84] See GW Bush, Address to a Joint Session of Congress and the American People, 20 September 2001: 'Our war on terror begins with al-Qaeda, but it does not end there. It will not end until every terrorist group of global reach has been found, stopped and defeated', https://georgewbush-whitehouse.archives.gov/news/releases/2001/09/

It follows that the global war on terror cannot be categorised as an armed conflict, and is best understood as a metaphor or a political concept not warranting the application of IHL.[85]

The CIA programme is thus only subject to applicable rules of IHL when it is connected to those conflicts to which IHL applies *ratione materiae*, i.e., the conflicts in Afghanistan and Iraq.[86] Therefore, only those individuals captured during the time and on the territory of which such armed conflicts extended are protected by IHL, notwithstanding that the protections afforded by general international law and international human rights law remain applicable.[87]

3.3.3 Interstate Obligations

While the CIA rendition, detention, and interrogation programme mainly infringed upon the rights of individuals, its territorial scope, extending over dozens of states, raises the possibility that the rights of some of these states may have been breached too. That would be so whenever the territorial state did not consent to CIA conduct on its territory, including in its territorial airspace. This is a question of fact, the answer to which is often uncertain. Valid consent would preclude the wrongfulness of CIA conduct towards the consenting state.[88] Conversely, in the absence of valid consent, any breach by CIA agents of an obligation owed to the territorial state would engage the responsibility of the US.

20010920-8.html. Although the Obama administration declared the 'global war on terror' to be 'over' in 2013, there were some important continuities with the actions initiated by the Bush administration, and the rhetoric was picked up again by the Trump administration.

[85] On the dangers of adopting a war paradigm in combating terrorism, and in particular on the risks associated with a global armed conflict, see International Commission of Jurists (2009) 'Assessing Damage, Urging Action: Report of the Eminent Jurists Panel on Terrorism, Counter-terrorism and Human Rights' ('EJP Report 2009') 49–63.

[86] While it is not directly relevant to the present discussion, placing counterterrorism operations and measures under a war paradigm raises the possibility of linking the applicability of IHL to the person (and their belonging to a group) rather than to the territory. As the same reasoning is used to carry out lethal drone strikes in states where the threshold for an armed conflict is not met, this controversial position remains defended by some administrations. Manfred Nowak and Anne Charbord, 'Key Trends in the Fight against Terrorism and Key Aspects of International Human Rights Law' in Manfred Nowak and Anne Charbord (eds), *Using Human Rights to Counter Terrorism* (Edward Elgar Publishing 2018) 19–20.

[87] *Legal Consequences of the Construction of a Wall in the Occupied Palestinian Territory, Advisory Opinion* [2004] ICJ Reports 2004 136 (International Court of Justice) [109–111]; UN Human Rights Committee (n 66) para 11.

[88] ASR Article 20.

In this regard, several sources of law are applicable in the relations between the US and other states. The first relevant principle is that of territorial sovereignty, enshrined in Article 2(4) of the UN Charter.[89] Rights of third states may also have been breached with regard to the Chicago Convention on International Civil Aviation, as well as the Vienna Convention on Consular Relations.[90]

3.3.4 Rights and Obligations Affected by the CIA Programme

3.3.4.1 Liberty and security of the person

The CIA detention, rendition, and interrogation programme constitutes a complete violation of the right to liberty and security of the person as enshrined in various international legal instruments.[91] The practice of secret detention, which implies incommunicado, unacknowledged, and potentially indefinite detention, cannot be reconciled with the rights of its victims not to be subjected to arbitrary detention and to be afforded due process.[92] Such denial of essential guarantees also sets the path for further violations, including of the right to a fair trial[93] and the right not to be tortured or subjected to cruel, inhuman, and degrading treatment.[94]

3.3.4.2 Torture and cruel, inhuman, and degrading treatment

There is no doubt whatsoever that the 'enhanced interrogation techniques' developed by the CIA and approved at the highest levels of government amounted, by themselves and in combination, to torture and ill-treatment.[95] The modus operandi of rendition operations has also been found to constitute

---

[89] See Chapter 2, section 2.4.
[90] ibid.
[91] ICCPR Article 9; ECHR Article 5; ACHR Article 14; ACHPR Article 6.
[92] See ECtHR, *Kurt* v. *Turkey* (Merits), App. No. 15/1997/799/1002, 25 May 1998, para 124; and Working Group on Arbitrary Detention, Opinion No. 12/2006 (A/HRC/4/40/Add.1).
[93] Human Rights Council (n 38) 16.
[94] ibid 20.
[95] See, e.g., United States Senate Select Committee on Intelligence (n 5) Finding 3; 'Report of the Special Rapporteur on the Promotion and Protection of Human Rights and Fundamental Freedoms While Countering Terrorism: Addendum: Mission to the United States of America', UN General Assembly, November 2007, A/HRC/6/17/Add.3. See also UN Committee against Torture, 'Conclusions and Recommendations of the Committee against Torture to the United States of America', CAT/C/USA/CO/2, 25 July 2006, para 17; ICRC (n 37) 46; ECtHR, *Al-Nashiri* v. *Poland*, 24 July 2014, App. No. 28761/11; *Husayn (Abu Zubaydah)* v. *Poland*, 24 July 2014, App. No. 7511/13.

cruel, inhumane, and degrading treatment,[96] as have the conditions of detention in CIA-run prisons.[97] In addition, incommunicado detention has consistently been found to constitute torture or inhumane treatment due to the extreme distress induced by the secret and arbitrary nature of the detention.[98]

3.3.4.3 Enforced disappearance

The prohibition of enforced disappearance is non-derogable[99] and is increasingly recognised as constituting *jus cogens*.[100] The practice of extraordinary rendition and secret detention constitutes a perfect match with the definition of enforced disappearance set down in the CPED:[101]

> The arrest, detention, abduction or any other form of deprivation of liberty by agents of the State or by persons or groups of persons acting with the authorization, support or acquiescence of the State, followed by a refusal to acknowledge the deprivation of liberty or by concealment of the fate or whereabouts of the disappeared person, which place such a person outside the protection of the law.[102]

The UN Joint Study on Secret Detention emphasises that, essentially, 'every instance of secret detention also amounts to a case of enforced disappearance'.[103] This statement is supported by the extreme level of secrecy over the programme and the repeated efforts of the Bush administration to remove all legal protections for CIA detainees. Both aspects underscore the CIA programme's method and purpose: to remove its victims from the protection of the law. International human rights bodies have all confirmed that enforced disappearances constitute violations of multiple human rights, among them the rights to liberty, to humane conditions of detention and to recognition before

---

[96] *El-Masri* (n 37) para 211; *Alzery* v. *Sweden* (n 37) para 11.6.
[97] United States Senate Select Committee on Intelligence (n 5) Finding 4.
[98] *El-Masri* (n 37), paras 202–203; Human Rights Council (n 38) 20; ICRC (n 37) 7–8.
[99] International Convention for the Protection of All Persons from Enforced Disappearance, UNGA Res. 61/177, adopted 20 December 2006, in force 23 December 2010 (CPED), Article 1.
[100] In addition to the IACtHR in, e.g., *Goiburú et al.* v. *Paraguay* (n 63), recent scholarly work also tends to argue for the recognition of the prohibition of enforced disappearance as *jus cogens*. Jeremy Sarkin, 'Why the Prohibition of Enforced Disappearance Has Attained *Jus Cogens* Status in International Law' (2012) 81 Nordic Journal of International Law 537; Nikolas Kyriakou, 'An Affront to the Conscience of Humanity: Enforced Disappearance in International Human Rights Law' (PhD Thesis, European University Institute 2012).
[101] Kyriakou (n 100) 226–233.
[102] CPED, Article 2.
[103] Human Rights Council (n 38) 17.

the law, as well as the right not to be tortured, and, in some cases, the right to life.[104] Further, the rights of family members of victims of enforced disappearances may also be violated due to the anguish caused by the disappearance.[105]

3.3.4.4 Non-refoulement to serious violations

The practice of extraordinary rendition is in direct violation of the obligation of non-refoulement to serious human rights violations and of the various due process rights safeguarding the right not to be refouled. The prohibition also covers refoulement from a third-party territory,[106] therefore encompassing extraordinary renditions. It is increasingly acknowledged that not only refoulement to torture is prohibited, but also refoulement to enforced disappearance,[107] arbitrary detention,[108] the death penalty,[109] or an unfair trial.[110] In addition, diplomatic assurances have been judged not to constitute a sufficient safeguard against the risk of torture, meaning that state responsibility can be engaged for refoulement even where diplomatic assurances were obtained.[111]

3.3.4.5 Positive obligations and the rights to remedy and reparation

The abuse of doctrines of state secrecy and immunities, in addition to the high level of secrecy over the programme and the denial of procedural rights to CIA detainees, mean that there still are no effective means to obtain redress at the domestic level for the abuses committed. Victims are therefore prevented from satisfying their right to remedy and reparation.

This overreaching approach to national security has also been flagrant in the absence of effective investigation and prosecution, and in the refusal to disclose or declassify information, even when the information is already in the public domain.[112] Such shortcomings mean that the obligations to conduct

---

[104] *Sarma* v. *Sri-Lanka*, CCPR/C/78/D/950/2000, 16 July 2003; *Coronel* v. *Columbia*, CCPR/C/76/D/778/1997, 24 October 2002; *Velásquez Rodriguez* v. *Honduras*, IACtHR 29 July 1988, Series C, No. 4; *Mouvement Burkinabé des Droits de l'Homme et des Peuples* v. *Burkina Faso*, 204/97, 14th Activity Report of the ACommHPR (2001); *Kurt* v. *Turkey*, ECtHR (n 92).

[105] *Mojica* v. *Dominican Republic*, CCPR/C751/D/449/1991, 25 July 1994.

[106] 'Special Rapporteur on torture: Study on the phenomena of torture, cruel, inhuman or degrading treatment or punishment in the world, including an assessment of conditions of detention', UN Doc. A/HRC/13/39/Add.5, 5 February 2010, para 241.

[107] CPED, Article 16.

[108] ECtHR, *Abu Zubaydah* v. *Poland* (n 95) and *Al-Nashiri* v. *Poland* (n 95).

[109] ECtHR, *Al-Saadoon and Mufdhi* v. *United Kingdom* (n 78), para 123.

[110] ECtHR, *Othman (Abu Qatada)* v. *United Kingdom*, App. No. 8139/09, 17 January 2012.

[111] UNCAT, *Agiza* v. *Sweden* (n 37), para 13.4.

[112] The most recent example is the US Supreme Court decision in *United States* v. *Husayn a.k.a. Zubaydah*, No. 20–827, 3 March 2022. The Supreme Court decided that

an effective investigation and to sanction and remedy violations are not fulfilled,[113] and neither is the right to truth and justice of the victims and their families.[114]

3.3.4.6 Other human rights

Many other rights of detainees were infringed by the operation of the CIA programme, among them the rights to private and family life, to life, to a fair trial, and to freedom of expression and movement. The violation of these rights is a direct consequence of the violation of detainees' right to liberty and security of the person and of the prohibitions of torture, refoulement, and enforced disappearance.

3.3.4.7 International humanitarian law

Where and to the extent that it is applicable in addition to IHRL, IHL prohibits the torture and ill-treatment of prisoners and civilians alike.[115] It further prohibits their transfer to situations where there is a clear risk of torture or ill-treatment,[116] as well as forced transfer between detaining powers and in occupation.[117] There are furthermore a number of procedural safeguards

---

the existence of a CIA black site in Poland, and the fact that Abu Zubaydah was held and tortured there, were state secrets.

[113] See e.g., ECHR Article 3, CAT Articles 4 to 9. See also *Velásquez Rodriguez* v. *Honduras* (n 104) paras 172–175; *Assanidze* v. *Georgia*, ECtHR, App. No. 71503/01, 8 April 2004; *Abu Zubaydah* v. *Poland* (n 95) and *Al-Nashiri* v. *Poland* (n 95).

[114] *El-Masri* (n 37), para 192. For a discussion, see Federico Fabbrini, 'The European Court of Human Rights, Extraordinary Renditions and the Right to the Truth: Ensuring Accountability for Gross Human Rights Violations Committed in the Fight Against Terrorism' (2014) 14 Human Rights Law Review 85, 99–102.

[115] For IACs, Article 17 GC III (prisoners of war), Article 27 GC IV (protected persons), and Article 75 AP I; for NIACs, Common Article 3 to the four Geneva Conventions and Article 4 AP II. See: Geneva Convention Relative to the Treatment of Prisoners of War (adopted 12 August 1949, entered into force 21 October 1950) ('GC III'); Geneva Convention Relative to the Protection of Civilian Persons in Time of War (adopted 12 August 1949, entered into force 21 October 1950) ('GC IV'); Protocol Additional to the Geneva Conventions of 12 August 1949 and Relating to the Protection of Victims of International Armed Conflicts (Protocol I) (adopted 8 June 1977, entered into force 7 December 1978) ('AP I'); Protocol Additional to the Geneva Conventions of 12 August 1949 and Relating to the Protection of Victims of Non-international Armed Conflicts (Protocol II) (adopted 8 June 1977, entered into force 7 December 1978) ('AP II'). Although the US has not ratified either of the Additional Protocols, the general consensus is that the standards of AP I have been so widely accepted by states that they constitute customary international law.

[116] Common Article 3.

[117] Article 12 GC III permits the transfer of prisoners of war only into the hands of a party to the conflict where the transferring power has satisfied itself 'of the willing-

applicable in cases of detention, including fair trial guarantees[118] and the registration of detainees with, and access by, the ICRC. Violations of some of these provisions constitute grave breaches of the Geneva Conventions,[119] which carry with them positive obligations to investigate and repress the relevant conduct.[120] The CIA programme, when and where it operated in armed conflict situations, thus involved violations of the above-mentioned IHL rules.

3.3.4.8 Interstate obligations

The CIA programme may also have infringed on the rights of other states. In the absence of valid consent from the territorial state,[121] any incursion on its territory by CIA agents – for instance to abduct an individual – would arguably constitute a violation of Article 2(4) of the UN Charter and of the principles of territorial sovereignty and non-intervention.[122] The CIA programme also conflicts with Article 36 of the Vienna Convention on Consular Relations, which purports to afford consular protection to individuals in detention in a state other than their state of nationality.[123]

The modus operandi of extraordinary renditions would also be in violation of the Chicago Convention on International Civil Aviation.[124] The Convention regime facilitates the entry of civilian aircrafts,[125] but state aircrafts are excluded from that regime and may only enter the airspace of another state if so authorised under special (ad hoc or standing) agreements concluded with

---

ness and ability of such transferee Power to apply the convention'. See likewise Article 49(1) GC IV for transfer of civilians in occupation: 'forcible transfers as well as deportation of protected persons' are 'prohibited, regardless of their motive'.

[118] Common Article 3.

[119] For a list of grave breaches, see ICRC, 'Grave Breaches Specified in the 1949 Geneva Conventions and in Additional Protocol I of 1977', available at: https://www.icrc.org/en/doc/resources/documents/misc/57jp2a.htm.

[120] Common Article 1 and AP I.

[121] Under Article 20 ASR, to preclude the wrongfulness of an otherwise wrongful act, consent must be valid and given in advance or at the time of the commission of the act.

[122] See Chapter 2, section 2.4 for details over the international legal framework governing intelligence activities. The most famous example is the abduction of Adolf Eichmann in Argentina by Israeli agents, condemned by the UN Security Council as a violation of Argentina's territorial integrity. UN Doc. S/RES/138, 23 June 1960.

[123] Vienna Convention on Consular Relations, adopted 24 April 1963, in force 19 March 1967.

[124] Venice Commission, Opinion on the international legal obligations of Council of Europe Member States in respect of secret detention facilities and inter-state transport of prisoners, CDL-AD(2006)009. See also Duffy (n 43) 797.

[125] Chicago Convention on International Civil Aviation, 7 December 1944, Article 3.

that state.[126] The CIA's practice of concealing the public nature of its flights, and/or of landing state aircrafts without such special agreement with the territorial state, would therefore be in violation of Articles 3(c) and 4 of the Chicago Convention.[127] In that respect, it bears mentioning that the measure regarding blanket overflight clearance, agreed under the NATO framework, only concerned military flights. Hence, even states that agreed to it would in theory be entitled to invoke the responsibility of the US under the Chicago Convention. However, were that the case, there is an argument to be made for the invocation of consent as a circumstance precluding the wrongfulness[128] of the breach of Article 3(c) and/or Article 4 of the Chicago Convention towards at least some of these states. Indeed, consent may be implicit, as long as it is not presumed, is given by a person authorised to consent on behalf of the state, and does not conflict with a peremptory norm. It is therefore arguable that, where the territorial state's air authority was aware of the non-civilian nature of the flights and yet let them enter, cross their airspace and/or land, the territorial state thereby consented to the military or public use made of civil aircrafts by the US.[129]

3.4   STATE COMPLICITY

The CIA rendition, detention, and interrogation programme was designed and authorised at the highest levels of the US government, and it was operated for the most part by the CIA. However, it was carried out with the complicity of many other states and private actors, and depended heavily on their continued cooperation. The CIA programme therefore exhibits unique levels of intelligence cooperation, raising complex legal questions regarding the responsibility of the states involved in the violation of CIA detainees' rights. This section endeavours to map the responsibility of cooperating states based on the conduct they adopted.

The extent of cooperation varied widely. Some states thus 'simply' provided blanket overflight clearance to the US allowing CIA flights to cross their

---

[126] Article 3(c).

[127] Article 4 of the Chicago Convention provides that: 'Each contracting State agrees not to use civil aviation for any purpose inconsistent with the aims of this Convention'. See, as supporting state practice in that context, the argument by Portugal in its response of 5 August 2015 to Communication PRT 1/2015 by special mandate holders regarding the case of Abou Elkasim Brittel.

[128] ASR Article 20.

[129] Consent would however never preclude the wrongfulness of (even foreseeable) human rights violations deriving from the breach since the scope of Article 20 is limited to interstate relations, thus excluding the possibility that a state may validly consent to the violation of individuals' rights.

airspace while carrying out renditions – while others went as far as to take custody of CIA detainees or host secret detention sites on their territory. Yet, even seemingly minimal forms of cooperation proved essential to the functioning and survival of the programme. Further, they can constitute instances of state complicity in the violation of the rights of CIA detainees.

Participation of foreign states in the CIA programme can engage their responsibility in various ways:

- As a breach of a primary negative obligation of that state (obligation to respect); or
- As a breach of a primary positive obligation of that state (obligation to protect); or
- As aid or assistance under Article 16 ASR; or
- As a breach of a secondary obligation of that state in respect of peremptory norms of international law as provided under Article 41 ASR.

It should be noted here already that an internationally wrongful act can be committed in a variety of ways, including direct commission, aid or assistance, support, inaction, acquiescence, or wilful blindness.[130]

The present section analyses various forms of state complicity against the background of international law. Whilst the analysis is for the most part conducted *in abstracto*, and despite high levels of secrecy and remaining uncertainty regarding state complicity, it is alleged that foreign states have participated in the programme in the following ways:[131]

(1) By taking custody of CIA detainees for the purpose of interrogation and detention without charge ('proxy detention'): Jordan, Egypt, Morocco, the Syrian Arab Republic, Pakistan, Djibouti, Ethiopia, and possibly other states.
(2) By hosting CIA black sites on their territory: Afghanistan, Lithuania, Morocco, Poland, Romania, Thailand, and possibly other states.
(3) By participating in the arrest and/or initial detention and transfer of individuals into CIA custody: Afghanistan, Bosnia and Herzegovina, Egypt, the Gambia, Georgia, Hong Kong, Indonesia, Iran, Iraq, Italy,

---

[130] ASR Articles 12, 16 and 41.
[131] Data retrieved from Human Rights Council (n 38); and Raphael, Black and Blakeley (n 8). Ross Bellaby conducted a similar analysis of state complicity based on the same list of conducts, but from a moral rather than legal perspective, and reached substantially identical conclusions: Ross W Bellaby, 'Extraordinary Rendition: Expanding the Circle of Blame in International Politics' (2018) 22 The International Journal of Human Rights 574.

Macedonia, Pakistan, South Africa, Sweden, Tanzania, Thailand, United Arab Emirates, and possibly other states.
(4) By allowing CIA rendition flights to cross their airspace, or refuel and stop at their airports or military bases, with and/or without detainees aboard: many states.
(5) By sending agents to participate in the interrogation of CIA detainees abroad and/or providing intelligence for the programme and/or relying on intelligence extracted through it: Australia, Belgium, Canada, Germany, the United Kingdom, and many others.

In situations (3) to (5), state responsibility would normally not be engaged if the participating state had no awareness whatsoever of the CIA programme and of the specific illegality of the acts being committed.[132] Due to the high level of secrecy over the programme, a timeline is needed to establish from which point onward foreign states could have reasonably been expected to know about the CIA programme and the wrongful acts it entailed. Because some foreign intelligence agencies had knowledge of (aspects of) the CIA programme well before information came into the public domain, the timeline may differ from state to state.[133] The timeline presented in Table 3.2 reflects the increasing state of public knowledge about the programme – notwithstanding that, for states that cooperated with the CIA, earlier and higher levels of knowledge can sometimes be demonstrated.

Official confirmation of the existence of the programme came on 6 September 2006 when US President George W Bush admitted to the existence of secret CIA prisons and to the use of enhanced interrogation techniques.[134]

---

[132] See Marko Milanovic, 'Intelligence Sharing in Multinational Military Operations and Complicity under International Law' (2021) 97 International Legal Studies 136 for an analysis of the element of knowledge to establish complicity in intelligence-sharing settings.

[133] As regards the United Kingdom, the timeline drafted in Intelligence and Security Committee (n 10) section 5 should be followed. See, in respect of the increased level of knowledge of states cooperating with the CIA, ECtHR, *Al-Nashiri* v. *Poland* (n 95), para 517.

[134] A transcript of his speech is available at: https://www.npr.org/templates/story/story.php?storyId=5777480.

96   The regulation of intelligence activities under international law

Table 3.2   Public knowledge timeline concerning the CIA programme

Date	Disclosure	About	State of Knowledge
12 March 2002	IACHR 'Precautionary Measure 259/02 – Persons held by the United States in Guantánamo Bay'	Unlawful detention (Guantánamo Bay)	*
26 December 2002	*Washington Post* article: 'U.S. Decries Abuse but Defends Interrogations; "Stress and Duress" Tactics Used on Terrorism Suspects Held in Secret Overseas Facilities'	Torture; CIA secret detention sites (Bagram and other unnamed sites); extraordinary rendition; proxy detention/interrogation/ torture in Egypt, Jordan, Saudi Arabia, Morocco, Syria	*
26 June 2003	PACE Resolution 1340 (2003) 'Rights of persons held in the custody of the United States in Afghanistan or Guantánamo Bay'	Detention conditions; ill-treatment by the US; unlawful detention; Afghanistan and Guantánamo Bay.	**
1 November 2003	Associated Press Report about detention conditions in US detention sites in Iraq (incl. Abu Ghraib)	Detention conditions and ill-treatment by the US; Iraq.	***
28 April 2004	CBS Documentary about Abu Ghraib	Detention conditions; torture (Abu Ghraib).	***
8 June 2004	Human Rights Watch Report 'The Road to Abu Ghraib'	Detention conditions (Guantánamo, Iraq, and Afghanistan); torture; extraordinary renditions; unlawful detention.	***
2 November 2005	*Washington Post* article: 'CIA Holds Terror Suspects in Secret Prisons'.	CIA black sites (Thailand, Afghanistan, Guantánamo Bay, unnamed 'Eastern European democracies'); torture; unlawful detention; state complicity; rendition to proxy detention; HVD programme.	****
4 April 2006	Amnesty International Report 'USA: Below the Radar: secret Flights to Torture and "Disappearance"'.	Extraordinary renditions; secret detentions; torture; rendition flights circuits and numbers.	*****

* Early on, the US gathered support from a large number of foreign states for its 'war on terror'; and some agreed to specific forms of collaboration, or collaboration under specific frameworks (UN Security Council authorisation; NATO). By the end of December 2002, however, these states should have become aware that CIA methods may not be fully in line with rule of law and human rights principles, and they should have become cautious and inquisitive about what exactly they were supporting. I therefore submit that, from

26 December 2002 and the publication of the *Washington Post* article,[a] foreign states cooperating with the CIA ought to have known that there was a risk that the CIA could be using extra-legal methods of detention, transfer, and interrogation. In particular, it has been judged that foreign states ought to have known that 'a person in US custody under the [High-Value Detainee] programme could be exposed to a serious risk of treatment contrary to the principles [of the European Convention on Human Rights]'.[b] In light of these elements, I submit that from 2003 onward, foreign states had a duty to inquire about interrogation methods, detention conditions, and lawfulness of detention before and while cooperating with the CIA.

** From mid-2003 onward, public knowledge of unlawful detention and abusive detention conditions in Guantánamo Bay, Afghanistan and Iraq-based US detention sites is considered to be established.[c] This means that, from that date, states cooperating with the CIA knew or ought to have known, at least, that detainees held in CIA prisons were held arbitrarily and in degrading and inhumane conditions.

*** From early 2004 onward, public knowledge that torture was being used by US interrogators and routinely by US prison guards in Afghanistan, Iraq, and Guantánamo Bay is considered established. Any state cooperating with the CIA thus knew or ought to have known that the risk of torture being applied was serious.[d] In addition, with the publication of Human Rights Watch's report in June 2004[e] and considering its substantiated allegations regarding extraordinary renditions, foreign states should have become cautious and inquisitive about allowing US aircrafts unrestricted access to their airspace and airbases.

**** From November 2005 onward,[f] public knowledge of the existence of the rendition, detention, and interrogation programme is considered established, so that foreign states cooperating with the CIA did so with (actual or constructive) knowledge of the programme and of the specific illegality of its components.

***** The matter of rendition flights, and in particular the specifics of the modus operandi of renditions, including the tail number and front companies used for the aircrafts, became clear enough to impute knowledge to all foreign states only slightly later, with the publication of Amnesty International's report in April 2006.[g]

Notes: [a] Priest and Gellman, 'U.S. Decries Abuse but Defends Interrogations; "Stress and Duress" Tactics Used on Terrorism Suspects Held in Secret Overseas Facilities' Washington Post, 26 December 2002, available at: http://www.hartford-hwp.com/archives/27a/092.html [b] ECtHR, Al-Nashiri v. Poland (n 95), para 441 with reference to the period between January 2002 and August 2003. [c] CoE, PACE Resolution 1340 (2003) 'Rights of persons held in the custody of the United States in Afghanistan or Guantánamo Bay'. [d] See: Associated Press Report about detention conditions in US detention sites in Iraq, 1 November 2003, available at: http://legacy.sandiegouniontribune.com/news/world/iraq/20031101-0936-iraq-thecamps.html; CBS Documentary about Abu Ghraib, 28 April 2004, available at: https://www.cbsnews.com/news/abuse-of-iraqi-pows-by-gis-probed/. [e] Human Rights Watch, 'The Road to Abu Ghraib', 8 June 2004. Available at: https://www.hrw.org/report/2004/06/08/road-abu-ghraib. [f] D Priest, 'CIA Holds Terror Suspects in Secret Prisons', Washington Post, 2 November 2005 available at: https://www.washingtonpost.com/archive/politics/2005/11/02/cia-holds-terror-suspects-in-secret-prisons/767f0160-cde4-41f2-a691-ba989990039c/. [g] Amnesty International, 'USA: Below the Radar: Secret Flights to Torture and "Disappearance"', 4 April 2006, Index number: AMR 51/051/2006.

3.4.1 Taking Custody of CIA Detainees (Proxy Detention)

Proxy detention entails a state (in this case the US) transferring an individual to a partner state that has agreed to detain and interrogate the individual and return the fruits of that interrogation to the transferring state.[135] It covers situations whereby the CIA took custody of a detainee and rendered them to a detention site in a third country (neither the country of capture nor the detainee's state of nationality) or in their country of origin. Proxy detention should be distinguished from 'pre-CIA detention', which refers to the period of detention of an individual before entering CIA custody, usually in the country of capture. The distinction may however be harder to maintain in individual cases.[136]

Proxy detention raises a variety of human rights concerns, especially as states used as proxy detention sites for the CIA were allegedly picked for the brutality of their interrogation methods.[137] In most cases, CIA personnel had unrestricted access to detainees but they were officially in the custody of the foreign government. In consequence, the territorial state's jurisdiction is not at issue and all violations of detainees' rights can be attributed to the territorial state as principal wrongdoer – in addition to the US as co-perpetrator or complicit state where appropriate. In some situations, the powers of direction and control of the US over the state providing proxy detention may be such that the US would bear responsibility for their wrongful acts under Article 17 ASR. However, as Article 19 ASR underlines, acting under the influence of direction and control does not constitute an excuse or a circumstance precluding wrongfulness. Hence, the directed state would still incur primary responsibility for its wrongful acts.

In proxy detention situations, the territorial state would in most cases be held responsible for a breach of the prohibition of torture, cruel, inhuman, and degrading treatment in respect of interrogation methods and detention conditions; and of the right to liberty and security of the person in respect of detention without charge. In some cases, the conditions for a violation of the right to life, of the right to a fair trial, or of the prohibition of enforced disappearance may also be met.

---

[135] Margaret L Satterthwaite and Alexandra M Zetes, 'Rendition in Extraordinary Times', *Human Rights and America's War on Terror* (Routledge 2018) 2.

[136] Crofton Black, 'Foreign "Liaison Partners" and the CIA's Economy of Detention', *Extraordinary Rendition* (Routledge 2018) 57.

[137] Human Rights Council (n 38) paras 141–143.

3.4.2 Hosting CIA Black Sites

In contrast with proxy detention, host states of CIA black sites did not take custody of CIA detainees. Instead, they provided the CIA with all the necessary guarantees and protections to establish its own detention centre(s) on their territory. In most if not all cases, host state authorities never came in contact with CIA detainees.

The territorial state normally retains full jurisdiction over any place of detention on its territory, so that its responsibility should be engaged if the detainees' detention and treatment are not in accordance with international law. The ECtHR has ruled generally that 'the acquiescence or connivance of the authorities of a Contracting State in the acts of private individuals which violate the Convention rights of other individuals within its jurisdiction may engage the State's responsibility under the Convention'.[138] This naturally also applies to acts by agents of foreign states.

The bilateral Statute of Forces Agreements (SOFAs) concluded under the NATO-SOFA model between the US and various NATO Allies in the context of the invocation of Article 5 of the North Atlantic Treaty granted criminal jurisdiction to the US on part of the territory of these states (so-called 'foreign military bases').[139] However, secret detention constitutes a violation of the laws of all NATO members. Hence, despite its normally limited criminal jurisdiction over foreign military bases, if the territorial state is informed or has reasonable grounds to suspect that a person is held incommunicado on a foreign military base in its territory, it retains criminal jurisdiction. In consequence, the host state's duty to put an end to and investigate criminal offences committed by the sending state on its territory is not affected by the NATO-SOFA. Unless

---

[138] ECtHR, *Ilascu and others v. Moldova and Russia*, App. No. 48787/99, 8 July 2004, para 318. See also IACtHR, *Velásquez Rodríguez v Honduras* (n 104), para 172 and UN Human Rights Committee (n 66) para 8.

[139] SOFAs are normally bilateral; there exists in addition a multilateral SOFA with NATO members, the NATO Status of Forces Agreement (SOFA) of 19 June 1951 (Agreement between the Parties to the North Atlantic Treaty Regarding the Status of their Forces, available at: http://www.nato.int/docu/basictxt/b510619a.htm). Pursuant to Article VII of the NATO SOFA, when only the sending state's law is violated, the sending state has the power to exercise sole criminal jurisdiction. When only the receiving state's law is violated, the receiving state has the power to exercise sole criminal jurisdiction. When a crime violated the laws of both countries, there is concurrent criminal jurisdiction: the receiving state maintains primary jurisdiction except for offences committed solely against the property or security or member of the sending state force, or for offences arising out of any act or omission done by the sending state service member in the performance of official duty. In all other cases, the receiving state has the primary right to exercise jurisdiction.

the host state takes all measures within its power to put an end to and remedy such violations, its responsibility is engaged.

Having established that human rights jurisdiction is not affected by concurrent criminal jurisdiction, I now move to assessing the obligations of the territorial state towards CIA detainees. The acts of torture and secret detention are not attributable to the territorial state under the law of state responsibility,[140] meaning that it cannot be held responsible for a breach of its negative obligations. However, because the territorial state retains both criminal and human rights jurisdiction over CIA black sites, it is under an obligation to protect CIA detainees. This obligation to protect is aggravated in situations in which the state enables third-party actors to violate rights,[141] as did the states providing land, buildings, security clearance and other protections to the CIA to help it run its black sites.

A state under an obligation to protect – inherent in various human rights treaties and provisions[142] – can discharge the obligation by taking all reasonable measures at its disposal. What is reasonable and sufficient to discharge the obligation is necessarily context-specific and the obligation is one of conduct, but there must be some sort of appropriate action by the state to *try* to restrain the primary rights-violator.[143] A reasonable measure in the present case could consist of searching the premises in which the detention sites are located; revising the agreements with the CIA; or simply putting an end to those agreements, as several host states did when the existence of the sites became public. Hence, CIA black sites hosts would be in breach of their obligations to protect against torture, arbitrary detention, and other rights violations if they passively or actively abstained from preventing the CIA using their territory to that end. In addition, failure by the state to inform monitoring bodies such as the European Committee for the Prevention of Torture (ECPT) or the ICRC of the existence of detention centres and to grant them access would constitute violations of the relevant IHRL and IHL provisions.[144] Finally, an obligation to

---

[140] The ECtHR came to the opposite conclusion in the *Al-Nashiri* and *Abu Zubaydah* cases against Poland, Romania and Lithuania, but confused attribution and obligation to protect. Under the ASR, there is no basis for attribution of the acts of the CIA to the authorities of the territorial state.

[141] By analogy see: *Application of the Convention on the Prevention and Punishment of the Crime of Genocide (Bosnia and Herzegovina v Serbia and Montenegro)* [2007] ICJ Reports 2007 43 (International Court of Justice) [386 and 438]. See also Monica Hakimi, 'State Bystander Responsibility' (2010) 21 European Journal of International Law 341, 364.

[142] E.g., ICCPR Art. 2(1); CAT Art. 2; ACHR Art. 1(1); ECHR Art. 1.

[143] ECtHR, *Ilascu* (n 138), para 318. See also IACtHR, *Velásquez Rodríguez v. Honduras* (n 104), para 172.

[144] Article 3, ECPT; Article 126, GC III and Article 143, GC IV.

protect also entails adequately investigating and prosecuting third-party violations of human rights under one's jurisdiction once they have become known to the host state, as well as providing an effective remedy.

It is also possible to conceive of the territorial state's responsibility as one for aid or assistance to the principal wrongful act under Article 16 ASR. Providing one's territory and security protections for the establishment of a secret detention site would undoubtedly qualify as a 'significant contribution' to the commission of the wrongful act. The issue is then to assess the level of knowledge and intent of the territorial state.[145] In so far as a detention centre can be 'secret' vis-à-vis the national authorities, if any branch of the state is involved in or informed about the detention site,[146] irrespective of their acting ultra vires, the responsibility of the state as a subject of international law is engaged. It is then a question of fact whether any official of the state was aware of, or wilfully blind to the fact that secret detention was taking place on the state's territory.

3.4.3 Cooperation in the Arrest, Detention, and Transfer of Individuals into CIA Custody

States are presumed to exercise jurisdiction over their entire territory. Therefore, when an individual is arrested by foreign authorities on the territory of a state, that state is presumed to be responsible unless it can be proven that the foreign authorities have acted extraterritorially without consent, violating the sovereignty of the territorial state.[147]

However, this latter state of affairs would not release the territorial state from its positive obligations towards the individual and their relatives. The territorial state would notably be required to take reasonable measures to prevent the violation and do everything in its power to bring ongoing violations to an end.[148] In addition, in the face of plausible claims or information indicative of serious rights violations, the state would be under an obligation to carry out a prompt, thorough, independent, and effective investigation and, where appropriate, to proceed to hold those responsible to account.[149] Furthermore,

---

[145] On the various frameworks to be used to assess knowledge and intent, see Milanovic (n 132).

[146] E.g., the application of the strict NATO need-to-know policy, in conjunction with the choice of military intelligence as a partner by the CIA, means that knowledge of the operation of the HVD programme in Poland was restricted to a few individuals only. See Marty (n 20) paras 167–179.

[147] ECtHR, *Öcalan* v. *Turkey* (n 78), para 90.

[148] ECtHR, *Ilascu* (n 138), para 318.

[149] E.g., Article 3 ECHR, Articles 5 and 12 CAT.

the state would be required under IHRL to provide an effective remedy to the victims.[150] A failure to fulfil these obligations to protect and remedy the original wrong would engage the responsibility of the territorial state under applicable human rights provisions, and trigger a new set of obligations to remedy the secondary wrong attributable to the state.

When the territorial state cooperates with the foreign state in the arrest of an individual under its jurisdiction, its responsibility is engaged as principal wrongdoer for all violations of its negative obligations towards the individual taking place on its territory thereafter.[151] Its responsibility for a breach of its obligations to protect (in that case non-refoulement) will also be engaged in respect of the transfer of custody to foreign agents if there is a risk that such transfer will expose the individual to torture, arbitrary detention, or other serious human rights violations.[152]

There is a third variant to this situation, whereby the territorial state proceeds with the arrest on its own and later surrenders custody of the detainee to the CIA. These are cases of 'pre-CIA detention'. The territorial state's responsibility is here engaged as principal wrongdoer for all the breaches of its negative obligations while it holds custody. As in the previous situation, it is also engaged for a breach of its obligation to protect when it surrenders the detainee to the CIA. The ECtHR went further and held that, in such cases, the territorial state's responsibility is engaged for arbitrary detention under Article 5 ECHR (right to liberty and security of the person) for the whole duration of the detention abroad following the transfer.[153] However, the ECtHR's demonstration regarding attribution of conduct is weak, and it is doubtful whether such a conclusion would be reached by another court as it constitutes a significant departure from the basic principle of the law of state responsibility, embedded in Article 1 ASR, that a state is only responsible for its own wrongful acts. A more convincing demonstration could have been made under

---

[150] The right to an effective remedy is explicit in IHRL treaties, e.g., Article 2(3)(a) ICCPR and Article 13 ECHR, and inherent in the duty to 'ensure' the protection of rights in human rights and humanitarian law treaties.

[151] On the rendition of Mohammed Alzery from Sweden to Egypt with the cooperation of CIA agents, and regarding Alzery's treatment by CIA agents at Bromma airport in Sweden, the CCPR made the following determination: 'the acts complained of, which occurred in the course of performance of official functions in the presence of the State party's officials and within the State party's jurisdiction, are properly imputable to the State party itself, in addition to the State on whose behalf the officials were engaged'. CCPR, *Alzery* v. *Sweden* (n 37), para 11.6.

[152] See, on a set of facts identical to the situation under scrutiny: CCPR, *Alzery* v. *Sweden* (n 37), para 11.5; UNCAT, *Agiza* v. *Sweden* (n 37), para 13.4.

[153] ECtHR, *El-Masri* (n 37), para 239; and *Nasr and Ghali* v. *Italy*, App. No.44883/09, 23 February 2016, para 302.

the 'security of the person' fragment of Article 5 ECHR. The extension in time of Macedonia's and Italy's responsibility could then have been justified as a continuous breach of their positive and negative obligations to protect and not deliberately endanger the security of the claimants under Article 5(1).

3.4.4 Allowing CIA Aircrafts to Stop, Refuel, and Fly through National Airspace

The Chicago Convention on International Civil Aviation sets out in its Article 1 the principle that every state has complete and exclusive sovereignty over the airspace above its territory. As has been emphasised by the Venice Commission, the decision by NATO allies to grant blanket overflight clearance to the US does not diminish the human rights obligations they owe to all persons within their jurisdiction.[154] However, to protect the rights of individuals within their respective jurisdictions, NATO allies may have to act in apparent breach of the agreement(s) through which they provided the US with blanket overflight clearance.

The North Atlantic Treaty provides, through a conflict prevention clause in Article 7, that 'This Treaty does not affect, and shall not be interpreted as affecting in any way the rights and obligations under the Charter of the Parties which are members of the United Nations'. Thus, even if NATO allies undertook obligations towards the US in application of Article 5 of the North Atlantic Treaty, they should interpret such obligations in a manner compatible with their human rights obligations.[155] There is also a general presumption, independent of NATO membership, that the US would be acting in compliance with its human rights obligations. Hence, because agreeing to provide overflight clearance to the US would not, per se, involve any breach of human rights obligations there is, in essence, no conflict of norms. Notwithstanding,

---

[154] Venice Commission (n 124), para 115.
[155] See, in the context of an alleged conflict between a UN Security Council resolution and the ECHR, the rationale of the ECtHR finding that the protection of human rights forms an integral part of the purposes and principles of the United Nations, in *Al-Jedda* v. *United Kingdom*, App. No. 27021/08, 7 July 2011, para 102: 'In its approach to the interpretation of Resolution 1546, ... the Court must have regard to the purposes for which the United Nations was created. As well as the purpose of maintaining international peace and security, set out in the first subparagraph of Article 1 of the United Nations Charter, the third subparagraph provides that the United Nations was established to "achieve international cooperation in ... promoting and encouraging respect for human rights and fundamental freedoms". Article 24(2) of the Charter requires the Security Council, in discharging its duties with respect to its primary responsibility for the maintenance of international peace and security, to "act in accordance with the Purposes and Principles of the United Nations".'

the breach of treaty obligations by the territorial state for the purpose of complying with a peremptory norm would be required, both under customary law and to comply with UN Charter obligations. It would therefore not constitute an internationally wrongful act.[156]

The first situation examined here is one whereby a state has reasons to suspect that the mission of an aircraft crossing its airspace is to carry prisoners with the intention of transferring them to countries where they would face ill-treatment.[157] As long as an aircraft is in the air, individuals aboard are subject to the concurrent criminal jurisdiction of both the aircraft's flag state and the territorial state.[158] The territorial state is entitled to,[159] and must[160] take all possible measures in order to prevent the commission of criminal acts constituting human rights violations within its jurisdiction, including its airspace. Thus, the territorial state has an obligation to protect CIA detainees from violations of their right to liberty and security of the person, freedom from torture, and right to life. It can only discharge this obligation by taking reasonable measures to prevent the violation. What is required from the territorial state in this specific situation will depend greatly upon its degree of knowledge or awareness of the aircraft's status and purpose. If the territorial state has reasons to suspect that the aircraft is rendering detainees to secret detention and/or ill-treatment, its responsibility will be engaged under relevant human rights provisions unless it takes all preventive measures within its power, such as requiring the aircraft to land, and searching and inspecting it. In contrast, if the territorial state has no awareness of the CIA programme and its modus operandi, and has no reason to suspect that the aircraft crossing its airspace is violating any laws, then the state cannot reasonably be required to make the aircraft land. Its obligations to protect could then be discharged by taking more limited measures, such as ensuring that the aircraft crossing its airspace has filed a flight plan and is not violating international aviation laws.

---

[156] See Venice Commission (n 124), para 153, advancing a similar argument without reference to the UN Charter: 'the Commission recalls that if the breach of a treaty obligation is determined by the need to comply with a peremptory norm (*jus cogens*), it does not give rise to an internationally wrongful act'. Support for this position can be found, indirectly, in Article 53 of the Vienna Convention on the Law of Treaties; Article 41(2) ASR; and customary international law.

[157] Public knowledge of extraordinary rendition is considered established from early 2006 onward. However, states that cooperated with the CIA often had earlier knowledge of the programme's specifics, including rendition.

[158] ICAO, Convention on offences and certain other acts committed aboard aircraft, 14 September 1963 (Tokyo Convention), Articles 3 and 4.

[159] Chicago Convention, Articles 3bis(b) and 16 and Tokyo Convention, Article 4(b).

[160] See, e.g., ICCPR Art. 2(1); CAT Art. 2; ACHR Art. 1(1); ECHR Art. 1.

Where knowledge of the purpose and mission of the flight is established, the territorial state's responsibility could also be engaged for aiding or assisting in the commission of the principal wrongful act under Article 16 ASR. Indeed, allowing an aircraft carrying detainees to cross one's airspace constitutes a significant enough contribution to the wrongful act of rendition. Hence, if the territorial state is aware of the circumstances or specific illegality of the wrongful act, then the requirements of Article 16 are satisfied.

The second situation considered concerns so-called stopover states. Despite the military or public nature of most CIA flights, the flag state is estopped from claiming state aircraft status because, in order to circumvent the requirement to obtain special permissions to enter national airspace, the public purpose of the flight was not declared. In consequence, the aircraft is deemed to be civil and thus falling within the Chicago Convention's scope of application.[161] Crucially, when a civil aircraft lands, its passengers come under the sole criminal jurisdiction of the territorial state, in addition to its human rights jurisdiction under the spatial model. Crofton Black classifies stopover states within three categories – those whose territory was used for: mid-rendition stop-offs; a mid-rendition switch; or a pre/post-rendition stop-off.[162]

According to Black's definitions and the data compiled by the Rendition Project, a mid-rendition stop-off refers to situation whereby the aircraft transferring a CIA detainee between two rendition sites stops in a third country midway. Stop-offs occurred in Italy, Dubai, Egypt, Sri Lanka, the Canaries (Spain), Poland, Romania, Morocco, Jordan and the territory of Diego Garcia, under British sovereignty at the time.[163] In this situation, there is no attribution of the wrongful act of rendition to the territorial state, hence no responsibility for a breach of the territorial state's negative obligations. However, once again, this does not release the state from its obligation to protect, inherent in the exercise of jurisdiction. To discharge the obligation, the territorial state would thus be required to, for instance, search the plane or carry out an identity check of all persons aboard. In the absence of such reasonable measures, only a complete lack of awareness and knowledge of the CIA programme would prevent the engagement of responsibility for a breach of the state's obligation to protect,[164] and only in so far as there was no reasonable basis to suspect that a detainee was aboard or that the flight was carrying out a rendition.

---

[161] Venice Commission (n 124), para 103.
[162] Black (n 136).
[163] *Legal Consequences of the Separation of the Chagos Archipelago from Mauritius in 1965 (Advisory Opinion)* [2019] ICJ Reports 2019 95 (International Court of Justice).
[164] A complete lack of awareness could only be invoked before 2003, and not by all states.

Mid-rendition switches happened more rarely. They involved a detainee being taken off of one plane and moved onto another during a stop-off in a third country. States that acted as switch points include Jordan, Albania, and Egypt. Again, there can be no responsibility for a breach of the state's negative obligations as there is no attribution of the wrongful act of rendition to the territorial state. Similar reasonable measures as for mid-rendition stop-offs would be required from the territorial state, but it is arguable that the territorial state's knowledge will be harder to deny in such cases. Indeed, as the detainee(s) did set foot on the airport's tarmac, constructive knowledge may be more easily inferred and responsibility for breach of the obligation to protect consequently harder to evade.

In both mid-rendition stop-offs and switches, the territorial state's responsibility could also be engaged under Article 16 ASR if it can be shown that the state had constructive knowledge that the aircraft landing was a CIA aircraft carrying out a rendition. Allowing the CIA to use one's airports or airbases to carry out a rendition would normally qualify as a substantial contribution to the commission of the wrongful act of rendition, so that the only difficulty would lie in establishing state officials' knowledge.

The last type of stopover state was the most common. A pre/post-rendition stop-off is a pause in a rendition plane's journey without a detainee aboard, either just before a detainee was picked up or after one was dropped off. Passengers (the crew, US personnel and CIA agents) usually disembarked, sometimes for lengthy periods of time, and checked into hotels. There is no jurisdictional link between CIA detainees and the territorial state in such cases, hence no obligation owed to CIA detainees.[165]

However, there is a jurisdictional link with potential perpetrators of torture (CIA agents). The UN Convention against Torture[166] (CAT) imposes on contracting states positive obligations in relation to the prosecution or extradition of persons suspected of torture.[167] The obligation to prosecute or extradite is an obligation of result and it is only triggered if the territorial state knew or

---

[165] However, with regard to the ICCPR, see the potential for disregarding the necessity of a jurisdictional link in a case concerning the wrongful failure to act of Romanian authorities while the applicant was tried in Iraq and in US custody. *Munaf* v. *Romania* (n 68), para 14.2: 'The Committee recalls its jurisprudence that a State party may be responsible for extra-territorial violations of the Covenant, if it is a link in the causal chain that would make possible violations in another jurisdiction. Thus, the risk of an extra-territorial violation must be a necessary and foreseeable consequence and must be judged on the knowledge the State party had at the time'.

[166] UN General Assembly, Convention Against Torture and Other Cruel, Inhuman or Degrading Treatment or Punishment, opened for signature 10 December 1984, 1465 UNTS 85 (entered into force 26 June 1987) ('CAT').

[167] CAT, Articles 6 and 7.

ought to have known that individuals on its territory were actively taking part in a state programme involving torture. Awareness of the CIA programme and of the disembarking passengers' nature (CIA agents) could arguably be said to constitute constructive knowledge, thereby triggering positive obligations under the CAT.

Alternatively, where the territorial state has at least constructive knowledge of the flight's mission and of the broader context of the CIA programme, state responsibility could be engaged for aid or assistance under Article 16 ASR. Indeed, it is arguable that the concrete support received by the CIA in the form of airspace and airport access was essential to the operation of the programme. Hence, if awareness of the wrongful act's circumstances can be shown, then the territorial state's responsibility can be engaged for aid or assistance. In addition, because the wrongful acts of rendition, secret detention, torture, and enforced disappearance were of a systematic nature and constituted continuing breaches, Article 41(2) ASR could apply concurrently. The territorial state's responsibility could therefore also be engaged for aid or assistance to the maintenance of an unlawful situation (impunity) deriving from the serious breach of the prohibitions of torture and enforced disappearance. Knowledge is not formally required under Article 41(2), but given the extreme secrecy surrounding the programme and the rationale for the absence of a knowledge requirement,[168] constructive awareness could reasonably be required for responsibility to arise.

3.4.5 Intelligence Sharing with the CIA

Intelligence sharing raises remarkable legal issues. The collection, sharing, receipt, and use of intelligence can engage the responsibility of both the sending state and the receiving state under various legal frameworks, but especially under IHL and IHRL.[169] Particularly salient issues concern the right to privacy, the right to life, and the prohibition of torture. Given the facts of the CIA programme, the current section focuses mainly on the latter. The prohibition of torture is recognised as *jus cogens*, a peremptory norm of international law suffering no derogation for any purpose.[170] The CAT further imposes on states parties to the Convention direct positive obligations to investigate and punish, in their territory and jurisdiction, participation and complicity in tor-

---

[168] ASR, commentary to Article 41, para 11: 'it is hardly conceivable that a State would not have notice of the commission of a serious breach by another State'.

[169] See generally Milanovic (n 132).

[170] ASR, commentary to Article 26, para 5 and commentary to Article 40, para 5; ICJ, *Questions relating to the Obligation to Prosecute or Extradite* (Belgium v. Senegal), Judgment, ICJ Reports 2012, 422, para 99.

ture.[171] In addition, the Convention obliges states to criminalise such acts under domestic law[172] and to take effective measures to prevent them.[173]

In intelligence cooperation, state responsibility for an internationally wrongful act relating to the prohibition of torture may arise in a straightforward way from actions by foreign intelligence agencies on a state's own territory;[174] from refoulement to torture;[175] or from the lack of effective domestic investigation and remedies for allegations of torture by a state official – even when committed abroad.[176] Slightly more indirectly, it may also arise from the receipt and use of intelligence obtained through torture, in court[177] or by the executive, and from the interrogation of detainees abroad where there exists a serious risk that they are being tortured in detention. These last two situations form the subject of important legal debates, and constitute the focus of the current subsection.

The starting point for the argument is that actionable use of intelligence obtained through or tainted by torture creates a market for such intelligence and goes against the spirit of the CAT.[178] However, one can go further and

---

[171] CAT, Articles 12 and 13.
[172] CAT, Article 4.
[173] CAT, Article 2.
[174] ECtHR, *Al-Nashiri v. Poland* (n 95); *Husayn (Abu Zubaydah) v. Poland* (n 95); *Al-Nashiri v. Romania*, App. No.33234/12, 31 May 2018; *Abu Zubaydah v. Lithuania*, App. No.46454/11, 31 May 2018.
[175] ECtHR, *El-Masri* (n 37); *Nasr and Ghali v. Italy* (n 153); UNCAT, *Agiza v. Sweden* (n 37); CCPR, *Alzery v. Sweden* (n 37).
[176] CAT, Articles 4 to 9. CCPR, *López-Burgos v. Uruguay*, CCPR/C/13/D52/1979, 29 July 1981, para. 12.3: 'States are accountable for violations of rights under the [ICCPR] which [their] agents commit upon the territory of another State'; and by analogy with procedural obligations under the right to life: ECtHR, *Jaloud v. The Netherlands*, App. No.47708/08, 20 November 2014. In addition, a state's failure to investigate, criminally prosecute or allow civil proceedings – or efforts to block or hinder such proceedings – relating to allegations of torture or other forms of ill-treatment constitutes a de facto denial of an effective remedy: UN Committee against Torture, 'General Comment No. 3 : Convention against Torture and Other Cruel, Inhuman or Degrading Treatment or Punishment : Implementation of Article 14 by States Parties' (2012) CAT/C/GC/3.
[177] CAT, Article 15.
[178] See Martin Scheinin and Mathias Vermeulen, 'Unilateral Exceptions to International Law: Systematic Legal Analysis and Critique of Doctrines to Deny or Reduce the Applicability of Human Rights Norms in the Fight against Terrorism' (2011) 8 Essex Human Rights Review 20. This position is also supported by the 'Report of the Special Rapporteur on Torture and Other Cruel, Inhuman or Degrading Treatment or Punishment, Juan E. Méndez' (2014) A/HRC/25/60 ('Méndez Report 2014'); EJP Report 2009 (n 85), para 85; and Martin Scheinin, 'Report of the Special Rapporteur on the Promotion and Protection of Human Rights and Fundamental Freedoms While Countering Terrorism, Martin Scheinin' (UN General Assembly, Human Rights Council 2009) A/HRC/10/3.

inquire whether the collection, receipt, demand, or use of torture-tainted intelligence constitute acts which, taken individually, are susceptible to engaging the international responsibility of the states involved.

3.4.5.1 Overview of the applicable legal framework

Contrary to the claim that executive use of torture-tainted intelligence is unregulated in international law, I submit here that there exists an interlocking set of primary and secondary rules prohibiting collection, demand, provision, passive receipt, and actionable use of such intelligence. In none of the situations under scrutiny did the state itself torture – i.e., there can be no attribution of the acts of torture to the state – and in none of them did the acts of torture occur on the territory of the state. The inquiry should therefore begin with looking at complicity under international law. The general customary law provision is reflected in Article 16 ASR.[179] It imposes a stringent threshold of responsibility for aid or assistance that requires knowledge,[180] intent[181] and significant contribution[182] to the commission of the wrongful act.[183]

As *lex specialis* to Article 16, or simply as less tenuous ways to establish state responsibility – especially while respecting the *Monetary Gold* principle[184] – international humanitarian and human rights law provide various legal avenues to hold states responsible for acts they did not themselves commit. These constitute stricter standards of conduct to which states have committed

---

[179] Article 16. *Aid or assistance in the commission of an internationally wrongful act*
A State which aids or assists another State in the commission of an internationally wrongful act by the latter is internationally responsible for doing so if:
(a) that State does so with knowledge of the circumstances of the internationally wrongful act; and
(b) the act would be internationally wrongful if committed by that State.

[180] ASR, commentary to Article 16, para 4. See also, ICJ, *Bosnian Genocide* case (n 141) paras 420–423.

[181] ASR, commentary to Article 16, para 9.

[182] ibid para 5.

[183] For a discussion of the knowledge and intent elements of Article 16, see Harriet Moynihan, 'Aiding and Assisting: The Mental Element under Article 16 of the International Law Commission's Article on State Responsibility' (2018) 67 International and Comparative Law Quarterly 455; Milanovic (n 132).

[184] The essence of the principle as expressed by the ICJ is that it cannot decide on the international responsibility of a state if, in order to do so, 'it would have to rule, as a prerequisite, on the lawfulness' of the conduct of another state in the latter's absence and without its consent. *Monetary Gold Removed from Rome in 1943*, Judgment, ICJ Reports 1954 32. The issue posed by the principle in proceedings invoking Article 16 is acknowledged by the ILC at paragraph 11 of the ASR commentary. However, it is less problematic in proceedings invoking direct responsibility of the 'complicit' state through breach of its obligation to protect, such as positive obligations, obligations to prevent, and the prohibition of non-refoulement.

themselves, and which consequently impose lower thresholds for holding states responsible in a direct form (rather than derivatively as under Article 16 ASR). Of particular interest to the current inquiry are obligations to prevent and positive obligations; Common Article 1 to the 1949 Geneva Conventions; and Article 41 ASR.

One of the most important positive obligations of states, inherent in the prohibition of torture itself and therefore not territorially limited,[185] is the obligation to refrain from action that exposes individuals to a risk of torture. It is often equated with the prohibition of refoulement to torture, explicitly stated in Article 3 CAT and read in the more general provisions prohibiting torture in various human rights treaties. Under the prohibition of refoulement, it is sufficient that there are serious grounds to believe that the individual will be subjected to wrongful treatment for refoulement to engage state responsibility.[186] In contrast, for responsibility to be engaged under Article 16 ASR, it would be required that the individual has actually been subjected to wrongful treatment.[187] In addition to the prohibition of refoulement, the prohibition of *any* action exposing individuals to a risk of torture should also be read within the general prohibition of torture. This prohibition concerns actions by state agents abroad, but also actions taken on the territory of the state, such as intelligence sharing, which have effects abroad.[188] Thus, despite the individual not coming under the state's jurisdiction, the state would be in breach of the general prohibition of torture by exposing them to a risk of torture from its own territory.[189]

In addition, Article 4 CAT requires states to ensure that all acts of torture and 'complicity and participation' therein are criminalised under domestic

---

[185] See 'Report of the Special Rapporteur on torture and other cruel, inhuman or degrading treatment or punishment Theo van Boven' (2004) A/59/324, para 28; Méndez Report 2014 (n 178), paras 40–58. See generally on the extraterritoriality of the prohibition of torture, UNHRC, 'Interim report of the Special Rapporteur on torture and other cruel, inhuman or degrading treatment or punishment Juan E. Méndez' (2015) A/70/303 ('Méndez Report 2015'), especially para 27.

[186] For the weight to be given to diplomatic assurances in precluding the wrongfulness of refoulement, see UNCAT, *Agiza* v. *Sweden* (n 37), para 13.4.

[187] Helmut Philipp Aust, *Complicity and the Law of State Responsibility* (Cambridge University Press 2011) Chapter 14.

[188] The ECtHR has consistently found that states' responsibility 'can be involved because of acts of their authorities, whether performed within or outside national boundaries, which produce effects outside their own territory'. *Loizidou* v. *Turkey*, Admissibility, App. No.15318/89, 23 March 1995, para 62.

[189] Méndez Report 2015 (n 185), paras 20 and 33. This position is also defended by Jackson with regards to Article 3 ECHR and the jurisdiction of the ECtHR: Miles Jackson, 'Freeing *Soering*: The ECHR, State Complicity in Torture and Jurisdiction' (2016) 27 European Journal of International Law 817.

law. While the term 'complicity' is not defined in the Convention, the definition of torture in Article 1 provides that acts will constitute torture if they are committed 'by or at the instigation of or with the consent or acquiescence of a public official or other person acting in an official capacity'. By reference to Article 1, therefore, complicity in Article 4 has been interpreted as including incitement; instigation; superior orders or instructions; consent; acquiescence; and concealment.[190] The concept of acquiescence, which requires only constructive knowledge of the occurrence of torture associated with a failure to object, is the most relevant for the issues at hand. Thus, as acquiescence constitutes complicity in torture, and as the state has an obligation to criminalise complicity in torture, it must constitute a wrongful act for the state to be complicit in torture itself.[191] In that sense, albeit indirectly, Article 4 imposes an obligation on states to refrain from being complicit in torture through the acts of their officials, without territorial limitation.[192] In consequence, public officials' acquiescence to torture committed abroad can trigger the state's responsibility for a breach of Article 4.

In its General Comment No. 31, the Human Rights Committee emphasised that, regarding the general prohibition on torture imposed on states by the ICCPR, 'it is implicit in Article 7 that State Parties have to take positive measures to ensure that private persons or entities do not inflict torture or cruel, inhuman or degrading treatment or punishment on others within their power', adding that 'this applies to those within the power or effective control of the forces of a State Party acting outside its territory'.[193] The general obligation contained in Article 7 ICCPR therefore implies a positive obligation to prevent torture by public officials of the state whenever they have 'effective control' over an individual in a foreign country.

Whereas Article 2 CAT is, like Article 7 ICCPR, explicitly restricted to persons and territories under the jurisdiction of the state, Article 5 CAT imposes on states an obligation to prosecute and punish acts of torture, no matter where they may have been committed (Arts 6 and 7). As this is one of the most effective ways of preventing torture wherever it occurs, state conduct that would raise the overall risk of torture abroad would be incompatible with the obligation to criminalise (Art. 4) and punish (Art. 5). It could therefore be argued that the state is under an obligation of conduct to prevent the wrongful

---

[190] Manfred Nowak, Moritz Birk and Giuliana Monina (eds), *The United Nations Convention against Torture and Its Optional Protocol: A Commentary* (2nd ed, Oxford University Press 2019) 236–237; Human Rights Council (n 38) para 39.

[191] By analogy with the Genocide Convention, see *Bosnian Genocide* (n 141) para 167.

[192] Méndez Report 2014 (n 178), para 48 and Méndez Report 2015 (n 185), para 21.

[193] UN Human Rights Committee (n 66) para 8.

acts using all the means available to it.¹⁹⁴ This is supported, by analogy, by the ICJ decision in the *Bosnian Genocide* case¹⁹⁵ and, with regard to the customary prohibition of torture, by the ICTY judgment in *Furundzjia*.¹⁹⁶ By merely requiring a failure to act and a low degree of awareness for finding a breach of an obligation to prevent – the criteria for which are rather vague – the threshold of responsibility is consequently much easier to reach than that of complicity under Article 16 ASR. In addition, claims alleging the breach of an obligation to prevent, as with other positive obligations, absolve the judicial forum from having to formally assess the conduct of another state against international law, thus dismissing potential issues related to the *Monetary Gold* principle.¹⁹⁷

Linked to this is Common Article 1 to the 1949 Geneva Conventions, which imposes on states an obligation to 'ensure respect' for the rights protected in the Conventions, including the right not to be subjected to torture, cruel, inhuman, or degrading treatment.¹⁹⁸ This has been interpreted as an obligation not to encourage violations of IHL by other states or actors, together with an obligation to exert all possible influence to put an end to such violations.¹⁹⁹ This obligation applies to all states regarding acts committed as part of an armed conflict, regardless of whether states are engaged in it.²⁰⁰ In all the situations analysed below, if the torture-tainted information was obtained during and as part of an armed conflict situation, acts by other states amounting to a failure to meet their obligation to prevent or their obligation of non-recognition would also amount to a breach of Common Article 1.

Finally, Article 41 ASR sets out a strict standard of conduct for all states regarding serious breaches of peremptory norms of international law, including the prohibition of torture.²⁰¹ Article 41(1) provides that, in such cases, all states 'shall cooperate to bring to an end through lawful means' breaches of

---

[194] Sarah Fulton, 'Cooperating with the Enemy of Mankind: Can States Simply Turn a Blind Eye to Torture?' (2012) 16 The International Journal of Human Rights 773, 785–786; Hakimi (n 141) 376–379.

[195] *Bosnian Genocide* (n 141) paras 426–431.

[196] ICTY, *Prosecutor* v. *Furundzjia*, IT-95-17/1-T, Judgment, 10 December 1998, paras 147–157 with reference to the customary prohibition of torture.

[197] Aust (n 187) 403.

[198] Geneva Conventions of 1949, Common Article 3.

[199] Aust (n 187) 385–389. ICRC Study on Customary International Humanitarian Law, Rule 144.

[200] Jean Pictet (ed), *Commentary on the Third Geneva Convention*, ICRC, Geneva, 1960, 18; *Military and Paramilitary Activities in and against Nicaragua (Nicaragua v United States)* [1986] ICJ Reports 1986 14 (ICJ) [46].

[201] On Article 41, see generally Eric Wyler and León Castellanos-Jankiewicz, 'Serious Breaches of Peremptory Norms' in André Nollkaemper and Ilias Plakokefalos (eds), *Principles of Shared Responsibility in International Law: An Appraisal of the State of the Art* (Cambridge University Press 2014).

peremptory norms amounting to 'a gross or systematic failure by the responsible State to fulfil the obligation'.[202] There is therefore a duty of cooperation, and a failure to respect it would engage state responsibility.[203] In the context of intelligence sharing, Article 41(1) would thus impose on states a duty to exert all possible influence and use all available means to put an end to ongoing policies of torture by their intelligence partners – including by putting an end to intelligence sharing.

The obligation of cooperation becomes redundant in the case of a non-continuing breach, but states are nevertheless under additional obligations of non-recognition and non-assistance regarding the continuing effects of the breach. Article 41(2) thus provides that 'no State shall recognize as lawful a situation created by a serious breach ... nor render aid or assistance in maintaining that situation'. With regard to *jus cogens* norms, therefore, there appears to be a lower threshold for complicity, *ex post facto*.[204] Indeed, when states assist the principal wrongdoer in maintaining the illegal situation (e.g., impunity) created by the serious breach, their responsibility may be engaged for a violation of the obligation of non-assistance. Notwithstanding that if the aid or assistance is substantial enough, it may also satisfy the requirements of Article 16 ASR. In addition, it could be argued that treating torture-tainted information as lawfully-obtained information would amount to recognising the situation created by the serious breach as lawful, and thus amount to a violation of the obligation of non-recognition.[205]

3.4.5.2 Intelligence sharing as an internationally wrongful act

Sending agents to interrogate detainees abroad

Several states have sent agents to interrogate CIA detainees held in Guantánamo Bay, at Bagram airbase, or in other detention sites managed by the CIA or foreign services. This situation raises jurisdictional issues that may preclude the establishment of the sending state's responsibility under human rights law. Specifically, states that send agents do not have custody of the detainees. For Council of Europe states, according to recent ECtHR case-law, it depends

---

[202] ASR, Article 40(2).
[203] The commentary notes that it may be open to question whether general international law at present prescribes a positive duty of cooperation and observes that Article 41(1) may, in that respect, reflect the progressive development of international law. But see Méndez Report 2014 (n 178), para 49; Méndez Report 2015 (n 185), para 22; UNHRC, 'Report of the Special Rapporteur on the Promotion and Protection of Human Rights and Fundamental Freedoms while Countering Terrorism, Ben Emerson' (2012) A/67/396, para 48; and Human Rights Council (n 38) para 42.
[204] Méndez Report 2014 (n 178), para 52.
[205] ibid para 54, referring to 'acts that would imply such recognition'.

upon the level of control and power over the individual *and* over the geographical area whether the individual is within the jurisdiction of the sending state.[206] Hence, except in situations where the sending state is the occupying power or exercises elements of governmental authority in the area, current case-law in this respect does not favour the existence of a jurisdictional link. The situation may however be slightly different before the CCPR with its broader conception of jurisdiction, provided a factual link between the sending state and the ill-treatment can be drawn.[207]

However, even without detainees coming under its jurisdiction, by sending agents to interrogate detainees that are being tortured by the detaining authority, the sending state may become complicit in their ill-treatment in various ways. First, by interrogating the detainee, state agents may be exposing them to further risk of torture, in contravention of the sending state's obligations under the CAT. In addition, because the detainee is still in the custody of the authorities administrating torture, any information obtained by the sending state's agents would necessarily be tainted by previous torture and the risk of future torture should the detainee not behave as demanded or expected.[208] The sending state would thus be profiting from past and future torture, thereby condoning and acquiescing to it. The sending state's degree of knowledge matters only to the extent that complete lack of knowledge would prevent the engagement of responsibility.[209] However, in so far as the sending state's constructive knowledge can reasonably be inferred – due to information in the public domain or in intelligence cables, or according to what agents on the ground have observed or been told by detainees – then the state's responsibility will be engaged if it carries on with the interrogation.[210]

---

[206] The ECtHR indeed seems to have adopted a double spatial-personal model of jurisdiction in situations where the respondent state does not have custody of the individual. *Al-Skeini* (n 72), paras 149–150.

[207] See, e.g., *Munaf* v. *Romania* (n 68), para 14.2.

[208] A DoD-run military commission judge recently ruled in agreement with the principle that the taint of torture carries over, judging that all statements to the FBI made by the five detainees charged with crimes relating to the 9/11 attacks were inadmissible in court because of the detainees' treatment by the CIA during previous interrogations. Charlie Savage, 'Judge Bars Statements Made by Guantánamo Detainees During F.B.I. Interrogations', *The New York Times* (18 August 2018), available at: https://www.nytimes.com/2018/08/17/us/politics/guantanamo-detainees-fbi-interrogations.html (accessed 14 June 2022).

[209] It would only be possible to assert complete lack of knowledge prior to 2003, and it is unlikely that states that sent agents to CIA-run prisons would be able to prove such lack of knowledge.

[210] Intelligence and Security Committee (n 10) conclusions G and H (Annex A).

Furthermore, carrying out an interrogation when the state knew or ought to have known that there was a serious risk that the detainee had been or would be tortured[211] constitutes a breach of the state's obligations to prevent and bring to an end the violation under the CAT and Article 41(1) ASR, as well as under Common Article 1 GC where applicable.[212]

In addition, in situations where the detainee does come under the jurisdiction of the sending state,[213] human rights treaties become applicable, in whole or in part.[214] Assuming that the sending state's agents do not commit torture themselves, the state cannot be held responsible for a breach of negative obligations owed to detainees. However, if agents of the sending state have witnessed ill-treatment, been told about ill-treatment, or are aware of secret detention (the conditions of which amount to ill-treatment) and carry on with the interrogation, the state would become complicit in torture under Article 4 CAT.

Moreover, the obligation to respect and ensure the rights of individuals within its jurisdiction would oblige the state to take reasonable measures to that end, such as inquiring about detainee treatment, abstaining from participating in an interrogation if there has been or exists any risk of mistreatment, and ensuring through all means available that detainees are not mistreated by a third party.[215] Any failure to fulfil these positive obligations would engage the state's responsibility under applicable human rights treaties. Other human rights provisions, such as the right to life and the right to liberty and security of the person, may also require the state to take positive steps to protect the rights of the detainees they interrogate.

---

[211] This would be the case for all foreign states from early 2004 onward. Constructive knowledge of abusive detention conditions, and specific knowledge of abusive interrogation methods by several foreign intelligence services can however be established earlier.

[212] A large number of detainees in CIA detention sites were captured during the conflicts in Afghanistan and Iraq and are therefore protected under IHL.

[213] That could be the case, for instance, for US-held detainees interrogated by British agents while the US and the UK were occupying powers in Iraq or while the US-led coalition 'Operation Enduring Freedom', in which UK armed forces took part, was exercising elements of governmental power in Afghanistan. Intelligence and Security Committee (n 10) 17–20.

[214] ECHR provisions would potentially be 'divided and tailored' to the situation (see *Al-Skeini* (n 72), para 149) while some CAT provisions are only applicable on the territory (and not within the jurisdiction) of the state. Other applicable human rights treaties have not been judged to be dividable by competent bodies.

[215] ECHR, Article 3; ICCPR, Article 7; CCPR, General Comment No. 31 para 8. See also Intelligence and Security Committee (n 10) 43 and conclusions F, G, and H (Annex A).

Demand

Sending questions to a foreign state for the interrogation of a detainee constitutes an explicit form of demand for information held by that detainee. This is both a lawful and common cooperation practice. However, in cases where the detainee is held by a state with a poor human rights record including wide or systematic use of torture of (certain categories of) detainees, the demand concerns torture-tainted intelligence. If the state sending questions knows or ought to know about the detaining state's human rights record, then it also knows or ought to know that the information it is demanding will likely be obtained through torture. Thus, if there is a pattern of systemic torture in the receiving state,[216] constructive knowledge on the part of the sending state is sufficient for responsibility to arise. The sending state should reasonably have known that torture would be applied in order to obtain answers to its questions. It also ought to have known that the sending of questions would likely induce new acts of torture: but for sending such questions, the detainee would not have been tortured to answer them.[217]

I submit that, where it is established that torture was applied to obtain answers to the questions sent, sending questions may amount, depending on the factual situation, to participation, incitement, instigation, or complicity to the commission of torture (Article 4 CAT); or to providing aid or assistance to the commission of torture (Article 16 ASR). In the latter case, constructive knowledge could be deemed sufficient.[218]

I further submit that, where it cannot be established that torture was applied in that specific instance, there is nevertheless a breach of the state's positive obligation to refrain from actions that would expose individuals to a risk of torture, wherever it occurs. Sending questions for the interrogation of a detainee to a foreign state known to systematically torture detainees appears clearly in breach of this obligation, irrespective of whether torture was ultimately used. Indeed, the sending state exposed the individual to a high risk of torture by asking the detaining state, despite its known interrogation methods, to obtain answers from the detainee. In addition, by not enquiring about the means through which information was obtained, and not investigating or ques-

---

[216] Public knowledge of such a systematic pattern is considered established for the US regarding detainees held in Iraq, Afghanistan, and Guantánamo Bay from early 2004 onward.

[217] Matt Pollard, 'Rotten Fruit: State Solicitation, Acceptance, and Use of Information Obtained through Torture by Another State' (2005) 23 Netherlands Quarterly of Human Rights 349, 356.

[218] Moynihan (n 183) 8–12; Vladyslav Lanovoy, *Complicity and its Limits in the Law of International Responsibility* (Hart Publishing 2016) 100–101. See also Méndez Report 2014 (n 178), para 53.

tioning the methods employed to extract it, the sending state would impliedly recognise the lawfulness of the torture-tainted information, in breach of Article 41(2) ASR.[219]

Finally, when torture was indeed applied but the torturing state is not one that can be considered to widely or systematically use torture,[220] actual knowledge would have to be established for the responsibility of the sending state to arise, this time for aid or assistance under Article 16 ASR.[221] However, constructive knowledge that there was a real risk that demand would lead to torture in that instance may sometimes be deemed sufficient.[222]

Provision

Provision here refers to the 'clean-hands' sharing of torture-tainted information, such as would occur if state A shares with state B information it has obtained from state T, knowing or wilfully blind to the fact that it has been obtained through torture. By doing so, state A is treating the information as if it had been obtained lawfully, and is thus aiding or assisting state T in maintaining impunity. It is arguable that, where state T is known to systematically use torture, this may amount to a breach of the obligation contained in Article 41(2) ASR not to render aid or assistance in maintaining a situation (here, impunity) created by a serious breach in the sense of Article 40 ASR. It may be further argued that, by sharing the tainted information, state A is condoning torture and thus acting in breach of its obligation to prevent torture, and of its positive obligations to investigate, prosecute, and punish it under the CAT.

Passive receipt

States receiving torture-tainted information from a state known to use torture on a wide or systematic scale, usually as part of an established intelligence-sharing relationship but sometimes in an ad hoc manner, may be condoning torture when they know or ought to know about the methods employed to obtain the information and do not protest. By not speaking out against such methods, they are in fact acquiescing to it, and become complicit in contravention of Article 4 CAT.[223] In addition, they participate in the main-

---

[219] Méndez Report 2014 (n 178), para 56.
[220] It was the case for the US until 2004, when the general presumption that the US would be acting in compliance with its human rights obligations was displaced by revelations about the treatment of detainees in US-run detentions centres worldwide and the methods used in interrogating those detainees.
[221] Méndez Report 2015 (n 185), para 22.
[222] Regarding US-held detainees in Iraq, Afghanistan, and Guantánamo Bay, there was public knowledge of a serious risk of torture from early 2004 onward.
[223] Fulton (n 194) 786.

tenance of the situation of impunity, which is contrary to the requirements of Article 41(2) ASR.[224] By doing so, they also encourage continuation of the receipt, and therefore the collection, of torture-tainted information.

Executive Use

Following (passive) receipt, states may wish to use the tainted information. Article 15 CAT prohibits the invocation as evidence 'in any proceedings' of 'any statement which is established to have been made as a result of torture' 'whenever and by whomever obtained'.[225] While this has been interpreted by many states as applying only to judicial proceedings, both the drafting history and UNCAT opinions favour a broader interpretation.[226]

In *G.K.* v. *Switzerland*, the Committee confirmed the broad scope of Article 15, which 'is a function of the absolute nature of the prohibition of torture and implies, consequently, an obligation for each state to ascertain whether or not statements admitted as evidence in any judicial or administrative proceedings for which it has jurisdiction, including extradition proceedings, have been made as a result of torture'.[227] The application of Article 15 presupposes the assessment of evidence in a formal procedure that leads to a decision of the respective court or administrative agency.[228] Therefore, preventive detention, extradition, control orders, and other administrative measures such as the granting of citizenship, a residence permit or a visa will be covered by the exclusionary rule of Article 15.

Several reasons underlie the prohibition of using torture-tainted evidence in *any* proceedings. First, the prohibition removes the incentive for officials to use torture, and thus has a strong preventive effect. Second, torture-tainted evidence is unreliable. Using it against an individual would be unfair and severely damage the integrity of the proceedings, whether judicial or administrative, in addition to the rule of law. But using it at all, outside any formal proceedings, would also amount to 'impliedly recognising the lawfulness of such conduct, in contravention of the duty of states under [customary international law]'.[229] Therefore, it may be argued that preventive police or security action relying on tainted intelligence that does not result from formal proceedings covered by Article 15 may still be unlawful under customary international law as reflected

---

[224] Méndez Report 2014 (n 178) para 55; Scheinin (n 178) para 55; Fulton (n 194) 777.
[225] UNCAT 'Conclusions and Recommendations, United Kingdom' (2004) UN Doc CAT/C/CR/33/3, para 4.
[226] Nowak, Birk and Monina (n 190) 420, 426–427.
[227] CAT/C/30/D/219/2002, 12 May 2003, para 6.10.
[228] Nowak, Birk and Monina (n 190) 430.
[229] Scheinin (n 178) para 55.

by Article 41 ASR because it creates a demand for torture-tainted information and elevates its operational use to a policy.[230]

3.5 CONCLUSIONS: THE APPLICABILITY OF INTERNATIONAL LAW TO INTELLIGENCE ACTIVITIES

The present chapter constitutes the first part of the case-study on the CIA-led 'global war on terror', which aims to demonstrate how the first two layers of regulation apply to intelligence activities in practice. In this chapter, the focus was on showing how international law governs the conducts operationalising the programme, and on establishing state responsibility for these conducts.

On the basis of the legal and policy background of the CIA programme and its facts as established in the SSCI Study and other reliable sources, I comprehensively mapped state responsibility for participation in the CIA programme. I first identified the applicable legal framework and determined the conditions of its breach by the programme's operation. The analysis covered primarily US responsibility as principal wrongdoer, which is engaged under an impressively high number of human rights norms, humanitarian law rules where applicable, and a few interstate obligations.

Then, I focused on establishing cooperating states' international responsibility based on the conduct that they adopted: acting as proxy detention site; acting as black site host; surrendering custody of a detainee to the CIA; acting as a stopover point for CIA flights; and/or sharing intelligence with the CIA. Whilst the analysis was conducted for the most part *in abstracto*, it is easily transferable to the concrete situations examined in the second part of the case-study (Chapter 6). In this respect, I put forward a public knowledge timeline (Table 3.2) according to which the knowledge of any state can be assessed to establish responsibility in the absence of elements showing state-specific knowledge.

This systematic analysis of state complicity in the programme is the first of its kind. Beyond its direct utility for the case-study, it also provides a strong illustration of the applicability and application of the law of state responsibility to intelligence cooperation. This conclusion is particularly valuable regarding intelligence sharing, which has for too long been considered as outside the realm of international law but does, in fact, trigger the international responsibility of states in a variety of ways. This proves especially true when shared information is tainted by torture.

---

[230] Méndez Report 2014 (n 178), para 56. For a discussion, see Nowak, Birk and Monina (n 190) 426–430.

Overall, the case-study demonstrates that intelligence activities, no matter their nature, are comprehensively governed by international law and engage state responsibility when they breach the state's international obligations. The analysis additionally clarifies the nature of the responsibility of states engaging in intelligence cooperation in forms that are often wrongly considered too distant from the principal wrongful act to engage state responsibility. The CIA-led global war on terror encompassed a multitude of participating states and a variety of forms of participation, ranging from 'active inaction' to clear cooperation in torture. Yet, even in such a wide-reaching and complex web of activities, it is possible to systematically apply the primary and secondary rules of international law and successfully determine whether state responsibility is engaged. The case-study thus confirms that the first layer of regulation – legality – encompasses and applies to all intelligence activities and forms of cooperation.

PART II

Accountability

4. International legal accountability for an internationally wrongful act resulting from intelligence activities

4.1 INTRODUCTION

Intelligence activities are characterised primarily by their secret nature. This ontological secrecy has led some authors to claim that 'the very notion that international law is currently capable of regulating intelligence gathering is dubious'.[1] Yet, I clearly established in Part I that intelligence activities are comprehensively addressed by international law. Further, states can be responsible for breaches of international law resulting from intelligence activities of all sorts, including intelligence gathering and cooperation. Nonetheless, there is an inherent tension between the need for confidentiality, which remains an essential feature of effective intelligence operations, and the enforcement of international legality, requiring transparency, oversight, and accountability. In addition, whereas intelligence cooperation requires trust and assigns value to complete secrecy, effective national security measures require compliance with human rights law and the rule of law.

In the pre-9/11 paradigm, this tension was partially resolved through reliance on domestic oversight and review mechanisms. Domestic mechanisms are in theory (at least somewhat) able to ensure the legality of intelligence activities while protecting confidentiality and guaranteeing that intelligence matters are dealt with domestically. In recent decades, however, and especially when international counterterrorism cooperation has been at stake, domestic mechanisms have proven highly ineffective in preventing and remedying gross breaches of international law. Their failure to ensure international legality and to remedy violations has resulted in the engagement of state responsibility in respect of intelligence activities constituting internationally wrongful acts. Furthermore, the lack of effective oversight has led to unreliable intelligence being circulated and acted upon, harming the national security and intelligence

---

[1] Glenn Sulmasy and John Yoo, 'Counterintuitive: Intelligence Operations and International Law' (2007) 28 Mich. J. Int'l L. 625, 626.

reputation of the states involved in addition to domestic and international counterterrorism efforts.[2]

Whilst a state can be responsible for an internationally wrongful act without being held to account for it, international legal responsibility is a prerequisite for international legal accountability. Andreas Schedler usefully differentiates between responsibility *to* someone, which presupposes responsibility for something; and responsibility *for* something, which can go entirely without responsibility to someone.[3] Using these notions, the international legal responsibility of states as established under the law of state responsibility constitutes responsibility for something. It exists in a vacuum, arising as soon as a state commits an internationally wrongful act. International legal accountability, in contrast, entails responsibility to someone: the account-holder.[4] The presence and active role of an account-holder make responsibility for something become tangible and produce consequences. It is what transforms the mere engagement of responsibility into accountability; what takes us from the first to the second layer of regulation.

In the twenty-first-century security landscape, reliance on other states to enforce international legality through the rules on invocation of state responsibility has only led to general impunity.[5] Meanwhile, domestic accountability has failed in almost all attempts, leaving wide and numerous accountability gaps. As Richard Aldrich pointed out, 'intelligence liaison and accountability have never mixed well ... [but] the "black hole" presented by liaison is now too big to ignore'.[6] In the wake of the global war on terror and as terrorism and other national security threats are still leading to intelligence activities

---

[2] In the context of the war on terror, the SSCI Study documents numerous instances of fabrication of intelligence by CIA detainees as a result of enhanced interrogation techniques amounting to torture. Intelligence was then shared with other states, who acted upon it. United States, Senate Select Committee on Intelligence [2014] Committee Study of the Central Intelligence Agency's Detention and Interrogation Program, declassified executive summary ('SSCI Study').

[3] Andreas Schedler (ed), *The Self-Restraining State: Power and Accountability in New Democracies* (Lynne Rienner Publ 1999) 19.

[4] I follow a series of scholars writing on accountability in using this term to refer to the actor holding the power wielder to account. See notably Ruth W Grant and Robert O Keohane, 'Accountability and Abuses of Power in World Politics' (2005) 99 American Political Science Review 29 ('accountability holder'); Mark Bovens, 'Analysing and Assessing Accountability: A Conceptual Framework' (2007) 13 European Law Journal 447 ('account-holder'); Jennifer Rubenstein, 'Accountability in an Unequal World' (2007) 69 The Journal of Politics 616 ('accountability holder').

[5] Impunity is here understood as the lack of accountability rather than the lack of punishment.

[6] Richard J Aldrich, 'Global Intelligence Co-Operation versus Accountability: New Facets to an Old Problem' (2009) 24 Intelligence and National Security 26, 54.

in breach of international law, recent developments in international courts and bodies allow me to theorise on how accountability takes place following the engagement of state responsibility for intelligence activities in breach of international law.

In practice, and particularly when the primary norms infringed protect non-state actors, the International Law Commission's (ILC) interstate regime of invocation of responsibility[7] is unusable in intelligence matters. A broader and more flexible conceptualisation is therefore required to analyse existing and potential instances of state accountability for intelligence activities, taking into account the role played by non-state actors in holding states to account. In consequence, one of this chapter's undertakings is the development of the missing part of the ILC Articles on State Responsibility (ASR): the enforcement of state responsibility by non-state actors and entities.

In this chapter, I put forward the concept of international legal accountability to theorise how states are held accountable for their intelligence activities in breach of international law. I begin by conceptualising international legal accountability (section 4.2). I then proceed with a detailed account of the necessity and relevance of the concept in the intelligence cooperation context (section 4.3), followed by an exploration of its objectives (section 4.4). Finally, I highlight the place of international legal accountability as the second layer in the model of regulation of intelligence activities under international law (section 4.5).

4.2　INTERNATIONAL LEGAL ACCOUNTABILITY

In 1999, Andreas Schedler began his conceptualisation of accountability by writing that 'accountability represents an underexplored concept whose meaning remains evasive, whose boundaries are fuzzy, and whose internal structure is confusing'.[8] The present section endeavours to build upon the various conceptualisations of the term attempted since then, and to define the meaning, boundaries, and forms of the sub-type of accountability that forms the second layer of regulation: international legal accountability.

In its most basic form, accountability is conceived as a tool to hold power wielders[9] to account and control how they exercise such power. In law as in politics, accountability is used as a tool to constrain power and its exercise.

---

[7] International Law Commission, Draft Articles on the Responsibility of States for Internationally Wrongful Acts, November 2001, Supplement No. 10 (A/56/10), chp. IV.E.1 ('ASR'), Part Three.

[8] Schedler (n 3) 13.

[9] I follow Grant and Keohane in using the term 'power wielder' to refer to the actor whose exercise of power is supposed to be constrained by the accountability mecha-

The famous claim that 'power breeds responsibility'[10] implies that only when an actor holds power is it able to commit an act warranting the engagement of its responsibility and, in consequence, be held to account for it. The theoretical link between responsibility and accountability is thus made evident through the notion of power. Power, in its different forms, 'breeds' potential responsibility, and its exercise (including the decision not to exercise it) 'entails' both responsibility and accountability. Practically speaking, accountability refers to the consequences of the engagement of responsibility or, put more simply, the enforcement of responsibility.

In the ASR, Part Three deals with the implementation of a state's international responsibility, i.e., the invocation of that responsibility (Chapter I) and the modalities of countermeasures by injured states (Chapter II). The notion of 'injured state' is central to this part of the ASR as it entitles a state to invoke the responsibility of another state, resorting to all judicial and extra-judicial means provided for in the ASR. The Articles also envisage the right of 'non-injured' states to invoke the responsibility of a state in certain situations: where the obligation is owed *erga omnes partes* (Article 48(1)(a)); or *erga omnes* (Article 48(1)(b)).

It is clear from the text of the ASR that the system of invocation of responsibility thus codified is of an exclusively interstate nature. James Crawford justified this restriction by stating that 'the law of implementation by entities other than states is embryonic'. He nevertheless tempered his comment by noting that the ASR's 'silence on the implementation of responsibility by non-states does not mean that such entities will never have standing to claim against a state in response to its internationally wrongful act'.[11] The saving clause of Article 33(2) indeed safeguards the entitlement to claim of non-state entities under primary norms, but such right is not covered by the ASR. The next section of this chapter aims at integrating this missing part of the ASR within an analysis of the general framework of enforcement of state responsibility, or what I call 'international legal accountability'.

4.2.1 Basic Elements

International legal accountability is necessarily linked to the idea of international legality. As Jutta Brunnée explains, 'the existence of an international

---

nism. This does not prejudge the power relationship between such an actor and the one holding them to account (the account-holder). Grant and Keohane (n 4).

[10] Clyde Eagleton, *The Responsibility of States in International Law* (New York University Press 1928) 206.

[11] James Crawford, *State Responsibility: The General Part* (Cambridge University Press 2013) 549.

legal order presupposes that the conduct of international actors is constantly measured against existing legal standards'.[12] The concept of international *legal* accountability thus excludes accountability for reasons (political, professional, ethical, religious, corporate) other than the breach, attributable to the state, of a positive legal norm.[13] While different fields of international law inevitably entail different purposes and functions for accountability, the notion of power remains at the core. The conduct of an actor is only evaluated and measured against existing legal standards if the actor is exercising enough power to warrant it, that is, if the actor is able to breach applicable norms of international law.

To comprehend the concept of international legal accountability properly, the following questions must be answered: *Who* is being held to account? For *what*? By *whom*? *Why* are they obliged to render account? And *how* are they held accountable?

Who is being held to account? States' intelligence activities are the exclusive focus of the present book. However, any actor possessing international obligations can potentially be held legally accountable. International organisations are a prime example,[14] but debates on the possibilities for holding to account other non-state actors, such as non-state armed groups and transnational corporations, are topical in international law.

For what is the state being held to account? Because of its legal nature, the concept of international legal accountability intrinsically builds upon the legal obligations of states, the breach of which triggers the engagement of their international responsibility. States can therefore only be held legally accountable for the breach, attributable to them under the law of state responsibility, of a valid legal obligation.

By whom is the state held to account? State obligations are owed to other actors: states, international organisations, individuals, private parties, etc. These actors are the primary account-holders. If the obligation owed to them is breached, they are entitled to hold the wrongdoing state to account. They may do so directly[15] or make use of an international accountability mechanism. Indeed, primary norms are by their nature often linked to a specific review, oversight, judicial or other mechanism established by the relevant source of

---

[12] Jutta Brunnée, 'International Legal Accountability through the Lens of the Law of State Responsibility' (2005) 36 Netherlands Yearbook of International Law 21, 55.

[13] Notwithstanding that non-state actors can also be held accountable for an internationally wrongful act.

[14] E.g., International Law Commission, *Draft Articles on the Responsibility of International Organizations*, UN Doc. A/66/10.

[15] Although direct recourse to the regime of invocation of state responsibility as set out in the ASR is reserved to states.

obligations. This creates a legal relationship between the state and this international mechanism, which I term 'external forum'. The state will then have to justify its conduct before the forum, who will be entitled to assess and pass judgement upon it based on the conduct required by the primary norm allegedly breached, and to impose consequences upon the state. Since obligations are not owed to it, the forum is not the primary account-holder. Nevertheless, it can be empowered by the primary account-holder to act as such and to provide an authoritative and impartial assessment of the dispute, the law, or the consequences that should follow.

Why is the state obliged to render account? International obligations necessarily entail a corollary obligation to render account if the legal commitment made to the beneficiary of the obligation is breached. In addition, the formal source of legal obligations (treaty, convention) against which the conduct of the state should be measured will often include a dispute resolution clause, referring to a particular mechanism or institution, or establish a monitoring mechanism of some sort empowered to evaluate the state's compliance with its legal obligations. Such a mechanism will usually be the external forum. Because of the legal nature of the relationship between the state and the forum,[16] the state is under a legal obligation to render account to the forum: this is what makes it an accountability mechanism. This third party is extremely useful as it allows primary account-holders to hold states to account using the legal authority of the forum, to which the power wielder state consented, while (partially) circumventing power imbalances and/or lack of international standing.

4.2.2   Accountability Forms: How is the State Held Accountable?

In general public international law, states have established mechanisms to enforce their rights vis-à-vis other states. The power one state can exercise over another is constrained both by primary norms that states have consented to be bound by and by the right of an injured state to invoke the responsibility of another state and hold it accountable. In contrast, international human rights law (IHRL) was originally developed to protect the individual against state power, and primary norms of IHRL purport to restrain the exercise of state power over individuals within their territory and/or jurisdiction. The accountability of states for their human rights performances therefore aims to restrain the power that a state can exercise over the individuals within its jurisdiction, in accordance with the human rights law standards that the state consented

---

[16] In the sense that the forum is legally empowered to perform its mission through state consent.

to be bound by. Therefore, whereas in general public international law states are the primary account-holders (as the concept of 'injured state' in the ASR demonstrates), in specific fields of law, such as IHRL, the individual becomes the account-holder.

Forms of accountability in which individuals (or other non-state actors such as foreign investors) are account-holders are not provided for in the ASR but have become very common in practice. The relative lack of individual standing in the international legal order, and especially the lack of power of the individual relative to the state, has led to the use of international forums as accountability mechanisms in IHRL, and to actors other than the individual being allowed to hold states to account. It is crucial to consider these developments for the present conceptualisation of accountability. Although there already exist various classifications of accountability forms,[17] the sub-type of state accountability that is international legal accountability requires more precise analysis criteria and fitted classifications. The following paragraphs thus frame an original and multidimensional taxonomy of international legal accountability. Several forms of accountability can be distinguished, on the basis of: the nature of the account-holder and their relationship to the state; the type of interest giving standing to the account-holder; and the way in which the account-holder is holding the state to account.

Relationship. A first distinction can be made based on whether the primary account-holder, to whom the obligation is owed, is a state or a non-state actor. State-to-state accountability will be deemed horizontal, based on the sovereign status of both actors rather than on their power relationship.[18] In contrast, non-state-to-state accountability will normally be vertical, again without prejudging of the power relationship between the two parties: vertical accountability can be bottom-up (e.g., individual account-holder) or top-down, for example in situations where international institutions or corporations are more powerful than the state they are holding to account.[19] When the account-holder is not the one to whom the obligation is owed, as is the case in surrogate accountability,[20] the relationship cannot be classified as either horizontal or vertical: it is a different kind of legal relationship, which is based solely on state consent. However, the primary account-holder, on behalf of whom the forum is acting, will be in a horizontal or vertical relationship with the state.

---

[17] See Bovens (n 4); Grant and Keohane (n 4); Schedler (n 3).
[18] See Schedler (n 3) 23–24 for a discussion on the impossibility of truly horizontal power relationships.
[19] E.g., the 'Troika' composed by the European Commission, the International Monetary Fund, and the European Central Bank held Greece to account for its failure to meet its international obligations during the sovereign debt crisis.
[20] See Table 4.1.

Standing. A second distinction can be made based on the type of interest giving standing to the account-holder. Linked to the nature of the primary norms breached, this allows us to first distinguish between injured states as defined by Article 42 ASR;[21] and non-injured states, who have a legal interest in seeing the obligation respected but have neither been 'specially affected' nor put in a 'radically' different position by the breach. In the latter case, for non-injured states to become account-holders, the primary norm necessarily has to be an obligation *erga omnes* (Article 48(1)(b)), or *erga omnes partes* (Article 48(1)(a)). Non-state actors that have standing to invoke a state's responsibility before an international forum must have had a particular interest or right violated by the breach in order to have standing. In that sense, they are in the same situation as injured states: their status as account-holders derives from their injury.

Method. A third distinction can be made based on the involvement of an external forum and the role attributed to it. Direct accountability makes no use of an external forum. It is necessarily an interstate form of accountability since only states have standing to directly invoke the responsibility of other states and impose consequences upon them. Mediated accountability, in contrast, makes use of an external forum. Reasons for using an external forum include lack of international standing (individuals, private actors) preventing the direct invocation of responsibility but allowing complaints before the forum; or more simply the willingness, need or obligation to refer to an impartial authority to interpret the law or impose sanctions. Surrogate accountability goes further as the external forum becomes the account-holder on behalf of the primary account-holder. It has been termed a 'second-best' form of accountability, in part because it can take away the voice of the primary account-holder and may not adequately represent their interests.[22] Notwithstanding, it remains a useful substitute to compensate for the lack of power of certain actors relative to the state and, often, for their lack of international status and/or standing or access to more direct (including mediated) accountability mechanisms.

---

[21] Article 42. *Invocation of responsibility by an injured State*
A State is entitled as an injured State to invoke the responsibility of another State if the obligation breached is owed to:
(a)   that State individually; or
(b)   a group of States including that State, or the international community as a whole, and the breach of the obligation:
  (i)   specially affects that State; or
  (ii) is of such a character as radically to change the position of all the other States to which the obligation is owed with respect to the further performance of the obligation.

[22] Rubenstein (n 4) 616.

Table 4.1   Forms of international legal accountability

Form	Account-holder	Relationship	Basis for account-holder status	Use of external forum
Interstate Direct	Injured state	Horizontal	Injury	No
Interstate Mediated	Injured state	Horizontal	Injury	Yes
Erga Omnes	Non-injured state	Horizontal	Legal interest	Not necessarily
Mediated	Injured non-state actor	Vertical	Injury	Yes
Surrogate	Actor acting on behalf of an injured party	N/A	State consent	Forum becomes account-holder

Table 4.1 summarises the five possible forms of international legal accountability based on these distinctions

The first form, *interstate direct* accountability, is the form embodied in Part Three of the ASR. An example would be state A taking countermeasures, as provided for in Part Three, Chapter II, against state B in order to incite state B to cease its wrongful act, provide reparation for the breach, and comply with its legal obligations owed to state A. Another common example is the delivery of a diplomatic démarche by the embassy of state A to host state B, protesting state B's policy or conduct and aiming to persuade state B to comply with the legal obligations it owes to state A.

The second form, *interstate mediated* accountability, is very similar to the first but makes use of an external, often judicial, forum. It is featured in Part Three, Chapter I, of the ASR. An example would be state A filing a complaint against state B before the ICJ alleging state B's breach of its legal obligations owed to state A. Both forms are horizontal and rely on the injured state status of the account-holder.

The third form is the one foreseen in Article 48 ASR. I term it *erga omnes* accountability. *Erga omnes* accountability refers to situations whereby non-injured states assume the position of account-holders towards a state in breach of an *erga omnes* (*partes*) obligation. The non-injured state's entitlement to act as account-holder is based on the legal interest it has to see the *erga omnes* (*partes*) obligation respected. This hybrid form of accountability is horizontal and can be classified as direct or mediated and/or surrogate, depending on how the non-injured state invokes the responsibility of the power-wielding state. Indeed, the invocation of responsibility can be direct, as with injured states, but also mediated when the non-injured state acts through a forum.²³ Finally, it can also be considered surrogate when the non-injured state acts not only on the basis of its own legal interest but also on behalf of those to whom the obligation is primarily owed.²⁴ Examples include state A filing a complaint against state B before the ICJ for breach of the prohibition to commit genocide (mediated);²⁵ state C filing a complaint against state D before a regional human rights body for breach of the prohibition to commit torture (mediated) and asking for reparations for the victims (surrogate);²⁶ and state E deciding to end diplomatic relations with state F for breach of the prohibition of apartheid (direct).²⁷

While all *jus cogens* obligations are by nature *erga omnes* obligations, the opposite does not hold true. *Erga omnes* accountability can thus take place following the breach of legal obligations not of a peremptory nature but which are 'established for the protection of a collective interest of the group' or 'owed to the international community as a whole'.²⁸ Such non-peremptory *erga omnes* obligations can be treaty-based (*erga omnes partes*) and include things such as passage rights for foreign vessels,²⁹ or human rights generally under relevant

---

[23] ASR Article 48 foresees both possibilities.

[24] ASR Article 48(2)(b) allows non-injured states to claim reparation 'in the interest of the injured state or *of the beneficiaries of the obligation breached*' (emphasis added). The invocation of responsibility is however subject to the nationality of claims rule in those cases where it is applicable. See ASR Article 48(3) with reference to Article 44(a).

[25] *Application of the Convention on the Prevention and Punishment of the Crime of Genocide (Bosnia and Herzegovina v Serbia and Montenegro)* [2007] ICJ Reports 2007 43 (International Court of Justice) 43.

[26] E.g., ECtHR, *Ireland v. The United Kingdom*, App. No. 5310/71, 13 December 1977. On the dual nature (*erga omnes* and surrogate) of the accountability process, the Commentary to Article 48 ASR para 12 notes that 'certain provisions, for example in various human rights treaties, allow invocation of responsibility by any State party. In those cases where they have been resorted to, a clear distinction has been drawn between the capacity of the applicant State to raise the matter and the interests of the beneficiaries of the obligation'. See also Article 2(b) of the Institute of International Law (IDI) 'Resolution on Obligations and Rights erga omnes in International Law', Resolution I/2005.

[27] E.g., the isolation of South Africa on the diplomatic scene during the Apartheid (1948–1993), and especially resolution 1761 (XVII) of the UN General Assembly (1962) requesting states to 'break off diplomatic relations with the Government of the Republic of South Africa'.

[28] ASR Article 48(1)(a) and (b).

[29] See the position of Japan, who had no economic interest at stake in this dispute, as account-holder in the *S.S. 'Wimbledon'* case (*France, Great Britain, Italy, and Japan v. Germany*) (1923) P.C.I.J., Ser. A, No. 1.

treaties, without conditions of nationality.[30] In the latter case, it should be clear that states have no human rights of their own. Rather, they possess a procedural right to invoke the responsibility of other states under the relevant treaty.

The fourth form, termed *mediated* accountability, has as account-holder an individual or private party. Here, accountability is vertical and is necessarily mediated because non-state actors cannot invoke the responsibility of a state under the customary law of state responsibility. Account-holder status derives from the injury suffered by the non-state actor as a result of the breach. An example would be a complaint by individual X against state A in front of a regional human rights court for the breach of X's rights.

In mediated accountability processes, account-holder status is highly restricted due to procedural requirements. Especially in complaint procedures, international accountability mechanisms have rules regarding *locus standi*, *ratione personae*, and *ratione materiae* in addition to other admissibility requirements such as the exhaustion of domestic remedies. Indeed, in IHRL, as in other fields of international law, the presumption is that domestic legal systems provide an effective remedy for the violation of individuals' rights. It is only when domestic remedies are exhausted, or when they are not available or effective,[31] that there is an internationally wrongful act opening the possibility to hold the state to account before an international forum.[32] However, procedural requirements restricting account-holder status for non-state actors do not bar other forms of accountability, for example arising from the *proprio motu* investigation of a situation by the forum (surrogate), or from referral by other states (interstate mediated or *erga omnes*) or other non-state actors (mediated or surrogate).

The fifth and final form, *surrogate* accountability, has a third party acting as account-holder on behalf of the actor to whom the obligation is owed. This form of accountability is neither horizontal nor vertical per se and is not based on any injury suffered by the account-holder. Rather, it is the result of a legal relationship between the state and a forum (which can be of any nature), allowing the forum to act as account-holder on behalf of other parties to whom the

---

[30] European Commission on Human Rights, *Austria v. Italy*, App. No. 788/60, Admissibility Decision, 1961, para 19; *Questions relating to the Obligation to Prosecute or Extradite (Belgium v Senegal), Judgment* [2012] ICJ Reports 2012 422 (International Court of Justice) [69].

[31] In cases of serious and massive violations, the requirement may be waived. See e.g., ACHPR, *Malawi African Association and Others v. Mauritania*, Comm. Nos. 54/91, 61/91, 98/93, 164/97 to 196/97 and 210/98, 11 May 2000, para 85.

[32] ASR Article 44(b). See also e.g., ECHR Article 35(1); ICCPR Article 41(1)(c); ACHR Article 46(1)(a). For a discussion on the substantive or procedural character of this rule, see James Crawford and Thomas Grant, 'Local Remedies, Exhaustion Of', *Max Planck Encyclopaedia of Public International Law* (2007).

state's obligations are owed or who have a legal interest in seeing these obligations respected. Often, the external forum will act as account-holder, but states can also act on behalf of the primary account-holders.[33] For the sake of clarity, this latter form of surrogate accountability will be analysed in further sections under the relevant interstate forms, and 'surrogate accountability' will only be used to refer to non-interstate processes. Examples for both types include the UN Human Rights Committee acting as account-holder on behalf of individuals having their rights violated by state A through state A's reporting obligations; the UN General Assembly asking the ICJ for an Advisory Opinion on the compliance of State C's conduct with international law;[34] or a claim by state A against state B before a regional human rights court, asserting the systematic use of torture against detainees in state B and demanding reparation for the victims (*erga omnes*, mediated, and surrogate).[35]

4.2.3 Definition

The definition I propose builds upon the constitutive elements detailed above and follows from Mark Bovens' conceptualisation of accountability[36] and Jutta Brunnée's definition of international legal accountability:[37]

> International legal accountability is the process by which a state legally justifies its performance vis-à-vis other international actors,[38] in which an assessment or judgement of that performance against international legal standards is rendered, and through which consequences can be imposed if the state fails to live up to applicable international legal standards.

---

[33] See above, interstate and *erga omnes* forms of accountability. The most obvious example of interstate surrogate accountability is diplomatic protection.

[34] E.g., *Legal Consequences of the Construction of a Wall in the Occupied Palestinian Territory, Advisory Opinion* [2004] ICJ Reports 2004 136 (International Court of Justice).

[35] E.g., ECtHR *Denmark v. Turkey* (friendly settlement), Judgment of 5 April 2000, Reports of Judgments and Decisions 2000-IV.

[36] 'Accountability is a relationship between an actor and a forum, in which the actor has an obligation to explain and to justify his or her conduct, the forum can pose questions and pass judgement, and the actor may face consequences', Bovens (n 4) 450. Note that in Bovens' definition, the forum is the account-holder, not the accountability mechanism.

[37] 'International legal accountability involves the legal justification of an international actor's performance vis-à-vis others, the assessment or judgment of that performance against international legal standards, and the possible imposition of consequences if the actors fails to live up to applicable legal standards', Brunnée (n 12) 24.

[38] The state is indeed only justifying its performance vis-à-vis another state (interstate direct or *erga omnes*) or before an external forum having international status.

Accountability is therefore premised upon the engagement of the state's international responsibility, with its two constitutive elements of breach and attribution. While not all accountability mechanisms are based upon the formal invocation of state responsibility (reporting mechanisms, for instance, are more geared towards improving implementation and compliance with states' obligations), the determination of responsibility nevertheless forms part of their tasks. This competence explains why such mechanisms also achieve the status of accountability mechanisms. In addition, consequences, which can be positive or negative, are not necessarily brought about by the forum itself. They can also result from the publicity of the forum's decision or even from the mere commencement of an accountability process.

By nature, international legal accountability processes take place *ex post facto*. However, they can have *ex ante* effects. The consequences imposed by a forum can indeed be forward-looking, such as recommendations by a UN treaty body to ensure better compliance in the future, or a judgment demanding reform of a domestic law or system at the origin of a breach. Hence, in addition to the *ex post facto* evaluation of state conduct, international legal accountability is also about prevention and anticipation. Consequences imposed in accountability proceedings can likewise consist of precautionary or interim measures. Despite their apparent *ex ante* and preventive nature, these measures are nevertheless *ex post* in relation to a fact, such as a detention or judgment, which has already happened. In such situations, accountability proceedings concern the purpose of that fact (e.g., enforcement of a death sentence or extradition) and the state's intention to enforce this purpose. Precautionary proceedings thus also constitute *ex post facto* accountability processes.

4.3 INTERNATIONAL LEGAL ACCOUNTABILITY FOR INTELLIGENCE ACTIVITIES

Several factors play into the necessity of adopting a broader concept of accountability for wrongful acts resulting from intelligence activities than that embedded in Part Three of the ASR, especially in the context of intelligence cooperation. As secrecy rules the world of intelligence cooperation, domestic oversight mechanisms have been side-lined, and forms of interstate accountability made practically unusable by the necessities of cooperation. Hence, while it may be true that 'intelligence liaison and accountability have never mixed well',[39] and even that applying international law to intelligence activities is 'counter-intuitive',[40] the conceptual oxymoron that international legal

---

[39] Aldrich (n 6) 54.
[40] Sulmasy and Yoo (n 1) 626.

accountability for intelligence activities may appear to be has now become a necessity, in addition to becoming a reality.[41] To analyse how states are held to account for their intelligence activities, the present section presents the main empirical and theoretical factors justifying the adoption of a broader conceptualisation of accountability than that of interstate invocation of responsibility.

4.3.1 The Inadequacy of Domestic Oversight Mechanisms

It is a relatively undisputed reality that states must engage in intelligence collection and cooperation to protect their populations against terrorism and other credible threats to their national security. Since the attacks of 11 September 2001 (9/11), intelligence cooperation has been encouraged and even made binding by UN Security Council Resolution 1373,[42] and operations and exchanges of information with foreign partners have increased exponentially. States have pledged to implement a global counterterrorism agenda and have made legally binding commitments to cooperate in fighting international terrorism.[43] Intelligence cooperation in its various forms – the most important of which are information sharing; covert operational cooperation; hosting facilities; and the provision of training, advice, hardware and software – is therefore a staple of modern international counterterrorism policies and practice.

Yet, the necessity of such forms of cooperation does not erase the fact that several of the means and methods adopted in recent decades, and particularly since 9/11, are problematic from a legal perspective. Under IHRL, states have an obligation to protect their citizens from terrorist attacks. However, this obligation neither excuses nor justifies human rights violations in countering (potential) terrorist threats. And yet, for preventative and intelligence gathering purposes, intelligence cooperation has given rise to gross human rights violations, including violations of the prohibitions of torture, arbitrary detention, and enforced disappearance; routine extra-judicial killings; overwhelming privacy violations; and many other wrongful acts.[44]

International cooperation and information sharing have also opened the possibility for intelligence communities to circumvent domestic law by getting

---

[41] Chapter 6 provides a detailed analysis of international practice with regard to the CIA-led global war on terror.
[42] UN Doc. S/RES/1373 (2001), paras 2(b), 2(e) and 3.
[43] See Arianna Vedaschi and Kim Lane Scheppele (eds), *9/11 and the Rise of Global Anti-Terrorism Law: How the UN Security Council Rules the World* (Cambridge University Press 2021).
[44] See generally: OHCHR, Factsheet No. 32 'Human Rights, Terrorism and Counter-terrorism'. For a detailed account of the practices used by the CIA and its partners in the 'global war on terror' see SSCI Study (n 2).

their intelligence partners to collect, use, or process information in ways that would have been unlawful under domestic law.[45] This includes practices ranging from a sort of 'legal shopping' to establish cooperation centres[46] or the collection of data on a state's citizens by a foreign state at the demand of the former,[47] to the outsourcing of torture.[48]

Domestic oversight and accountability mechanisms have proven largely ineffective in preventing and remedying abuses of power and violations of international law when faced with doctrines of state secrecy and national security, immunities, statutes of limitation, and the general lack of transparency surrounding intelligence activities.[49] In addition, the deference of national

---

[45] Hans Born and others, *Making International Intelligence Cooperation Accountable* (DCAF – The Geneva Centre for the Democratic Control of Armed Forces 2015) 48–50; Martin Scheinin, 'Report of the Special Rapporteur on the Promotion and Protection of Human Rights and Fundamental Freedoms while Countering Terrorism, Martin Scheinin. Compilation of Good Practices on Legal and Institutional Frameworks and Measures that Ensure Respect for Human Rights by Intelligence Agencies while Countering Terrorism, Including on their Oversight' (UN General Assembly, Human Rights Council 2010) A/HRC/14/46 29.

[46] The establishment of joint counterterrorism intelligence centres by the CIA in more than two dozen countries in the immediate aftermath of 9/11 is a prime example. The infamous Alliance Base centre was therefore established in Paris, chosen for the protection and lack of oversight afforded by French legislation to intelligence cooperation and classified information. Dana Priest, 'Foreign Network at Front of CIA's Terror Fight' *Washington Post* (18 November 2005) http://www.washingtonpost.com/wp-dyn/content/article/2005/11/17/AR2005111702070.html accessed 12 November 2021.

[47] In the framework of the ECHELON Programme, the Five Eyes (Australia, Canada, New Zealand, the United Kingdom and the United States) regularly circumvent domestic safeguards regarding data collection on citizens by collecting from the 'global information infrastructure' shared between them. Craig Forcese, 'The Collateral Casualties of Collaboration: The Consequences for Civil and Human Rights of Transnational Intelligence Sharing' in Hans Born, Ian Leigh and Aidan Wills (eds), *International Intelligence Cooperation and Accountability* (Routledge 2011) 80. European Parliament, 'Report on the Existence of a Global System for the Interception of Private and Commercial Communications (ECHELON Interception System)', (2001/2098(INI)), A5-0264/2001, 11 July 2001.

[48] Jordan, Egypt, Morocco, the Syrian Arab Republic, Pakistan, Ethiopia, and Djibouti are alleged to have received detainees from the US for the purpose of using interrogation techniques amounting to torture. Human Rights Council, 'Joint Study on Global Practices in Relation to Secret Detention in the Context of Countering Terrorism of the Special Rapporteur on the Promotion and Protection of Human Rights and Fundamental Freedoms While Countering Terrorism' (UN General Assembly 2010) A/HRC/13/42.

[49] Peter Gill, 'Of intelligence oversight and the challenge of surveillance corporatism', (2020) 35 Intelligence and National Security 7, 970–989. See also Human Rights Council (n 48); Dick Marty, 'Abuse of State Secrecy and National Security: Obstacles

courts to the executive has allowed intelligence cooperation to remain mostly unchecked by the judiciary.[50] These legal and factual barriers have resulted in the general impunity of the authors of human rights violations committed as part of counterterrorism intelligence activities, first among which stands intelligence cooperation.

An inadequate domestic legal framework – i.e., the failure to construct and implement satisfactory oversight and review mechanisms and institutions at the national level, thus allowing the exercise of unrestricted intelligence powers – will also engage state responsibility independently of the wrongful acts committed as a result.[51] In such cases, a supra-national mechanism of accountability would be necessary to successfully induce the state into reforming the structure of its intelligence services.

Intelligence cooperation poses increased challenges to national oversight mechanisms. This is first due to their lack of capacity to oversee the actions of foreign intelligence agencies and intelligence operations abroad.[52] It is further due to the extensive use of the third-party rule,[53] which prevents disclosure of foreign intelligence information to third parties, including to oversight bodies if domestic law considers them third parties.[54] While the rule is crucial to ensure trust between intelligence partners, protect their sources and avoid multiple sharing, it also allows intelligence agencies to escape oversight of

---

to Parliamentary and Judicial Scrutiny of Human Rights Violations' (Parliamentary Assembly of the Council of Europe 2011) PACE Doc. 12714; Martin Scheinin, 'Report of the Special Rapporteur on the Promotion and Protection of Human Rights and Fundamental Freedoms While Countering Terrorism, Martin Scheinin' (UN General Assembly, Human Rights Council 2009) A/HRC/10/3.

[50] John Ip, 'The Supreme Court and the House of Lords in the War on Terror: Inter Arma Silent Leges?' (2010) 19 Michigan State Journal of International Law; Ian Leigh, 'National Courts and International Intelligence Cooperation' in Hans Born, Ian Leigh and Aidan Wills (eds), *International Intelligence Cooperation and Accountability* (Routledge 2011).

[51] Iain Cameron, 'Oversight of Intelligence Agencies: The European Dimension' in Zachary K Goldman and Samuel J Rascoff (eds), *Global Intelligence Oversight: Governing Security in the Twenty-First Century* (Oxford University Press 2016) 79.

[52] See Gill (n 49). In that respect, the German Constitutional Court's decision of 19 May 2020, ruling that the Basic Law applies to extraterritorial intelligence activities, in that case surveillance operations targeting foreigners abroad, is an encouraging development. Further, the judgment adopts a more expansive conception of extra-territorial jurisdiction than the ECtHR, which could prove important in setting European standards for the protection of human rights infringed by surveillance operations. See BVerfG, Urteil des Ersten Senats vom 19 Mai 2020 - 1 BvR 2835/17 -, Rn. 1-332, especially para 97.

[53] Also known as 'operator control' or 'originator control principle'.

[54] Forcese (n 47).

international cooperation.[55] Even where the third-party rule does not apply to oversight bodies,[56] it is often not possible for them to know whether the information received from abroad was collected lawfully. All they can do is assess whether the domestic intelligence service they are overseeing provided or received information in accordance with domestic law.[57] In addition, policies such as the 'need-to-know'[58] and 'plausible deniability'[59] have been overused and in some cases misused to ensure secrecy over extra-legal activities and evade unwanted domestic oversight and accountability.

This problem is widely recognised. As Craig Forcese explains, the very nature of intelligence cooperation can render national oversight systems futile: 'information is inherently fungible, and national systems designed to guard how it is used may prove ineffective once that information is in international circulation'.[60] Iain Cameron also emphasizes the tension between the need for timely exchange of information and the dangers of inaccurate information, which are multiplied by international circulation.[61] Due to the disparity of domestic regulations regarding intelligence agencies' oversight, in addition to the disparity of collection, processing, and use of intelligence, and the wide variations in states' human rights records, states must actively legislate and negotiate with their intelligence partners in order to ensure that information exchanged will be collected or processed in accordance with human rights norms. For this purpose, states can implement precautionary measures and policies, such as: the prior assessment of intelligence partners' human rights records; the request of assurances from foreign services when sending information; or the inclusion of caveats regarding the reliability and use to be made

---

[55] In the EU, most parliamentary committees do not have access to classified information received from foreign secret services. See European Union Fundamental Rights Agency (2017) *Surveillance by intelligence services: fundamental rights safeguards and remedies in the EU – Volume II: Field perspectives and legal update*, 106–107.

[56] In the EU, this concerns Belgium, the Netherlands, and Luxembourg. ibid, 107.

[57] See the Netherlands, CTIVD, *Annual Report 2014–2015*, 35.

[58] Under need-to-know restrictions, even if one has all the necessary official approvals (such as a security clearance) to access certain information, one would not be given access to such information, or read into a clandestine operation, unless one has a specific need to know; that is, access to the information must be necessary for one to conduct one's official duties.

[59] According to the *Oxford Essential Dictionary of the U.S. Military*, plausible deniability is, 'with respect to clandestine operations, the state of being capable of being denied by those in authority'.

[60] Forcese (n 47) 73.

[61] Iain Cameron, 'Beyond the Nation State: The Influence of the European Court of Human Rights on Intelligence Accountability' in Hans Born, Loch K Johnson, and Ian Leigh (eds), *Who's Watching the Spies? Establishing Intelligence Service Accountability* (Potomac Press 2005) 54.

of information shared. In practice, however, precautionary measures and policies are scarcely used. Further, they rarely outweigh the need for information exchange and cooperation.

Alongside the inadequacy of domestic legal frameworks, other factors such as national security concerns, peer pressure and reputational interests[62] all favour timely exchange and minimum oversight against reliability and risk assessments. This becomes particularly worrisome once one realises that information shared with or received from foreign partners can be used to justify arrests, arbitrary detentions, renditions, torture, or lethal drone strikes, notwithstanding the fact that mistaken identity[63] and trumped-up[64] cases have been numerous.

4.3.2 Accountability Gaps and Shared Accountability

International legal accountability, as conceptualised here, has become crucial to address modern intelligence activities and fill international and transnational accountability gaps. The latter concept, borrowed from Kent Roach,[65] is used to describe a situation whereby domestic accountability in one state fails to hold to account foreign states that participated in the commission of the internationally wrongful act under scrutiny, so that accountability is partial and does not extend beyond borders. International accountability gaps similarly arise when a plurality of states is responsible for one wrongful act but not all of them are held accountable for it at international level. The potential of international legal accountability proceedings to ignore domestic sovereignty-related procedural bars, but also to hold several states responsible and accountable for

---

[62] Aidan Wills and Hans Born, 'International Intelligence Cooperation and Accountability: Formidable Challenges and Imperfect Solutions' in Hans Born, Ian Leigh and Aidan Wills (eds), *International Intelligence Cooperation and Accountability* (Routledge 2011) 283–289.

[63] See, among many others, the emblematic stories of Maher Arar or Khaled El-Masri.

[64] The most emblematic example is that of Abu Zubaydah, portrayed as No. 2 in al Qaeda and used as such for the counterterrorism communication strategy of the US, when, in reality, he had few to no links with al Qaeda. Numerous other examples deriving from unreliable shared intelligence have occurred during the United States' war on terror. Dick Marty highlights some of them in his 2006 report for the Parliamentary Assembly of the Council of Europe (n 112); and the SSCI Study (n 2) details the systematic issue of 'imputed knowledge' in the CIA programme.

[65] Kent Roach, 'Public Inquiries as an Attempt to Fill Accountability Gaps Left by Judicial and Legislative Review' in Fergal F Davis and Fiona De Londras (eds), *Critical Debates on Counter-Terrorism Judicial Review* (Cambridge University Press 2014).

the same wrongful act or harmful outcome,[66] is what makes these proceedings so valuable in the context of intelligence cooperation where, by nature, wrongful acts involve the participation of a plurality of states.

Shared accountability can be defined as holding several states to account, either in the same or, more commonly, in differentiated proceedings, through one or several accountability mechanisms for a wrongful act or harmful outcome in which they participated together through joint or cumulative action. Proceedings need not involve all implicated states at the same time, nor be of the same nature or come before the same accountability forum. They need simply concern the same wrongful act or harmful outcome. Shared accountability can therefore extend over time and involve a variety of accountability forms and mechanisms before reaching completion. In that sense, it is more flexible than the current doctrine of invocation of shared responsibility before international mechanisms (interstate mediated),[67] which requires joint proceedings or risks being dismissed in application of the *Monetary Gold* principle.[68]

The notion of harmful outcome[69] is preferred to that of injury when analysing shared responsibility and accountability. However, it must be carefully apprehended and should be differentiated from the wrongful acts composing it. Indeed, each actor is individually responsible for its own wrongful acts, regardless of whether multiple actors also contributed to the resulting harmful outcome.[70] In joint action situations (joint and several responsibility), there

---

[66] This is also called the 'transboundary reach' of international review bodies. Wills and Born (n 62) 302.

[67] See Annemarieke Vermeer-Künzli, 'Invocation of Responsibility' in André Nollkaemper and Ilias Plakokefalos (eds), *Principles of Shared Responsibility in International Law: An Appraisal of the State of the Art* (Cambridge University Press 2014).

[68] The essence of the principle as expressed by the ICJ is that it cannot decide on the international responsibility of a state if, to do so, 'it would have to rule, as a prerequisite, on the lawfulness' of the conduct of another State in the latter's absence and without its consent. *Monetary Gold Removed from Rome in 1943*, Judgment, ICJ Reports 1954 19 (International Court of Justice), 32.

[69] See André Nollkaemper and Dov Jacobs, 'Shared Responsibility in International Law: A Conceptual Framework' (2012) 34 Mich. J. Int'l L. 359, 367: 'We thus opt for a definition referring to a contribution to harmful outcomes that the law seeks to prevent, irrespective of the question whether such an outcome causes injury to a particular actor'. In the field of ethics, the notion of 'spectrum of blame' proposed by Ross Bellaby regarding the CIA rendition, detention, and interrogation programme serves a similar purpose; Ross W Bellaby, 'Extraordinary Rendition: Expanding the Circle of Blame in International Politics' (2018) 22 The International Journal of Human Rights 574.

[70] The principle of individual attribution is embedded in ASR Article 1.

often is no obstacle to accountability because the harmful outcome is the result of any and all states' wrongful act at the same time.[71] Each state is individually responsible for the harmful outcome. In this situation, shared accountability is about ensuring that all states involved are held accountable. However, there is no material accountability gap in the sense that, even if only one state is held accountable, this automatically pertains to the harmful outcome itself.

In contrast, the notion of harmful outcome becomes useful when analysing situations involving cumulative acts performed by different actors (multi-states composite act) but amounting to a single harmful outcome made up of the aggregate of individual acts.[72] The issue is that, necessarily, under the principle of individual attribution only those acts that constitute internationally wrongful acts can engage the responsibility of the states committing them, thereby shielding from responsibility the states that collaborated in the harmful outcome in a lawful way, and preventing any accountability for the harmful outcome itself. This also means that there is no responsibility 'when the accumulation of conduct is wrongful, but the separate and individual contributions are not'.[73] Such can be the case for composite acts, which are constituted of 'a series of acts or omissions defined in aggregate as wrongful'.[74] Article 15 ASR provides that a composite act committed by a single state will engage the responsibility of that state. Indeed, the aggregate (harmful outcome) is wrongful and all the acts composing it can be attributed to one state. However, no adaptation is made for cases in which the harmful outcome is the product of several states' acts. In such situations, there is no responsibility for the aggregate, but only for those acts, if any, that were individually wrongful.[75] The result is a material accountability gap: it is not possible to hold anyone (or any combination of actors) legally responsible either for the harmful outcome or for all the acts composing it.

---

[71] ASR Article 47. See also André Nollkaemper and others, 'Guiding Principles on Shared Responsibility in International Law' (2020) 31 European Journal of International Law 15 Principle 7.

[72] This will particularly be the case in situations of aid or assistance under ASR Article 16.

[73] Vermeer-Künzli (n 67) 261.

[74] ASR Article 15(1).

[75] A slightly different position was adopted by the authors of the Guiding Principles on Shared Responsibility in International Law. According to them, when the composite act is the result of a single wrongful act committed by a multiplicity of international persons, it will engage their shared responsibility (Principle 3, commentary para 6). They however recognise that 'an act or omission of an international person that is per se lawful' would not be rendered unlawful 'on account of it having been aggregated with other acts and omissions attributable to other international persons'. Nollkaemper and others (n 71).

The issue also lies further ahead. Even when responsibility is engaged and shared by all implicated actors,[76] in practice and under positive international law, states are being held accountable on an individual basis, for their individual wrongful acts only.[77] This means that, often, there is no accountability for the harmful outcome they contributed to, which is different in nature and degree from the sum of the individual acts composing it.

This issue is especially salient when serious breaches of peremptory norms of international law are involved. The aggravated regime of state responsibility that such breaches trigger[78] can only be invoked against states individually, meaning that at least one state's wrongful acts should reach the high threshold of constituting 'a gross or systematic failure by the responsible state to fulfil the obligation' imposed by a peremptory norm.[79] Yet, as Eric Wyler and León Castellanos-Jankiewicz emphasise, such breaches 'are hardly ever committed singlehandedly, and often involve a host of actors to plan and execute or stand idly by'.[80] The result is that, while cumulatively they result in a single harmful outcome constituting a serious breach of a peremptory norm, taken individually, wrongful acts committed by several states often do not reach this high threshold and can even appear quite minor. As a remedy to this unsatisfying state of affairs, Wyler and Castellanos-Jankiewicz suggest attributing conduct for serious breaches in light of harmful outcomes and taking shared responsibility as the standard for assessing the gravity of the breach.[81] The Guiding Principles on Shared Responsibility in International Law, conscious of the issue, also 'extend the existing rules of international responsibility'. They thus consider that, 'in situations of shared responsibility, a serious breach of a peremptory norm may also consist of the wrongful conduct of multiple international persons that cumulatively constitutes a serious breach of a peremptory norm of international law, but which would not reach the threshold of a serious breach when considered independently'.[82] Were this position to become representative of customary international law, it would be a welcome development. Under the current state of the law, however, the aggravated regime of Article

---

[76] As provided by ASR Articles 16–18, in situations of joint action, or through the creation of joint organs.
[77] ASR Article 1. For instance, in practice, ICJ cases are not joined and, in the ECtHR cases that are joined, the determination of responsibility is individualised.
[78] ASR Part Two, Chapter III.
[79] ASR Article 40(2).
[80] Eric Wyler and León Castellanos-Jankiewicz, 'Serious Breaches of Peremptory Norms' in André Nollkaemper and Ilias Plakokefalos (eds), *Principles of Shared Responsibility in International Law: An Appraisal of the State of the Art* (Cambridge University Press 2014) 291.
[81] Wyler and Castellanos-Jankiewicz (n 80) 291–292.
[82] Nollkaemper and others (n 71) Principle 13, commentary para 3.

41 ASR is still based on the principle of individual attribution. It follows that *erga omnes* forms of accountability under this regime[83] will not only be rare, but also rarely shared.

International legal accountability is no magic cure. It is based upon the engagement of state responsibility and is bound to follow the customary law of state responsibility, including the principle of individual attribution. The conceptualisation of international legal accountability proposed here is therefore not a remedy to material accountability gaps, nor can it remedy all of the issues raised by the individualisation of responsibility in situations involving composite acts or the serious breach of a peremptory norm. Shared accountability may thus only consist of the sum of the accountability processes targeting individual states. Nevertheless, because it is not necessary that shared responsibility be invoked for shared accountability to take place (provided the *Monetary Gold* principle is respected in all proceedings), the possibility to extend shared accountability over time and through various proceedings and forums allows us to take the harmful outcome as a standard for evaluating the completion of the process, i.e., the absence of international accountability gaps relating to a single harmful outcome. This means that shared accountability is fully reached when all the actors who participated in the harmful outcome have been held accountable for their own wrongful acts. International legal accountability can thus function as a tool to remedy international and transnational accountability gaps in so far as it provides several ways to ensure that all actors are held accountable for their own wrongful acts.

4.3.3 Practical Limits of Interstate Accountability

While intelligence activities are undoubtedly subject to the law of state responsibility, the rules of invocation of state responsibility are generally ill fitted, and particularly so in the intelligence cooperation context. This is mainly due to a practical issue: states are expected to hold one another to account under Part Three of the ASR. The interstate, horizontal forms of accountability embodied in the ASR therefore suffer from a serious lacuna stemming from the fact that states are not equally powerful, so that it is highly unlikely that a small, weak state will be able or willing to hold a more powerful one to account. Furthermore, even powerful states have no incentive to hold other states to account if their own security interests are not at stake. The sanctioning dilemma is thus at its peak in intelligence matters.

---

[83] Although *erga omnes* obligations constitute a wider category than *jus cogens* norms, in practice few claims based on legal interest concern non-peremptory norms.

In the intelligence cooperation context, the costs of holding another state to account are so high that no state will do so (and none has so far done so) for fear of losing its reputation as a reliable intelligence partner, and of ultimately putting its national security in jeopardy.[84] As Sir Stephen Lander, former Director General of the British Security Service (1996–2002), puts it, 'collaboration is not an end in itself. It is utility that drives collaboration'.[85] In the post-9/11 context, utility also seemed to call for collusion between states to evade oversight and review. Further, international pressures to frustrate accountability processes (whether at domestic or international level) have been solidly documented.[86] These observations converge with what Ruth Grant and Robert Keohane highlight regarding transnational networks generally, but with great relevance to instances of cooperation between foreign intelligence services having similar national security concerns: 'abuses of power might in some instances be controlled by the fragmentation of power and conflicts of interest between the participants, but cooperation among the members of such networks could easily become collusion against the interests of outsiders'.[87] Notwithstanding active collusion efforts, when national security is at stake, all actions are driven by national interest. As a result, if calling another state to account increases the risk of endangering a state's own national security through consequences such as the interruption of intelligence sharing or backlash from terrorist groups, the state will refrain from doing so.

Academic literature has identified several challenges specific to accountability in the intelligence cooperation context. Of particular importance are the third-party rule (and especially its institutionalised overclaim);[88] the reputational concerns of states who want to keep being perceived as reliable and

---

[84] Wills and Born (n 62). See also the statement by the England and Wales High Court in *(R) (Binyam Mohamed)* v. *Secretary of State for Foreign and Commonwealth Affairs* (No. 4) [2009] EWHC 152 (Admin.), paras 69–70.

[85] Stephen Lander, 'International Intelligence Cooperation: An inside Perspective' (2004) 17 Cambridge Review of International Affairs 481, 484.

[86] An emblematic example is the cooperation framework established by the classified NATO agreement of 4 October 2001, in effect making NATO 'a platform from which the United States obtained the essential permissions and protections it required to launch CIA covert action in the war on terror'. Dick Marty, 'Secret Detentions and Illegal Transfers of Detainees Involving Council of Europe Member States' (Parliamentary Assembly of the Council of Europe 2007) PACE Doc. 11302 rev. 90; see also Hans Born and Aidan Wills, 'International Responses to the Accountability Gap: European Inquiries into Illegal Transfers and Secret Detentions' in Hans Born, Ian Leigh and Aidan Wills (eds), *International Intelligence Cooperation and Accountability* (Routledge 2011) 210.

[87] Grant and Keohane (n 4) 39.

[88] There is a growing tendency on the part of intelligence agencies to invoke the third-party rule against oversight bodies in order to protect intelligence cooperation

trustworthy intelligence partners;[89] collusion to evade oversight, review, and ultimately accountability; and the inadequate legal frameworks establishing the terms of cooperation (secret legal agreements and classified memorandums of understanding).[90] In other words, the main challenges to accountability are states themselves: they do not want to be held accountable for their intelligence practices. In consequence, we must move beyond the horizontal interstate system of invocation of responsibility embodied in the ASR to understand how the international legal order still manages to address internationally wrongful acts resulting from intelligence activities.

4.3.4 The Necessity of Mediated and Surrogate Forms of Accountability in the Intelligence Context

Obligations breached by intelligence activities, and especially counterterrorism cooperation, are predominantly international human rights norms. Indeed, interstate obligations are normally waived in cooperation contexts. Further, the nature of intelligence operations themselves, particularly in the twenty-first-century security landscape, means that individuals will be their main and most numerous targets. In consequence, individuals should be able to hold states to account when their rights are wrongfully infringed. However, state secrecy and immunities often bar domestic accountability, and diplomatic protection and *erga omnes* claims are very unlikely in intelligence matters. Hence, to hold states to account, individuals and other non-state actors need to have standing, i.e., be allowed procedurally to become account-holders.

If domestic remedies have been exhausted and have not resulted in domestic accountability of all the states involved in the violation of individual rights,[91] complaint procedures before human rights institutions (mediated accountability) are the only avenues left for an individual to hold a state to account. If the state has consented to complaint procedures before international and/or regional human rights courts and bodies, then account-holder status is dependent upon standing. Standing is determined in accordance with the requirements imposed by the relevant convention or treaty.

---

relationships but also to avoid review of their own actions. It is almost impossible for oversight bodies to assess whether the rule was used legitimately or not.

[89] Pepijn Tuinier, Thijs Brocades Zaalberg and Sebastiaan Rietjens, 'The Social Ties That Bind: Unraveling the Role of Trust in International Intelligence Cooperation' [2022] International Journal of Intelligence and CounterIntelligence 1, 14.

[90] Wills and Born (n 62) 283–284.

[91] Domestic remedies accordingly need to be exhausted in all states against which a complaint is raised. See discussion in Vermeer-Künzli (n 67) 267–270.

In situations in which the state has not consented to relevant individual complaint procedures or where the claim is declared inadmissible, an accountability gap may subsist. Account-holder status can however be taken over by an international forum (surrogate accountability), often a human rights body, in the course of non-complaint procedures. These include, for example, reporting obligations of the state under a treaty; UN General Assembly requests for an ICJ Advisory Opinion; or *proprio motu* investigations of a situation by the forum. Conceptualising surrogate accountability in international relations, Jennifer Rubenstein distinguishes three stages of surrogacy: at the standards-setting stage and/or the information stage and/or the sanctions stage.[92] In contrast, surrogacy is absolute in international law. Individuals lack the requisite international legal status to (directly) hold states to account. Hence, if they do not have standing for mediated accountability, they can play no active role in the accountability process.

Mediated and surrogate accountability constitute the only two forms of accountability allowing individuals to hold states to account, and the only forms likely to be used in the context of intelligence cooperation. In consequence, a correct assessment of international practice and of the potential of the international legal order to hold states accountable requires their inclusion in the conceptualisation and analysis of state accountability for intelligence activities. Further, while accountability is conceptually only concerned with the consequences for the state of the engagement of its international responsibility, a process of accountability based upon the establishment of state responsibility for a breach of its human rights obligations can often, through the consequences imposed on the state, participate in remedying the human rights violations suffered by the victims.

4.4 OBJECTIVES

If international law is to regulate intelligence activities meaningfully, it should have effects on state behaviour. The first purpose of accountability must therefore be to deter the wrongdoer state from committing further violations, as well as to deter all states from engaging in conduct violating international law. In addition, accountability aims at (at least partially) remedying the wrongful act. Indeed, once responsibility is engaged, providing satisfactory

---

[92] Rubenstein (n 4).

reparation[93] is a legal obligation that flows from the breach[94] and is owed to the account-holder.[95]

At the level of intelligence services, accountability constitutes an incentive to improve intelligence practices and the structure of the agencies. Compliance with human rights law in intelligence matters enhances the reliability of the intelligence produced and shared, as well as the legitimacy of intelligence work. Finally, at the level of victims and society as a whole, accountability is particularly valuable when it contributes to enhancing transparency and uncovering the truth.

4.4.1 Enforcing International Legality

The first and main aim of accountability is to preserve international legality by ensuring that state responsibility is enforced and does not simply exist in a vacuum. The ILC introduced the protection of legality as a freestanding legal objective by eliminating damage as a condition of responsibility in the ASR. Enforcing international legality entails fighting state impunity through the declaration of state responsibility and the imposition of consequences.

Consequences have a deterrent potential: rational states will comply with the law through fear of sanctions if they believe that sanctions will be enforced in case of breach. Enforcement can activate social and normative motivations for compliance because it stigmatises and shames those who are caught in noncompliance and it acts as a reminder to others that the general community values compliance.[96] On the other hand, enforcement that is not effective, that is ignored by the community or that seems pointless can encourage non-compliance. The deterrent potential of consequences is therefore only activated if sanctions are actually enforced, and often enough.[97] Experiments in various contexts have confirmed the efficacy of decentralised sanctioning systems such as the international legal order.[98]

Another important quality of accountability proceedings is the clarification, benefiting the entire community of states, which stems from the decisions

---

[93] ASR Part Two, Chapter II, details various forms of reparation for internationally wrongful acts: restitution, compensation, and satisfaction.
[94] ASR Article 31.
[95] ASR Article 33.
[96] On deterrence theory, see especially Christine Parker and Vibeke Nielsen, 'Compliance: 14 Questions' in Peter Drahos (ed), *Regulatory Theory* (ANU Press 2017).
[97] See Chapter 5 for further analysis.
[98] Anne van Aaken, 'Experimental Insights for International Legal Theory' (2019) 30 European Journal of International Law 1237, 1256.

on what expectations a legal norm entails. Accountability for internationally wrongful acts deriving from intelligence cooperation further clarifies what types and levels of risk should preclude cooperation, and what evidence of risk is sufficient for responsibility to be engaged.

The enforcement of international legality also has a secondary, indirect purpose. Accountability aims at forcing the state to provide reparations for its wrongful act, a legal duty that stems directly from the breach.[99] Where the fight against impunity concerns human rights norms, state accountability thus also aims at ensuring a remedy for victims. At the very least, accountability mechanisms do so by giving credit to victims' allegations and by recognising their victim status. In processes where individual victims act as account-holders, more concrete remedies may also be ordered by the forum as an integral part of the consequences imposed on states.

4.4.2 Reliable Intelligence

The United States' Army Field Manual of 1992 was quite clear in stating the commonly held view[100] pre-9/11 regarding interrogation methods:

> Experience indicates that the use of prohibited techniques is not necessary to gain cooperation of interrogation sources. Use of torture and other illegal methods is a poor technique that yields unreliable results, may damage subsequent collection efforts, and can induce the source to say what he thinks the interrogator wants to hear.[101]

Instances of state accountability for the use of illegal interrogation and intelligence gathering methods – including facilitation, aid, assistance, and any other form of state complicity – contribute to ensuring that such methods are not used again. State accountability thus improves the quality and reliability of intelligence and helps to prevent unreliable or fabricated intelligence[102] being put in international circulation and/or being acted upon – whether in lawful or unlawful ways.

Accountability provides incentives for states to seek assurances and include caveats on the authorised use and/or the reliability of the intelligence they share in order to prevent the engagement of their responsibility for actions by the

---

[99] ASR Part Two.

[100] For worldwide illustrations of the international consensus on the matter, see Darius M Rejali, *Torture and Democracy* (Princeton University Press 2007) 461–462.

[101] US Army Field Manual 34–52, 1992, 1-8. See also SSCI Study (n 2) 18–19 on US policy and practice pre-9/11.

[102] See the numerous instances of fabrication of intelligence by CIA detainees as a result of 'enhanced interrogation techniques' reported in the SSCI Study (n 2).

receiving state. Indeed, state responsibility may be engaged for the sharing of intelligence which is then acted upon unlawfully where the sending state knew or was 'wilfully blind' to the fact that this was a near-certain possibility.[103] In addition, the receipt and actionable use of intelligence obtained through unlawful means, especially torture, may also engage state responsibility.[104] Holding states accountable for executive use of torture-tainted intelligence would ensure that intelligence services perform more thorough checks on their partners' human rights records. In turn, this would constitute an incentive for intelligence services worldwide to operate within a rule of law framework, improving the reliability of the intelligence produced and circulated.

In addition, lawful methods of intelligence gathering and interrogation allow the information obtained to be used in judicial proceedings, if need be. Indeed, intelligence obtained through torture 'shall not be invoked as evidence in any proceedings',[105] and information obtained through unlawful surveillance operations would not be admissible in court in most jurisdictions.[106] Even though the task of intelligence agencies stops well before trial and is sometimes mistakenly reduced to the disruption of terrorist plots, the importance of collecting intelligence through lawful means should not be overlooked by intelligence agencies. The conviction of terrorist suspects identified through intelligence work improves agencies' reputation and the trust they obtain from foreign intelligence agencies. Such indirect benefits can prove to be decisive in concluding cooperation agreements.[107]

---

[103] It is indeed arguable that such a situation would be covered by ASR Article 16. See Harriet Moynihan, 'Aiding and Assisting: The Mental Element under Article 16 of the International Law Commission's Article on State Responsibility' (2018) 67 International and Comparative Law Quarterly 455; Marko Milanovic, 'Intelligence Sharing in Multinational Military Operations and Complicity under International Law' (2021) 97 International Legal Studies 136.

[104] See Chapter 3, section 3.4.5.

[105] UN Convention Against Torture, Article 15.

[106] This is particularly so for surveillance without a warrant in common law jurisdictions, but various types of unlawfulness will trigger inadmissibility in civil law jurisdictions, too. For illustrations, see United Nations Office of Drugs and Crimes, *Current Practices in Electronic Surveillance in the Investigation of Serious and Organized Crime* (United Nations 2009).

[107] The US practice of detaining (and interrogating with methods amounting to torture) individuals solely for their alleged intelligence value has been rightly criticised as infringing greatly on the dignity and rights of the victims and has immensely harmed the US reputation as a model in human rights, as well as its counterterrorism efforts. See SSCI Study (n 2) and Anna-Katherine Staser McGill and David H Gray, 'Challenges to International Counterterrorism Intelligence Sharing' (2012) 3 Global Security Studies 76, 79–80.

The constitutional aspect of accountability – i.e., accountability for the failure to implement sufficient oversight and accountability mechanisms at the domestic level[108] – also plays a role in improving states' legal framework, the structure of their intelligence services, and, in turn, the quality of the intelligence produced. This is particularly the case for member states of the Council of Europe, which have been subjected to increased oversight by the ECtHR, the Venice Commission, and the Commissioner for Human Rights.[109] The ECtHR has especially been keen to demand from states that they enact clear and detailed legislation regarding surveillance and law enforcement powers, and, in particular in the area of surveillance, that they implement independent control and remedy mechanisms in addition to procedural safeguards.[110] The European Parliament[111] and PACE[112] inquiries into the CIA-led rendition, detention, and interrogation programme have also put pressure on EU and Council of Europe member states to open domestic inquiries into allegations of cooperation with the CIA-led programme, highlighting structural failures and reform needs.

Beyond Europe, the compatibility of states' intelligence policies and practices with international law has come under international institutions' scrutiny in the counterterrorism context. Such scrutiny has given rise to increased demands that the states concerned provide mechanisms to bring their intelligence legislation and practice into conformity with human rights law.[113]

---

[108] See above, section 4.3.1 'The Inadequacy of Domestic Oversight Mechanisms'. Generally, see Cameron (n 51).

[109] See, e.g., Muižnieks, 'Report by Nils Muižnieks, Council of Europe Commissioner for Human Rights, following his visit to Poland, from 9 to 12 February 2016', CommDH(2016)23 (2016), 12; Venice Commission, Report on the Democratic Oversight of the Security Services, CDL-AD(2015)010.

[110] E.g., *Roman Zakharov* v. *Russia*, App. No. 47143/06, 4 December 2015; *Szabo and Vissy* v. *Hungary*, App. No. 37138/14, 12 January 2016; *Big Brother Watch and Others* v. *the United Kingdom* [GC], App. No. 58170/13, 62322/14 and 24960/15, 25 May 2021.

[111] The inquiry led to the publication of the Fava Report on the alleged use of European countries by the CIA for the transportation and illegal detention of prisoners (2006/2200(INI)) of 30 January 2007.

[112] The inquiry led to the publication of three reports by Rapporteur Dick Marty ('Marty Reports') to the Parliamentary Assembly of the Council of Europe: Dick Marty, 'Alleged Secret Detentions and Unlawful Inter-State Transfers of Detainees Involving Council of Europe Member States' (Parliamentary Assembly of the Council of Europe 2006) PACE Doc. 10957; Marty, 'Marty Report 2007' (n 86); Marty, 'Marty Report 2011' (n 49).

[113] See, e.g., Scheinin (n 45); UN General Assembly, Resolution A/RES/60/158 (2005) 'Protection of human rights and fundamental freedoms while countering terrorism'.

4.4.3 Truth, Transparency, and Legitimacy

One of the most valuable effects of accountability is that it sheds light upon the exercise of power. As Andreas Schedler wrote, 'the demand for accountability originates from the opacity of power'.[114] In intelligence matters as in other forms of power exercise, accountability provides incentives for adopting good practices through the necessary exposure of facts that takes place in accountability proceedings. Truth and transparency thus constitute both indispensable conditions and objectives of accountability proceedings.

In addition, states' wilful (*ex post facto*) transparency[115] and the subjection of their intelligence agencies and practices to (domestic) oversight contribute to making them legitimate and rule-of-law-compliant, or at least perceived as such. When the state acts or is perceived to act in compliance with international law and the rule of law, it is more likely to receive both domestic and international support, i.e., intelligence sharing and cooperation from like-minded states and willing informants and sources at the domestic level. Lawful and non-stigmatising practices yield enhanced cooperation and better results,[116] in addition to being a necessary condition for the achievement of peace and security.[117] In contrast, policies targeting specific communities or perceived as unfair or unlawful have been shown to be counter-productive.[118] International

---

[114] Schedler (n 3) 20.

[115] Transparency does not necessarily entail declassification but should involve at least genuine *ex post* explanations about decisions and actions.

[116] The best modern example is probably the arrest of the five London bombers of 21 July 2005 within ten days of the attacks. The first one, Mukhtar Said-Ibrahim was identified after his parents contacted the police, and the investigation proceeded from there. It is doubtful that Ibrahim's parents would have contacted the police had they feared that their son would be mistreated or receive an unfair trial. Empirical research in the Israel-Palestine conflict has also shown that repressive actions are either unrelated to terror or related to subsequent increases in terror whereas conciliatory actions are generally related to decreases in terror; Laura Dugan and Erica Chenoweth, 'Moving Beyond Deterrence: The Effectiveness of Raising the Expected Utility of Abstaining from Terrorism in Israel' (2012) 77 American Sociological Review 597.

[117] Seung Whan Choi, 'Fighting Terrorism through the Rule of Law?' (2010) 54 Journal of Conflict Resolution 940. See also: UN Security Council, Resolution S/RES/2178 (2014), 'Addressing the growing issue of foreign terrorist fighters'; UN Security Council, Resolution S/RES/1963 (2010) 'Threats to international peace and security caused by terrorist acts'; UN General Assembly, Resolution A/RES/60/288 (2006) 'UN Global Counter-Terrorism Strategy and Plan of Action', Pillar IV.

[118] E.g., UNDP, 'Journey to Extremism in Africa', 2017 emphasising the importance of human rights violations as drivers of violent extremism; UK House of Commons, 'Communities and Local Government Committee, Preventing Violent Extremism', Sixth Report of Session 2009–10, Evaluation the UK Prevent programme; UN General Assembly, Resolution A/70/674, 24 December 2015. See also James E Baker, 'What's

accountability proceedings should therefore endeavour to enhance transparency by circumventing state secrecy doctrines and authoritatively exposing facts. The main benefit will be that, to avoid public exposure and reputational damages, states will have to reform their institutional frameworks and ensure sufficient transparency, oversight, and accountability at the domestic level.

In addition, international accountability mechanisms (especially but not limited to judicial proceedings) can establish facts authoritatively and publicly. This creates a platform for victims to launch remedial action at both the domestic and international levels. Uncovering the truth should therefore be considered a self-standing objective of accountability. Consideration of accountability proceedings' potential to thereby enforce a 'right to truth' belonging both to victims of gross human rights violations and to society at large regarding counterterrorism operations[119] has similarly emerged in scholarship, case-law, and institutional documents.[120] This feature also concerns non-judicial accountability mechanisms such as truth commissions and fact-finding inquiries,[121] and links with what Bovens identified as a collateral objective of accountability: catharsis.[122]

International Law Got to Do With It? Transnational Law and the Intelligence Mission Symposium: State Intelligence Gathering and International Law' (2006) 28 Michigan Journal of International Law 639, 656.

[119] See Federico Fabbrini, 'The European Court of Human Rights, Extraordinary Renditions and the Right to the Truth: Ensuring Accountability for Gross Human Rights Violations Committed in the Fight Against Terrorism' (2014) 14 Human Rights Law Review 85, 99–102 for a discussion in relation to the El-Masri case before the ECtHR.

[120] Fabbrini (n 119). More generally, see: UNHRC Resolution 9/11, 24 September 2008 and UNHRC Resolution 12/1, 12 October 2009; *Velasquez Rodriguez v. Honduras*, IACtHR Series C 4 (1988); *Contreras et al. v. El Salvador*, IACtHR Series C 232 (2011); *Myrna Mack Chang v. Guatemala*, Series C No. 101 (2003), paras 75-77; Council of Europe, *Guidelines of the Committee of Ministers on Eradicating Impunity for Serious Human Rights Violations* (2011) and UN Human Rights Council, *Report of the Special Rapporteur on the promotion and protection of human rights and fundamental freedoms while countering terrorism Ben Emmerson*, A/HRC/22/52, paras 23–26, all mentioning the importance of truth in eradicating impunity and providing a remedy to victims and their relatives.

[121] The Canadian inquiry into the facts of Maher Arar's rendition can be cited as exemplary in the context of intelligence cooperation. For an empirical analysis of the 'differences' made by international commissions of inquiry in specific contexts, see Michael A Becker and Sarah MH Nouwen, 'International Commissions of Inquiry: What Difference Do They Make? Taking an Empirical Approach' (2019) 30 European Journal of International Law 819.

[122] Bovens (n 4) 464.

4.5 CONCLUSIONS: ACCOUNTABILITY AS THE SECOND LAYER OF REGULATION

The engagement of a state's responsibility for an internationally wrongful act resulting from intelligence activities is an automatic process. Accountability, however, requires the presence and active engagement of an account-holder. In the regulation process, international legal accountability entails a move from legality to the active enforcement of responsibility by external actors, making it the second layer of regulation.

This chapter first developed the conceptual framework of state accountability, taking into account the role that non-state actors and entities play in the enforcement of state responsibility. To reflect the actual functioning of this second layer of regulation, I conceptualised state accountability beyond the rules on invocation of responsibility provided by the ASR. I thus developed an empirically grounded, original, and multidimensional taxonomy of the forms of international legal accountability.

The particular relevance, and even necessity, of this specific conceptualisation in the intelligence context was then demonstrated through references to the failures of both domestic and interstate accountability mechanisms; the necessity of mediated and surrogate forms of accountability to fill the accountability gaps created by such failures; and the added value of the concept to achieve shared accountability. The analysis also demonstrated that, at least in theory, international legal accountability mechanisms can adequately address states' intelligence activities. This conclusion is tested empirically in Chapter 6, which evaluates the accountability of five states for their participation in the CIA global war on terror.

Finally, I articulated the objectives of the concept in the context of international intelligence activities and cooperation. I grouped the objectives of state accountability for intelligence activities into three clusters, namely: enforcing international legality and preventing impunity; reliable intelligence and intelligence services; and truth, transparency, and legitimacy. These objectives interconnect, and, while highly specific to the context at stake, they are coherent with the objectives identified in more general studies of accountability.

While this chapter conceptualised international legal accountability as the second layer of regulation, it left open the question of its effectiveness and operationalisation. The following chapter will identify the conditions necessary for international legal accountability to become an effective tool to regulate intelligence activities and will present an evaluative framework.

5. Effective accountability

5.1 INTRODUCTION

The influence of international law over state behaviour is an oft-studied yet never quite solved question. It links to the issue, well known to modern international lawyers, of the functioning and effectiveness of the international legal order as a social order.[1] How is order sustained in a decentralised system composed of *de jure* sovereign equals who have renounced the use of force? How can legality be enforced absent a centralised enforcement mechanism? Are states 'rational' when they interact with one another, make international law, abide by it, violate it, and enforce it? Various international legal theories compete and complement each other in attempting to explain why states behave the way they do or, to put it otherwise, why states comply or do not comply with international law in their daily activities.

In this chapter, I aim to decipher the conditions under which international legal accountability is effective to regulate states' intelligence activities. What is required for state accountability to influence state behaviour in the international legal order? To answer this question, I theorise 'effective accountability', relying on regulatory theory and behavioural insights applied to the international legal order. Drawing on behavioural international law scholarship, I focus first on the influence of international law in the absence of external regulatory interventions such as sanctions (internal regulation). This allows me to draw implications regarding the role played by legality (the first layer) in regulation. Then, integrating behavioural approaches with regulatory theory, I analyse the supplemental role and influence of such regulatory interventions on state behaviour (external regulation). This second step allows me to analyse the role of accountability (the second layer) and identify the conditions of its effectiveness as a regulatory tool.

---

[1] As emphasised by Oona Hathaway and Scott Shapiro, the problem of enforcement 'is so vexing in part because it is so new. During the Old World Order [before 1945], international law did not need police. International law was backed by the very real threat of war'. Oona Anne Hathaway and Scott Shapiro, *The Internationalists: How a Radical Plan to Outlaw War Remade the World* (Simon & Schuster 2017) 61.

In section 5.2, I analyse the influence of international law on states' preferences, interests, and motives. In section 5.3, I apply theories of regulation, supplemented by behavioural insights, to the international legal order conceived of as the regulator of states' acts. In this section, my aim is to explain how the international legal order functions and sustains order. Drawing on these insights, in section 5.4, I put forward a theory of effective accountability as nodal, networked responsive regulation. In section 5.5, finally, I propose a framework to evaluate the theoretical potential of the international legal order, as a regulator, to provide accountability in the intelligence context. Section 5.6 provides concluding remarks regarding the role of effective accountability as a bridge between the second and third layers of regulation, i.e., between accountability and compliance.

5.2 THE INFLUENCE OF INTERNATIONAL LAW ON STATES' PREFERENCES, INTERESTS, AND MOTIVES

Empirical evidence shows that states are neither purely self-interested nor genuine altruist entities. Depending on the context and the stakes, they usually fall somewhere between these two extremes. The challenge thus becomes identifying the factors and reasons underlying states' behaviour in the international legal order in the absence of explicit external constraints such as sanctions. In other words, what is the influence of international law *as law* on state behaviour?

Anne van Aaken stresses the role of the law itself in shaping states' beliefs, motives, and interests.[2] Legal norms act as a frame[3] by enhancing beliefs regarding what others will do in a situation, and by expressing a view on what 'the right thing to do' is. These two aspects are crucial in shaping states' social preferences and, in turn, their behaviour in cooperative and social contexts. Experiments thus show that, depending on how a situation is framed, behaviours may be more or less cooperative.[4]

When the law presents a course of conduct as the default one, it creates a belief, or normative expectation, that most states will adopt that course of

---

[2] Anne van Aaken, 'Experimental Insights for International Legal Theory' (2019) 30 European Journal of International Law 1237, 1247–1251.

[3] A framing effect exists when different ways of describing the same choice problem change the choices that people make, even though the underlying information and choice options remain essentially the same.

[4] van Aaken (n 2) 1248.

conduct.⁵ States will therefore be more inclined to cooperate if they believe others are also willing to and will follow the rules.⁶ In addition, a law's existence provides information about other states' opinions.⁷ This 'attitudinal signalling'⁸ function of law has at least one important implication for state behaviour. Information about what other members of a community (either the majority, the most powerful, or any section thereof) believe affects one's own beliefs. This can be due to a taste for agreeing with the majority or with powerful actors, or because going with the majority is rational.⁹ The framing effect of the law also goes further: legal norms can activate moral sentiments and create moral expectations, and the internalisation of legal norms triggers emotional responses in decision-makers.¹⁰

Moral preferences and concerns about fairness and equality are commonly based on social and internalised (legal) norms. Yet, law is generally considered to be more reliable than social norms in generating normative expectations, both because it is governed by authority and because of its expressive function.¹¹ Of particular relevance here, law can be perceived as a public expression of what one ought to do, especially if it is chosen endogenously.¹² In turn, this may activate the (social) norm of conditional cooperation.¹³ The internalisation

---

⁵ This is for instance the case with opt-in and opt-out arrangements in treaty regimes: due to a strong status quo bias, most states stick with the default option even though other options may not be more costly. See Jean Galbraith, 'Treaty Options: Towards a Behavioral Understanding of Treaty Design' (2013) 53 Virginia Journal of International Law 309; Doron Teichman and Eyal Zamir, 'Nudge Goes International' (2019) 30 European Journal of International Law 1263, 1269–1270.

⁶ Jean-Robert Tyran and Lars P Feld, 'Achieving Compliance When Legal Sanctions Are Non-Deterrent' (2006) 108 Scandinavian Journal of Economics 135. The negotiation and continued functioning of arms control treaties forms a prime example: states only accept reducing their arsenal if other states do so, and they will resume armament when other states breach the provisions of the treaties.

⁷ Tyran and Feld (n 6) explain that endogenously chosen law drives higher rates of compliance than exogenously-imposed law in part because it allows citizens to signal to one another their willingness to cooperate.

⁸ Richard H McAdams, *The Expressive Powers of Law: Theories and Limits* (Harvard University Press 2015).

⁹ Eric Rasmusen, 'Law, Coercion, and Expression: A Review Essay on Frederick Schauer's *The Force of Law* and Richard McAdams's *The Expressive Powers of Law*' (2017) 55 Journal of Economic Literature 1098, 1111 explains that, as most people are politically uninvolved, and hence have weak priors, going with the majority is rational. In contrast, blind conformity would not be.

¹⁰ van Aaken (n 2) 1250.
¹¹ See generally McAdams (n 8).
¹² Tyran and Feld (n 6) 138.
¹³ ibid 139. Conditional cooperation is the tendency of individuals to engage in cooperation depending on the degree of cooperation of other individuals.

of legal norms perceived as dictating the right course of conduct transforms the decision-making process by rendering alternative courses of conduct less attractive. Further, if the norm is internalised, the choice of such alternative courses of conduct will trigger emotions of guilt[14] – and possibly shame[15] – in the decision-maker. Guilt is described by van Aaken as an internal sanctioning mechanism, relying on the self-image of decision-makers.[16] Actors' guilt aversion thus influences their behaviour absent any external enforcement mechanism. In contrast, shame is an external sanction, imposed by peers,[17] and is partially a function of the importance that the actor gives to others' image of them.[18]

Beliefs have an effect on a wide range of state behaviours in the international legal order. Van Aaken thus highlights that states' beliefs about the intentions of other actors will influence whether an act is perceived as cooperative or retaliatory.[19] Such perception will then influence states' willingness to reciprocate, retaliate, or sanction, even if costly to them.[20] Relatedly, it can be posited from experiments with individuals that, when states expect other states to comply with a rule, they tend to also do so themselves.[21] This position, termed 'conditional cooperation', represents an important part of states' behaviour in the international legal order and is crucial for the functioning of the system. Further, beliefs about equality and fairness[22] explain (to a certain extent) why states cooperate in fields such as IHRL, and why they take action against non-complying states in the absence of direct injury to them.[23] In addition, beliefs in other actors' trustworthiness also affect decisions related to cooperation, and thus cooperative outcomes. These insights highlight the

---

[14] Guilt is defined as mental pain felt aside from the existence of other people or actors.

[15] Shame is defined as mental pain from other people or actors seeing what one has done, or from one imagining them seeing it.

[16] van Aaken (n 2) 1250.

[17] Notwithstanding that shame can arise from *imagining* others witnessing our actions. Even in that case, however, it remains an external sanction as it relies on the existence of others.

[18] Nathan Harris, 'Shame in Regulatory Settings' in Peter Drahos (ed), *Regulatory Theory* (ANU Press 2017) 64 describes shame as a 'social threat'.

[19] van Aaken (n 2) 1252–1253.

[20] Anne van Aaken, 'Behavioral International Law and Economics' (2014) 55 Harvard International Law Journal 62, 471–474.

[21] Tyran and Feld (n 6).

[22] Also called 'bounded self-interest'. See van Aaken (n 20) 432–435; Tomer Broude, 'Behavioral International Law' [2015] 163 U. Pa. L. Rev. 1099 1118.

[23] van Aaken (n 20) 472–473.

importance of communication and trust-enhancing devices, not least to ensure the participation of conditional cooperators.[24]

This brief overview of some applications of experimental insights to international law, which is by no means comprehensive, highlights the significant role played by legal norms on state behaviour in the absence of any external enforcement mechanism. Legal norms, by their very existence, shape states' beliefs, motives, and interests through various cognitive and social processes. In turn, these beliefs shape state behaviour in the international legal order. Undoubtedly, the framing effect of the law is not always enough to ensure state compliance with legal norms. External intervention may thus become necessary. The efficacy of such regulatory interventions is, as for legal norms, a function of aspects of states' bounded rationality at play, which can either enhance or hinder it.

5.3 REGULATION IN THE INTERNATIONAL LEGAL ORDER

Anne-Marie Slaughter famously described the modern international order as a 'Lego world':[25] a network of modular ad hoc organisations encompassing state and non-state actors, thus replacing the previous Westphalian order. The international *legal* order has followed similar transformations, with governmental international organisations first acquiring international legal personality, followed by a variety of other non-state actors. Non-state actors thus became the subjects of international norms, acquiring rights, standing, and even some duties, in the international legal order. Hence, while the original actors remain sovereign states, the composition and power distribution of the international legal order are in fact much more varied.

How does this modern international legal order maintain order and enforce legality? Or, more simply, how does international law work? To answer these questions, I propose to apply theories of regulation, supplemented by behavioural insights, to the international legal order. Indeed, the international legal order is a social order. With regard to international law as a normative order, I argue that the international legal order should be conceived of as a regulator, or rather *the* regulator of states' actions. This regulatory perspective highlights crucial aspects of the international legal order's functioning, which match empirical behavioural insights regarding the reasons underlying state behaviour in the same legal order.

---

[24] van Aaken (n 2) 1254.
[25] Anne-Marie Slaughter, 'Remarks, The Big Picture: Beyond Hot Spots & Crises in Our Interconnected World' (2012) 1 Penn St. J.L. & Int'l Aff. 286, 294.

5.3.1 Networked Governance

The international legal order can first be conceived of as a *network* of enforcement of international legality. This conception contrasts with the usual scholarly legal approach, which looks at individual accountability mechanisms, such as courts or treaty bodies, in isolation. This mainstream approach prevents any accurate assessment and analysis of the influence that the isolated actor's actions have on state behaviour because it ignores the role played by other actors in the social order that is the international legal order.

5.3.1.1 Networks of accountability mechanisms

The previous chapter demonstrated that, both empirically and theoretically, international legal accountability cannot be reduced to the purely interstate forms codified in the ILC Articles on the Responsibility of States (ASR).[26] This observation necessarily leads one to reconsider the Westphalian vision of the international legal order still implied by the customary law of state responsibility. Hence, I offer a new perspective: for each state, all the competent accountability mechanisms constitute a network, with a set of tools at their disposition.

This *network of accountability mechanisms*, thus encompassing all other states and competent supra-national accountability mechanisms, is unique to each state. Indeed, states have not all consented to an identical set of international legal norms and to the competence of the same supra-national accountability forums. In addition, the nature, extent, and depth of their relations with other states (individually and as groups) are also unique. With regard to human rights, for instance, the relevant part of a state's network would include all other states (although not at the same level) and courts and bodies with universal jurisdiction that the state has recognised as competent, as well as a combination of the 56 United Nations special procedures, ten UN human rights treaty bodies, three principal regional human rights systems (each with various components), and their respective 'parent' intergovernmental organisations. The strength of the network comes through the addition of the individual competences and powers of each of its members, which complement and reinforce one another.

Networked governance functions through nodes of activity or interest, earning the label of 'nodal governance'. Nodal governance is defined as 'an elaboration of contemporary networks theory explaining how a variety

---

[26] International Law Commission, *Draft Articles on the Responsibility of States for Internationally Wrongful Acts*, November 2001, Supplement No. 10 (A/56/10), chp. IV.E.1 ('ASR'), Part Three.

of actors operating within social systems interact along networks to govern the system they inhabit'.[27] Nodes are made up of any type(s) of actor(s) (individuals, groups, institutions, organisations, states, sub-entities, etc.) that can mobilise resources and 'tie together strands in networks of power'.[28] Nodes are not generally fixed entities, and their size, membership, activity, and degree of specialisation may vary greatly over time, space, and between them. Coordination between nodes is made possible via networks, leading to a governance that is 'networked' rather than the product of any single node's activity.[29]

Nodes may have differing interests and priorities. Therefore, effective networked governance depends heavily upon the management of dissonances – if not upon straightforward coordinated action – between them. In the international legal order, one might conceive of nodes as groups of states with similar concerns; groups of international institutions with similar *ratione materiae* competence; member states of an international organisation; etc. For a particular state, its network of accountability mechanisms could thus be composed of the states with whom it regularly trades as one node, competent human rights bodies as another, states who have invested in the country as a third node, etc. Members of the network can be actors in more than one node, and this overlapping membership may help in reducing dissonances and achieving concerted action.

Since nodes have different interests, competences, and powers, they also have different enforcement capabilities. Effective networked governance supposes that the regulator knows which nodes to activate at any one time so that the network, like a web, becomes animated and able to constrain the state into complying. In the case of the international legal order, the regulator is the network itself, which implies some sort of self-governance and a minimum level of coordination by its many members if effectiveness is to be achieved. Sometimes, intervention by only one of the nodes may be sufficient, but cumulated action by several nodes – even if their interests and motives differ – creates more diffuse and usually stronger regulatory pressure.[30] Applying

---

[27] Scott Burris, Peter Drahos and Clifford Shearing, 'Nodal Governance' (2005) 30 Australian Journal of Legal Philosophy 5.

[28] Cameron Holley and Clifford Shearing, 'A Nodal Perspective of Governance: Advances in Nodal Governance Thinking' in Peter Drahos (ed), *Regulatory Theory* (ANU Press, 2017) 168.

[29] ibid 167.

[30] Think of a situation in which a US threat of economic sanctions could be enough to coerce a non-complying state, but in which a resolution of the UN Security Council, or General Assembly, coupled with concerted action by other states and potentially other organisations would add more weight to US economic sanctions and have stronger prospects of success.

pressure by acting on various interests of the regulated state also creates more opportunities for touching a sensitive interest. Further, one of the nodes may have irresistible bargaining power, thus making it a solid enforcement partner for other nodes.

5.3.1.2 Behavioural insights into international legal networked governance

To understand how such a decentralised enforcement system may influence a state's behaviour, it is useful to combine networked governance theory with experimental behavioural insights applied to the international legal order. International law is a system that lacks a centralised enforcement mechanism and relies on mostly mild and symbolic sanctions. Yet, empirical knowledge confirms that non-material sanctions can be effective provided that they satisfy several conditions. Of particular importance are consent to the rule, guilt and shame, and procedural fairness.

In the first place, international law as a system relies on state consent. The most fundamental principle of international law is *pacta sunt servanda*. A sovereign state is thus only bound by rules it consents to be bound by.[31] However, as Ian Hurd explains, it cannot escape the expectation of adherence to law.[32] Because political legitimacy comes from being seen as compliant, states deploy extensive legal resources to frame their behaviour as legal, evidencing their pervasive shared ideological commitment to rule following – whether genuine or instrumental.[33] States also signal their obedience to the law (or rather, the law as they interpret it), seeking validation and stigmatising those that they consider non-compliant.[34] Their motive for complying, from this perspective, is the prize of political legitimacy that comes from being seen as rule-complying. The hegemony of the international rule of law is therefore manifest in the universality of law as a source of justification and contestation of state behaviour.[35] This fundamental and foundational principle of international law explains, by itself, much of state compliance.

---

[31] This general statement naturally does not purport to affect debates regarding state consent in situations of decolonisation or state succession.
[32] Ian Hurd, *How to Do Things with International Law* (Princeton University Press 2017) 130.
[33] ibid 130–134.
[34] Rasmusen (n 9) 1113–1114.
[35] Hurd (n 32) 134; see also Monica Hakimi, 'Why Should We Care About International Law?' (2020) 118 Michigan Law Review 1283; Michael Zürn, *A Theory of Global Governance: Authority, Legitimacy, and Contestation* (Oxford University Press 2018) 6.

Crucial to the functioning of the international legal order, experimental insights confirm that endogenously chosen law is more effective than exogenous law in that it is better accepted and drives higher compliance rates.[36] This is the case irrespective of whether attached sanctions are considered severe or mild.[37] Two main interrelated cognitive factors explain this state of affair. The first one relates to the perceived legitimacy of the rule: if I have drafted it, or have explicitly consented to it, then I see it as legitimate and will be more inclined to follow it.[38] In turn, such attitudinal signalling by unconditional cooperators triggers conditional cooperation from other actors, increasing general compliance rates.[39]

The second factor conceives of consent as a promise. Promises, as a commitment system, have been shown to activate promisers' internal value system, so that people may keep their promises in the absence of external enforcement mechanisms and reputational effects.[40] Experiments show that individuals keep their promises for three reasons:

1) People feel duty bound to keep their promises regardless of whether promisees expect them to do so (promising per se effect);
2) They care about not disappointing promisees' expectations regardless of whether those expectations were induced by the promise (expectations per se effect);
3) They are even more motivated to avoid disappointing promisees' expectations when those expectations were induced by a promise (interaction effect).[41]

Hence, transferring these insights to states as actors of the international legal order, states' consent to a rule would be akin to a promise, which they may feel bound to keep for internal, perceived, or external reasons. In the first case,

---

[36] Tyran and Feld (n 6) 147–153. Exogenous law can however still be useful to resolve coordination problems, rather than cooperative ones; see Iris Bohnet and Robert D Cooter, 'Expressive Law: Framing or Equilibrium Selection?' [2003] SSRN Electronic Journal http://www.ssrn.com/abstract=452420 accessed 19 October 2021.

[37] Tyran and Feld (n 6) 149. The experiment unfortunately did not include symbolic sanctions, but we can hypothesise that this conclusion would also apply to law that is formally only backed by symbolic or reputational sanctions, as is often the case in the international legal order.

[38] This is confirmed by field experiments in a variety of contexts, all confirming that active participation in the making of rules increases compliance, contribution to the public good, and the efficiency of such contributions.

[39] Tyran and Feld (n 6) 150–153.

[40] Florian Ederer and Alexander Stremitzer, 'Promises and Expectations' (2017) 106 Games and Economic Behavior 161, 20.

[41] Dorothee Mischkowski, Rebecca Stone and Alexander Stremitzer, 'Promises, Expectations, and Social Cooperation' (2019) 62 The Journal of Law and Economics 687, 687.

breaching a promise would activate emotions of guilt. This internal sanctioning device (guilt aversion) thus motivates states to keep their promises, irrespective of promisees' expectations. In the second case, both guilt and shame are expected, rightly and hypothetically, were the promise to be breached. The promising state holds beliefs about the expectations of promisees,[42] which influence its beliefs about the possible consequences of its actions (disappointing promisees' expectations). To avoid triggering emotions of guilt, and potentially of shame, the state then keeps its promise. The third case is mostly reliant on shame (although guilt may be underlying) due to the certainty that the promise induced promisees' expectations.

Shame constitutes an external sanctioning device, which can be conceived of as an emotional response to external social pressures. As such, shame is a response to a social threat. It relies on the need to be accepted by others and the fear of rejection. Shame thus constitutes an extremely powerful device to induce actors to self-monitor and comply with social expectations.[43] In the international legal order, informal sanctions involving shame are common. States exist in a social order, and are sensitive to the evaluation of others. Thus, a simple declaration of illegality can induce a state to reverse its behaviour. Further, expressive adjudication, showing disapproval of the behaviour and publicly shaming the rule violator in a judgment, has also been shown to influence the behaviour of the parties to the dispute and of other members of the social order.[44]

Another form of decentralised sanctioning, outcasting, has proven particularly effective in changing state behaviour. Anne van Aaken defines outcasting as 'the use of techniques to deny noncompliant states the benefits of social cooperation and membership or the use of markets'.[45] Outcasting is a non-violent sanctioning device, which threatens to deny the benefits of cooperation in order to encourage cooperation. It is the most pervasive sanctioning device in international law. Outcasting can first take a direct form, like in the WTO with authorised countermeasures, effectively entitling the victorious party to suspend the benefits of membership in the community.[46] Outcasting

---

[42] In economics terms, the expectations of promisees are first-order beliefs, while the promiser's beliefs about those expectations are second-order beliefs. See Ederer and Stremitzer (n 40) 20–23.

[43] Harris (n 18) 64–65.

[44] For a discussion, see Veronika Fikfak, 'Changing State Behaviour: Damages before the European Court of Human Rights' (2018) 29 European Journal of International Law 1091, 1106.

[45] van Aaken (n 2) 1257.

[46] The WTO authorises state parties with legitimate complaints to retaliate against non-compliant states through a limited denial of the 'Most Favoured Nation' status. Such a system provides for outcasting by first parties only. A testimony to the success

can also take an indirect form, as in some human rights institutions, which can make compliance with their decisions a condition of continued membership.[47] Van Aaken explains that outcasting is effective because it is both a cheap and impactful sanctioning device, which works as a shaming device and sets a normative benchmark.[48] In addition, outcasting enhances cooperation between members of the group, which can now see themselves as a 'club', contributing to what have become club goods[49] instead of a more diffuse and non-excludable public good. Further, van Aaken notes that when the exclusion is reversible, it contributes to achieving larger contributions to the public (now club) good.[50] Because of its dependence on cooperative benefits, however, the effectiveness of outcasting is usually proportional to the number of participants in the regime.

The effectiveness of mild and non-material sanctions also depends upon their perceived fairness. The bottom line of experiments on the subject is that, when 'individuals are treated respectfully by an authority, are dealt with in an unbiased fashion, believe the authority has demonstrated trustworthy motives and has taken the individual's concerns into account before reaching a decision, then individuals will evaluate the interaction as more procedurally just'.[51] This evaluation matters because procedural fairness promotes voluntary compliance. Indeed, compliance is more often related to normative concerns linked to the perceived legitimacy of the system than to instrumental concerns.[52] The perceived legitimacy of the authority becomes even more crucial to ensure compliance with laws that might be incompatible with one's values. Consequently, authorities that govern with procedural justice will be better able to foster voluntary compliance, thus avoiding relying too heavily on

---

of the WTO system can be seen in the change of position of the Bush Administration regarding steel tariffs (one of President Bush's main campaign promises) after the WTO allowed the EU to retaliate with tariffs of its own, worth two billion dollars, in 2002. This shows that even the most powerful states can be successfully outcast. For a detailed analysis, see Oona Hathaway and Scott J Shapiro, 'Outcasting: Enforcement in Domestic and International Law' [2011] Yale Law Journal 98.

[47] An example can be found in the successful threat by the Council of Europe's Committee of Ministers to expel Turkey from the organisation if it did not implement the ECtHR's decision in *Loizidou* v. *Turkey* by paying damages to the victim. See Interim Resolution ResDH(2003)174, 12 November 2003.

[48] van Aaken (n 2) 1258.

[49] According to James Buchanan's original terminology, club good are non-rivalrous (like public goods) but excludable (like private goods). James M Buchanan, 'An Economic Theory of Clubs' (1965) 32 Economica 1.

[50] van Aaken (n 2) 1258–1259.

[51] Kristina Murphy, 'Procedural Justice and Its Role in Promoting Voluntary Compliance' in Peter Drahos (ed), *Regulatory Theory* (ANU Press 2017) 47.

[52] Tom R Tyler, *Why People Obey the Law* (Yale University Press 1990).

measures of deterrence.⁵³ The influence of procedural justice over behaviour is explained by Kristina Murphy as involving factors related to social identity and emotions. Receiving fair treatment generates a positive sense of the individual's place in society and motivates them to legitimate the authority and do right by it.⁵⁴ On the contrary, receiving unfair treatment may trigger negative emotions that can lead the individual to question the authority's legitimacy and engage in retaliatory, non-compliant behaviour.⁵⁵

Legitimacy in international law is intimately linked to consent, to the norm itself but also to the competence of an external authority, whatever its nature, to assess and judge the behaviour of the state against the normative standard. This is why a state's network of accountability mechanisms only comprises other states (its sovereign equals) and the non-state actors that the state has consented to recognise as competent. Further, how states perceive the fairness of sanctions also depends on third-party involvement, highlighting the crucial role of international courts, tribunals, and bodies in keeping the international order functioning.⁵⁶ Indeed, as third-party sanctioning devices, they guarantee fair procedures (in contrast with sanctions imposed by other states). In addition, supra-national mechanisms are restricted in the range of sanctions they can impose. The symbolic and mild sanctions they impose are perceived by states as more procedurally fair,⁵⁷ meaning that states will then continue to engage with the authority, perceive it as legitimate, and try to do right by it.⁵⁸ Veronika Fikfak further highlights that, as state compliance is voluntary and international human rights courts have low enforcement authority, courts have to rely on the persuasive strength of their judgments to not only induce compliance with the remedies ordered but also to ensure that states internalise their

---

⁵³ Tyler (n 52).
⁵⁴ Murphy (n 51) 49.
⁵⁵ ibid 49.
⁵⁶ van Aaken (n 2) 1257.
⁵⁷ ibid 1257; and Yuval Shany, 'Assessing the Effectiveness of International Courts: A Goal-Based Approach' (2012) 106 The American Journal of International Law 225, 261 positing that the less objectionable the substantive portion of the judgment to the losing party and the less onerous the remedies issued, the greater the judgment's compliance pull will be. However, the impact of these cheap remedies on state behaviour is likely to be minimal.
⁵⁸ Notwithstanding the poor rates of compliance with regional human rights courts' decisions, especially when non-monetary remedies are imposed as these are considered more costly to implement for the state. See Fikfak (n 44) for the ECtHR; and Darren Hawkins and Wade Jacoby, 'Partial Compliance: A Comparison of the European and Inter-American Courts of Human Rights Engagement and Escape: International Legal Institutions and Public Political Contestation' (2010) 6 Journal of International Law and International Relations 35 for a comparison between the ECtHR and the IACtHR and between various types of remedies.

interpretation of the rule.[59] Procedural fairness and the substantive quality of legal reasoning are thus necessary elements of effective third-party sanctioning. Disinterested unilateral sanctioning by other states may also enjoy some of the benefits of third-party sanctioning due to the perceived legitimacy of the intentions, as does centralised procedurally fair sanctioning by other states, such as outcasting.

The counterparts of sanctions, rewards, have recently triggered interest in international legal scholarship.[60] Analysing the typology and functions of rewards in the international legal order, Anne van Aaken and Betül Simsek put forward a powerful claim: rewards can produce better results than penalties, both on efficiency grounds (Pareto optimality)[61] and on psychological grounds (behavioural differences).[62] Van Aaken and Simsek further show that rewarding is inherent in existing compliance mechanisms such as reciprocity, reputation, and outcasting. From a behavioural perspective, rewards are perceived differently than penalties and their effects are asymmetrical.[63] While penalties are perceived negatively and are likely to trigger resistance and escalation (rather than compliance), rewards are evaluated positively and are often reciprocated.[64] In consequence, rewards tend to increase trust and cooperation and produce de-escalatory behaviour.[65] To enhance compliance, effective regulation therefore needs to account for states' sensitivity to rewarding. The theory of responsive regulation provides the conceptual framework to apprehend both sanctions and rewards within the same regulatory environment.

---

[59] Fikfak (n 44) 1101.

[60] Anne van Aaken and Betül Simsek, 'Rewarding in International Law' (2021) 115 American Journal of International Law 195; Jeffrey L Dunoff, 'Introduction to the Symposium on Anne van Aaken & Betül Simsek, "Rewarding in International Law"' (2021) 115 AJIL Unbound 207; 'Rewarding in International Law (Symposium)' (*Voelkerrechtsblog*), https://voelkerrechtsblog.org/symposium/rewarding-in-international-law/ (accessed 18 June 2021).

[61] Pareto optimality is a situation where no individual or preference criterion can be better off without making at least one individual or preference criterion worse off or without any loss thereof.

[62] van Aaken and Simsek (n 60) 197.

[63] This is explained by prospect theory. Introduced by Kahneman and Tversky, prospect theory is a psychology-based utility theory that characterises decisions among risky alternatives with known probabilities. Prospect theory applies an S-shaped value function that assumes the value of zero at the reference point and is concave on the space of gains and convex on the space of losses. The S-shaped value function embeds loss aversion, according to which a gain generates a utility increase lower than the disutility caused by the same-sized loss. Daniel Kahneman and Amos Tversky, 'Prospect Theory: An Analysis of Decision under Risk' (1979) 47 Econometrica 263.

[64] van Aaken and Simsek (n 60) 227–228.

[65] ibid 227–235.

5.3.2 Responsive Regulation

The essence of responsive regulation is that 'governance should be responsive to the regulatory environment and to the conduct of the regulated in deciding whether a more or less interventionist response is needed'.[66] Responsive regulation can be presented through different models,[67] but its core principle remains that, by having the capacity to escalate to tough enforcement, most regulation can be about collaborative capacity-building. Building on responsive regulation as theorised by Ian Ayres and John Braithwaite,[68] Peter Drahos proposed a theory of networked, or nodal, responsiveness.[69] Drahos' model is applicable in situations whereby an individual regulator does not have the capacity, by itself, to ensure responsive regulation through escalation of supporting activities and sanctions. In networked, nodal responsiveness, the regulator escalates by networking regulatory pressure from other actors.

Networked, nodal responsiveness can suitably be applied to networks of accountability mechanisms to explain their functioning. For instance, following a finding by a supra-national body that a state has committed a wrongful act, other states may take action to enforce the decision and coerce the non-compliant state into complying. Hence, states commonly threaten or impose (targeted) economic sanctions; refuse to recognise certain situations as lawful; break off diplomatic ties; etc. Other supra-national bodies may also decide to wield their own set of tools and adopt resolutions; issue decisions; threaten exclusion; remove some or all of the benefits of membership (such as voting rights); etc. Enforcement may be further reinforced by the actions of individuals, NGOs, and other non-state actors such as transnational corporations, which form part of other nodes.[70]

A theoretical application[71] of networked, nodal responsiveness to the international legal order leads me to describe the process of international legal

---

[66] John Braithwaite, 'Types of Responsiveness' in Peter Drahos (ed), *Regulatory Theory* (ANU Press 2017) 117; see generally John Braithwaite, 'The Essence of Responsive Regulation' (2011) 44 UBC Law Review 475.

[67] For an examination of different types of responsiveness, see Braithwaite, 'Types of Responsiveness' (n 66).

[68] Ian Ayres and John Braithwaite, *Responsive Regulation: Transcending the Deregulation Debate* (Oxford University Press 1992).

[69] Peter Drahos, 'Intellectual Property and Pharmaceutical Markets: A Nodal Governance Approach Symposium on SARS, Public Health, and Global Governance' (2004) 77 Temple Law Review 401.

[70] Reactions against Russia's invasion of Ukraine in February 2022 provide illustrations for all these possibilities.

[71] Broude (n 22) 1132: 'theoretical applications take research scenarios in which a divergence from perfect rationality is noted on the basis of general empirical evidence, and then apply the ramifications to a legal rule or institution'.

accountability. As conceptualised in the previous chapter, international legal accountability is 'the process by which a state legally justifies its performance vis-à-vis other international actors, in which an assessment or judgement of that performance against international legal standards is rendered, and through which consequences can be imposed if the state fails to live up to applicable international legal standards'.[72] The definition does not require that all steps be undertaken by a single actor. In the international legal order, it is recognised that, on the contrary, accountability will be more effective if different actors undertake different steps. Hence, third parties such as international courts and tribunals have more legitimacy to carry out the assessment or judgement of state conduct against legal standards, in addition to ensuring procedural fairness. In contrast, the imposition of consequences, whether rewards, support activities, or sanctions, can be better carried out by international organisations and other states.

Effective responsive regulation implies flexibility in the choice of responses, procedural fairness, signalling the possibility of escalation, and enrolling powerful regulatory partners in networks.[73] These are all attributes that the international legal order possesses. Indeed, the range of available rewards, support activities, and sanctions in international law is limited only by the creativity of the actors involved (unlawful use of force excepted), thus signalling at all times the possibility of escalation to tougher sanctions. The rules of procedure of supra-national judicial and quasi-judicial bodies ensure the procedural fairness of accountability processes, giving a voice to participating states and taking into account their concerns and specific situations. The same can be said, to a lesser extent, of the customary rules on state responsibility, imposing several procedural requirements before countermeasures can be taken and limiting their material and temporal scope.[74]

Finally, because states rely on continued cooperation for survival in a wide variety of domains, powerful enforcement partners almost always exist. Whether they will be willing to participate in enforcing international legality is another matter, but a less difficult one than realists may anticipate. In fact, empirical evidence shows that states routinely act to sanction other states, even if they expect no direct gain from doing it.[75] This is explained by their concerns

---

[72] Chapter 4, section 4.2.3.
[73] See generally Braithwaite, 'The Essence of Responsive Regulation' (n 66); Braithwaite, 'Types of Responsiveness' (n 66).
[74] ASR Part Three, Chapter II.
[75] Apart from the highly mediatised judicial cases involving obligations *erga omnes*, states often act in less visible ways to sanction other states for violations that do not directly affect their rights or interests, or for violations that affect them but for which sanctioning is costly. They do so by using their bargaining power in their inter-

about equality and fairness; by their moral beliefs about what the right thing to do is and the legitimacy of the rule broken; and by the pervasiveness of shaming and outcasting, which are generally cheap sanctioning mechanisms.

5.4 A THEORY OF EFFECTIVE ACCOUNTABILITY

Building upon empirical and theoretical knowledge about networked governance and responsive regulation, it thus becomes possible to identify the factors that make a process of international legal accountability effective, in the sense that it induces a desired change in state behaviour. To that end, I apply the theories of regulation presented above to networks of accountability mechanisms as regulators. I therefore theorise effective accountability as networked, nodal responsive regulation by the international legal order. In the intelligence context, effective accountability should additionally fulfil the objectives of accountability, identified in the previous chapter as (a) enforcing international legality; (b) reliable intelligence; and (c) truth, transparency, and legitimacy.

Thus conceived of, effective accountability becomes possible if and when the network, as a regulator, is able to: (1) respond to states' motivational postures in order to engage them constructively; (2) establish trust-building and communication institutions as part of the network; and (3) effectively deter non-compliant behaviour. The combination of these qualities and abilities provides the regulator network with a range of responses (rewards, support activities, and sanctions) needed to achieve (networked, nodal) responsive regulation in the form of effective accountability.

Effective regulation is sometimes mistakenly assumed to consist solely of deterrence. The idea behind deterrence theory is that, generally, actors will be deterred from breaching the law when the legal or social penalty they would receive for a breach, multiplied by the likelihood of swift detection and conviction, outweighs the gain. Deterrence-based policies thus aim at lowering the anticipated gains of illegal behaviour by raising its costs. More than the actual risk of being held accountable, however, the *perception* of the risk is what deters actors from breaching the law.[76] The severity and variety of sanctions at

---

actions with other states and in the negotiation of treaties, and often impose economic sanctions that are detrimental to their interests (e.g., the economic sanctions imposed on Russia after the annexation of Crimea and after the invasion of Ukraine; or the (few) arms embargoes against Saudi Arabia). They also do so through diplomatic démarches; official statements; decisions to continue or suspend trade activities; investigations and reports on specific situations or incidents; the exercise of universal jurisdiction; etc.

[76] Christine Parker and Vibeke Nielsen, 'Compliance: 14 Questions' in Peter Drahos (ed), *Regulatory Theory* (ANU Press 2017) 228.

the disposal of the regulator influence this perception,[77] as does the apparent willingness of the network to use them. Yet, a regulator relying exclusively on the fear of sanctions would be neither efficient nor effective. Further, behavioural approaches show that raising the anticipated value of legal behaviour relative to illegal ones, i.e. rewarding, is often more effective.[78] In consequence, although deterrence is an important component of effective regulation, it cannot constitute its only strategy. Further, the deterrent effect pursued by a regulator is enhanced by previous and continuous supportive actions from that regulator. Deterrence thus forms part of a wider set of strategies and tools that a regulator may use, depending on context.

Context, aside from obvious exogenous elements, is mostly made up by the motivational postures adopted by states, which should direct the type of response adopted by the regulator. Motivational postures, as conceptualised by Valerie Braithwaite, are the signals or messages that actors send to the regulator about the control it purportedly has over them. They thus communicate various levels of social distance, liking, and deference.[79] Braithwaite identifies five motivational postures, from easiest to most challenging for the authority: commitment; capitulation; resistance; disengagement; and game-playing.[80]

Because motivational postures are not only shaped by stable world-views, but also by contextual variables, the regulatory authority has the power to influence them.[81] Hence, the regulator needs to adapt its response to meet the motivational posture of the actor before it. While the first two postures (commitment and capitulation) signal accommodation to the authority, resistance signals dissatisfaction with the way the authority is doing its job. Increased procedural justice should therefore be the response to a posture of resistance. Both disengagement and game-playing threaten the authority of the regulator, its enforcement capacity, and its legitimacy. The challenge then concerns the regulator's moral authority, i.e., its power to decide what the right thing to do is. Braithwaite thus explains that, to positively influence actors adopting these challenging postures, regulation requires the force of the law, credible

---

[77] In this respect, unpredictable damages/sanctions have a better deterrent effect than fully predictable or certain damages/sanctions. Fikfak (n 44) 1113.

[78] Laura Dugan and Erica Chenoweth, 'Moving Beyond Deterrence: The Effectiveness of Raising the Expected Utility of Abstaining from Terrorism in Israel' (2012) 77 American Sociological Review 597; van Aaken and Simsek (n 60).

[79] Valerie Braithwaite, 'Closing the Gap between Regulation and the Community' in Peter Drahos (ed), *Regulatory Theory* (ANU Press 2017) 33.

[80] ibid 33–35.

[81] ibid 35.

enforcement, and society's backing to add normative moral strength to the regulator's actions.[82]

Regardless of the motivational posture, but especially if it challenges the regulator, procedural fairness is key. It is the main source of legitimacy and can drive resistant and game-playing actors to capitulation when coupled with credible enforcement. Together, procedural fairness and credible enforcement signal the moral importance of the rule, and the fair but nevertheless punitive treatment to which non-compliers expose themselves. Braithwaite thus highlights the necessity for the regulator to elicit moral obligations, ensure justice, and provide benefits in order to obtain and maintain compliance from a variety of actors with differing interests.[83]

In order to engage with dissenting voices constructively, a networked regulator needs more than legitimacy and procedural fairness. It also needs to enhance trust and communication, through institutional devices and mechanisms. This is especially true in the international legal order, as the beliefs that states hold about the intentions of other actors determine, to a great extent, their willingness to cooperate.[84] Communication between actors is crucial to ensure a shared understanding of the rules and to uphold trust that others will comply with them and cooperate to enforce them. In the international legal order, the argumentative value of, for instance, justifying one's actions through legal interpretation of an international obligation, reaffirms one's commitment to the rule.[85] It is not merely cheap talk.[86] Instead, it provides all other actors with credible reassurances of a continued willingness to cooperate and abide by the rules. Most of international law can be considered an incomplete contract,[87] and it often relies on promises not backed up by a high probability of direct sanctions. Therefore, upholding communication and trust is crucial to the (good) functioning of the system.[88] Further, communication displays a posture of engagement with the system of international law, allowing the regulator to be responsive and adapt its strategy accordingly.

---

[82] ibid 35–37.
[83] ibid 36.
[84] van Aaken (n 2) 1251–1252.
[85] Hakimi (n 35) 1300.
[86] See generally Hurd (n 32). Note, however, that this does not apply to absurd uses of international law rhetoric: Fuad Zarbiyev, 'Of Bullshit, Lies and "Demonstrably Rubbish" Justifications in International Law' (*Voelkerrechtsblog*, 18 March 2022) https://voelkerrechtsblog.org/of-bullshit-lies-and-demonstrably-rubbish-justifications-in-international-law/ accessed 19 March 2022.
[87] On this aspect, see van Aaken (n 20) 460:'International law is incomplete due to its long-term nature and multilateral character and often lacks specified sanctions for non-compliance'.
[88] van Aaken (n 2) 1255.

In the international legal order, which is a consent-based system, the regulator can provide a variety of rewards, supporting activities, and sanctions, thereby embodying the qualities necessary to make it an effective responsive regulator. As states seek to legitimate their behaviour and choices of policies through legal justification, the regulator also has a role to play in shaping common understandings of legality. International courts and bodies, in their advisory and contentious capacities, participate in developing and accrediting legal interpretations, either legitimating or undermining states' justifications. The evolving nature of international law and its incomplete character require that courts and bodies do so in a constantly self-adapting and responsive manner, hearing and taking into account states' arguments fairly. Hence, in order to engage with all states, including those expressing dissenting positions as to the interpretation of a legal rule, accountability mechanisms must exemplify independence and procedural fairness. Upon this depends states' acceptance of their decisions as fair and legitimate, and thus states' willingness to comply and share their concerns transparently. In addition, where the interpretation of a legal rule is at stake (as is often the case in international law), procedural fairness and legitimacy will ensure that the authority's chosen interpretation is accepted as 'true', triggering capitulation on the part of resistant states.

Following the representation of responsive regulation through the pyramids of supports and sanctions offered by John Braithwaite,[89] I propose a simplified generic representation of effective accountability as responsive regulation in the international legal order in Figure 5.1.

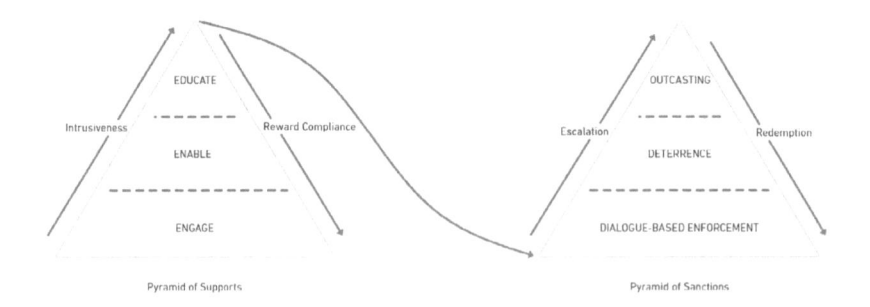

Figure 5.1   *Pyramids of supports and sanctions*

---

[89] See Braithwaite, 'Types of Responsiveness' (n 66) for a summary and http://johnbraithwaite.com/responsive-regulation/ for examples of topical pyramids of supports and sanctions.

The principle is that the regulator should first go through the available support activities (pyramid of supports), starting with the least intrusive intervention and moving up the pyramid to stronger support activities, as necessary. Only when these fail or when support activities would be useless should the regulator move to the pyramid of sanctions. Following this order underlines the value of persuasion (engagement), capacity-building (enabling), and education as the first steps to achieve compliance. This applies to all field of international law and proves especially true in IHRL.[90] Clarification of legal norms and expectations, open communication, and trust-enhancing devices are crucial at this stage. Examples of such support activities include, for instance, non-contentious procedures such as reporting obligations and the resulting concluding observations of treaty bodies; the universal periodic review (UPR); the activities of UN special mandate holders; or, in other fields, OSCE field missions and training activities; WHO country cooperation strategy; or EU cooperation and development policies. All are accountability processes, but they do not directly involve sanctions. Rather, they constitute support activities and may trigger the imposition of consequences, which may be positive (rewards) or negative (escalation). If the escalation of support activities fails to induce compliance, the regulator may then move to the pyramid of sanctions.

The pyramid of sanctions is designed in such a way that the very possibility of escalation reduces the need to escalate to tougher sanctions. The base of the pyramid represents restorative justice and dialogue-based enforcement. It embodies the necessity of engaging resistant actors with fairness, to give them a voice, and to address each situation with flexibility. To some extent, this first stage overlaps with support activities in the international legal order. 'Restorative justice' sanctions thus include dialogue-based procedures such as reporting obligations, the UPR, special mandate holders' procedures, but also mediation, facilitation, integrative negotiation, and many other mechanisms well known to the international legal order. They differ from support activities mostly in the fact that the possibility of escalation to stronger sanctions is made clear. Yet, by signalling (but not threatening) this possibility, the regulator demonstrates fairness, builds its legitimacy, and encourages compliance with the decision taken at the dialogue stage.

The second stage of the pyramid is deterrence. There, sanctions should be strong enough that the (perceived) costs would deter any rational actor from pursuing the non-compliant behaviour. It is thus useful to enlist and activate powerful regulatory actors in the network to increase these costs. Deterrence

---

[90] For a theoretical application to the international human rights system, see Hilary Charlesworth, 'A Regulatory Perspective on the International Human Rights System' in Peter Drahos (ed), *Regulatory Theory* (ANU Press 2017).

functions as a rational choice problem. As Equation 5.1 shows, a rational state will comply with international law if the costs of compliance outweigh the benefits of non-compliance minus the costs of non-compliance:

$$Costs\ C\ /\ Benefits\ NC - Costs\ NC > 1^* \qquad (5.1)$$

*With C = Compliance; NC = Non-Compliance; and all values > 0

In the international legal order, these costs can take at least two main forms. They can be direct costs (countermeasures, economic sanctions, authorised use of force, suspension of voting rights, etc.), usually imposed by other states directly or through intergovernmental organisations. They can also be of a reputational (sometimes called 'symbolic') nature and participate in politically delegitimising the state, as is the case when another state and/or supra-national institution declares that the state has violated its obligations. Direct and reputational costs are not exclusive of one another. Rather, they reinforce each other through the various emotions and responses they respectively and conjointly trigger in the non-compliant state.

The success of a deterrence strategy depends largely upon the state's perception of the costs. This variable is a function of the value accorded by the state to relevant aspects of its reputation and to (continued) cooperation with other states. It is also a function of the state's perception of the legitimacy of the rule breached and of the sanction, amongst other things. Hence, it is once again the state's perception that matters most, meaning that fairness, responsiveness, and flexibility in the choice of sanctions are all necessary to achieve deterrence. In this regard, experiments have shown that when fines are publicly presented as a punishment or a sanction, they are more likely to have a deterrent effect than when they are presented as compensation or lack publicity.[91] In international law, retributive sanctions should however not be perceived as unfair if constructive engagement with the state is to be maintained. Yet, at least in human rights law, even if high-value punitive damages might not be paid, 'they may nevertheless encourage states to conduct a cost-benefit analysis and conclude that it is best to get rid of structural/systemic problems than to continue the

---

[91] Tim Kurz, William E Thomas and Miguel A Fonseca, 'A Fine Is a More Effective Financial Deterrent When Framed Retributively and Extracted Publicly' (2014) 54 Journal of Experimental Social Psychology 170. Note, however, that punitive sanctions are the exception in public international law, and that the reparation for a wrongful act entails and is limited to appropriate compensatory action. See ASR, Article 31.

violation'.[92] Deterrence may thus benefit from retributive sanctions in certain cases, through their effect on states' calculations.

The tip of the pyramid of sanctions is incapacitation. In the international legal order, this mostly refers to outcasting, potentially accompanied by other sanctions. This sometimes costly punitive measure is reserved for situations in which all other persuasive and deterring tools fail or would otherwise be ineffective. Exclusion from a group is the ultimate sanction that the network can take, effectively preventing the non-compliant state from being considered an equal with the right to participate and access group-exclusive benefits. These benefits may be economic, military, reputational, or of another nature. Hence, a state could be excluded from trading privileges or from a military-support organisation such as NATO; or it could lose the political legitimacy of membership in a human rights organisation; or face targeted economic and political sanctions resulting in its isolation on the international scene; etc.

Without the possibility of incapacitation (and thus of true escalation), however, the network's regulatory power is often less effective. Indeed, a calculating state may realise that the costs of available lower-level sanctions do not outweigh the benefits of noncompliance, and will therefore endure lower-level sanctions without altering its behaviour.[93] Similarly, the state may simply be unable to comply. Provided all supporting activities have previously failed, incapacitation in the form of outcasting would be the only appropriate response in both cases. Otherwise, regulation becomes costly and would have to rely on constant surveillance and coercion – yet without guarantees of effectiveness – resulting in it being perceived as less legitimate. This loss of legitimacy in turn affects effectiveness. Indeed, as the system is based upon the capacity to escalate, credible and sufficiently regular escalation is essential for the system to function effectively, i.e., enforcing legality mostly through collaborative capacity-building.

In addition, the possibility of redemption, or de-escalation, is crucial to give hope to disengaged and/or excluded actors and re-engage them constructively. As Braithwaite puts it, 'the pyramid is firm yet forgiving in its demands for compliance'.[94] De-escalation, or the removal of a penalty, produces the effect

---

[92] Fikfak (n 44) 1125 with regard to seemingly punitive damages awarded by the ECtHR in the case of *Cyprus* v. *Turkey*.

[93] Fikfak (n 44) 1115–1116 gives as an example of this type of calculation Russia's budgeting for ECtHR compensation, which increased substantially between 2010 and 2016 without the sources of the violations being addressed. She concludes that, 'rather than invest money into addressing systemic problems and breaches ..., Russia instead puts money towards compensating human rights violations'.

[94] Braithwaite, 'Types of Responsiveness' (n 66) 119.

of a reward and should thus be a key part of a responsive regulatory strategy.[95] Further, by rewarding compliance, the regulator increases the benefits of such compliance relative to non-compliance.[96] Whereas sanctions may be perceived as unfair and trigger disengagement or backlash, rewards that support fairness perceptions can increase positive engagement and compliance.[97]

Furthermore, rewarding compliance not only alters the calculations made by states who behave according to a rational-choice model, but naming and praising also validates the social status of states whose motive for complying is to be perceived as rule-compliant. Rewarding compliance likewise motivates the remaining actors and ensures their continued cooperation. Indeed, as van Aaken explains, following the outcasting of one member, remaining actors begin seeing public goods as club goods (group benefits) and consequently better perceive the advantages of belonging and of cooperating.[98]

5.5 EVALUATING ACCOUNTABILITY: A FRAMEWORK

In this section, I translate empirical and theoretical insights about effective accountability into factors that can be qualitatively evaluated. I further tailor these factors to state accountability for wrongful acts resulting from intelligence activities. The evaluative framework thus developed aims to assess the theoretical potential of the international legal order, as a regulator, to provide accountability in the intelligence context. Such accountability, when it exists, will not necessarily be effective in inducing compliance. However, the stronger the potential of the network to provide accountability, the higher the chance that the resulting accountability will be effective.

Insights regarding international legal accountability can be broadly classified as belonging to one of three types: those related to the capacity of the network of accountability mechanisms to constrain and escalate sanctions; those related to the legitimacy of the network as a regulator and regulating authority; and those concerned with the accessibility and publicity of both the regulator and the proceedings. These three categories are then sub-divided into factors informing the theoretical strength of the network and used to evaluate that strength. Table 5.1 presents the evaluative framework. I examine each factor in the following subsections.

---

[95] van Aaken and Simsek (n 60) 196.
[96] van Aaken and Simsek (n 60).
[97] ibid 231.
[98] van Aaken (n 2) 1258.

Table 5.1   Evaluation factors

	Evaluation Factors
Capacity to Constrain and Escalate	Jurisdiction *ratione materiae*
	Jurisdiction *ratione personae*
	Investigatory powers
	Powers to sanction non-cooperation
	Capacity to order remedies
	Capacity to sanction
	Reputation of account-holder state:
	– Standing in the international legal order
	– Relative power
	– Human rights records
	Capacity of account-holder state to constrain compliance:
	– Interdependencies
	– Leverage tools
Legitimacy	Overall reputation
	Participation of the state under scrutiny
	Capacity to reward compliance or de-escalate
	Independence:
	– Budget and resources
	– Formal independence
	– Judicial independence
	– Relative power (state)
Publicity and Accessibility	Representation of public interest
	Publicity of proceedings
	Publicity of outcomes
	Accessibility to non-state account-holders:
	– Information
	– Financial and geographical accessibility
	– Procedural accessibility

5.5.1   The Capacity to Constrain and Escalate

This first set of factors is the one in which the networked interaction between indirect and direct forms of accountability is the most important. In the current state of the international legal order, individual accountability forums rarely possess a deep escalation capacity or even the capacity to formally sanction at all. Yet, their decisions may still have a strong compliance pull. This may be because their decisions have an impact on other actors' conduct, who possess a stronger capacity to escalate; because the expressive power of the forum's decisions is so strong that it is enough in and of itself to induce compliance; or because of a myriad of other reasons and combinations thereof. The bottom line is that, as the sanctioning tools of all the actors of the network add up, so does the capacity of the network as a whole to constrain a state into compliance. The capacity to constrain and escalate comprises several evaluative factors, some of which may be better embodied by specific actors of the international legal order.

First, a mediated accountability forum is better able to induce compliance if it possesses a broad enough jurisdiction *ratione materiae* that allows it to hold the state accountable for all components of the wrongful act or harmful outcome. In addition, it is desirable that, together, the network's forums hold a jurisdiction *ratione personae* that allows them to (potentially) hold all – or as many as possible – involved states to account. The deterrent effect of a decision by a forum with universal jurisdiction will thus be stronger, as potentially all states could be held to account by that forum for similar acts. Jurisdiction *ratione personae* is also linked to the forum's standing and legitimacy, examined below, because the forum's reputation for procedural fairness helps induce states to consent to its jurisdiction.

A mediated accountability forum will also be better at inducing compliance if it possesses investigatory powers allowing it to, for instance, compel witnesses or order the disclosure of (classified) documents.[99] Such powers allow the forum to obtain the information necessary for the establishment of truth and to make an informed judgement on the regulated state's conduct. Investigatory powers are one of the main strengths of supra-national accountability mechanisms compared to domestic ones: they are not bound by doctrines of state secrecy and can even impose consequences on the state for a failure to cooperate with the investigation.[100] The power to impose interim remedies and sanctions in cases of non-cooperation constitutes an incentive for states to cooperate with the investigation. It also enhances the forum's ability to enforce

---

[99] ECtHR, *Roman Zakharov* v. *Russia*, App. No. 47143/06, 4 December 2015, para 281; Martin Scheinin, 'Report of the Special Rapporteur on the Promotion and Protection of Human Rights and Fundamental Freedoms While Countering Terrorism, Martin Scheinin. Compilation of Good Practices on Legal and Institutional Frameworks and Measures that Ensure Respect for Human Rights by Intelligence Agencies While Countering Terrorism, Including on Their Oversight' (UN General Assembly, Human Rights Council 2010) A/HRC/14/46 Good Practice 7.

[100] See, e.g., the ECtHR cases against Poland, finding a violation of Article 38 for failure to cooperate with the Court. ECtHR, *Al-Nashiri* v. *Poland*, App. No. 28761/11, 24 July 2014, para 376; *Husayn (Abu Zubaydah)* v. *Poland*, App. No. 7511/13, 24 July 2014, para 369.

international legality and establish the truth. If a forum is able to authoritatively establish the truth by compelling disclosure and state cooperation with the investigation, its findings will then be useful to the other actors of the accountability network.

At least some of the network's actors need to have the capacity to order direct sanctions.[101] Here, sanctions are distinguished from mere consequences, which can be positive or negative and simply result from the publicity of the decision taken by a forum, or of the proceedings. Consequences can be sufficient to induce further compliance.[102] However, the deterrent effect of reputational and material sanctions and the possibility of their direct imposition by one of the actors help to make them an effective tool to respond to breaches of international law and induce compliance, both *ex ante* and with the remedies ordered.[103] In mediated accountability proceedings, in addition to the consequences common to all forms of accountability, it is also desirable that the forum can order remedies for account-holder victims.

A state's perception of the likelihood and severity of enforcement procedures and of sanctions is more likely to influence its behaviour than the mere existence of penalties and enforcement procedures that are disregarded. Therefore, if it appears that the general community of states is not willing to use their sanctioning tools against a state in breach of its obligations, it is all the more important that institutional accountability mechanisms possess a capacity to order sanctions and use it regularly enough. In contrast, if other states are willing to assist in enforcing international legality, then the role of sanctions in mediated accountability proceedings is less crucial: a symbolic finding of illegality can be enforced by other states.

How effectively states can constrain one of them into compliance depends on two main factors. The first one is the reputation of the account-holder state. This includes its standing in the international order (e.g., membership of relevant international institutions); its power relative to the power wielder state (the more the better); and its human rights record if the legal standard at stake is a human rights norm.[104] The second factor is the capacity of the account-holder state to constrain the power wielder in practice. This refers to the tools available to the account-holder to pressure the power wielder into complying with its legal obligations. This factor takes into account the specific

---

[101] ECtHR, *Roman Zakharov* v. *Russia* (n 99), para 282; Venice Commission 'Report on the Democratic Oversight of Signals Intelligence Agencies' CDL-AD(2015)011-e.

[102] Andreas Schedler (ed), *The Self-Restraining State: Power and Accountability in New Democracies* (Lynne Rienner Publ 1999) 21.

[103] Ruth W Grant and Robert O Keohane, 'Accountability and Abuses of Power in World Politics' (2005) 99 American Political Science Review 29, 30.

[104] ibid 40.

relationships and dependencies between the two states which may play a role independently of general power imbalances and provide for negotiation constraints (e.g., trade or intelligence).[105]

5.5.2 Legitimacy

Actors belonging to an accountability network will be more effective in inducing compliance when they are perceived as legitimate in this function, i.e., when they have authoritative standing.[106] Their legitimacy rests on their overall reputation; the procedural fairness of their decision-making; and their (perceived) independence. Legitimacy increases engagement by states, who will endeavour to appear compliant with both the law and the decision of the forum or of other states. When states value approval of their conduct by a forum or another state because they perceive them as legitimate authorities, accountability processes are more meaningful and the network's decisions or enforcement measures are more readily accepted and respected. This feeling of fairness is further enhanced if the network can de-escalate the sanctions when compliance is achieved, and if it can reward compliance.

The network's actors should be independent from the power wielder state.[107] Interdependence between states of the international community is the norm, and independence is therefore heavily linked to the power relationship between two states. A state that relies on another for survival or protection will not be in a position to call that state to account for human rights violations. Powerful states are thus more likely to be independent enough to call others to account, as will be the case for states that are part of a powerful group of states (such as the EU or NATO) with regard to states outside the group.

When it comes to mediated accountability forums, independence does not exclude the possibility that the state under scrutiny will be the 'creator' of an accountability mechanism, nor that its funding is provided by this state or its members elected by it. What matters is that the state under scrutiny cannot influence the outcome of accountability proceedings by pressuring individual members or the forum as a whole. Other structural considerations come into

---

[105] ibid 40.

[106] See Principle 31(a) of the UN OHCHR 2011 Guiding Principles on Business and Human Rights ('Effectiveness criteria for non-judicial grievance mechanisms').

[107] ECtHR, *Roman Zakharov* v. *Russia* (n 99), para 275. For judicial mechanisms, see the indicators of independence developed in the European Network of Councils for the Judiciary's 2017 Report: 'Report on Independence, Accountability and Quality of the Judiciary – Performance Indicators' ('ENCJ 2017'). Those indicators apply by analogy to quasi-judicial mechanisms and all accountability mechanisms performing similar functions.

play, such as the budget of the accountability mechanism.[108] The forum should have adequate, and if possible independent, resources allowing it to conduct the proceedings without withdrawal of funding being a threatening tool at the disposal of the state under scrutiny.[109] The forum's efficiency of functioning, an important evaluative criterion,[110] is therefore necessarily linked to its funding and independence, in addition to state cooperation, which depends heavily on the forum's legitimacy and standing. For judicial and quasi-judicial mechanisms, the independence of the judges (or members performing functions akin to judicial ones) is a crucial feature of independence. It is ensured and measured through various factors, such as: the qualification of judges; the basis of appointment or promotion; tenure (period of appointment and irremovability); remuneration; and freedom from undue external influence.[111]

5.5.3 Publicity and Accessibility

Publicity is a twofold criterion. It first concerns the accountability process and refers to the accountability mechanism's agency. Publicity enhances the legitimacy of the proceedings and ensures that the public interest is represented. Representation can take several forms depending on the form of accountability. In mediated accountability proceedings, at the minimum, a public watchdog such as an ombudsperson will act as a public interest defender. However, public hearings and the publication of parties' submissions throughout the proceedings should be preferred when possible. In direct accountability proceedings, publicity regarding the account-holder state's reasons for holding the state to account is fundamental to ensure public knowledge, drive support and leverage, and, ultimately, induce compliance.

In addition, and fundamentally, publicity concerns the outcome of the proceedings. Without publicity surrounding the decisions taken by the accountability network, there is no accountability.[112] Accountability exposes states' actions to view and makes public how they compare to applicable legal standards. It is a consequence in itself, but also goes beyond: it provides information to the international community about the consequences that certain conduct may trigger and is thus crucial to the efficacy of the whole system of enforce-

---

[108] ENCJ 2017 (n 107) 11.
[109] Scheinin (n 99) Good Practice 7.
[110] ENCJ 2017 (n 107).
[111] ECtHR, *Campbell and Fell* v. *United Kingdom*, Apps. No. 7819/77 and 7878/77, 28 June 1984, para 78; Venice Commission, 'Report on the Independence of the Judicial System. Part I: The Independence of Judges', CDL-AD(2010)004.
[112] Schedler (n 102) 21.

ment of international legality.¹¹³ Further, publicity surrounding a forum's decision or a state's reasons for action is necessary for other actors of the network to take enforcement action.

In addition, mediated accountability forums should be accessible to account-holders.¹¹⁴ First, individuals and non-state actors need to be informed about their existence. Then, financial or geographical concerns should not disproportionately hinder access to the forum, and neither should impairments attributable to the power wielder (e.g., detention of the individual or enforcement of state secrecy or impunity doctrines) bar access. To remain accessible, forums may thus need to adapt their rules of admissibility, procedure, and evidence to the specificities of intelligence cases.¹¹⁵

5.6 CONCLUSIONS: EFFECTIVE ACCOUNTABILITY AS A BRIDGE BETWEEN ACCOUNTABILITY AND COMPLIANCE

This chapter theorised effective accountability, identifying the conditions required for international legal accountability to constitute an effective regulatory tool. Being relevant to both Parts II (Accountability) and III (Compliance) of the book, the theoretical framework put forward in this chapter forms the basis of the analysis conducted in Chapters 6 and 7.

As actors of the international legal order, states often adopt courses of action or make choices that may appear erroneous or irrational to an external observer. General theories of international law fail to capture the triggers, influences, and emotional responses underlying much of states' choices. These are, however, well described and evidenced by cognitive psychology and behavioural economics. Insights from these two disciplines can be merged into behavioural approaches to international law, and their experimental findings carefully applied or replicated using states as units of analysis.

In this chapter, I first analysed the role of legality as the first layer of regulation. By itself, law can be enough to influence state behaviour towards compliance. States are bounded rational entities, and legal norms – even without any enforcement mechanism – often suffice to trigger compliant behaviour through states' various biases and heuristics. Second, interpreting applicable behavioural insights through the lens of regulatory theory, I proposed that the international legal order be conceived of as the regulator of states' actions.

---

¹¹³ Grant and Keohane (n 103) 41; Schedler (n 102) 21.
¹¹⁴ UN Guiding Principles on Business and Human Rights, Principle 31(b). See also ENCJ 2017 (n 107).
¹¹⁵ ECtHR, *Szabo and Vissy* v. *Hungary*, App. No. 37138/14, 12 January 2016, para 33.

Conceptualised as a network of accountability mechanisms unique to each state, the international legal order obeys a networked, nodal mode of governance. I further analysed international legal accountability as a form of responsive regulation, regulating states' decisions through supporting activities, rewards, and escalating sanctions. Third, combining behavioural insights and regulatory theory, I put forward a theory of effective accountability. I theorised effective accountability as networked, nodal responsive regulation by the international legal order.

The interaction and integration of cognitive and behavioural mechanisms, social factors, and theories of regulation into a single theoretical framework provides the necessary background to apprehend effective accountability as a means to effectively regulate states' activities in the international legal order. This theoretical framework lays the ground for an empirical description of state behaviour and of the factors influencing it, and leads to an evidence-based description of the factors underlying states' decision-making processes in intelligence matters in Chapter 7. The third layer of regulation (compliance), building on this theoretical framework, will be further theorised and modelled there.

Finally, translating these general empirical and theoretical insights into the field of intelligence and into evaluative factors, I operationalised international legal accountability and proposed an evaluative framework. The theoretical strength of any network of accountability mechanisms (i.e., the international legal order as a regulator) may therefore be assessed according to three groups of factors: the network's capacity to constrain and escalate; its legitimacy; and the publicity and accessibility of the network and of its procedures. The evaluative framework provides the means to assess the potential of the international legal order to hold a state accountable in intelligence matters. In the following chapter, such potential will be compared against actual accountability for five states in the CIA-led war on terror. This comparison will allow me to assess the role and limits of accountability in the regulation of intelligence activities under international law.

6. International legal accountability in the CIA war on terror

6.1 INTRODUCTION

A state can be responsible for an internationally wrongful act without being held to account for it. But what determines whether a state will be held accountable? In this chapter, focusing on the second layer of regulation (accountability), I critically assess whether a strong network of accountability mechanisms necessarily correlates with higher rates of accountability for international wrongful acts resulting from intelligence activities. For this purpose, I build on the mapping exercise of state responsibility in the CIA war on terror (Chapter 3) and analyse the accountability levels of five states: the United States of America (US); Djibouti; Poland; the Gambia; and the United Kingdom (UK).

As recently highlighted by the current UN Special Rapporteur on the promotion and protection of human rights and fundamental freedoms while countering terrorism, Fionnuala Ní Aoláin, accountability in the war on terror remains a crucial and salient issue.[1] The lack of meaningful accountability for the practices of the war on terror has normalised such practices all around the world and entrenched its trade-offs philosophy. In consequence, using the CIA war on terror as a case-study is particularly appropriate. Not only are its facts public, but two decades of hindsight allow me to analyse where accountability is still lacking and identify the reasons why. Pinpointing the factors hindering or improving accountability in this context thus holds significant implications for the regulation of intelligence in the twenty-first-century security landscape.

The states selected for this case-study represent typical cases along a dual scale: the variety of conducts adopted by states in the CIA programme; and the variety of accountability networks. This case selection method (typical

---

[1] 'Follow-up report to the joint study on global practices in relation to secret detention in the context of countering terrorism. Report of the Special Rapporteur on the promotion and protection of human rights and fundamental freedoms while countering terrorism, Fionnuala Ní Aoláin', A/HRC/49/45, 25 March 2022.

cases)[2] allows for the selection of states whose conduct in the CIA programme covers all possible forms of wrongful participation identified in Chapter 3. In addition, I selected these five states among the pool of possible states for each type of conduct based on the variety of their accountability networks, in terms of membership but also of theoretical strength. Together, these five states thus represent the full range of conducts and the widest variety of accountability networks. This case-study thus aims at presenting a representative picture of the state of accountability in the CIA war on terror both in terms of state conduct and in terms of accountability networks.

Using a grid of competent institutional accountability mechanisms regarding the CIA war on terror (see Appendix 6.1), I identify the competent network of accountability mechanisms (referred to as 'accountability networks' hereinafter) for each state. I then analyse the theoretical potential of each state's network, applying the evaluation factors developed in Chapter 5. I qualitatively evaluate accountability networks under each of the factors, on a scale comprising three levels: weak – medium – strong. In this way, a general appraisal of the network's potential is made possible. Then, I assess international practice against the theoretical potential of each accountability network. The chapter is first divided into state-specific sections, all of which follow an identical structure:

(1) Identification of the wrongful acts committed by the state and its corresponding international responsibility;
(2) Identification of the competent institutional accountability network for the state;
(3) Evaluation of the accountability network;
(4) Assessment of international practice against the potential of the accountability network.

Finally, in section 6.7, I draw conclusions from the analysis and seek to explain discrepancies between the theoretical potential of the network and actual accountability by identifying additional factors influencing accountability. The case-study further highlights that, although there exists a correlation between the theoretical potential of a network and actual accountability, a good network alone is insufficient to provide effective accountability. The theoretical potential of the network represents the upper limit of what effective regulation can

---

[2] Under this case selection method, the selected cases (one or more) are typical examples of some cross-case relationships. John Gerring, 'Case Selection for Case-Study Analysis: Qualitative and Quantitative Techniques' in Janet M Box-Steffensmeier, Henry E Brady and David Collier (eds), *The Oxford Handbook of Political Methodology* (Oxford University Press 2008).

achieve, but extra-legal factors must be taken into account for regulation to be effective at inducing compliance.

6.2 THE UNITED STATES OF AMERICA

6.2.1 State Responsibility

The United States' responsibility is engaged for conduct by the CIA and private contractors (performing similar activities)[3] that constitutes internationally wrongful acts. These include violations of interstate obligations, violations of IHRL in respect of the 131 identified victims of the programme, and violations of IHL in respect of those victims captured during the time and on the territory of the armed conflicts in Afghanistan and Iraq.[4] US responsibility is engaged as principal wrongdoer in most, if not all, instances of collaborative breaches. Save in extremely specific and exceptional situations,[5] there is no circumstance precluding wrongfulness that can be successfully invoked to excuse US agents' conduct.

6.2.2 Accountability Network

The US's accountability network is not particularly strongly endowed. Its institutional network, as presented in Figure 6.1, could be described as minimalist. The US has not consented to the jurisdiction of any optional judicial or quasi-judicial mechanism with regard to individual complaints. In consequence, only special mandate holders and the Human Rights Council (HRC) can receive individual communications – a faculty that requires no consent from states. Interstate complaints are not likely either: the interstate complaint procedures of the Human Rights Committee (CCPR) and the Committee against Torture (UNCAT), the only ones to which the US has consented, have never been used.

Nevertheless, ad hoc acceptance of jurisdiction in interstate and individual complaint cases remains possible before the Inter-American Commission on Human Rights (IACHR). Similarly, acceptance of the ICJ's jurisdiction

---

[3] Their acts are attributable to the state under Article 5 of the International Law Commission, Draft Articles on Responsibility of States for Internationally Wrongful Acts 2001 (Supplement No 10 (A/56/10), chpIVE1) 76.

[4] See Chapter 3, section 3.3.2 for details.

[5] Chapter 3, section 3.3.4.8 envisages the possibility of consent being invoked as a circumstance precluding the violation of breaches of Articles 3(c) and 4 of the Chicago Convention towards some NATO member states.

remains possible, both in individual cases and through treaties' jurisdictional clauses. In addition to the ICAO Council in respect of violations of the Chicago Convention,[6] the ICJ and the ICC are the only actors of the network with the competence to issue decisions binding upon the US and its nationals, respectively. Indeed, while the US is not a state party to the Rome Statute,[7] US nationals may still appear before the ICC if they are accused of having committed international crimes on the territory of a state party;[8] or if a situation in which US nationals are implicated is referred to the ICC prosecutor by the Security Council acting under Chapter VII of the Charter of the United Nations.[9]

After the Cold War, the US assumed a privileged role as the sole remaining 'superpower' and furthered its strategic position in international organisations. In addition, successive US administrations have invested in defence and national security in monumental proportions. These factors mean that the role (if any) to be played by other states as account-holders or enforcers does not depend upon a general power relationship (unavoidably favouring the US), but rather upon how much the US needs their cooperation. In intelligence matters, and especially in counterterrorism matters, no state can be self-sufficient.[10] The necessities of cooperation might thus provide bargaining power and influence to the US's foreign intelligence partners, although not necessarily favouring compliance.[11]

Figure 6.1 visually presents the United States' institutional accountability network.

---

[6] International Civil Aviation Organization, Convention on Civil Aviation (Chicago Convention) 1944 (15 UNTS 295).

[7] UN General Assembly, Rome Statute of the International Criminal Court (last amended 2010), 17 July 1998, in force 1 July 2002.

[8] Notwithstanding Rome Statute, Article 12(2)(b). However, the requirement of consent of the state of nationality is dispensed with if there is another basis for jurisdiction, e.g., if there is consent by another state, such as the territorial state, for ICC jurisdiction over the situation under scrutiny.

[9] Rome Statute, Article 13(b). This is notwithstanding the unlikeliness of such a referral, given the US position in the Security Council.

[10] The utmost dependence of the US on foreign states for the very existence of its detention, rendition and interrogation programme is an ironic but nevertheless striking illustration of the necessities of cooperation.

[11] Power struggles in the intelligence world have alternatively led to a spreading of good practices or to races to the bottom and collusion.

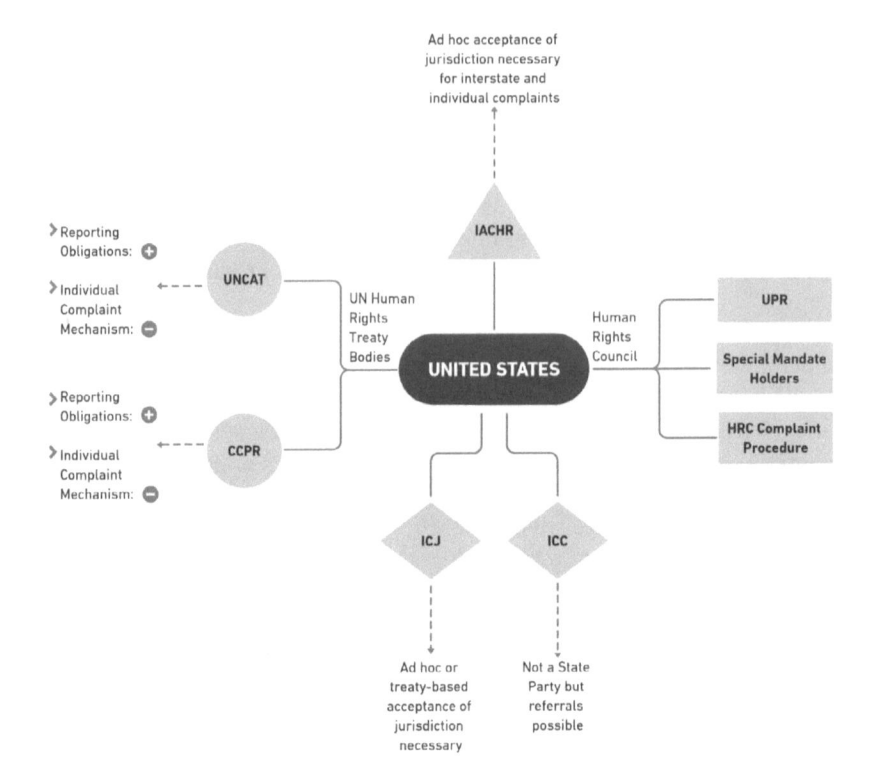

Figure 6.1   The United States' accountability network

6.2.3   Evaluation

Table 6.1 evaluates the United States' accountability network following the framework developed in Chapter 5.

The lack of US consent to almost all optional mechanisms means that the US's accountability network has an extremely weak capacity to constrain and escalate, as evidenced in Table 6.1. The non-binding character of actors' decisions, with the exception of the ICJ and ICC, illustrates this weakness. This is made worse by the relative lack of power and leverage of other states, which cannot effectively supplement institutional mechanisms.

In contrast, the network's legitimacy is quite strong. The main caveat in this respect relates to the nature of the few actors to which access is unrestricted: they are intergovernmental or expert bodies, not judicial or quasi-judicial mechanisms. This impacts assessments of the network's reputation and the

Table 6.1 Evaluation of the United States' accountability network

UNITED STATES	Evaluation Factors	Evaluation
Capacity to Constrain and Escalate	Jurisdiction *ratione materiae*	MEDIUM. The network as a whole does not have universal competence in the absence of ad hoc acceptance of jurisdiction.
	Jurisdiction *ratione personae*	STRONG. All actors of the network but the IACHR have near-universal jurisdiction.
	Investigatory powers	MEDIUM. Some powers but consent necessary (IACHR, Special Mandate Holders) or already denied (ICC).
	Powers to sanction non-cooperation	WEAK. No actor with compulsory jurisdiction has the capacity to sanction non-cooperation.
	Capacity to order remedies	WEAK. No actor with compulsory jurisdiction has the capacity to order remedies.
	Capacity to sanction	WEAK. No actor with compulsory jurisdiction has the capacity to impose sanctions.
	Reputation of account-holder state – Standing in the international legal order – Relative power – Human rights records	WEAK for all states due to the disproportion of power and standing between most states and the US. Further, states whose economic and/or defence power could compare to the US's (e.g., China, Russia, India) do not have a strong human rights record or agenda.
	Capacity of account-holder state to constrain compliance – Interdependencies – Leverage tools	MEDIUM for certain key states with leverage in the field of intelligence cooperation; WEAK for the rest.

UNITED STATES	Evaluation Factors	Evaluation
Legitimacy	Overall reputation	MEDIUM. The actors with the strongest reputation are those for whom access is restricted (ICJ, IACHR, UN treaty-bodies).
	Participation of the state under scrutiny	STRONG. Participation of the state is encouraged, if not necessary, in all procedures.
	Capacity to reward compliance or de-escalate	STRONG. Reporting obligations and interim measures are strong features of the US's network.
	Independence – Budget and resources – Formal independence – Judicial independence – Relative power (state)	MEDIUM. Actors of the network are mostly intergovernmental and expert bodies deprived of their quasi-judicial function by the lack of consent to individual complaints. Yet, most of those actors are formally independent and have relatively stable resources. Where applicable, the independence of judges or experts is also satisfactorily guaranteed. Other states, however, are almost all strongly dependent on the US for security, trade, etc.
Publicity and Accessibility	Representation of public interest	MEDIUM. In the absence of individual complaint procedures, the public interest is represented mostly through reporting obligations and shadow reporting by civil society organisations.
	Publicity of proceedings	STRONG. Reports are public and most hearings also are, in some form (video streaming or written records).
	Publicity of outcomes	STRONG. Decisions by all actors, except the HRC in its complaint procedure, are public.
	Accessibility to non-state account-holders – Information – Financial and geographical accessibility – Procedural accessibility	WEAK. In the absence of individual complaint procedures before a judicial or quasi-judicial mechanism, non-state account-holders have close to no access to accountability mechanisms. However, the two procedures that are available are free and relatively easy to understand and complete, mitigating slightly the absence of other mechanisms.

actors' independence. Foreign states are subject to the same limitations due to their high dependency on the US.

Publicity of the proceedings and outcomes is relatively strong, but representation of the public interest is hindered by the lack of accessibility to non-state account-holders. This lacuna is partially mitigated by the active role played by some of the network's actors in representing the public interest and in allowing other non-state actors to do so (in shadow reporting, for instance). Accessibility, finally, is evidently weak, and only very moderately mitigated by the existence of Human Rights Council (HRC) procedures.

6.2.4 Assessment of Practice

Owing to the network's lack of accessibility, one could naturally expect the number of cases to be relatively low compared with the scope of the programme and the number of identified victims (131). However, the total absence of any successful judicial or quasi-judicial proceedings against the US more than 20 years after the beginning of the programme, whether at domestic or supra-national level, cannot be considered anything but astounding. This absence is particularly remarkable because, as detailed below, almost all available international accountability mechanisms have been used. The question, then, is whether this minimalist accountability network might be able to provide meaningful accountability but has yet to reach its potential, or whether it is simply too weak to ever do so.

6.2.4.1 The Inter-American Commission on Human Rights

In March 2002, the Inter-American Commission on Human Rights (IACHR) was the first international institution to explicitly call upon the US to respect Guantánamo Bay detainees' human rights, two months after the first prisoners were transferred there from US detention sites overseas. While not focusing on CIA detainees specifically, those who transited through Guantánamo Bay were covered as such by the proceedings and actions before the IACHR. The Commission has made use of all the powers granted to it under the Organization of American States (OAS) Charter and its rules of procedure to monitor the situations of detainees at Guantánamo Bay. This includes in particular its power

> to examine communications submitted to it and any other available information, to address the government of any member state not a Party to the Convention for information deemed pertinent by this Commission, and to make recommendations to it, when it finds this appropriate, in order to bring about more effective observance of fundamental human rights.[12]

In addition, although the US has not ratified the American Convention on Human Rights and has not consented to the Inter-American Court of Human Rights' (IACtHR) jurisdiction, the Commission has jurisdiction to hear indi-

---

[12] Statute of the Inter-American Commission on Human Rights, OAS Res. 448 (IX-0/79) Article 20(b).

vidual petitions alleging violations of the American Declaration of the Rights and Duties of Man[13] if the respondent state consents to its jurisdiction in individual cases.

Throughout the years, the Commission's attempts to hold the US to account for the continued extra-judicial detention, mistreatment, and lack of due process afforded to Guantánamo Bay detainees have taken several forms. Precautionary measures[14] have been granted with regard to 'detainees held by the United States at Guantánamo Bay' since 2002. They have been extended and amplified several times since then as new information came to light and detainees' situations evolved.[15] Precautionary measures have also been granted individually in favour of Omar Khadr (2006), Djamel Ameziane (2008), Moath al-Alwi (2015), and Mustafa Adam Al-Hawsawi (2015).

Through press releases, the Commission has expressed its concerns, given publicity to the situation, and repeatedly called for the closure of the site. Since 2007, it has also repeatedly (though unsuccessfully) sought unconditional consent from the US to conduct a visit.[16] The Commission has issued several resolutions – binding on the US as an OAS member state – urging the US to give effect to the precautionary measures and indicating that its failure to do so had resulted in irreparable prejudice to the detainees' rights.[17] Finally, in a 2015 report entitled 'Towards the Closure of Guantánamo',[18] the Commission

---

[13] IACHR, American Declaration of the Rights and Duties of Man, 2 May 1948. On the legal value accorded to the Declaration, see OC-10/89, Advisory Opinion, IACtHR Series A 10 (1989) para 45, stating that 'the American Declaration is for [OAS member states] a source of international obligations related to the Charter of the Organization'.

[14] The IACHR's authority to issue precautionary measures in respect of Member States of the OAS is provided for under Article 25 of the Commission's Rules of Procedure. The Commission has affirmed at several occasions the 'international obligation that [OAS] member States have to comply with precautionary measures issued by the Inter-American Commission on Human Rights' (IACHR Resolution 1/05, 8 March 2005, para 1).

[15] For an early account of the role played by precautionary measures in the Guantánamo Bay situation, see BD Tittemore, 'Guantanamo Bay and the Precautionary Measures of the Inter-American Commission on Human Rights: A Case for International Oversight in the Struggle Against Terrorism' (2006) 6 Human Rights Law Review 378. On IACHR precautionary measures generally, see Diego Rodriguez-Pinzon, 'Precautionary Measures of the Inter-American Commission on Human Rights: Legal Status and Importance' [2013] Human Rights Brief 20, no. 2, 13.

[16] See OAS website – 'Decisions regarding the US Detention Centre in Guantánamo – Requests of permission for a visit': http://www.oas.org/en/iachr/pdl/decisions/Guantánamo.asp#Visita

[17] IACHR Resolution 2/06 on Precautionary Measures for Guantánamo Detainees, July 28, 2006; Resolution 2/11 on the Situation of Detainees at Guantánamo Bay, United States; Precautionary Measures 259-02, July 22, 2011.

[18] IACHR 'Towards the Closure of Guantánamo', 2015.

provided an extensive legal analysis of the various documented violations of detainees' rights under the American Declaration. On several occasions in the report, the Commission determined that there had been 'a violation' of the Declaration, as well as of various international obligations of the US.[19] Where appropriate, the Commission cited similar findings of violations by competent bodies under the UN Convention against Torture and the ICCPR – both binding on the US.

Hence, even before the opportunity for a formal quasi-judicial determination of US responsibility for acts related to Guantánamo Bay arose with the *Ameziane* case in 2020,[20] the Commission had not shied away from asserting that the US was responsible for violations of the Declaration, and from demanding that the US government takes steps to remedy its wrongful conduct. Although the Commission's jurisdiction is not compulsory, the various proceedings before the Commission nevertheless qualify as a process of international legal accountability. As a member state of the OAS, the relationship between the US and the Commission is well established and gives rise to the US's obligation to justify its conduct with regard to the rights guaranteed by the Declaration. There are several hearings and submission opportunities before decisions are issued, allowing for oral and written exchanges between the US and the Commission. Finally, if it judges that the US's performance does not meet the standards imposed by the Declaration, the Commission can impose consequences on the US, in the form of precautionary measures, decisions, resolutions, reports, and publicity.

The case of Djamel Ameziane was declared admissible in 2012,[21] and the confidential merits report was communicated to the US on 26 February 2019. As the US failed to comply with the recommendations in the report, the Commission had the requisite mandate to publish the final decision, dated 22 April 2020. There, it found the US responsible for the violation of multiple articles of the Declaration.[22] The Commission's report constitutes the first-ever

---

[19] E.g., para 96 'the indefinite detention of persons still held at Guantánamo without charge after more than a decade, mainly for the purpose of obtaining intelligence, constitutes a serious violation of their right to personal liberty guaranteed under Article I of the American Declaration'.

[20] See below for an analysis. IACHR, Report No. 29/20. Case 12.865. Merits Report (Publication). *Djamel Ameziane* v. *United States*. April 22, 2020 (hereinafter '*Ameziane*').

[21] Report 17/12. Petition 900-08. Report on Admissibility. *Djamel Ameziane* v. *United States*. OEA/Ser.L/V/II.144. Doc. 21. 20 March 2012.

[22] Articles I (life, liberty, and security), II (equality before the law), III (religious freedom and worship), IV (freedom of expression), V (protection of honor, personal reputation, and private and family life), VI (right to family and protection thereof), XI (protection of health and well-being), XVIII (fair trial), XXI (assembly), XXIII (prop-

breach in the US cloak of impunity for its acts in the global war on terror, and it also has implications for the CIA rendition, detention, and interrogation programme. Although Ameziane was not a CIA detainee, he was detained in Guantánamo Bay under US military custody between 2002 and 2013 and was subjected to the same regime of 'enhanced interrogation' and incommunicado detention as CIA detainees. Hence, the factual and legal findings in his case hold significance for future findings in CIA-related cases.[23] In particular, the US also consented to the Commission's jurisdiction in former CIA detainee Khaled El-Masri's case, which was declared admissible in 2016 and is now pending.[24] Most recently, on 9 July 2020, the Commission declared admissible the complaint by former CIA detainees Binyam Mohamed, Abou Elkassim Britel, Mohamed Farag Ahmad Bashmilah, and Bisher al-Rawi.[25]

In its report in *Ameziane*, the Commission first rejected the US's contention that Guantánamo Bay was only subjected to IHL, affirming instead the continued relevance and applicability of IHRL protections to Guantánamo Bay detainees.[26] Then, it determined that Ameziane's detention was entirely arbitrary.[27] The Commission also found that the conditions of detention and the treatments to which Ameziane was subjected in Guantánamo Bay constituted torture, generally as well as, regarding most of the acts under consideration, taken in isolation.[28] Further, the IACHR held that the US had an 'aggravated international responsibility'[29] – which it failed to meet – to protect Ameziane from torture and inhumane treatment. Such aggravated responsibility arose by reason of the US government's systemic practices and policies that permitted acts of torture to occur in Guantánamo, and from the US's failure to comply

---

erty), XXIV (petition), XXV (protection from arbitrary detention), and XXVI (due process). See IACHR. Report No. 29/20. Case 12.865. Merits (Publication).

[23] For a lengthier analysis of the IACHR report, the procedural history of the communication, and the possible impact of the decision, see Lisa Reinsberg, 'IACHR condemns Guantánamo Abuses in First War on Terror Decision', Just Security, 7 July 2020. Available at: https://www.justsecurity.org/71150/iachr-condemns-guantanamo-abuses-in-first-war-on-terror-decision/

[24] Report 21/16. Petition 419-08. Report on Admissibility. *Khaled El-Masri* v. *United States*. OEA/Ser.L/V/II.157. Doc. 25. 15 April 2016.

[25] Report 154/20, Petition 1638-11. Report on Admissibility. OEA/Ser.L/V/II. Doc 164, 9 June 2020.

[26] *Ameziane* (n 20) paras 114–116.

[27] ibid paras 125–134.

[28] ibid paras 168–205.

[29] The IACtHR has adopted the concept of aggravated state responsibility to qualify violations that are especially grave because they are perpetrated by those specifically responsible for certain obligations of respect and guarantee of human rights. See e.g., Separate Opinion of Judge Sergio García Ramírez concerning *Goiburú et al.* v. *Paraguay*, Judgment, 22 September 2006, para 6.

with the precautionary measures that the IACHR had granted in favour of Ameziane in 2008.[30] As a result of this failure, Ameziane continued to be subjected to torture and was returned to Algeria in violation of the principle of non-refoulement.[31] The IACHR concluded that the US has a legal framework characterised by amnesty laws and a lack of effective access to courts, thus allowing for acts of torture to be committed and preventing their 'effective investigation and punishment'.[32]

The Commission then issued recommendations to the US with regard to Ameziane and aimed at providing 'material and moral reparation' to him, but also beyond the circumstances of his case.[33] The Commission thus recommended that the US establish a truth commission to investigate acts that took place at Guantánamo Bay, and prosecute all those implicated in acts of torture between 2002 and 2008. It also urged the US to comply with the recommendations set forth in its 2015 report 'Towards the Closure of Guantánamo', which include providing detainees with adequate medical, psychiatric, and psychological care, access to justice and, ultimately, closing the Guantánamo Bay detention centre.

These findings and recommendations represent an authoritative quasi-judicial determination of US responsibility for its acts in the war on terror and in Guantánamo Bay. It also clarifies the nature of its obligations to remedy the numerous violations of the Declaration that these acts triggered. As of August 2022, 34 men were detained in Guantánamo, with 24 having never been charged and 20 of these having been cleared for release. A quasi-judicial finding that their initial and continued detention violates multiple Declaration articles is at least a symbolic victory and a recognition of detainees' victim status. In addition, the report constitutes legal precedent and an authoritative source for the establishment of facts. The Commission itself, but also domestic and international bodies, will thus be able to rely on the findings and conclusions of the report in the rare cases that reach them. Other actors of the US' accountability network may also decide to enforce the decision.

The all-encompassing accountability process that has taken place since 2002 at the IACHR has resulted in significant and authoritative legal analyses of the issues at stake. It has participated in making facts public and in mobilising public opinion from the start, and it probably contributed to the (unheeded) commitment of the Obama administration to close Guantánamo Bay. More importantly, it put the US in the position of having to legally defend and justify

---

[30] *Ameziane* (n 20) paras 275–278.
[31] ibid para 277.
[32] ibid.
[33] ibid para 285.

its policy from the early years of the war on terror. The US has suffered consequences as a result of the process. Its domestic case-law and legislation had to be (slightly) adjusted in response;[34] its international reputation and intelligence capacity have been affected by the publicity of the facts; and the accountability process has opened the door to individual petitions by Guantánamo detainees, which should lead to further consequences.

It remains to be seen what political and legal impact the development of the IACHR case-law on the war on terror in the *Ameziane* case and in the two pending cases will have. As the first international quasi-judicial precedent declaring the international responsibility of the US almost 20 years after the beginning of the war on terror, the Commission's report in *Ameziane* can be perceived as a more formal and authoritative condemnation than previous reports and press releases. Yet, it is anything but certain whether the report and attached recommendations will constitute enough incentive for the US to finally provide redress to victims. The stain of a formal condemnation, however symbolic, will nevertheless remain.

6.2.4.2 UN treaty bodies and the Human Rights Council

Both the CCPR and the UNCAT have extensively addressed the legal implications of the CIA programme in their concluding observations on the state's reporting obligations. The CCPR's concluding observations of September 2006 (revised December 2006) address as many aspects of the programme as were known at the time. The CCPR therefore commented and issued legal determinations upon the practice of secret detention; enhanced interrogation techniques; the lack of independent, impartial and effective investigations into allegations of torture; the lack of due process of Guantánamo Bay detainees under the Detainee Treatment Act 2005; the ICCPR's applicability in armed combat situations and extraterritorially; and the US's position that rendition is not contrary to the ICCPR.[35] Unsurprisingly, it found all aspects of the US's legal stance and of the CIA programme to be contrary to the provisions of the ICCPR.

A few months earlier, in July 2006 (hence before the official recognition of the existence of the programme by the Bush administration on 6 September 2006), the UNCAT issued similar concluding observations,[36] devoting them almost entirely to the CIA programme and Guantánamo Bay. The UNCAT

---

[34] See in particular the Detainee Treatment Act of 2005; and the Supreme Court decisions in *Hamdan* v. *Rumsfeld* 548 US 557 (2006) and *Boumediene* v. *Bush* 553 US 723 (2008).

[35] CCPR/C/USA/CO/3/Rev.1 (18 December 2006), paras 10 and 12–16.

[36] CAT/C/USA/CO/2 (25 July 2006).

found that the programme in all its strands constituted 'a violation' of the CAT, and that US legislation on torture came short of the requirements of the CAT.[37]

It is worth noting that both committees emphasised the US administration's cooperation, which can be interpreted as a posture of capitulation.[38] They highlighted the uncontested nature of the allegations and facts under scrutiny and made legal determinations upon them, thereby holding the US to account. However, and rather worryingly, they also noted the US administration's strong and persistent objection to universally accepted legal interpretations of the treaties and provisions thereof.[39] This posture of resistance constitutes an obstacle to effective accountability as the US does not consider the treaty bodies' legal interpretation to be binding or as overriding its own. Owing to this, the US can maintain that it is acting in accordance with its international obligations and refuse to acknowledge its international responsibility, preventing any prospect of accountability and redress.

Yet, the treaty bodies' legal determinations upon its conduct forced the US to justify itself, both in the initial reporting process and in the follow-up exchanges. Concluding observations commonly start by highlighting 'positive aspects', thereby rewarding progress and changes made by the state, and encouraging the implementation of recommendations issued in previous reports. Thus, the concluding observations issued by the CCPR and the UNCAT in 2014 provide an opportunity to assess whether and how the US's position evolved between the two cycles of reporting.[40]

Both Committees started by welcoming the executive orders issued by the Obama administration, which effectively put an end to the CIA programme and its excrescences, Guantánamo Bay excepted. They also applauded the US Supreme Court's decision in *Boumediene* v. *Bush*,[41] which recognised the extraterritorial application of constitutional habeas corpus rights to aliens detained by the military as 'enemy combatants' at Guantánamo Bay. In addition, the UNCAT welcomed 'the firm and principled position adopted by the State party with regard to the applicability of the Convention during armed conflict', as well as the US's acceptance of the extraterritorial applicability of

---

[37] ibid.
[38] On motivational postures, see Chapter 5, section 5.4.
[39] E.g., on the applicability of the ICCPR and CAT extra-territorially and in times of war, but also on the prohibition of refoulement, or on the definition of psychological torture.
[40] It should however be noted that the US's country reports were delayed by several years, a timeframe that witnessed the end of the CIA programme and the drafting and approval of the SSCI Study.
[41] 553 U.S. 723 (2008).

the CAT[42] (in contrast with its unchanged opposition to the ICCPR's extraterritorial applicability).[43]

In the second part of its 2014 report, the CCPR reserved one paragraph to regretting the lack of accountability of persons involved in the CIA programme, emphasising the lack of effective, independent, and impartial investigation into the crimes committed.[44] In contrast, the UNCAT dedicated half its report to the aftermath of the CIA programme, ongoing violations at Guantánamo Bay, and the confusing domestic legislation constituting a barrier to ensuring non-repetition.[45] Both committees also encouraged the declassification of the SSCI Study[46] – which happened at the end of the same year, albeit only for its executive summary.

Several patterns are noticeable throughout the cycles of state reports, concluding observations, and follow-up reports. First, the US is constantly engaging with the process and advocating for the Committees to issue positive findings. The US is therefore adamant that its legislation is in full conformity with the conventions, and that its current practice is in full conformity with how it interprets its obligations. This shows an effort to appear compliant and be judged as such, demonstrating that the US values the procedure and the determinations made by the Committees at least in so far as it tries to avoid bad publicity. The timeframe of the state reports delivered by the US, delayed but coinciding with the approval and declassification of the SSCI Study and the recognition by President Obama that acts of torture had been committed, supports this observation. This domestic *mea culpa* does not create any additional reputational damage when reproduced at international level, and is even presented as progress before the Committees. However, this is only as far as the US is willing to admit guilt: for past events that have been publicly repudiated.

Second, the Committees do not shy away from addressing any and all aspects of the CIA programme, a faculty they possess thanks to the flexible non-judicial nature of the reporting procedure. This lack of judicial character allows the Committees to make determinations upon US conduct (and thus responsibility) following standards of evidence and judicial reasoning that are much less stringent than in individual complaint procedures. Naturally, this also represents an obstacle to the concluding observations' authoritativeness, which is on a par with the Committees' lack of sanctioning power. Hence,

---

[42] CAT/C/USA/CO/3-5 (19 December 2014), para 10.
[43] CCPR/C/USA/CO/4 (23 April 2014), para 4.
[44] ibid para 5.
[45] CAT/C/USA/CO/3-5 (19 December 2014), paras 11–17.
[46] United States Senate Select Committee on Intelligence, *Torture Report: Committee Study of Central Intelligence Agency's Detention and Interrogation Program: Executive Summary* (2014).

the consequences that derive from concluding observations are exclusively reputational. However, they relate to a wide variety of 'concerning' practices and are reinforced by similar findings in Human Rights Council procedures.

Indeed, in an almost parallel endeavour, the first universal periodic review (UPR) cycle (2010) witnessed a number of remarks and recommendations by other states concerning the CIA programme, the prohibition of torture, and Guantánamo Bay, adopting the arguments and vocabulary of UN treaty bodies.[47] The second cycle (2015) focused more on the closure of Guantánamo Bay and accountability for the CIA programme, again matching recent concluding observations.[48] While it is doubtful that states would be willing and able to effectively constrain the US into compliance, and while a high number of interventions are solely politically motivated and have very little impact, the wide variety of states using the UPR procedure to speak up about the CIA programme is encouraging inasmuch as it constitutes another public forum and adds to the accountability network's soft coercion power.

On the other end of the political spectrum, reports by special mandate holders have been valued for their independence and the quality of their fact-finding and legal analysis. In various reports, but most importantly in a 2010 Joint Study on Secret Detention, special mandate holders have addressed the legal implications of the CIA programme and arrived at findings similar to those of the CCPR and UNCAT.[49] Reports by special mandate holders complement and reinforce the legal authority of treaty bodies' concluding observations, in addition to representing an authoritative statement of what compliance with international law entails. They also provide a valuable opportunity to engage with the US and raise attention about individual cases.

At the same time, indeed, special mandate holders – including the working group on arbitrary detentions (WGAD), which can receive individual com-

---

[47] A/HRC/16/11 (4 January 2011), paras 92.136 to 92.161.
[48] A/HRC/20/12 (20 July 2015), paras 176.239 to 176.256.
[49] Human Rights Council, 'Joint Study on Global Practices in Relation to Secret Detention in the Context of Countering Terrorism of the Special Rapporteur on the Promotion and Protection of Human Rights and Fundamental Freedoms While Countering Terrorism' (UN General Assembly 2010) A/HRC/13/42. See also Martin Scheinin, 'Report of the Special Rapporteur on the Promotion and Protection of Human Rights and Fundamental Freedoms While Countering Terrorism, Martin Scheinin' (UN General Assembly, Human Rights Council 2009) A/HRC/10/3; Martin Scheinin, 'Report of the Special Rapporteur on the Promotion and Protection of Human Rights and Fundamental Freedoms While Countering Terrorism, Martin Scheinin. Compilation of Good Practices on Legal and Institutional Frameworks and Measures that Ensure Respect for Human Rights by Intelligence Agencies While Countering Terrorism, Including on Their Oversight' (UN General Assembly, Human Rights Council 2010) A/HRC/14/46.

plaints – have received communications concerning a total of nine CIA detainees.[50] The communication procedure can only be considered an accountability mechanism when the US engages in the process, i.e., replies to the communication. This has been the case more often under the Obama administration than before or after.[51] Responses of the Obama administration match the country reports under the UNCAT and CCPR procedures, emphasising the changes implemented by the administration and refusing to accept responsibility for continued violations or to hold anyone accountable.[52] A worrisome pattern can also be observed more generally in the references to domestic legislation and to domestic litigation, either struck out due to national security concerns or conducted before military commissions, as a means to reply to and dismiss the allegations of violations raised in the communications.[53]

---

[50] Ammar al-Baluchi (USA 22/2017 and 5/2020); Mohammed al Qahtani (A/HRC/WGAD/2019/70); Mustafa Al-Hawsawi (USA 5/2016); Abou Elkassim Britel (USA 12/2015); Khalid Sheikh Mohammad, Mohammad al-Qahtani, Ramzi bin al-Shibh, Ali Abd al-Aziz Ali (a.k.a. Ammar al-Baluchi), Mustafa Ahmed al-Hawsawi, and Walid bin Attash (USA 31/2012, A/HRC/10/3/Add.1); Mohamed Basmilah and Salah Nasser Samil Ali (a.k.a. Saleh Qaru) (E/CN.4/2006/98).

[51] Compare the lengthy response and justification of the Obama administration before the WGAD to the communication concerning Al-Hawsawi in 2014, to the absence of response to the communication concerning al-Qahtani in 2019. Opinions adopted by the Working Group on Arbitrary Detention at its seventy-first session (17–21 November 2014) No. 50/2014 concerning Mustafa Al-Hawsawi (United States of America and Cuba), A/HRC/WGAD/2014/50; Opinions adopted by the Working Group on Arbitrary Detention at its eighty-sixth session, 18–22 November 2019. Opinion No. 70/2019 concerning Mohammed al Qahtani (United States of America), A/HRC/WGAD/2019/70. Further, when it did respond, the Trump administration reproduced almost word-for-word the previous responses of the Obama administration. See the US response, dated 8 March 2018, to communication 22/2017 concerning Ammar al-Baluchi, and compare with the above-mentioned 2014 response reproduced in A/HRC/WGAD/2014/50 concerning Al-Hawsawi.

[52] See e.g., Reply by the US to communication USA 1/2015 on the role of health professionals in the CIA detention and interrogation programme; or Report of the Special Rapporteur on the promotion and protection of human rights and fundamental freedoms while countering terrorism, Martin Scheinin – Addendum – Communications to and from Governments (From 1 January to 31 December 2011) A/HRC/16/51/Add.1, paras 221–224.

[53] See especially the numerous references to the Military Commissions Acts of 2006 and 2009; and for litigation see e.g., Report of the Special Rapporteur on the promotion and protection of human rights and fundamental freedoms while countering terrorism, Martin Scheinin – Addendum – Communications with Governments A/HRC/10/3/Add.1 para 366.

6.2.4.3 The International Criminal Court on the Situation in Afghanistan

On 5 March 2020, the Appeals Chamber authorised an investigation on war crimes and crimes against humanity in Afghanistan, including into allegations that US forces and the CIA committed acts of torture there.[54] This was two and a half years after the Office of the Prosecutor (OTP) first requested authorisation, and almost a year after Pre-Trial Chamber II (PTC) denied it 'in the interests of justice'.[55]

Aside from the significance of the Appeals Chamber's reversal for the future work of the ICC – greatly imperilled by the implications of the PTC's ruling with regard to its assessment of the interests of justice[56] – its importance for present purposes rests upon the unrestricted authorisation to proceed with the investigation (Finding 2). With regard to the scope of the investigation, the Appeals Chamber thus concluded that

> the Prosecutor is authorised to commence an investigation in relation to alleged crimes committed on the territory of Afghanistan in the period since 1 May 2003, as well as other alleged crimes that have a nexus to the armed conflict in Afghanistan and are sufficiently linked to the situation and were committed on the territory of other States Parties in the period since 1 July 2002.[57]

These notably include incidents related to CIA black sites located in Poland, Lithuania, and Romania whenever the required nexus with the armed conflict in Afghanistan is satisfied. As submitted in the OTP request, reproduced in and endorsed by the Appeals Chamber's judgment, this could be the case for persons captured outside Afghanistan and later mistreated on the territory of a state party (e.g., Poland, Lithuania, Romania), provided they were suspected of being associated with al Qaeda or the Taliban.[58]

On 27 September 2021, however, ICC Prosecutor Karim Khan QC issued a statement on how his office plans to resume investigations into the situation in Afghanistan.[59] A key part of this statement is his decision to focus

---

[54] Judgment on the appeal against the decision on the authorisation of an investigation into the situation in the Islamic Republic of Afghanistan, ICC-02/17 OA4, 5 March 2020, hereinafter 'AC 02/17'.

[55] Decision Pursuant to Article 15 of the Rome Statute on the Authorisation of an Investigation into the Situation in the Islamic Republic of Afghanistan, ICC-02/17, 12 April 2019, hereinafter 'PTC 02/17'.

[56] The PTC's assessment can be summarised under the heading of feasibility. See PTC 02/17 (n 55) paras 90–96.

[57] AC 02/17 (n 54) para 79.

[58] ibid para 67.

[59] Statement of the Prosecutor of the International Criminal Court, Karim A. A. Khan QC, following the application for an expedited order under Article 18(2) seeking

his office's efforts 'on crimes allegedly committed by the Taliban and the Islamic State – Khorasan Province ("IS-K") and to deprioritise other aspects of this investigation.' The 'other aspects' referred to include, notably, allegations of US war crimes and crimes against humanity. Although the Appeals Chamber's decision sent an important signal that political concerns and threats could not be transformed into legal principles nor influence the ICC's decision to investigate a situation, the Afghanistan investigation had already induced strong political reaction from the US.[60] It also promised to be extremely long and complex, even before the Taliban's grab of power in August 2021. Yet, it appears almost cynical that, with US sanctions lifted in April 2021, the newly appointed ICC Prosecutor took the exact decision these sanctions sought to achieve in September 2021.

The inclusion of CIA black sites in Eastern Europe into the OTP investigation represented a new opportunity for accountability and justice for the victims of the programme detained there at some point, many of whom are considered 'high value detainees' and are still detained at Guantánamo Bay. One might have also hoped that the renewed attention given to the CIA programme would help trigger the long-awaited impartial and effective domestic investigations by ICC state parties who participated in the programme as black site hosts. In these ways, the Appeals Chamber's judgment represented a crucial first step towards accountability, reversing the PTC's apparent rewarding of the US's lack of cooperation under the guise of serving 'the interests of justice'.[61] Prosecutor Khan's strategy, if not revisited, effectively closes the door to any remaining hopes that the US will be held accountable for any of the crimes it committed as part of its global war on terror, and that its victims will obtain justice and reparations.

---

authorisation to resume investigations in the Situation in Afghanistan, 27 September 2021.

[60] See US President Trump's Executive Order 13928, 'Blocking Property of Certain Persons Associated with the International Criminal Court'. On 2 September 2020, in application of the executive order, the Trump administration added Fatou Bensouda and Phakiso Mochochoko to its 'Specially Designated Nationals and Blocked Persons List'. Sanctions were lifted by Biden administration in April 2021.

[61] This is indeed a direct consequence of including feasibility in the interests of justice assessment, a risk that the OTP was already warning against in a 2013 policy paper on preliminary examinations, para 70: 'In terms of whether effective investigations are operationally feasible, the Office notes that feasibility is not a separate factor under the Statute as such when determining whether to open an investigation. Weighing feasibility as a separate self-standing factor, moreover, could prejudice the consistent application of the Statute and might encourage obstructionism to dissuade ICC intervention'. Available at: https://www.icc-cpi.int/news/policy-paper-preliminary-examinations

6.2.4.4 Responsibility without accountability: the US as principal wrongdoer in third-party proceedings

In November 2006, the UN Human Rights Committee (CCPR) concluded that Sweden had violated Article 7, read alone and in conjunction with Article 2, of the ICCPR and Article 1 of the Optional Protocol in respect of the rendition of Mohamed Alzery to Egypt with the assistance of CIA agents.[62] Unlike the UNCAT in the twin case of *Agiza* v. *Sweden*,[63] the CCPR also addressed the treatment of Alzery by CIA agents at Bromma airport, and made the determination that 'the acts complained of, which occurred in the course of performance of official functions in the presence of the State party's officials and within the State party's jurisdiction, are properly imputable to the State party itself, in addition to the State on whose behalf the officials were engaged'.[64] Stopping short of explicitly declaring the international responsibility of the US (and indeed of naming it in the conclusions) for breach of the international prohibition of torture, the CCPR nevertheless touched upon shared responsibility issues arising from intelligence cooperation. It also laid the ground for future findings against the US in separate proceedings.[65]

In *El-Masri* v. *Macedonia*,[66] due to obvious jurisdictional limitations, the ECtHR could not hold the US accountable. However, its account of the facts and the attribution to Macedonia of wrongful conduct committed by CIA agents underlined the US's role in the violations of El-Masri's rights.[67] While not holding the US accountable and refraining from naming it as the primary rights violator in the conclusions, the case nevertheless solidly established its international responsibility for El-Masri's rendition and torture. The Court went further in the cases against Poland, where state responsibility was found for hosting a CIA black site and for generally collaborating with the CIA programme. In these cases, the Court made an explicit finding of US responsibility for torture in its conclusions,[68] and then went on to find Poland responsible for treatment inflicted on the applicants by the CIA, on account of its 'acquiescence and connivance'. While this led the ECtHR to consider the preliminary

---

[62] CCPR, *Alzery* v. *Sweden*, CCPR/C/88/D/1416/2005.
[63] UNCAT, *Agiza* v. *Sweden*, CAT/C/34/D/233/2003.
[64] ibid para 11.6.
[65] See e.g., CCPR/C/USA/CO/3 para 16 and CAT/C/USA/CO/2 paras 20–22.
[66] ECtHR, *El-Masri* v. *The Former Yugoslav Republic of Macedonia*, Judgment, 13 December 2012, App. No. 39639/09 ('*El-Masri*').
[67] See *El-Masri*, para 206.
[68] ECtHR, *Al-Nashiri* v. *Poland*, Judgment, 24 July 2014, App. No. 28761/11 para 516; ECtHR, *Husayn (Abu Zubaydah)* v. *Poland*, Judgment, 24 July 2014, App. No. 7511/13, para 511: 'the Court concludes that the treatment to which the applicant was subjected by the CIA during his detention in Poland at the relevant time amounted to torture within the meaning of Article 3 of the Convention'.

establishment of US responsibility necessary (and controversially so),[69] it also clarified that responsibility arises from intelligence cooperation activities as much as from direct commission of the wrongful acts. In the two most recent cases, against Romania and Lithuania, the Court reverted to the more cautious approach followed in *El-Masri*. While finding that the treatment to which the applicants were subjected amounted to inhuman treatment and despite ample references to the CIA in previous paragraphs, the Court refrained from naming the CIA as the primary rights violator in its conclusions.[70]

The ECtHR's lack of jurisdiction over the US means that, while it could declare the US responsible for the torture and arbitrary detention of Al-Nashiri and Abu Zubaydah in the Polish cases, this had few legal or practical consequences. The ECtHR could not order their release nor impose any direct consequence on the US. In contrast, both the UNCAT and CCPR have jurisdiction over the US in its reporting obligations under the relevant conventions, so that shared accountability remained a theoretical possibility, albeit under differentiated proceedings. While this may explain their more careful approaches to the US's (or indeed Egypt's) responsibility in the cases against Sweden as a potential indispensable third party that has not consented to their jurisdiction, it is also possible that both Committees made conscious efforts to avoid addressing the legal issues raised by the complex and elaborate framework of intelligence cooperation in which the acts under scrutiny were taking place.

6.2.4.5 Assessment

Available accountability mechanisms have been used thoroughly, even beyond US membership and consent. Yet, although the accountability network has managed to exercise some 'soft coercion' over the US, it has not achieved sufficient or adequate accountability. Most importantly, while the network has consistently established the US's international responsibility, it has proved unable to provide redress to victims and remedy the wrongful acts committed. This is not solely due to the inherent incapability of the network. Despite its pronounced weaknesses, the network has still demonstrated some potential at institutional level. However, it is not living up to its limited capacities. The unique jurisdictional opportunity offered by the ICC Appeals Chamber's decision to authorise the investigation in Afghanistan represented a strong breach in the cloak of impunity surrounding the programme. However, ICC Prosecutor Khan's decision to deprioritise US crimes in the Afghanistan

---

[69] Martin Scheinin, 'The ECtHR Finds the US Guilty of Torture – As an Indispensable Third Party?' (*EJIL Talk!* 28 July 2014) https://www.ejiltalk.org/the-ecthr-finds-the-us-guilty-of-torture-as-an-indispensable-third-party/.

[70] *Al-Nashiri v. Romania*, App. No.33234/12, 31 May 2018, para 675; *Abu Zubaydah v. Lithuania*, App. No. 46454/11, 31 May 2018, para 640.

investigation put an end to hopes for accountability before the ICC. The US's minimalist accountability network may still achieve small successes on other fronts, for instance with IACHR reports in individual cases, but its capacity to provide meaningful accountability and redress in its current state is extremely limited.

6.3 DJIBOUTI

6.3.1 State Responsibility

Djibouti's international responsibility is engaged in relation to the arrest and pre-CIA detention and/or proxy detention,[71] and rendition to CIA detention of at least three individuals: Suleiman Abdallah, Mohammed Al-Asad, and Guled Hassan Dourad. Available information reveals that the US used Djibouti – and most importantly the military base Camp Lemonnier, leased by Djibouti to the US since 2001 – as a hub for its renditions from East Africa.[72] In this respect, the US benefited from the collaboration of Djiboutian authorities.

Suleiman Abdallah, a Tanzanian national, was abducted in Mogadishu, Somalia, on or around 15 March 2003. He was handed to US and Kenyan officials in Bossasso, Somalia, and rendered to Kenya, Djibouti, and Afghanistan.[73] In 2008, after five years of incommunicado detention and torture, Abdallah was unconditionally released from Bagram Airforce Base, Afghanistan. Abdallah recounts being held and physically abused by American personnel at an airport in Djibouti before being forcibly rendered to CIA detention in Afghanistan, where he was subjected to a range of treatments amounting to torture and cruel, inhuman, and degrading treatment (CIDT).[74] The SSCI Study confirms that Abdallah was amongst 'at least six detainees [that] were stripped and shackled, nude, in the standing stress position for sleep deprivation or subject to other enhanced interrogation techniques prior to being questioned'

---

[71] See Chapter 3, section 3.4.1 for details on the practice of proxy detention and its legal implications.

[72] Justice Forum's 2015 Shadow Report to the ACommHPR on Djibouti Renditions affirms that three more individuals have been rendered from Djibouti to US DoD custody in Djibouti and then Guantánamo Bay. They are thus not among the CIA detainees, but their stories support the allegations of the three CIA detainees and constitute additional evidence of the role played by Djibouti in the US war on terror. Justice Forum et al., 'Ignorance is No Defence: Djibouti, Rendition & Torture' (14 April 2015).

[73] Human Rights Council (n 49) Annex II, Case 2, 154; Sam Raphael, Crofton Black and Ruth Blakeley, 'CIA Torture Unredacted' (2019) 199–200.

[74] Justice Forum (n 72) 9.

in 2003.[75] Abdallah is also listed as one of 17 CIA detainees subjected to enhanced interrogation techniques without the approval of CIA headquarters.[76] His claim before US courts against the two CIA-contracted psychologists (James Mitchell and John Jessen) who designed and implemented interrogation and torture for the CIA programme was the first claim to be allowed to proceed to trial. It was however settled out of court a few weeks before the planned jury trial.[77]

Mohammed Al-Asad, a Yemeni national, was arrested in Dar es Salaam, Tanzania, on 26 December 2003. The following day, he was secretly flown to Djibouti, where he was questioned by US officials. Al-Asad spent about two weeks in Djibouti before being forcibly rendered to Afghanistan, where he was held in several CIA black sites before being returned to Yemen in May 2005. The SSCI Study confirms that Al-Asad was held in CIA custody for between 480 and 489 days.[78]

With regard to Abdallah and Al-Asad, Djibouti's international responsibility is engaged as a proxy detention site, i.e., Djibouti is responsible as principal wrongdoer for their incommunicado detention on its territory. Indeed, while details of their rendition to and from Djibouti are not fully established, it nonetheless appears that Djiboutian authorities were involved and had some contact with the detainees.[79] In addition, Djibouti is responsible for their mistreatment during their detention in, and rendition from Djibouti,[80] whether at the hands of Djiboutian authorities (negative obligations) or of CIA or US agents (positive obligations). Djibouti is also responsible for their rendition to CIA detention, which implies a breach of the prohibitions of refoulement to torture, arbitrary detention, and enforced disappearance.

---

[75] United States Senate Select Committee on Intelligence (n 46) 491–492.
[76] ibid 101–102, 459.
[77] US District Court for the Eastern District of Washington, *Suleiman Abdallah Salim and Others* v. *Mitchell and Jessen*, 17 August 2017. The case was filed in October 2015, basing its legal claims on the declassified facts in the executive summary of the SSCI Study. During the lawsuit's discovery process, dozens of new documents detailing the torture program were unearthed, and the case forced former senior CIA officials Jose Rodriguez and John Rizzo – in addition to Mitchell and Jessen themselves – to testify about torture during depositions. The full terms of the settlement are confidential.
[78] Al-Asad appears under the name 'Muhammed Abdullah Saleh' as detainee #92 in the SSCI Study, Appendix 2. See also Raphael, Black and Blakeley (n 73) 225–226.
[79] This should be contrasted with the role played by the Polish authorities, detailed in section 6.4.1 below.
[80] Both Abdullah and Al-Asad were subjected to the usual rendition 'security check', recognised as constituting a violation of Article 7 ICCPR. See *Alzery* v. *Sweden*, CCPR/C/88/D/1416/2005, para 11.6.

With regard to the prohibition of refoulement, Djibouti's knowledge regarding the risks to which it was exposing Al-Asad and Abdallah by rendering them to CIA custody must be assessed against the public knowledge timeline developed in Chapter 3.[81] At the time of Abdallah's rendition through Djibouti, in late March 2003, knowledge about CIA secret detention sites was starting to emerge, as was knowledge about conditions of detention in CIA and US DoD custody. Djibouti should therefore have, at minima, inquired about interrogation methods, detention conditions, and the lawfulness of detention to discharge its obligation to protect. There are no elements showing that this has been the case. At the time of Al-Asad's rendition, in contrast, it was already widely known that detainees held in CIA prisons were held arbitrarily and in inhumane and degrading conditions, so that constructive knowledge can be imputed to Djibouti. The breach of the prohibition of refoulement is characterised in both instances of rendition.

In respect of Guleed Hassan Dourad, a Somali national captured by Djiboutian authorities on 4 March 2004 and rendered from Djibouti to CIA detention on 8 March 2004,[82] Djibouti's international responsibility is engaged on similar grounds. It is first engaged for Dourad's arrest and his incommunicado detention between 4 and 8 March 2004, a period during which he was in the custody of Djiboutian authorities and directly interrogated by CIA officers. Second, it is engaged for torture, CIDT, and complicity thereof, in relation to, at least, the rendition procedure to which Dourad was subjected at Djibouti-Ambouli International Airport.[83] Further, by allowing CIA officers to interrogate Dourad, Djibouti is responsible for exposing him to mistreatment, in breach of its obligation to protect.

Finally, Djibouti's responsibility is engaged for Dourad's rendition to arbitrary detention, torture, CIDT and enforced disappearance, in breach of the prohibition of refoulement.[84] Indeed, after being handed over to the CIA, Dourad was rendered from Djibouti on 8 March 2004 on a CIA-owned Gulfstream V jet. His destination remains unclear as the aircraft flew to Afghanistan, Morocco, and Guantánamo Bay after taking off from Djibouti.[85]

---

[81] Chapter 3, Table 3.2.
[82] Raphael, Black and Blakeley (n 73) 246; United States Senate Select Committee on Intelligence (n 46) 336–342; Justice Forum (n 72) 14–15.
[83] The procedure has been recognised as constituting a violation of Article 7 ICCPR. See *Alzery* v. *Sweden*, CCPR/C/88/D/1416/2005, para 11.6.
[84] Knowledge is not at issue in that case, as it is considered established that by early 2004 it was public knowledge that US detainees in the war on terror were held unlawfully and that torture was used by US interrogators.
[85] According to journalist Adam Goldman, Dourad was in secret CIA detention in Guantánamo Bay during March 2004, before being moved to Morocco with other high-value detainees. It may therefore be that the detainee was kept on the air-

Dourad disappeared in the CIA secret detention site network for two years, before reappearing in Guantánamo Bay on 4 September 2006, where he is still detained without charges. He is one of the 14 HVDs interviewed by the ICRC in 2006.[86] While it remains unclear whether he was subjected to enhanced interrogation techniques,[87] he may have been tortured while in CIA or proxy detention[88] and he is identified as one of the detainees for whom 'care [was] delayed for serious medical issues'.[89]

6.3.2 Accountability Network

Djibouti's accountability network is averagely endowed, institutionally speaking. One can regret the lack of consent to the UNCAT individual complaint procedure and to the statute of the ACtPHR. However, this is partially compensated by consent to the ICCPR individual complaint procedure, to the jurisdiction of the ICC and ICJ, and the competence of the ACommHPR to receive individual communications.

Regarding the interstate aspects of the network, Djibouti's history as the last French colony (until 1977) and its strategic geographical location mean that it conserves privileged relationships with Western and Asian powers, many of which use its territory as a military base in the Horn of Africa. The most important is Camp Lemonnier, the only permanent US military base in Africa. Camp Lemonnier hosts the 'Combined Joint Task Force – Horn of Africa' (CJTF-HOA) of the 'US Africa Command' (USAFRICOM); supports 'Operation Enduring Freedom – Horn of Africa'; and serves as a hub for aerial operations in the Persian Gulf region. In addition, the country hosts several other foreign military bases, including a Chinese naval base, a French airbase, and a Japanese base.

Djibouti's strategic location means that it possesses useful leverage in its discussions with other states. Yet, because Djibouti's economy is, in its own words, that of 'a rentier state relying on its port infrastructures and military

---

craft during its flight to Afghanistan and Morocco, where it may have picked up and/or dropped off further detainees. Goldman then surmises that Dourad was moved to Morocco with other HVDs at the end of March 2004, before the Supreme Court decision in *Rasul* v. *Bush*. A Goldman, 'Secret Jails: Terror Suspect's Odyssey Through CIA's "Black Sites"', Associated Press, 19 August 2010.

[86] ICRC, 'ICRC Report on the Treatment of Fourteen "High Value Detainees" in CIA Custody' (2007).

[87] United States Senate Select Committee on Intelligence (n 46) 338 affirms that he was not.

[88] Notwithstanding that extraordinary rendition, secret detention, and HVDs' conditions of detention have been widely recognised as constituting torture.

[89] United States Senate Select Committee on Intelligence (n 46) 493.

International legal accountability in the CIA war on terror 209

bases',[90] it is itself highly dependent upon other states' presence on its territory. In addition, its low economic power relative to other states will almost always make economic pressures possible and effective. Nevertheless, the concurrent dependency of other states on their military bases and port access in Djibouti means that they will be less likely to raise human rights concerns and enforce international decisions against Djibouti.

Figure 6.2 visually presents Djibouti's institutional accountability network.

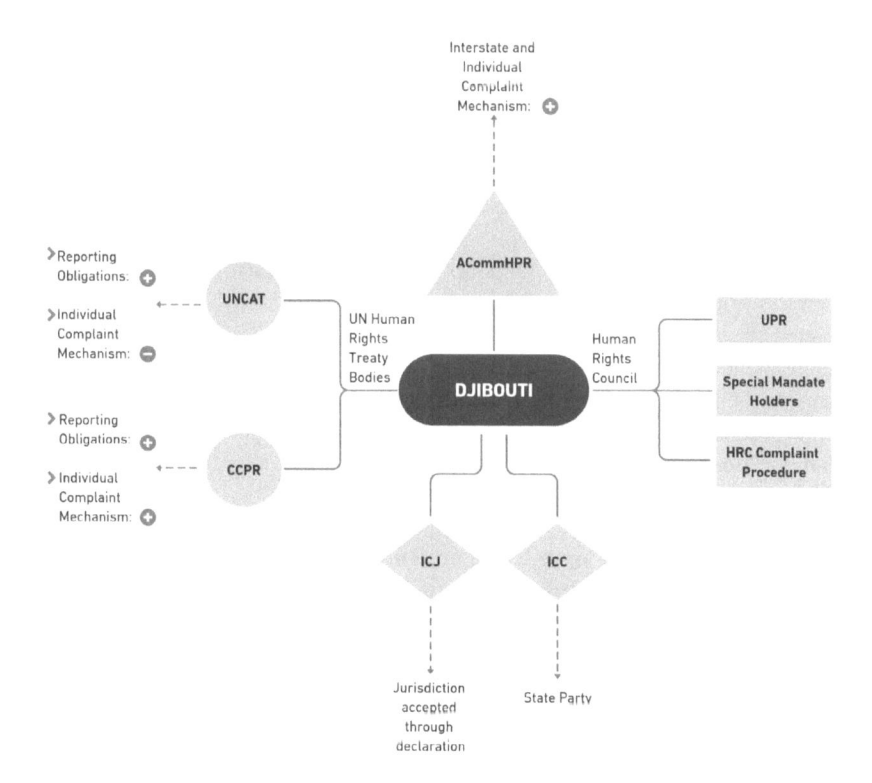

Figure 6.2   Djibouti's accountability network

---

[90] Republic of Djibouti, Combined Initial and Periodic Report under the African Charter on Human and Peoples' Rights, 2014.

6.3.3 Evaluation

Table 6.2 evaluates Djibouti's accountability network following the framework developed in Chapter 5.

As evidenced in Table 6.2, Djibouti's accountability network is very strong institutionally, with a good capacity to constrain and escalate and solid legitimacy. Despite the network's theoretical capacity to constrain based on relative power imbalances, interdependencies with other states somewhat undermine its strength and independence. It is therefore unlikely that states with economic or military interests in Djibouti will adopt an enforcer role in the human rights field, leaving it to institutional actors. Hence, the relative accessibility of institutional mechanisms to non-state account-holders and the publicity of their proceedings and decisions are important features of the network.

6.3.4 Assessment of Practice

By virtue of the strength of Djibouti's institutional network and its accessibility to non-state account-holders, expectations are higher than for the US. Naturally, the low number of cases in which Djibouti is implicated and its interdependence with the US, coupled with the reluctance of third states to involve themselves in holding either of them to account, should mitigate those expectations slightly. Yet, the absence of successful proceedings raises important questions in terms of procedural accessibility and equality in intelligence cooperation cases.

6.3.4.1 The African Commission on Human and Peoples' Rights

The only individual complaint against Djibouti was filed by Mohammed Al-Asad in December 2009 before the African Commission on Human and Peoples' Rights (ACommHPR). It was declared inadmissible by the Commission in 2014, on the ground that the complainant failed to 'conclusively establish that he was in Djibouti to the exclusion of the other alleged participating countries' of the CIA programme in the same region.[91] The Commission nevertheless rejected, as a matter of principle, Djibouti's argument that the Commission was unable to adjudicate the communication under the *Monetary Gold* principle, thus providing an important clarification for intelligence cooperation cases involving allegations of torture.[92]

---

[91] Communication 383/2010, *Mohammed Abdullah Saleh Al-Asad* v. *The Republic of Djibouti*, 14 October 2014, para 165.
[92] ibid para 180.

Table 6.2   Evaluation of Djibouti's accountability network

DJIBOUTI	Evaluation Factors	Evaluation and Comments
Capacity to Constrain and Escalate	Jurisdiction *ratione materiae*	STRONG. The network as a whole has universal competence.
	Jurisdiction *ratione personae*	STRONG. All actors but the ACommHPR have near-universal jurisdiction.
	Investigatory powers	STRONG. Consent to all optional investigatory powers has been given.
	Powers to sanction non-cooperation	STRONG. Several actors have compulsory jurisdiction and the power to sanction non-cooperation.
	Capacity to order remedies	STRONG. Several actors have compulsory jurisdiction and the capacity to order remedies.
	Capacity to sanction	STRONG. Several actors have compulsory jurisdiction and the capacity to impose sanctions.
	Reputation of account-holder state – Standing in the international legal order – Relative power – Human rights records	STRONG. Djibouti's economic and political power is weak; it is highly dependent upon other states; and it does not have a strong human rights record. Hence, other states are likely to be in a stronger position and have a more solid reputation.
	Capacity of account-holder state to constrain compliance – Interdependencies – Leverage tools	MEDIUM. Powerful states are almost all dependent upon Djibouti for its port and/or military bases and are therefore unlikely to call it to account.

DJIBOUTI	Evaluation Factors	Evaluation and Comments
Legitimacy	Overall reputation	STRONG. All actors have a strong reputation and their access is not restricted.
	Participation of the state under scrutiny	STRONG. Participation of the state is encouraged and necessary in almost all procedures.
	Capacity to reward compliance or de-escalate	STRONG. Most actors can impose interim measures, and Djibouti has reporting obligations under several mechanisms.
	Independence – Budget and resources – Formal independence – Judicial independence – Relative power (state)	MEDIUM. Most actors perform a judicial or quasi-judicial function. All are formally independent and possess relatively stable resources, which Djibouti cannot influence. Other states are relatively dependent upon Djibouti's geographical location, but this is mitigated by Djibouti's dependence upon their financial resources.
Publicity and Accessibility	Representation of public interest	STRONG. The public interest is represented in all judicial and quasi-judicial procedures, as well as by shadow reporting and reporting obligations.
	Publicity of proceedings	STRONG. Reports are public and most hearing also are, in some form (video streaming or written records).
	Publicity of outcomes	STRONG. Decisions by all actors, except the HRC in its complaint procedure, are public.
	Accessibility to non-state account-holders – Information – Financial and geographical accessibility – Procedural accessibility	STRONG Non-state account-holders have access to several individual complaint procedures, representing a spectrum of geographical and procedural accessibility. Information about the procedures is readily available and several are free of cost.

In its inadmissibility decision, the Commission was careful to distinguish *Al-Asad* from the ECtHR's *El-Masri* case.[93] It emphasised that, in *El-Masri*, 'there was overwhelming evidence placing the applicant both in the territory and under the jurisdiction of [Macedonia]', including the testimony of a former minister of interior.[94] Yet, if this factual difference could possibly justify a different decision when looking at the cases in isolation, it became apparent

---

[93] ECtHR, *El-Masri* (n 66).
[94] *Al-Asad* (n 91).

with the ECtHR's judgments against Poland in July 2014[95] that the two bodies had adopted very different procedural approaches to CIA-related cases. Even if the chronology of the decisions had been reversed, the ACommHPR could not have distinguished the Polish cases from *Al-Asad* based on the evidence provided by the applicants. Yet, despite their factual similarities and the high level of secrecy surrounding the facts, the cases yielded opposite outcomes. The ACommHPR's and ECtHR's opposite procedural approaches form the only plausible explanation for this difference.

In the Polish cases, as in *El-Masri*, the ECtHR articulated a framework for assessing the standard and burden of proof that takes into account the near-impossibility of discovering direct evidence in CIA-related cases. The ECtHR thus employs a burden-shifting analysis that requires the respondent state to substantively refute allegations and draws inferences from the state's failure to provide plausible explanations.[96] The absence of such a framework in *Al-Asad*, coupled with a few procedural errors and confusions by the Commission,[97] led to a decision that does not adequately take into account the particularities of CIA-related cases, and one that favours states who manage to keep all information about their participation in the programme secret.

In addition, the Commission went to great lengths to distinguish the requirement of jurisdiction *ratione loci*, read under Article 56(2) of the Charter,[98] from other jurisdictional criteria. It argued that jurisdiction *ratione loci* could only be established at the admissibility stage, and should therefore be established conclusively at that stage.[99] It is unclear what legal basis the Commission uses to justify this position, despite its direct impact upon its decision on admissibility.

It is however apparent from the Commission's decision that Djibouti successfully attempted to rely on the secrecy inherent to the CIA programme and its own failure to adequately investigate Al-Asad's allegations to shield itself from accountability. Instead of ensuring that these tactics did not result in the victory of states that cooperated in the CIA programme, the Commission's decision allowed Djibouti to prevail. By so doing, it denied victims of serious

---

[95] ECtHR, *Al-Nashiri v. Poland* (n 68); ECtHR, *Husayn (Abu Zubaydah) v. Poland* (n 68). See below section 6.4.4.1 for analysis.

[96] *El-Masri* (n 66) paras 151–153; *Al-Nashiri v. Poland* (n 68) paras 395–396; *Husayn (Abu Zubaydah) v. Poland* (n 68) paras 395-396.

[97] See NYU Global Justice Clinic, Request for Review of the Commission's Decision on Admissibility, December 2014, available at: https://chrgj.org/wp-content/uploads/2018/01/Al-AsadvDjibouti_RequestforReconsideration.pdf

[98] Stating that 'Communications relating to Human and Peoples' rights … shall be considered if they … are compatible with the Charter of the Organisation of African Unity or with the present Charter'.

[99] *Al-Asad* (n 91) paras 140–146.

human rights violations access to justice and even the opportunity to have their claims heard on the merits.

However, following a request for review of the Commission's 2014 decision,[100] the African Commission overturned it and found the case admissible in 2016.[101] As of August 2022, it had yet to issue a decision on the merits. The Commission held a hearing on the communication in May 2018[102] but, since then, it has deferred making a decision on multiple occasions.[103] The Commission only publishes final decisions on its website, meaning that only decisions dismissing cases as inadmissible or decisions on the merits are published. Therefore, while the Commission did note in its annual report that it granted the plaintiff's request for review, thereby overturning its previous inadmissibility finding, the only decision available on the Commission's website is the outdated 2014 decision finding the case inadmissible.

Finally, in its reporting obligations under the African Charter, Djibouti did not mention the allegations of secret detention or participation in the CIA programme.[104] Neither did the Commission in its 2015 concluding observations,[105] despite the 'new' incriminating elements provided by the publication of the SSCI Study regarding Djibouti's involvement in the programme.

6.3.4.2 UN treaty bodies and the Human Rights Council

The only mention of Djibouti's participation in the CIA programme is an allusion to the case of Al-Asad by the UNCAT in its 2011 concluding observations on Djibouti's initial report.[106] In this paragraph, the UNCAT recommends that Djibouti conduct an independent, impartial and thorough investigation into the incident, and adopt a legislative framework regulating expulsion, refoulement, and extradition in order to fulfil its obligation under Article 3 CAT. The CIA

---

[100] NYU Global Justice Clinic (n 97).

[101] 40th Activity Report of the African Commission on Human and Peoples' Rights 7, available at: https://www.achpr.org/activityreports/viewall?id=39

[102] 44th Activity Report of the African Commission on Human and Peoples' Rights 9, available at: https://www.achpr.org/activityreports/viewall?id=43

[103] 45th Activity Report of the African Commission on Human and Peoples' Rights 12, available at: https://www.achpr.org/activityreports/viewall?id=49; and 46th Activity Report of the African Commission on Human and Peoples' Rights 8, available at: https://www.achpr.org/activityreports/viewall?id=50

[104] Republic of Djibouti, Combined Initial and Periodic Report under the African Charter on Human and Peoples' Rights, 2014.

[105] Observations conclusives et Recommandations relatives aux Rapports initial et périodique combinés de la République de Djibouti sur la Mise en Œuvre de la Charte africaine des Droits de l'Homme et des Peuples (1993–2014), 56ème Session ordinaire 21 avril–7 mai 2015, à Banjul, Gambie.

[106] CAT/C/DJI/CO/1, 22 December 2011, para 14(c).

programme is not mentioned or alluded to anywhere else, nor is it in the concluding observations of the CCPR.[107] There was no mention or allusion to it either in any of the three UPR cycles concerning Djibouti.[108]

Djibouti is however listed in the 2010 UN Joint Study on Secret Detention as a proxy detention site,[109] and a full paragraph is dedicated to the facts of Al-Asad's case.[110] In addition, 'Case 2' of Annex II is based upon an interview with Suleiman Abdallah (corroborated by 'other credible sources'), who mentions Djibouti as one of the places through which he transited during his rendition from Somalia to Afghanistan.[111] A follow-up communication by the special mandate holders who conducted the UN Joint Study invited Djibouti to provide them with information on measures taken to investigate the allegations contained in the Joint Study and, if found true, to rectify the situation in compliance with international human rights norms and standards; to implement the related recommendations; and to provide any other relevant information.[112] The communication remains unanswered to this day.

6.3.4.3 Assessment

Despite the strength of its accountability network, Djibouti has not been held accountable for its participation in the CIA programme. Rather the opposite, the sole attempt made by a victim to obtain redress ended up rewarding the state for its policy of secrecy by declaring the petition inadmissible on account of the lack of direct evidence provided by the complainant, even as the state did not provide any substantive evidence to refute the allegations. The lack of use of the many available institutional accountability mechanisms, in their various aspects and procedures, is also quite surprising.

It is difficult to identify with certainty the reasons behind this lack of accountability, but also, and maybe more importantly, behind the lack of attention to Djibouti's role in the programme despite strong evidence of its participation. Djibouti's lack of engagement with institutional mechanisms, evidenced by the extreme delays with which it submits its reports (if at all) or answers communications, displays a posture of disengagement. Hence, it is possible that institutional mechanisms, when they manage to engage with the state, would prefer to prioritise domestic human rights issues. Interstate pressures and reputational concerns (especially regarding trustworthiness)

---

[107] CCPR/C/DJI/CO/1, 19 November 2013.
[108] A/HRC/39/10, 11 July 2018; A/HRC/24/10, 8 July 2013; A/HRC/11/16, 5 October 2009.
[109] Human Rights Council (n 49) para 143.
[110] ibid para 157.
[111] ibid Annex II, 154.
[112] DJI 3/2011, 21 October 2011.

might also play a role in Djibouti's disengagement and willingness to preserve secrecy over its partners' activities on its territory.

6.4 POLAND

6.4.1 State Responsibility

Poland's responsibility is engaged as a black site host. It is now established that the CIA used a base in the village of Stare Kiejkuty, near Szczytno-Szymany airport (now renamed Olsztyn-Mazury) as a secret detention site holding 'high value detainees' (HVDs) between December 2002 and September 2003.[113] CIA detainees were rendered through Szymany airport, with the complicity of Polish government and military intelligence officials.[114] Polish officials were never in contact with detainees. Poland was 'simply' the host state, providing cover-up and security but not 'treating' detainees.[115]

Poland has been implicated in at least eight[116] individual cases: Abd Al-Rahim Al-Nashiri, Abu Zubaydah, Khaled Sheikh Mohammed, Ramzi bin al-Shibh,[117] Walid bin Attash,[118] Ammar al-Baluchi,[119] Samr al-Barq,[120] and Abu Yasir al-Jaza'iri.[121] The first six are considered HVDs and are still

---

[113] The SSCI Study refers to it as [DETENTION SITE BLUE]. See Chapter 3, Table 3.1.

[114] See Dick Marty, 'Secret Detentions and Illegal Transfers of Detainees Involving Council of Europe Member States' (Parliamentary Assembly of the Council of Europe 2007) PACE Doc. 11302 rev. paras 180–196 for information on Polish complicity into air navigation and landing of CIA rendition flights; and para 197 on the transfer of HVDs at Szymany airport; Human Rights Council (n 49) paras 116–117 on the modus operandi of rendition flights in Poland.

[115] Marty (n 114) paras 198–200.

[116] Marty (n 114) and the Human Rights Council (n 49) also claim that at least eight CIA detainees were held in Poland, but they include Ahmed Ghailani, whose capture occurred almost a year after the closure of the Polish detention site.

[117] The SSCI Study details at length the detention and treatment of all four individuals in [DETENTION SITE BLUE]. Exact dates are as follows: Al-Nashiri (5 December 2002–6 June 2003); Abu Zubaydah (5 December 2002–22 September 2003); Khaled Sheikh Mohammed (7 March–22 September 2003); Ramzi bin al-Shibh (8 February–6 June 2003).

[118] Raphael, Black and Blakeley (n 73) 208 place him at Stare Kiejkuty from 5 June to 22 September 2003.

[119] Raphael, Black and Blakeley (n 73) 208 place him at Stare Kiejkuty from 29 July to 22 September 2003.

[120] Raphael, Black and Blakeley (n 73) 219 place him at Stare Kiejkuty from 29 July to 22 September 2003.

[121] Raphael, Black and Blakeley (n 73) 198 place him at Stare Kiejkuty from 25 March to 22 September 2003.

detained at Guantánamo Bay. All eight detainees were subjected to enhanced interrogation techniques (EITs) while held in Poland.

Through the provision of infrastructure, material support, and operational security, Poland enabled the US to violate CIA detainees' rights. Poland's international responsibility is therefore engaged for the breach of its obligation to protect CIA detainees on its territory from torture, arbitrary detention, enforced disappearance, and refoulement. Indeed, far from taking steps to discharge its positive obligations towards CIA detainees, the Polish state instead facilitated the violation of their rights. In that sense, Poland's conduct was not only passive, but also constituted active aid or assistance to the wrongful acts committed by the US under Article 16 ASR.[122]

6.4.2 Accountability Network

On paper, Poland has a perfect institutional accountability network. It has consented to the jurisdiction of all optional mechanisms, several of which have investigatory powers and/or can issue binding decisions. Further, their jurisdiction *ratione temporis* and *materiae* covers all aspects of Poland's participation in the CIA programme.

On the interstate level, Poland is (now) a member of the EU,[123] the Council of Europe (CoE) and NATO. Membership of European organisations, in particular, implies some pressure from fellow member states (directly or through institutional bodies) to behave in compliance with the values, laws, and rules of the organisation. Both the EU and the CoE place great emphasis on human rights and democratic values. Since respect for them is a formal condition of membership, this gives leverage to other member states.

On the other hand, at the time the US war on terror was launched, there was a 'special relationship' between the US and Poland,[124] and strong pro-American sentiment in the Polish administration.[125] In addition, 'the United States chose, in the case of Poland and Romania, to form special partnerships with countries that were economically vulnerable, emerging from difficult transitional periods in their history, and dependent on American support for their strategic development'.[126] In contrast with EU and CoE membership, therefore, NATO membership facilitated US pressures over Poland and continues to enable

---

[122] See Chapter 3, section 3.4.2.
[123] Poland only became a member of the EU in 2004.
[124] John Pomfret, *From Warsaw with Love: Polish Spies, the CIA, and the Forging of an Unlikely Alliance* (Henry Holt and Co 2021).
[125] Marty (n 114) paras 124–125.
[126] ibid para 123.

secrecy and lack of accountability.[127] In general, Poland's dependence upon its EU and CoE member state status makes it relatively sensitive to pressure for more transparency and accountability from other member states of these organisations. EU membership also provides Poland with additional economic and political strength on the global scene, something that was missing during its participation in the CIA programme, and makes it less vulnerable to extra-EU pressures. Yet, the strong anti-Russian and pro-American sentiment in Poland continues to make it particularly vulnerable to US pressures, including those that run counter to the rule of law and democratic values.

Figure 6.3 visually presents Poland's institutional accountability network.

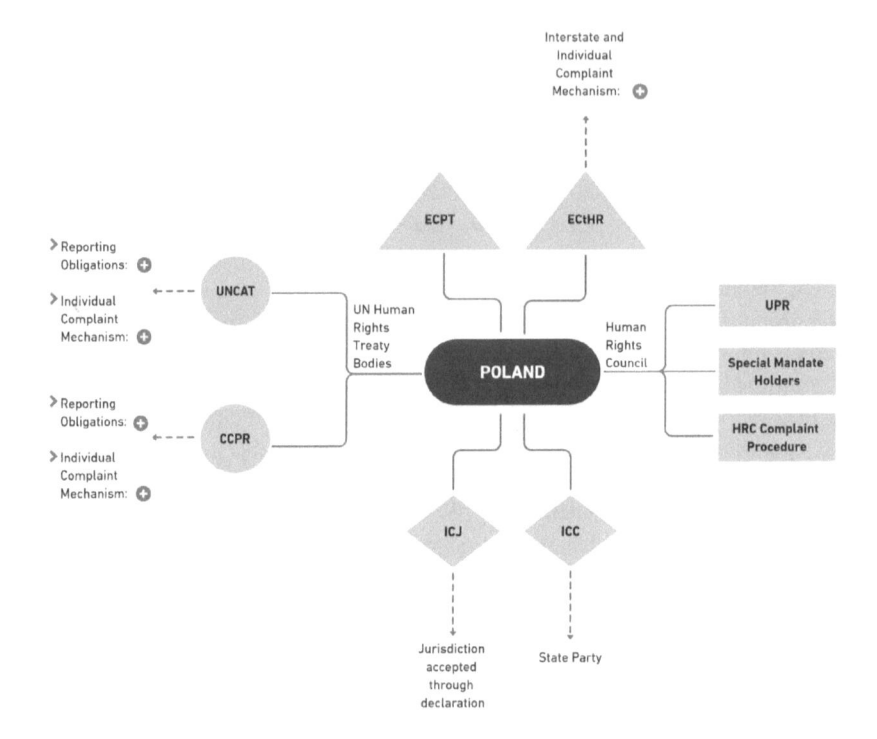

Figure 6.3   *Poland's accountability network*

---

[127] The SOFA between the US and Poland is classified at 'cosmic top secret' level, and NATO's secrecy and security of information regime was used to secure secrecy over all information relating to the CIA programme in the cooperation between the US and host states. Marty (n 114) para 179.

6.4.3 Evaluation

Table 6.3 evaluates Poland's accountability network following the framework developed in Chapter 5.

Table 6.3 evidences that Poland's accountability network is strong on all fronts. The sole caveat concerns the relative lack of interstate leverage for non-EU and non-NATO states. However, it is well compensated by the relative power imbalance favouring EU and most NATO states. The network's strength is embodied in the variety of available actors and procedures composing the institutional network, which altogether enhance its capacity to constrain and escalate, its legitimacy, and its accessibility. Nevertheless, the individual contributions of specific actors (such as the ECtHR) to the network's solidity should not be understated, even though they may not be sufficient by themselves.

6.4.4 Assessment of Practice

On account of its very strong accountability network, expectations regarding practice are very high. In fact, Poland is the only state among those featured in this chapter to have been held judicially accountable. Yet, no meaningful dialogue between the state and its accountability mechanisms has ever been established. In this situation, the importance of a strong capacity to constrain and escalate becomes apparent. Still, since not all states are subject to the jurisdiction of a strong international court, the fact that a state can effectively shut down all other accountability avenues through its lack of engagement is worrisome. Further, this leaves the issue of implementation unresolved.

6.4.4.1 The European Court of Human Rights

The ECtHR issued two judgments against Poland in the twin cases of *Abd al Rahim Al-Nashiri* v. *Poland* and *Husayn (Abu Zubaydah)* v. *Poland*.[128] Both cases concerned the extraordinary rendition, secret detention, and torture of the applicants by the CIA on Polish territory. On the substantive side, the Court found Poland responsible for the applicants' arbitrary detention on its territory, as well as for their transfer from its territory (refoulement to arbitrary detention).[129] In contrast with its earlier decision in *El-Masri*, however, it did not

---

[128] ECtHR, *Al-Nashiri* v. *Poland* (n 68); ECtHR, *Husayn (Abu Zubaydah)* v. *Poland* (n 68).

[129] The Court found Poland responsible under Articles 3, 5, 8 and 13, as well as under Articles 2 and 3 of the Convention taken together with Article 1 of Protocol No. 6 to the Convention in respect of Al-Nashiri. It also found Poland responsible for a breach of Article 38 due to its refusal to cooperate with the investigation.

Table 6.3   *Evaluation of Poland's accountability network*

POLAND	Evaluation Factors	Evaluation and Comments
Capacity to Constrain and Escalate	Jurisdiction *ratione materiae*	STRONG. The network as a whole has universal competence.
	Jurisdiction *ratione personae*	STRONG. All actors but the ECHR and ECPT have near-universal jurisdiction.
	Investigatory powers	STRONG. Consent to all optional investigatory powers has been given, and the ECPT is endowed with additional investigatory powers.
	Powers to sanction non-cooperation	STRONG. Several actors have compulsory jurisdiction and the power to sanction non-cooperation.
	Capacity to order remedies	STRONG. Several actors have compulsory jurisdiction and the capacity to order remedies.
	Capacity to sanction	STRONG. Several actors have compulsory jurisdiction and the capacity to impose sanctions.
	Reputation of account-holder state – Standing in the international legal order – Relative power – Human rights records	MEDIUM. Poland is not a superpower but being an EU member state gives it some credence economically, as does being a member of NATO in military terms. Other EU states will often have better human rights records and a higher relative power, but that is not necessarily the case for non-EU states.
	Capacity of account-holder state to constrain compliance – Interdependencies – Leverage tools	MEDIUM. Poland is part of the EU and NATO, providing it with strong protection against external pressures from non-EU and non-NATO states. Against EU and NATO states, however, Poland is quite vulnerable.
Legitimacy	Overall reputation	STRONG. All actors have a strong reputation and their access is not restricted.
	Participation of the state under scrutiny	STRONG. Participation of the state is encouraged and necessary in almost all procedures.
	Capacity to reward compliance or de-escalate	STRONG. Most actors can impose interim measures, and Poland has reporting obligations under several mechanisms.
	Independence – Budget and resources – Formal independence – Judicial independence – Relative power (state)	STRONG. Most actors perform a judicial or quasi-judicial function. All are formally independent and possess relatively stable resources, which Poland cannot influence. Other states, especially EU and NATO states, are in a strong position against Poland.

POLAND	Evaluation Factors	Evaluation and Comments
Publicity and Accessibility	Representation of public interest	STRONG. The public interest is represented in all judicial and quasi-judicial procedures, as well as by shadow reporting and reporting obligations.
	Publicity of proceedings	STRONG. Reports are public and most hearings also are, in some form (video streaming or written records).
	Publicity of outcomes	STRONG. Decisions by all actors, except the HRC in its complaint procedure, are public.
	Accessibility to non-state account-holders – Information – Financial and geographical accessibility – Procedural accessibility	STRONG. Non-state account-holders have access to several individual complaint procedures, representing a spectrum of geographical and procedural accessibility. Information about the procedures is readily available and several are free of cost.

find Poland responsible for the applicants' detention after they were rendered to another detention site. This can be explained by an important factual difference between the cases: in the Polish cases, the domestic authorities never came in direct contact with the applicants.[130]

On the procedural side, the applicants highlighted that the brief parliamentary inquiry into allegations of a CIA black site had been conducted behind closed doors and the results were never made public.[131] In addition, while criminal proceedings had been formally instituted against unknown persons concerning secret detention in March 2008, there had been no progress in the investigation and the state had unduly delayed the proceedings.[132] In its judgments on this issue, the ECtHR laid strong emphasis on the need to ensure that a refusal by states to disclose information in the course of an investigative process is subject to independent scrutiny. It noted in particular that the Polish government had refused, on grounds of national security, to supply the applicants' lawyers with information regarding its ongoing criminal investigations despite most of this information having already been published in detail in the national press.[133]

---

[130] The differentiated approach of the Court to this issue is confirmed by the latter case of *Nasr and Ghali* v. *Italy*, App. No.44883/09, 23 February 2016, which follows *El-Masri*, while *Al-Nashiri* v. *Romania* (n 70) and *Abu Zubaydah* v. *Lithuania* (n 70) follow the Polish cases.

[131] *Al-Nashiri* (n 68) para 121; *Abu Zubaydah* (n 68) para 122.

[132] *Al-Nashiri* (n 68) paras 141–172; *Abu Zubaydah* (n 68) paras 135–166.

[133] *Al-Nashiri* (n 68) para 494; *Abu Zubaydah* (n 68) para 488.

Because the ECtHR is a court of law and its jurisdiction is compulsory, state cooperation is not necessary for the ruling to proceed. In addition, the Court's international character means that it holds several procedural advantages for claimants. Of particular relevance in intelligence cooperation cases is that the state secret privilege does not apply. Further, the Court is not restricted by procedural barriers in the admission of evidence; and it has adopted a practice of shifting the burden of proof onto the state in situations where the respondent state is the only entity with exclusive knowledge of the facts. In CIA-related cases, the ECtHR therefore drew extensively on independent inquiries conducted by supra-national bodies and organisations to establish and corroborate the facts, which it left open to the respondent states to rebuke.

Yet, Poland also frustrated the proceedings before the ECtHR itself by refusing, again for reasons of national security, to follow the Court's procedures and accede to its repeated requests to view specific documentary material.[134] This obstructive attitude undoubtedly contributed to the Court's finding in both cases of a procedural breach of Article 3, read alone and in conjunction with Article 13. The importance and gravity of the issues at stake required, in the Court's view, 'particularly intense public scrutiny' of the investigations in order to secure proper accountability of those responsible for unlawful action.[135] The Court voiced further concern that the cases also pointed to a more general problem of democratic oversight of intelligence services, requiring appropriate safeguards in law and in practice to prevent further human rights violations arising from covert operations.[136]

6.4.4.2 UN treaty bodies and the Human Rights Council

In their concluding observations, both the UNCAT and CCPR expressed concerns regarding allegations of a secret detention site in Poland[137] and the persistent lack of effective investigation at domestic level.[138] In its 2019 concluding observations, the UNCAT reiterated its concerns about the enduring lack of accountability of Polish officials in relation to Poland's involvement in the CIA programme. Significantly, it also urged Poland to implement the ECtHR judgments, and insisted on its obligation to do so also 'in the context of the State party's ratification of the Rome Statute of the International Criminal

---

[134] *Al-Nashiri* (n 68) para 494; *Abu Zubaydah* (n 68) para 488.
[135] *Al-Nashiri* (n 68) para 497; *Abu Zubaydah* (n 68) para 491.
[136] *Al-Nashiri* (n 68) para 498; *Abu Zubaydah* (n 68) para 492. The Court found that the state had consequently failed to discharge its obligations under Article 38 ECHR in both sets of proceedings.
[137] CAT/C/POL/CO/4, 25 July 2007, para 11.
[138] CCPR/C/POL/CO/6, 15 November 2010, para 15; CAT/C/POL/CO/5-6, 23 December 2013, para 10; CCPR/C/POL/CO/7, 23 November 2016, paras 11–12.

Court'.¹³⁹ These recommendations evidence the networked functioning of the international legal order, with the UNCAT referring to obligations related to several other treaties and attempting to help enforce a decision by another mechanism.

Although Poland was explicitly named as a secret detention site in the 2010 UN Joint Study and details of its participation are abundantly provided,¹⁴⁰ no case or communication has been brought before any of the available UN mechanisms. A follow-up communication by the special mandate holders who conducted the UN Joint Study was sent in October 2011 but remains unanswered.¹⁴¹

Throughout the three UPR cycles to which Poland was subjected,¹⁴² mention of the secret detention site and rendition flights is made at various points. The lack of transparency of the investigations and their outcomes, in particular, is highlighted by several states.¹⁴³ Polish responses to questions on this topic are, expectedly, rather disappointing.¹⁴⁴ Yet, the added pressure towards transparency provided by interstate dialogue still contributes to the pressure placed on Poland by the network as a whole, especially since states refer to institutional reports and cases when asking questions and making recommendations. As such, they take up the role of enforcers.

6.4.4.3 Assessment

Despite the variety of mechanisms available in Poland's accountability network, only one – the ECtHR – has been used by victims. Given the Court's capacity to sanction compared to other mechanisms, this is rather unsurprising. Still, added pressure from UN treaty bodies could still have proven useful, especially as their competence *ratione personae* also covers the US. Yet, apart from a few paragraphs in concluding observations and a mention of Poland in the UN Joint Study, UN mechanisms have not been used, by victims or otherwise. Most importantly, UN mechanisms have not been successful in engaging a meaningful dialogue with Poland. The ECtHR was confronted with the same posture of disengagement, but its powers as an international court meant that

---

¹³⁹ CAT/C/POL/CO/7, 29 August 2019, para 22.
¹⁴⁰ Human Rights Council (n 49).
¹⁴¹ POL/1/2011, 21 October 2011.
¹⁴² A/HRC/8/30, 23 May 2008; A/HRC/21/14, 9 July 2012; A/HRC/36/14, 18 July 2017.
¹⁴³ E.g., by Russia A/HRC/8/30 para 30; by Switzerland, Cuba and Belarus A/HRC/21/14 paras 90.122, 90.123, and paras 58–59. Note however that none of those states are EU or NATO members.
¹⁴⁴ See A/HRC/8/30 para 32; A/HRC/21/14 paras 58–59; A/HRC/36/14 para 16.

it could bypass Poland's lack of cooperation (and even sanction it) in order to render justice.

The Polish cases are a striking example of accountability exclusively for intelligence cooperation, with violations established under multiple ECHR articles whilst the respondent state's authorities were never in contact with the applicants. Despite these strong judicial decisions, the first ones concerning black sites, implementation is proving to be problematic.[145] Difficulties stem mostly from the US's lack of cooperation, but the Polish government's reluctance to effectively investigate the facts should not be understated either.[146] The fragility of the rule of law[147] and of intelligence oversight in Poland is one of the reasons it was picked by the US as a privileged partner. This same fragility is now the cause of the diminished impact of institutional responses.

6.5 THE GAMBIA

6.5.1 State Responsibility

The Gambia's responsibility is engaged for the arrest, detention, and rendition to CIA detention of Iraqi citizen Bisher al-Rawi and Palestinian-Jordanian dual citizen Jamil el-Banna. Al-Rawi had indefinite leave to remain in the UK while el-Banna had refugee status there. Both were arrested by Gambian authorities at Banjul Airport on 8 November 2002, after extensive communication between MI5, the CIA, and the Gambian National Intelligence Agency (GNIA). It remains unclear whether Gambian authorities arrested the two men based on a hunch, on orders from the CIA, or on miscommunication between the three intelligence services. Indeed, according to the 2007 and

---

[145] In June 2022, Poland finally paid full compensation, in application of the damages award by the ECtHR, to Abu Zubaydah. It remains unclear whether compensation to Al-Nashiri has been paid in full or only partially. Other aspects of the judgments remain unimplemented.

[146] See HUDOC, Status of Execution, for the latest updates on the execution of the two judgments and the supervision by the Committee of Ministers: http://hudoc.exec.coe.int/eng?i=004-20624. For an analysis of the challenges in the implementation of the two judgments, see Barbara Grabowska-Moroz, 'The Polish Roadmap to Accountability: Why the Implementation of Al Nashiri and Abu Zubaydah Judgements Is so Highly Problematic' in Elspeth Guild and Didier Bigo (eds), *Extraordinary Rendition: Addressing the Challenges of Accountability* (Routledge 2018).

[147] In 2002, the fragility of the rule of law in Poland took a different form than it does now. Before joining the European Union in 2004, Poland had to implement important political and judicial reforms to fulfil membership criteria, which it had only partially achieved then. See European Commission, Regular report from the Commission on Poland's progress towards accession 2001. SEC (2001) 1752 final, 13 November 2001, 16–21.

2018 Intelligence and Security Committee (ISC) reports on British complicity in rendition, there is no evidence that MI5 intended the men to be arrested.[148]

In addition, Gambian responsibility is engaged for the arrest and arbitrary detention of the three men who were arrested in the company of al-Rawi and el-Banna: Abdullah El Janoudi, Wahab al-Rawi, and Omar Omeri. All three were detained by Gambian authorities for a period of between a few days to 27 days, and all were interrogated by the CIA during their detention. As they did not enter CIA detention, these three men are beyond the focus of this case-study, but their story brings credit to and additional circumstantial evidence regarding the Gambia's cooperation with the US.

According to information summarised by the Rendition Project,[149] the five men were initially taken to GNIA headquarters. They were questioned for two hours by Gambian officials. The next morning, two Americans interrogated and photographed each of the men. They remained at this location for two days before being transported to what their captors referred to as a 'safe house'. There, they were held in separate, small and windowless holding cells. The safe house was controlled by Americans, and they were interrogated by both Americans and Gambians.

Omeri was released relatively quickly, while El Janoudi was kept for 26 days and Wahab al-Rawi for 27 days. After a further two days, and despite habeas corpus proceedings pending in Gambian courts, Bisher al-Rawi and Jamil el-Banna were driven to the airport in Banjul. There, CIA officials performed their standardised 'rendition security check'[150] and al-Rawi and el-Banna were rendered to Afghanistan. The two men were further shuffled between CIA secret detention sites in Afghanistan before being transferred to Guantánamo Bay in February 2003. They were released and transferred back to the UK in 2007, five years after their arrest in the Gambia. No charges were ever brought against them.

Gambian responsibility is engaged for the arrest, detention, and transfer of al-Rawi and el-Banna into CIA custody. In view of the active role played by Gambian authorities, Gambian responsibility is engaged as principal wrongdoer for all the violations of its negative obligations towards al-Rawi and el-Banna that took place while they were in Gambian custody, whether at the hands of Gambian or US officials. It is engaged for the breach of its positive obligations (to protect and to prevent) with regard to the violations of

---

[148] Great Britain Intelligence and Security Committee, *Rendition* (2007) para 129, https://irp.fas.org/world/uk/rendition.pdf; Intelligence and Security Committee, 'Detainee Mistreatment and Rendition: 2001–2010' (2018) 86.

[149] Raphael, Black and Blakeley (n 73) 181–182.

[150] The procedure has been recognised as constituting a violation of Article 7 ICCPR. See *Alzery v. Sweden*, CCPR/C/88/D/1416/2005, para 11.6.

al-Rawi's and el-Banna's rights committed by CIA officials while they were in CIA custody on Gambian territory.

In addition, Gambian responsibility is engaged for breach of the prohibition of refoulement to torture, arbitrary detention, and other serious human rights violations in respect of the transfer of custody to CIA officials. The knowledge element of the violation is readily established by the treatment to which the two men had been subjected by the CIA while in the Gambia, in the presence of Gambian authorities.[151]

6.5.2 Accountability Network

The Gambia's accountability network is quite strongly endowed institutionally, with a variety of available accountability mechanisms that brings additional strength to the network. With the notable exception of the UNCAT,[152] the Gambia has consented to all optional mechanisms, including the jurisdiction of the ACtHPR. The Gambia is part of all relevant international and regional organisations – which means it has to abide by the rules of these organisations and is subject to their judicial competence where existent (e.g., ECCJ, ICC).

On the interstate level, membership also implies possible pressures by other members. Geographically surrounded by Senegal, the Gambia gained independence from the United Kingdom in 1965. President Yahya Jammeh was defeated after 22 years of dictatorship by Adama Barrow in the 2016 presidential election, but as Jammeh refused to step down, ECOWAS member states intervened militarily early in 2017 to force him to leave the country. The situation illustrates the Gambia's position vis-à-vis its neighbours.

The Gambia is not a superpower, not even regionally or within a hypothetical smaller zone of influence. Its economic dependency on exportations and foreign investments means that economic pressures are possible and usually effective. More generally, the Gambia can be easily pressured by most states and international organisations, which then have an interesting role to play as enforcers. However, the fragility and youth of its democratic institutions and economy also mean that it is vulnerable to foreign anti-democratic pressures, and it has close to no leverage to protect itself against them.

Figure 6.4 visually presents the Gambia's institutional accountability network.

---

[151] In a case with similar facts, the ECtHR has found Macedonia to be in breach of the prohibition of refoulement and responsible for the arbitrary detention of El-Masri at the hands of the CIA. ECtHR, *El-Masri* (n 66) para 239.

[152] In any case, the Gambia only ratified the CAT in September 2018, so the UNCAT would not have jurisdiction over anterior facts.

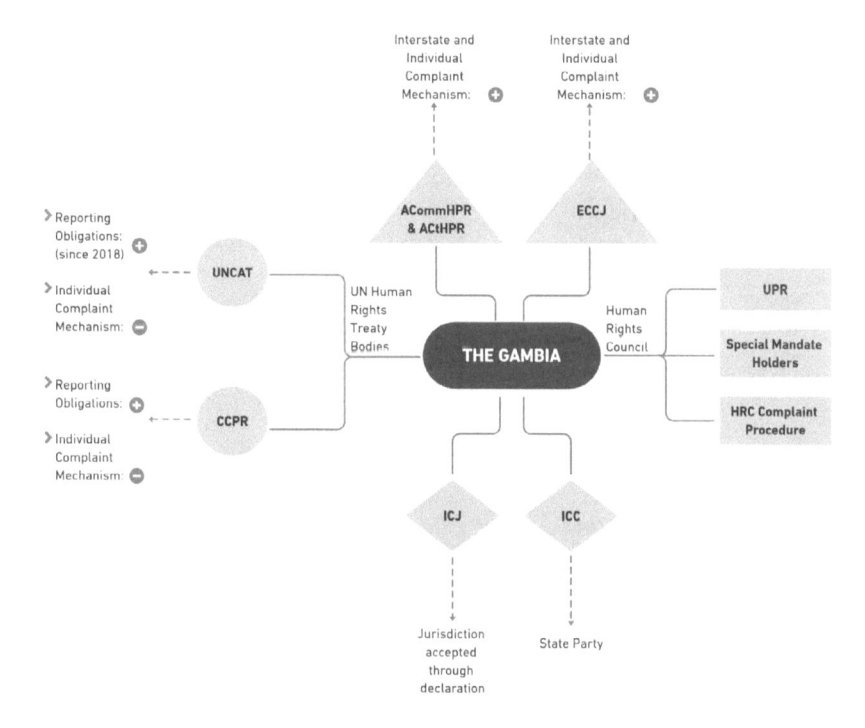

Figure 6.4   The Gambia's accountability network

6.5.3 Evaluation

Table 6.4 evaluates the Gambia's accountability network following the framework developed in Chapter 5.

As evidenced in Table 6.4, the Gambia's accountability network is powerful, due to both the institutional variety of the network and the power imbalances favouring other states. The network's capacity to constrain and escalate is therefore very strong, as are its legitimacy and the (theoretical) accessibility of the network to non-state actors.

6.5.4 Assessment of Practice

The theoretical strength of the network, even when seen in the context of the domestic political situation, would lead to some expectation of accountability practice. Although the low number of cases and the involvement of more wealthy and stable states in these cases have directed victims to look for

Table 6.4   Evaluation of the Gambia's accountability network

THE GAMBIA	Evaluation Factors	Evaluation and Comments
Capacity to Constrain and Escalate	Jurisdiction *ratione materiae*	STRONG. The network as a whole has universal competence.
	Jurisdiction *ratione personae*	STRONG. All actors but the ACommHPR, ACtHPR, and ECCJ have near-universal jurisdiction.
	Investigatory powers	STRONG. Consent to all optional investigatory powers has been given, UNCAT excepted.
	Powers to sanction non-cooperation	STRONG. Several actors have compulsory jurisdiction and the power to sanction non-cooperation.
	Capacity to order remedies	STRONG. Several actors have compulsory jurisdiction and the capacity to order remedies.
	Capacity to sanction	STRONG. Several actors have compulsory jurisdiction and the capacity to impose sanctions.
	Reputation of account-holder state – Standing in the international legal order – Relative power – Human rights records	STRONG. Other states are almost always in a stronger position than the Gambia in terms of economic and political power, as well as regarding human rights. Gambian membership of ECOWAS and AU does not impact that state of affairs.
	Capacity of account-holder state to constrain compliance – Interdependencies – Leverage tools	STRONG. Other states have no interdependencies with the Gambia, which is in a weaker economic and political position in relation to almost all states. Membership of regional institutions does not impact that state of affairs.

THE GAMBIA	Evaluation Factors	Evaluation and Comments
Legitimacy	Overall reputation	STRONG. All actors have a strong reputation and their access is not restricted.
	Participation of the state under scrutiny	STRONG. Participation of the state is encouraged and necessary in almost all procedures.
	Capacity to reward compliance or de-escalate	STRONG. Most actors can impose interim measures, and the Gambia has reporting obligations under several mechanisms.
	Independence – Budget and resources – Formal independence – Judicial independence – Relative power (state)	STRONG. Most actors perform a judicial or quasi-judicial function. All are formally independent and possess relatively stable resources, which the Gambia cannot influence. Other states are by default in a strong position in relation to the Gambia, which has no leverage against them.
	Representation of public interest	STRONG. The public interest is represented in all judicial and quasi-judicial procedures, as well as by shadow reporting and reporting obligations.
Publicity and Accessibility	Publicity of proceedings	STRONG. Reports are public and most hearing are too, in some form (video streaming or written records).
	Publicity of outcomes	STRONG. Decisions by all actors, except the HRC in its complaint procedure, are public.
	Accessibility to non-state account-holders – Information – Financial and geographical accessibility – Procedural accessibility	STRONG. Non-state account-holders have access to several individual complaint procedures, representing a spectrum of geographical and procedural accessibility. Information about the procedures is readily available and several are free of cost.

compensation elsewhere, it remains surprising that supra-national institutions have shown close to no interest in Gambian complicity in the CIA programme.

6.5.4.1 UN treaty bodies and the Human Rights Council
The Gambia is mentioned in the UN Joint Study as a country of pre-CIA detention[153] in the cases of Bisher al-Rawi[154] and Jamil el-Banna.[155] A follow-up

---

[153] Human Rights Council (n 49) 85.
[154] ibid 65 and Case 4 (Annex II).
[155] ibid 66.

communication was sent by the special mandate holders in October 2011[156] but remains unanswered to this day. No other direct mention of al-Rawi's and el-Banna's cases has been made in UN documents. However, recommendations regarding arbitrary and secret detention have been made generally, and attest to the general lack of respect for the rule of law by intelligence services. In particular, the then Special Rapporteur on extrajudicial, summary or arbitrary executions, Christof Heyns, devoted several paragraphs of his report on his 2015 mission to the Gambia to the lack of legal constraints upon the GNIA and to the numerous reports of persons being detained, tortured, and even disappeared or executed at the hands of the agency.[157] Similarly, the 2018 report of the Working Group on Enforced or Involuntary Disappearances on its mission to the Gambia highlights a general culture of detention without charges, secret detention, enforced disappearances, and a lack of accountability.[158] It also underlines that, despite positive steps taken by the new government, the legal framework is still inadequate to protect against gross human rights violations and provide accountability.[159]

6.5.4.2 Assessment

There is no instance of accountability for the arrest, detention, interrogation, and rendition of al-Rawi and el-Banna by the Gambia. On account of the heavy British and American involvement in that case, it is understandable that victims have preferred to focus on obtaining reparation from these more wealthy states, with a stronger judicial branch and democratic institutions, all of which promised better prospects of success.[160] Yet, if victims have been compensated,[161] the Gambia's responsibility and subsequent obligations are not diminished as a result.

---

[156] GMB 2/2011, 21 October 2011.
[157] A/HRC/29/37/Add.2 paras 44–47.
[158] A/HRC/39/46/Add.1.
[159] ibid paras 25–37.
[160] In 2010, the British government paid compensation to 12 Guantánamo Bay detainees, including al-Rawi and el-Banna, to settle a civil claim for damages that threatened to expose confidential information regarding British participation in the CIA programme. In August 2007, Bisher al-Rawi became the fifth plaintiff in a case filed against Jeppesen Dataplan before US courts and alleging complicity in his rendition and torture. However, after the US government intervened, asserting 'state secrets privilege' and claiming that the litigation would damage national security interests, the suit was dismissed. *Binyam Mohamed et al.* v. *Jeppesen Dataplan, Inc.*, dismissed February 2008.
[161] Whether a confidential settlement without an apology or recognition of responsibility constitutes a satisfactory remedy is another issue, addressed in section 6.6.1.2.

The lack of accountability in these two cases is not surprising when analysed in the context of the general lack of accountability for similar facts in the Gambia. The added visibility of CIA-related cases was not sufficient to bring about accountability or make these two cases stand apart from the hundreds of others within general reports and observations by institutional mechanisms. Moreover, in the cases under scrutiny, much of the international focus was directed at the UK and the US rather than at the Gambia, whose (important) executing role was relatively unsurprising based on its human rights record, in addition to being quite common in the grand scheme of the CIA programme. This does not diminish the importance of the Gambia's role, as the CIA programme relied on such vital foreign assistance. However, both the domestic context and the Gambia's relative lack of independent decision-making power in these cases made efforts towards accountability less likely, and seeking reparation from the UK and the US a better option.

6.6 THE UNITED KINGDOM

6.6.1 State Responsibility

On 28 June 2018, a report of the parliamentary Intelligence and Security Committee on 'Detainee Mistreatment and Rendition: 2001–2010' (hereinafter 'ISC Report')[162] found that British intelligence agencies had been complicit in the commission of torture, cruel, inhuman, and degrading treatment and punishment of detainees overseas in US detention facilities, including black sites in Iraq, Afghanistan, and Guantánamo Bay between 2001 and 2010.

The report records 13 incidents in which UK personnel were first-hand witnesses to acts of torture and ill-treatment committed against detainees by law enforcement officials. In at least 25 further incidents, UK personnel had been told by detainees that they had been mistreated by others. The report also recorded 232 cases where it appears that UK personnel continued to supply questions or intelligence to foreign liaison services despite the fact that they knew or had serious grounds to suspect that a detainee had been or was being subjected to torture and ill-treatment. There were a further 198 cases in which UK personnel received information obtained from detainees whom they knew had been subjected to torture and ill-treatment. The report also found that, in 28 cases, UK intelligence personnel had suggested, planned, or agreed to rendition operations proposed by other countries. In addition, it identified 22 cases in which the agencies provided intelligence to enable a rendition operation to take place, and 23 cases in which they failed to take action to prevent

---

[162] Intelligence and Security Committee (2018) (n 148).

a rendition. The present section analyses the international responsibility of the UK on two separate grounds: for rendition flights stop-offs on British territory; and for intelligence sharing with the CIA.

6.6.1.1 Stop-offs

The ISC Report states that, while there is 'no evidence that any US rendition flight transited the UK with a detainee on board', there is strong information that two detainees did transit through the British Overseas Territory of Diego Garcia (Chagos Archipelago).[163]

Notwithstanding the ongoing dispute between the UK and Mauritius on the status of the Chagos Islands Archipelago,[164] Diego Garcia was internationally considered to be British territory (part of the British Indian Ocean Territory) and under British sovereignty at the time of the CIA programme. The British government still considers it to be so and continues to exercise sovereign prerogatives over the island. Inasmuch as Diego Garcia could be considered British territory, British responsibility is engaged for wrongful acts taking place on the island at the hands of the CIA between 2001 and 2008. As emphasised by the ISC Report,

> the lease agreement between the UK and US Governments sets out agreed practices for the use of Diego Garcia, and clearly states that the US Government must consult the UK beforehand if it wishes to transit the island with a detainee on board. The UK remains fully responsible for ensuring that no activities contrary to international law take place on Diego Garcia.[165]

In particular, it is established that at least two instances of mid-rendition stop-offs took place in Diego Garcia in 2002.[166] The US government however denies that any other detainee has transited 'through the territorial land, air or seas of the United Kingdom or its territories'.[167] In the absence of compelling evidence to the contrary, the UK's responsibility would be engaged for wrongful acts that can be attributed to it as a stopover point in those two cases of rendition through Diego Garcia. In so far as there was a reasonable basis for the UK to suspect that the US was carrying out a rendition programme,[168] it should have displayed diligence in exercising its sovereign powers over

---

[163] ibid 98.

[164] *Legal Consequences of the Separation of the Chagos Archipelago from Mauritius in 1965 (Advisory Opinion)* [2019] ICJ Reports 2019 95 (International Court of Justice).

[165] Intelligence and Security Committee (2018) (n 148) para 194.

[166] Raphael, Black and Blakeley (n 73) 43.

[167] Intelligence and Security Committee (2018) (n 148) para 199.

[168] Especially so as the UK itself endorsed several instances of rendition by the US around that time. Intelligence and Security Committee (2018) (n 148) 98–107.

the island and military base. In particular, the UK was under an obligation, inherent to the exercise of jurisdiction, to protect the detainees that transited through its territory. This required the UK to take reasonable measures (such as searching the plane, recording flight numbers and passenger names, etc.) to ensure that its territory was not used to commit human rights violations. It does not appear that the UK took any such measures. On the contrary, the ISC Report underlines that 'the policy on recording flights was woefully inadequate' to the extent that 'the record review cannot be relied on to provide any assurances'.[169] In consequence, the UK's responsibility is engaged for the breach of its positive obligations in respect of the two detainees who transited through Diego Garcia.

In addition to the mid-rendition stop-offs, it is established that CIA aircrafts have refuelled at mainland UK airports hundreds of times. In the absence of evidence to the contrary, it will be assumed that no detainee was ever on board, making those instances of pre/post-rendition stop-off. In such cases, there is no jurisdictional link with the detainees, hence no obligation owed to them. However, there is a jurisdictional link with the CIA agents on board, which could arguably trigger a breach of the CAT if the UK had some awareness of the CIA programme and of the identity of the passengers disembarking.[170] It is established that, from the end of 2004 onward, all agencies and relevant governmental officials knew of the nature of the programme,[171] so that the UK's obligation to prosecute or extradite was triggered under Articles 6 and 7 CAT.

Furthermore, the UK's responsibility could be engaged under Article 16 ASR for its aid or assistance to the CIA programme in the form of airspace and airport access. Indeed, at least from early 2004 onward, the UK had extensive knowledge of the CIA programme.[172] It could even be argued that such knowledge was established from early 2002 on for British intelligence agencies.[173] Irrespective of which date is picked, several CIA aircrafts have landed and refuelled in British airports after 2004 – and many more between 2002 and 2004.[174] If it can be established that at least one government official knew about the nature of the flight, then the responsibility of the UK can be established for aid or assistance under Article 16 ASR.

---

[169] Intelligence and Security Committee (2018) (n 148) para 203.
[170] See Chapter 3, section 3.4.4.
[171] Intelligence and Security Committee (2018) (n 148) paras 132, 151.
[172] ibid para 151 confirms this.
[173] ibid 85.
[174] See The Rendition Project Flight Database: https://www.therenditionproject.org.uk/flights/flight-database.html

6.6.1.2 Intelligence sharing with the CIA

The United Kingdom is implicated in dozens of individual cases for the role its intelligence agencies played in the capture, rendition, or interrogation of CIA detainees. Short of committing torture themselves,[175] British officials did share extensive intelligence with the CIA, received information extracted by the CIA from its detainees, and participated in interrogations of detainees held by the CIA. In addition, it is likely that the UK has at some point shared information tainted by CIA torture with other states and/or made executive use of such information. As demonstrated in Chapter 3, section 3.4.5, all these courses of conduct constitute wrongful acts provided that at least constructive knowledge of a risk of torture can be established. Constructive (if not actual) knowledge can be shown very early on[176] for the UK as the closest intelligence partner of the US and, as a military ally, a direct witness of US actions and interrogation techniques on the ground.[177]

From mid-2004 onwards, British agencies slowly started to issue guidance and training to their agents regarding what constitutes 'mistreatment'. They also took some preventive measures to avoid being seen as condoning US methods of interrogation. However, this has been analysed as constituting an attempt 'to leave open the option of colluding in torture again'.[178] Further, the ISC Report sheds light on the balancing act in which the UK government and its intelligence agencies engaged during the war on terror. While aware of detainees' mistreatment and the unlawfulness of its continued cooperation with the CIA programme, the UK turned a blind eye to CIA practices and persisted in sending questions for interrogation; receiving and acting on intelligence obtained through mistreatment; and condoning renditions because it deemed the CIA programme 'absolutely vital for revealing threats' and would not risk being denied access to this source of information.[179] MI5 thus 'assessed that the legal and reputational risks were low and the intelligence it was receiving was highly valuable and therefore worth the risk'.[180] This position was maintained even after 2004, as British agencies seemed to still regard torture as a risk[181]

---

[175] Although this could be disputed. See Intelligence and Security Committee (2018) (n 148) para 42.
[176] Intelligence and Security Committee (2018) (n 148) 29–50.
[177] For an extensive analysis of British complicity in the CIA programme, and especially of British involvement in torture through intelligence cooperation, see Ruth Blakeley and Sam Raphael, 'Accountability, Denial and the Future-Proofing of British Torture' (2020) 96 International Affairs 691.
[178] ibid 708.
[179] Intelligence and Security Committee (2018) (n 148) paras 123–131.
[180] ibid para 129.
[181] Although it is probable that the real risk the agencies wanted to guard themselves against was to be seen as condoning torture.

to be balanced against the 'benefits derived from co-operation with the US', a balancing act that 'clearly' favoured continued cooperation.[182] The recourse to balancing still forms part of British intelligence's contemporary practice.[183]

Although there generally have been more domestic efforts towards establishing accountability than in other states, no CIA-related case before British courts has resulted in a substantive (rather than procedural) decision in favour of the claimants. Indeed, all claims with chances of success ended up being settled.[184] The UK thus chose to give the nine British nationals and six British residents released from Guantánamo Bay around one million pounds each to settle civil damages claims rather than contest in court allegations that British security services were complicit in their capture, rendition, detention, and torture. While the right to a remedy of some victims has been partially satisfied by monetary compensation, the UK has only issued an apology to two victims (Belhaj and Bouchar), but without admission of liability and only after spending £11 million to try and keep the case out of court. Further, there has been no criminal or civil conviction of any government or intelligence official for the UK's complicity in the CIA programme, despite its heavy involvement in rendition, interrogation, and intelligence sharing.[185]

The procedural aspects of the prohibition of torture, the right to life, and the prohibition of arbitrary detention have arguably not been satisfied[186] by

---

[182] Intelligence and Security Committee (2018) (n 148) para 159 quoting MI5: Classified MI5 internal document, 'Review of benefits and risks associated with the Service's intelligence co-operation with ***', 30 January 2006.

[183] Blakeley and Raphael (n 177) 707.

[184] Most claims have been settled in confidential, out-of-court settlements without acknowledgement of responsibility. The one exception is the case of Abdel Hakim Belhaj and his wife Fatima Bouchar, who obtained a public apology by Prime Minister Theresa May during proceedings before the Supreme Court. But, even in the Belhaj case, the proceedings were settled after argument before the Supreme Court. The Court still issued a judgment in view of the importance of the legal issue, namely whether a closed material procedure could be used for the appellants' application to require the DPP to prosecute Sir Mark Allen. *Belhaj and another (Appellants) v. Director of Public Prosecutions and another (Respondents)* [2017] UKSC 33, 4 July 2018.

[185] For a description and analysis of the steps taken by the British administration to prevent and limit public exposure of British complicity, see Blakeley and Raphael (n 177).

[186] Under the ECHR, allegations of a violation of Articles 2 and 3 require a prompt and effective investigation, in addition to the prosecution of responsible individuals and the award of an effective remedy to victims. Allegations of a violation of Article 5 requires positive steps to put an end to the arbitrary detention as well as compensation for wrongful detention. See Council of Europe (2013) 'Guide to good practice in respect of domestic remedies' 15–34.

the Gibson and ISC inquiries ordered by the government.[187] Nor is, or can be, victims' right to an effective remedy satisfied by the practice of financial compensation through a confidential settlement without an acknowledgement of the responsibility that the British government has adopted.[188] It follows that, even in those cases in which the UK has settled individual claims, its international responsibility remains engaged as the victims' right to an effective remedy has not been satisfied and the country's procedural obligations have not been discharged.

6.6.2 Accountability Network

The UK's accountability network is rather strong institutionally. The UK has ratified the ICC statute and issued a declaration recognising the compulsory jurisdiction of the ICJ, albeit with some reservations.[189] The lack of consent to the individual complaint mechanisms of the UNCAT and CCPR is (in theory) almost entirely substantively compensated by the compulsory jurisdiction of the ECtHR.[190] Nevertheless, it is regrettable that intelligence-sharing matters cannot be submitted to the UNCAT through individual complaints as the CAT goes further and is more precise than other instruments with regard to complicity in torture.[191] Further, the lack of variety is also unfortunate as a claim that is inadmissible before the ECtHR (for procedural or substantive reasons) may very well be admissible before other forums.[192]

---

[187] Both the Gibson inquiry and the ISC inquiry were closed prematurely. In the latter case, this was due to lack of access to key evidence, orchestrated by the government's refusal to provide access to witnesses from intelligence agencies. Despite the troubling findings of the ISC reports, no judicial inquiry was launched after their publication.

[188] See Council of Europe (2013) 'Guide to good practice in respect of domestic remedies' 15–34; UN General Assembly, 'Basic Principles and Guidelines on the Right to a Remedy and Reparation for Victims of Gross Violations of International Human Rights Law and Serious Violations of International Humanitarian Law', A/RES/60/147 (16 December 2005), especially paras 22–23.

[189] Declarations recognizing the jurisdiction of the Court as compulsory, United Kingdom of Great Britain and Northern Ireland, 22 February 2017.

[190] Notwithstanding the differing interpretations of the notion of jurisdiction, and the better applicability *ratione loci* of CAT provisions.

[191] See Chapter 3, section 3.4.5.

[192] Regarding the UNCAT, however, its recent inadmissibility decision in *M.Z.* v. *Belgium*, which reverses established case-law on the matter in respect of a case concerning intelligence cooperation, casts a doubt on that last statement. *M.Z.* v. *Belgium*, No. 813/2017, 29 August 2019. For an analysis, see Sophie Duroy, 'Chronique des Constatations des Comités Conventionnels des Nations Unies: Comité contre la

On the interstate level, the UK is a permanent member of the UN Security Council, making a resolution concerning its actions extremely unlikely. It is also a member of NATO, which means that it is unlikely to act against the security interests of another NATO member, and vice versa. In addition, the intelligence relationship between the UK and the US, as seen in agreements commonly referred to as UKUSA or Five Eyes, means that the interdependencies between the two states (although favouring the US) play against the prospect of a British action jeopardising this relationship. Hence, British cooperation in supra-national accountability processes is a lot less likely if the US opposes it – as it has done without exception until now– or if it could risk endangering another NATO member's interests.

However, this is partially mitigated by the UK's membership of the Council of Europe and the requirements of the ECHR, implemented in British domestic law through the Human Rights Act 1998. The UK is subject to the jurisdiction and oversight of the ECtHR and other CoE bodies, and generally cares about its human rights records and reputation as a rule-of-law-compliant state. Hence, the UK is relatively sensitive to pressure from the ECtHR, CoE institutions, and other CoE member states. This pressure has led to some changes in policies throughout the years, and to stronger domestic oversight of intelligence activities and cooperation in order to avoid having to render account at the supra-national level. The British government has therefore renounced its most aggressive counterterrorism policies and its intelligence community has evolved towards greater self-constraint to avoid being held accountable for its own and the US's wrongful acts. In addition, ECHR standards have prevented reliance on expansive doctrines of state secrecy and national security privileges in court, giving victims better prospects of success than before US courts.

Figure 6.5 visually presents the United Kingdom's institutional accountability network.

Torture, M. Z. c. Belgique, 2 Août 2019, Communication No 813/2017' (2020) 18 Revue Droits Fondamentaux 11.

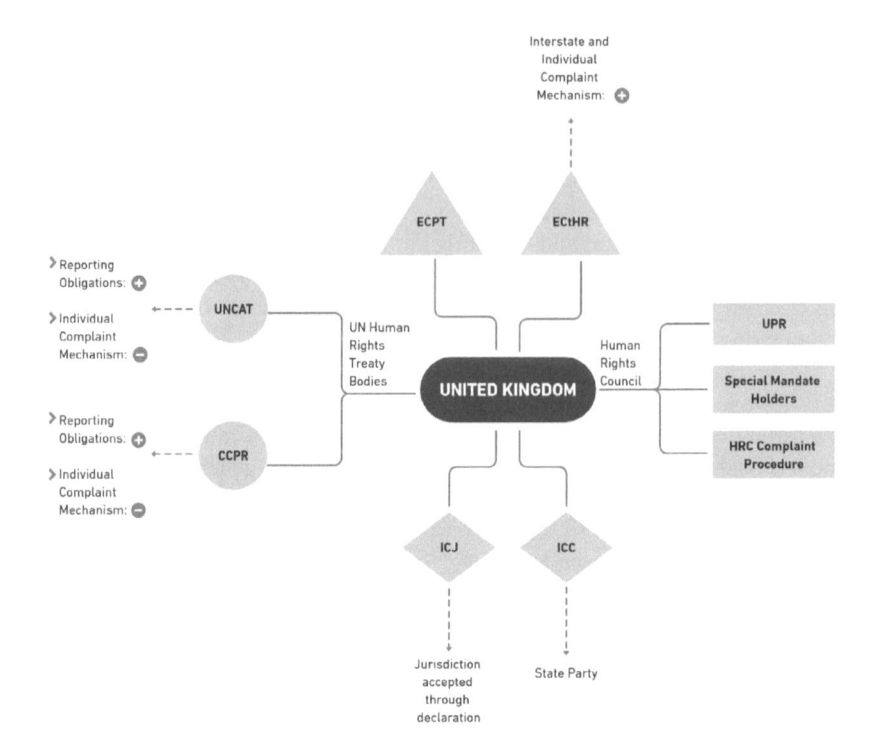

Figure 6.5   The United Kingdom's accountability network

6.6.3   Evaluation

Table 6.5 evaluates the United Kingdom's accountability network following the framework developed in Chapter 5.

As evidenced in Table 6.5, the UK's accountability network scores unequally depending on whether one looks at it from an institutional perspective or also includes interstate accountability. Institutionally, the network scores rather well under all three headings – thanks, mostly, to the competence of the ECtHR and despite the lack of other individual complaint mechanisms. At the same time, it seems extremely unlikely that other states will play any role in enforcing institutional decisions or acting to accept accountability. Indeed, all the caveats in relation to the strength of the network come from the relative position of other states: their relative lack of power or incentives to hold the UK to account and the UK's generally better human rights record relative to states that would have the capacity to hold it to account.

Table 6.5 Evaluation of the United Kingdom's accountability network

UNITED KINGDOM	Evaluation Factors	Evaluation and Comments
Capacity to Constrain and Escalate	Jurisdiction *ratione materiae*	STRONG. The network as a whole has universal competence.
	Jurisdiction *ratione personae*	STRONG. All actors but the ECHR and ECPT have near-universal jurisdiction.
	Investigatory powers	STRONG. Consent to all optional investigatory powers has been given, and the ECPT is endowed with additional investigatory powers.
	Powers to sanction non-cooperation	STRONG. Several actors have compulsory jurisdiction and the power to sanction non-cooperation.
	Capacity to order remedies	STRONG. Several actors have compulsory jurisdiction and the capacity to order remedies.
	Capacity to sanction	STRONG. Several actors have compulsory jurisdiction and the capacity to impose sanctions.
	Reputation of account-holder state – Standing in the international legal order – Relative power – Human rights records	WEAK as, except for other P5 states (permanent members of the UN Security Council), power imbalances and standing favour the UK. Even among the P5, the UK's human rights record and agenda play in its favour.
	Capacity of account-holder state to constrain compliance – Interdependencies – Leverage tools	MEDIUM. Certain states and international organisations (EU) have leverage in the economic, trade, and intelligence fields. Membership of CoE also gives leverage to CoE states in the human rights field.
Legitimacy	Overall reputation	STRONG. All actors have a strong reputation and their access is not restricted.
	Participation of the state under scrutiny	STRONG. Participation of the state is encouraged and necessary in almost all procedures.
	Capacity to reward compliance or de-escalate	STRONG. Most actors can impose interim measures, and the UK has reporting obligations under several mechanisms.
	Independence – Budget and resources – Formal independence – Judicial independence – Relative power (state)	MEDIUM. Most actors perform a judicial or quasi-judicial function. All are formally independent and possess relatively stable resources, which the UK cannot influence. However, with the exception of the US, other states are in a weak position power wise.

UNITED KINGDOM	Evaluation Factors	Evaluation and Comments
Publicity and Accessibility	Representation of public interest	STRONG. The public interest is represented in all judicial and quasi-judicial procedures, as well as by shadow reporting and reporting obligations.
	Publicity of proceedings	STRONG. Reports are public and most hearing also are, in some form (video streaming or written records).
	Publicity of outcomes	STRONG. Decisions by all actors, except the HRC in its complaint procedure, are public.
	Accessibility to non-state account-holders – Information – Financial and geographical accessibility – Procedural accessibility	STRONG. Non-state account-holders have access to several individual complaint procedures, representing a spectrum of geographical and procedural accessibility. Information about the procedures is readily available and several are free of cost.

6.6.4 Assessment of Practice

On account of the institutional strength of the network and its interstate weaknesses, one could safely expect some level of accountability. However, the lack of variety of available complaint mechanisms together with the British government's practice of settling civil claims temper these expectations. This bizarre state of affairs means that UN bodies are the only competent mechanisms, despite the UK having a theoretically stronger and more varied network. Thus, as they did for the US, UN mechanisms took up a very active role, and accountability has been partially achieved this way.

6.6.4.1 UN treaty bodies and the Human Rights Council

Both the CCPR and UNCAT have addressed at length the various aspects of British participation in the CIA programme in their concluding observations. Starting in 2004, the UNCAT first expressed concern that British law has been interpreted to exclude the use of evidence extracted by torture only where British officials were complicit.[193] In its following concluding observations, in 2013, the UNCAT highlighted several more issues regarding the possibility that torture-tainted intelligence could be used in closed material procedures[194] and in court more generally.[195] It also expressed concern regarding the continued use of diplomatic assurances, including in communications with foreign

---

[193] CAT/C/CR/3/33, 10 December 2004, para 4(a)(i).
[194] CAT/C/GBR/CO/5, 24 June 2013, para 12(b).
[195] CAT/C/GBR/CO/5, para 25.

intelligence services overseas.[196] The UNCAT further deplored the persistent lack of judicial inquiry into allegations of torture overseas, and regretted the shortcomings of the Gibson inquiry.[197] In its most recent concluding observations (2019), the Committee stressed that its previous recommendations regarding inquiries into allegations of torture overseas have not been implemented.[198] It further noted with concern that the ISC parliamentary inquiry had been prematurely closed due to the government's refusal to provide access to key witnesses from intelligence services, and that, despite the troubling findings of its reports, no judicial investigation had been opened.[199]

In 2008, the CCPR expressed concern at the use of Diego Garcia as a transit point for rendition operations[200] and regretted the UK's statement that the Covenant did not apply to British military detention facilities overseas, save in exceptional circumstances. It also noted that allegations of abuse in such facilities have been numerous and recommended that the UK investigate, prosecute, and sanction appropriately those responsible.[201] In its 2015 concluding observations, the CCPR deplored the slow progress of the parliamentary inquiry and its inadequacy as an investigation mechanism.[202]

Both Committees noted the cooperation of the British government in the reporting cycles, and the progress made in some areas. Yet, they also reported on the lack of implementation of many of their recommendations linked to the counterterrorism context and, in particular, to British complicity in torture and rendition. Nevertheless, repeated pressures for more transparency and accountability probably played a role in the launch and publication of the reports of the Gibson and the ISC inquiries.

Pressure has also been applied through communications to special mandate holders, which remains the only available UN complaint mechanism for individual victims. However, it has only been used as such in two cases: that of Seitmarian Nassar,[203] allegedly held in Diego Garcia in 2002; and for Shaker Aamer, the last British resident detained in Guantánamo Bay.[204] More often, communications to the government were initiated directly by the special mandate holders, and focused on British anti-terror legislation and action

---

[196] CAT/C/GBR/CO/5, paras 11 and 18.
[197] CAT/C/GBR/CO/5, para 15.
[198] CAT/C/GBR/CO/6, 7 June 2019, para 7.
[199] CAT/C/GBR/CO/6, para 34.
[200] CCPR/C/GBR/CO/6, 30 July 2008, para 13.
[201] CCPR/C/GBR/CO/6, para 14.
[202] CCPR/C/GBR/CO/7, 17 August 2015, para 9.
[203] A/HRC/10/37/Add.1, 18 February 2010, paras 121–123.
[204] GBR 6/2012.

towards accountability.²⁰⁵ Communication 11/2018, in particular, laid out the findings of the ISC Report and called for the UK government to launch a judicial inquiry, all while reminding it of its legal obligations under the ICCPR, CAT, and ECHR. The reply from the government is disappointing in its refusal to acknowledge the findings of the report as established, but nevertheless shows its respect both for the procedure and for appearances of compliance with the rule of law. The United Kingdom was also mentioned several times in the UN Joint Study, in particular in relation to Diego Garcia²⁰⁶ and for knowingly taking 'advantage of the situation of secret detention by sending questions to the State detaining the person or by soliciting or receiving information from persons who are being kept in secret detention' (i.e., demand for torture-tainted intelligence).²⁰⁷ The UK has also been called out in similar terms by other states in the UPR cycles it was subjected to.²⁰⁸

Special mandate holders' communications are a valuable addition to concluding observations as their mandate is wider in scope – they can address obligations under any treaty and do not depend upon reporting from the state – and they are more specific and timelier for the same reasons. With regard to the UK, they have acted as a constant source of supra-national oversight over counterterrorism legislation in the early years post 9/11, and then over inquiries and accountability processes in more recent years. Acting with a higher frequency than reporting obligations cycles, special mandate holders have been able to engage in a constructive dialogue with the British government over current issues. It is also arguable that their communications may have had (and could still have) some influence over the drafting of legislation, the launch of inquiries, or the publication of their reports.

6.6.4.2 Assessment

There has been no individual complaint against the UK at supra-national level for its participation in the CIA programme – with the exception of the communication by Nassar regarding his transfer through Diego Garcia. This can be partially explained by the British government's willingness to settle civil claims at the domestic level, in addition to the active role played by domestic courts and the Intelligence and Security Committee of Parliament. However,

---

²⁰⁵ E.g., E/CN.4/2006/98/Add.1, 23 December 2005; A/HRC/4/26/Add.1 15 March 2007; A/HRC/10/3/Add.1, 24 February 2009, all with regard to anti-terror legislation; GBR 6/2011 on the terms of reference of the Gibson Inquiry; and GBR 11/2018 and 12/2018 on the follow-up of the ISC Report.
²⁰⁶ Human Rights Council (n 49) para 127.
²⁰⁷ ibid para 159(b).
²⁰⁸ A/HRC/8/25 (23 May 2008); A/HRC/21/9 (6 July 2012). See also A/HRC/36/9 (14 July 2017), focusing more on surveillance legislation and practice.

neither the victims' right to a remedy nor the UK's procedural obligations have been satisfied by this course of action, so that the UK's responsibility remains engaged in the cases that have been settled – in addition to the many others that have not. Yet, settled claims prevent individual access to both domestic and supra-national mechanisms, leaving a substantial accountability gap.

The UK has still been held to account internationally through the more general procedure of reporting obligations before the CCPR and UNCAT, and through communications by special mandate holders. Despite their weak capacity to constrain and escalate, UN mechanisms have provided a valuable source of oversight and dialogue with the British government. In addition, as the only entities able to call the British government out for its actions in the war on terror, they have provided a constant reminder of the UK's international obligations in order to influence British policies and conduct regarding intelligence cooperation with the CIA. Yet, as was the case for the US, if the committees and special mandate holders did not shy away from addressing any and all aspects of British complicity in the CIA programme, their lack of judicial character represents an obstacle to the authoritativeness of their observations. This is on a par with their lack of sanctioning power and, as a result, the consequences that derive from their oversight are exclusively reputational. More importantly, no state has made any attempt to enforce their findings outside UPR procedures.

The threat of complaints before the ECtHR has played a similar role in influencing British policies and its management of civil complaints at domestic level, but it has had the unfortunate result of leaving accountability gaps in individual cases. In addition, the ECtHR's case-law on state and individual immunities for acts of torture committed by a foreign government,[209] together with its debatable stance on extraterritorial jurisdiction,[210] have so far favoured British courts' practice of throwing out all criminal cases (together with some civil claims for damages) for complicity implicating its own agents on account of the *Monetary Gold* principle.

6.7 CONCLUSIONS: THE ROAD TO EFFECTIVE ACCOUNTABILITY

The present case-study focused on the second layer of regulation (international legal accountability) with the aim of empirically identifying its strengths and

---

[209] ECtHR, *Al-Adsani v. The United Kingdom*, App. No. 35763/97, 21 November 2001 upholding state immunity; *Jones and Others v. The United Kingdom*, App. Nos. 34356/06 and 40528/06, 14 January 2014 upholding state officials' immunity.

[210] ECtHR, *Al-Skeini and Others v. The United Kingdom*, App. No. 55721/07, 7 July 2011, para 137. See Chapter 3, section 3.3.1.

limits. The analysis conducted in the chapter thus highlighted the differences between the potential of the international accountability networks of five states, and the actual accountability of the same states for their participation in the CIA programme. In this section, comparing state-specific findings, I draw some conclusions and identify some of the factors impacting accountability.

The starting point for the analysis is that both the variety of available individual complaint mechanisms and the capacity of a single mechanism to constrain and escalate have an impact on actual accountability. Poland possesses the largest variety and highest individual strength of accountability mechanisms of the five states. It is also the state that has been held accountable in the most effective way: through two judicial decisions (out of eight potential cases) affirming its international responsibility and awarding damages to the victims. On the opposite end of the spectrum is the US, for which there is no available individual complaint mechanism and for which no single mechanism has a capacity to constrain and escalate that can be considered better than average. The US has not been held accountable once out of 131 potential cases.

Yet, while a clear correlation can be observed between the strength of the network and actual accountability in these two instances (Poland and the US), for the other three states (Djibouti, the Gambia, and the UK) the correlation is weaker. The theoretical capacity of the accountability network may therefore be only one of several factors leading to accountability, a necessary yet insufficient factor.

General instances of accountability can partially mitigate the poor accessibility of individual complaint mechanisms. Despite a weak capacity to constrain and escalate and their lack of capacity to order remedies outside individual complaint procedures, competent UN treaty bodies and the Human Rights Council have played an important compensatory role when complaint mechanisms were unavailable. This was the case for the US and, to a lesser extent, for the UK due to domestic settlements and the jurisprudential barriers to the only available individual complaint mechanism, the ECtHR.

However, these general accountability mechanisms have played a very limited role in holding the two remaining states – Djibouti and the Gambia – to account. Apart from a mention in the UN Joint Study (which does not equate accountability in the absence of response and engagement by the state), Djibouti and the Gambia have escaped virtually untouched from UN mechanisms' oversight. The low number of individual cases in which they are respectively alleged to be involved (three and two) is only part of the explanation.[211] The other part is more complex.

---

[211] After all, Macedonia was only involved in a single case, with facts oddly similar to those of the Gambian cases, and yet held accountable by the ECtHR in *El-Masri* (n 66).

For both states, their usually poor human rights record is a factor that likely played a role in the UN's lack of interest in their ad hoc participation in the CIA programme. In addition, the Gambian and Djiboutian cases drew more attention to US's (and UK's, for the Gambia) actions than to their own. This might be because of the usually more positive human rights records of the US and UK. It may also be due to the practical nature of the role played by Djibouti and the Gambia, which was devoid of any self-interest – as opposed to those states, such as NATO members, that may have had intelligence or other interests in seeing the victims rendered to CIA custody. Djibouti's unique interdependencies with the US and other world powers using its territory as a military base have probably constituted a hindrance to achieving accountability within intergovernmental mechanisms, in addition to preventing any prospect of interstate accountability or enforcement. The Gambia's domestic situation, on the other hand, means that the uniqueness of the two cases rested only in US and UK cooperation rather than in the gross human rights violations committed. UN mechanisms could rightly consider that priority lay elsewhere, and victims' prospects for obtaining a remedy were much higher in the UK or US.

It appears, therefore, that on top of the theoretical strength of the network, other factors come into play and may negate or improve actual accountability. From this case-study, at least the following additional factors can be identified:

(1) The usual human rights record of the state – i.e., whether the acts complained of are of a nature to trigger public outrage or whether they only add to a long list of human rights violations;
(2) Interstate pressures and dependencies, including membership or lack thereof of certain international organisations, working both towards accountability and against it;
(3) The ad hoc or organised nature of the state's cooperation with the US and the CIA programme – i.e., whether there is an established intelligence relationship with the primary wrongdoer.

These factors, specific to the context at hand, interact with one another and with the potential of the accountability network. In isolation, they cannot explain a state's (lack of) accountability. However, they may be taken as additional cues that explain why a given state has or has not been held to account for its actions despite the strength of its accountability network predicting otherwise.

The identification of these and other potential extra-legal factors allows us to understand, to a certain extent, why there are still remaining accountability gaps. It also allows for research into solutions to fill these gaps as much as the theoretical strength of the network permits. Indeed, while the theoretical strength of the network constitutes the upper limit of what accountability can achieve, the current state of accountability is nowhere near that limit. And, without actual accountability being likely, neither accountability nor regulation can be effective.

The road to achieving accountability thus rests, first, on the evaluation of the strength of accountability networks; second, on the assessment of accountability gaps, through a comparison between the theoretical strength of the network and actual accountability; then, on the identification of the factors behind any discrepancy. Crucially, knowing what can be done for actual accountability to match the potential of the accountability network brings us a step closer to a more systematic enforcement of international law and state responsibility. However, achieving effective accountability further necessitates taking into account extra-legal factors and integrating them into a third layer of regulation: compliance.

APPENDIX 6.1   GRID OF ACCOUNTABILITY MECHANISMS

Table 6A.1   Competent institutional accountability mechanisms regarding the CIA war on terror

Competent Accountability Mechanisms regarding the CIA-led War on Terror	UN Human Rights Treaty Bodies				Regional Human Rights Courts and Bodies				
	CCPR	UNCAT	CED	AComHPR	ACtHPR	ECCJ	ECtHR	ECPT
Procedure	N/A	N/A	N/A	N/A	Contentious	Contentious	Contentious	On-site visits to places of detention
Legal basis	ICCPR Art. 28	CAT Art. 17	CPED Art. 26	ACHPR Art. 30	Protocol to ACHPR Art. 1	Articles 6 and 15 of ECOWAS Revised Treaty	ECHR Art. 19	ECPT Art. 1
Nature of Body/Procedure	Quasi-Judicial	Quasi-Judicial	Quasi-Judicial	Quasi-Judicial	Judicial	Judicial	Judicial	Preventative Inquiry Mechanism
Reporting Obligations	ICCPR Art. 40	YES - CAT Art. 19	YES - CPED Art. 29	YES - ACHPR Art. 62	NO	NO	NO	NO
Interstate Complaint Mechanism	YES ICCPR Art. 4 (49 State Parties)	YES - CAT Art. 21 (63 State Parties)	YES - CPED Art. 32	YES - ACHPR Art. 47	YES - Protocol Art. 5	YES	YES - ECHR Art. 33	NO
Individual Complaint Mechanisms	YES - Optional Protocol (116 State Parties)	YES - CAT Art. 22 (66 State Parties)	YES - CPED Art. 31 (21 State Parties)	YES - ACHPR Art. 55	YES if declaration by State - Protocol Art. 34(6)	YES	YES - ECHR Art. 34	NO
Interim Measures	YES - Rules of Procedure, Rule 92	YES - Rules of Procedure, Rule 108(1)	YES - CPED Art. 30 (request for urgent action)	YES - Rules of Procedure, Rule 111	YES - Protocol Art. 27(2)	YES - Rules of Procedure Art. 79 & Protocol Art. 21	YES - Rules of Court, Rule 39	NO
Jurisdiction ratione materiae	ICCPR provisions	CAT provisions	CPED provisions	ACHPR Provisions + other relevant international or African conventions (ACHPR Art. 60-61)	ACHPR provisions, its Protocol and any other relevant Human Rights instrument ratified by State (Protocol Art. 3)	ECOWAS Treaties. All relevant international HR treaties ratified (Protocol Art. 19)	ECHR and Protocols	Detainee Treatment (Art. ECPT)
Jurisdiction ratione personae	172 State Parties. 116 State Parties to OP	165 State Parties. 66 under Art. 22	59 State Parties, 21 under Art. 31	53 State Parties	24 State Parties	ECOWAS Member States	CoE Member States	CoE Member States
Jurisdiction ratione temporis (entry into force)	ICCPR: 23.03.1976 + OP: 23.03.1976	26.01.1987	23.12.2010	21.11.1986	25.01.2004	(06.07.1991)	03.09.1953	01.02.1989
Investigatory Powers	NO	Inquiry Procedure (CAT Art. 20 + 152 State Parties) and Subcommittee (OP)	Inquiry Procedure (CPED Art. 33 + 50 State Parties)	NO	YES - Protocol Art. 26	YES - Rules of Procedure Art. 41 & Protocol Art. 16	YES - Rules of Court Annex to the Rules	YES - CPT Art. 2
Type of Decision	Opinion	Views	Views	Decision	Judgment	Judgment	Judgment	Report
Decisions Public	YES	YES	YES	YES	YES	YES	YES	NO (except if state requests so - CPT Art. 11)
Decisions Binding	NO (but authoritative interpretation of treaty obligations)	NO (but authoritative interpretation of treaty obligations)	NO (but authoritative interpretation of treaty obligations)	YES if adopted by OAU (ACHPR Art. 54)	YES	YES	YES	NO
Sanctioning Powers	YES	YES	YES	YES	YES	YES	YES	NO
Follow-Up of Decisions	Special Rapporteur for Follow-upon Views	Follow-up experts		Letter by Secretariat	National Authorities	National Authorities	Committee of Ministers / referral to ECtHR	National Authorities

Competent Accountability Mechanisms regarding the CIA-led War on Terror	IACHR	IACtHR	HRC (UPR)	HRC (Special Procedures)	HRC (Complaint Procedure)	Other UN and Intergovernmental Accountability Mechanisms		ICAO Council	ICC	ICJ
						HRC				
Procedure	N/A	Contentious	UPR	Special Mandate Holders	Complaint Procedure	Complaint Procedure		Infraction procedure (Art 54) / Settlement of Disputes (Art. 84)	Individual Criminal Responsibility	Contentious
Legal Basis	OAS Charter Art. 106	OAS Res. No. 448	UNGA Res. 60/251	HRC Res. 5/1	HRC Res. 5/1	HRC Res. 5/1		Chicago Convention	Rome Statute	UN Charter
Nature of Body/Procedure	Quasi-Judicial	Judicial	Intergovernmental	Independent Experts	Complaint Procedure	Complaint Procedure		Intergovernmental	Judicial	Judicial
Reporting Obligations	YES - Statute Art. 18(d)	NO	YES	NO	NO	NO		NO	NO	NO
Interstate Complaint Mechanism	YES - Rules of Procedure Art. 50	YES	NO	NO	NO	NO		YES (Art. 84)	NO (but referral of situations possible)	YES
Individual Complaint Mechanism	YES - Rules of Procedure Art. 23	YES but only through IACHR	NO	YES	YES	YES		NO	NO	NO
Interim Measures	YES - Rules of Procedure Art. 25	YES - Rules of Procedure, Art. 27	NO	YES (urgent appeals)	NO	NO		N/A	YES (Provisional Arrest - Rome Statute Art. 92)	YES - Art. 41 Statute
Jurisdiction ratione materiae	All OAS Treaties ratified by State Party + American Declaration	All OAS Treaties ratified by State Party	All UN human rights treaties ratified by the State	Thematic or Country-specific	Patterns of gross violations of Human Rights			Chicago Convention	International crimes figuring in the Rome Statute	Universal
Jurisdiction ratione personae	OAS Member States (ad hoc acceptance of jurisdiction possible)	OAS Member States who ratified the ACHR (ad hoc acceptance of jurisdiction possible)	UN Member States	UN Member States	UN Member States			State Parties	Individuals	Universal (but acceptance of competence necessary)
Jurisdiction ratione temporis (entry into force)	13.12.1951	22.05.1979	First cycle began April 2008	N/A	27.05.1970			04.04.1947	01.07.2002	N/A
Investigatory Powers	YES - Rules of Procedure Art. 39	YES - Rules of Procedure Art. 58	NO	YES (Country-visits)	NO			N/A	YES	YES - Art. 50 Statute
Type of Decision	Decision	Judgment	Recommendations	Reports, Reasoned Opinions, Deliberations, General Comments	Confidential Report			Decision	Judgment	Judgment
Decisions Public	YES	YES	YES	YES	NO			YES	YES	YES
Decisions Binding	YES for State Parties to the ACHR - Not formally for the others	YES	NO	NO (but can constitute authoritative opinions and standards)	NO			YES	YES	YES
Sanctioning Powers	YES	YES	NO	NO	NO			YES	YES	YES
Follow-Up of Decisions	Report + Referral to IACtHR if State Party (Rules of Procedure Art. 45)	Tribunal - Rules of Procedure Art. 69	Voluntary Implementation Reports	Ad hoc - Follow-up visits or letters				Submission of dispute to arbitration possible		

PART III

Compliance

7. State compliance with international law in intelligence matters: a behavioural approach

7.1 INTRODUCTION

As I demonstrated in Part I, intelligence activities are comprehensively addressed by international legal rules. These rules indirectly govern the motives, methods, and conducts necessary to operationalise intelligence activities. Hence, when states violate their international legal obligations in conducting intelligence activities, their international responsibility is engaged. As Part II showed, states can be and have been held accountable for internationally wrongful acts resulting from intelligence activities. However, to constitute an effective regulatory tool, accountability needs to have an influence on state behaviour, i.e., induce compliance.

The third layer of regulation that I present in this chapter, compliance, constitutes a meta-layer. Indeed, it encompasses legality (first layer) and accountability (second layer), but also the extra-legal cognitive and social factors that need to be accounted for to make accountability effective. In this sense, this third layer can be conceived of as an effective regulatory strategy, the aim of which is compliance with international law.

Thus far, the role played by international law in intelligence decision-making and state (non-)compliance remains an open question. Having established in Chapter 5 that both legality and accountability can influence state behaviour, I now turn to the following question: what is the role of effective accountability in state compliance with international law in intelligence matters? Effective accountability embodies the potential of international law to influence state behaviour. Answering this question will thus allow me to assess how international law influences state behaviour in intelligence matters.

Intelligence decision-makers are often portrayed as following a rational choice model, impartially balancing the costs and benefits of a course of action for the nation's security.[1] Decision-makers are thus assumed to be rational, and international law to be of little relevance in this process. Yet, a behavioural approach to national security intelligence shows that intelligence analysts and decision-makers are subject to many biases and heuristics, making a simple rational choice model inadequate to represent decision-making accurately. Beyond the assumed simple costs-benefits analysis, a behavioural approach uncovers other extra-legal and legal factors influencing decision-making, and thus compliance. These factors need to be accounted for in any model claiming to represent decision-making accurately. One of these factors, the post-9/11 increase of state accountability for wrongful acts deriving from intelligence activities, has dramatically altered the costs and payoffs associated with these intelligence activities in recent years.

In this chapter, I demonstrate that the likelihood of effective accountability, a legal factor, now represents the most important variable to explain and determine whether a state will comply with international law in its intelligence activities. As I conceptualised it in Chapters 4 and 5, international legal accountability encompasses all supporting, rewarding, and sanctioning actions by the international legal order and includes persuasion, capacity-building, and education, as well as dialogue-based enforcement, deterrence measures, and outcasting. Accountability is deemed effective when it induces a desired change in state behaviour, namely compliance with international law. The likelihood of effective accountability should thus be understood as the extent to which a state's behaviour is affected by the likelihood that available supporting and sanctioning tools will be used. This variable can be measured. By modelling decision-making in intelligence matters through a bounded rational choice equation, I show that the likelihood of effective accountability explains and determines whether a state will comply with international law in its intelligence activities.

In the following sections, I first demonstrate the relevance of a behavioural approach to national security intelligence, highlighting several biases and heuristics affecting analysis and decision-making, and their implications for regulation (section 7.2). I then proceed by modelling executive decision-making in intelligence matters, integrating relevant legal and extra-legal factors into a bounded rational choice equation that accounts for these biases and heuristics

---

[1] The latest publicised example concerns MI5's 'Guidelines on the Use of Agents who participate in Criminality – Official Guidance', which stipulate that authorisation for an MI5 agent to commit a criminal act may be given where 'the potential harm to the public interest from the criminal activity is outweighed by the benefit to the public interest derived from the anticipated information the agent may provide'. This guidance was deemed lawful by the England and Wales Court of Appeal on 9 March 2021, Case No: T3/2020/0317 [2021] EWCA Civ 330.

(section 7.3). A comparative case-study using France and the United States as most-similar cases illustrates the functioning of the model and the explanatory role of the likelihood of effective accountability in intelligence decision-making (section 7.4). I conclude by highlighting compliance-enhancing paths and the necessity of a comprehensive model of regulation integrating all three layers to achieve compliance (section 7.5).

7.2 A BEHAVIOURAL APPROACH TO NATIONAL SECURITY INTELLIGENCE

States are bounded rational entities, in the sense that the determination of their interests, preferences, and motives is a function of the limits of their rationality and can be influenced by various cognitive and social factors.[2] This does not change in national security matters, which constitute the core of intelligence work. However, whereas in other issue areas states sometimes exemplify altruistic and fairness considerations, such is not the case in national security matters. Indeed, one cannot find any example of a state showing bounded self-interest when its national security is at stake. Rather, national security requires that one act in the *national interest*. States should therefore be considered self-interested when dealing with a (perceived or actual) threat to their national security.

In national security matters, the acute demands for a feeling of security and the need to show that 'everything' is being done to counter threats to the security of state institutions and its population often lead to responses that deviate from the rationality assumption in that they are ineffective to counter the threat. In the twenty-first-century security landscape, such responses frequently take the form of recourse to extra-legal measures such as torture and arbitrary detention, discriminatory laws and practices, unlawful surveillance, a reduction in rights and liberties, etc. Whereas these measures are generally ineffective in providing enhanced security to the population (national security in a broad sense),[3] they may nevertheless be considered effective in serving

---

[2] Anne van Aaken, 'Behavioral International Law and Economics' (2014) 55 Harvard International Law Journal 62; Tomer Broude, 'Behavioral International Law' [2015] 163 U. Pa. L. Rev. 1099; Anne van Aaken and Tomer Broude, 'The Psychology of International Law: An Introduction' (2019) 30 European Journal of International Law 1225.

[3] See e.g., Christian Bjørnskov and Stefan Voigt, 'When Does Terror Induce a State of Emergency? And What Are the Effects?' (2020) 64 Journal of Conflict Resolution 579; Seung-Whan Choi, 'Fighting Terrorism through the Rule of Law?' (2010) 54 Journal of Conflict Resolution 940; Laura Dugan and Erica Chenoweth, 'Moving Beyond Deterrence: The Effectiveness of Raising the Expected Utility of Abstaining from Terrorism in Israel' (2012) 77 American Sociological Review 597;

other purposes. In particular, they may enhance the security of governmental institutions (national security in a narrow sense) and provide domestic advantages to decision-makers. Therefore, responses that would, at first sight, appear irrational to counter national security threats may well be rational responses when considered from other perspectives, including that of institutional and individual decision-makers. A behavioural approach to intelligence decision-making is thus needed to understand the motives underlying states' responses and to redefine rational behaviour in intelligence matters (section 7.2.1). This approach further proves crucial to identifying how the likelihood of effective accountability can affect intelligence decisions-making (section 7.2.2).

7.2.1 A Behavioural Approach to Intelligence Decision-Making

A behavioural approach is first useful to understand the biases of intelligence analysts and decision-makers in assessing national security threats. Threat assessments are not produced by rational actors. This is primarily because intelligence analysts' interpretations are influenced by their general beliefs and theories.[4] Indeed, analysts' world-views and assessments are subject to most of the same biases and heuristics that can be found in an educated public. Further, the weakness and uncertainty of intelligence and the absence of clear feedback on analytic insights allow them to follow their own preferences and intuitions when interpreting ambiguous information,[5] and to do so with (over)confidence due to their insider position and expertise.[6]

Christian Bjørnskov and Stefan Voigt, 'You Don't Always Get What You'd Expect – On Some Unexpected Effects of Constitutional Emergency Provisions' (Social Science Research Network 2018).

[4] Martha Whitesmith, 'Experimental Research in Reducing the Risk of Cognitive Bias in Intelligence Analysis' (2020) 33 International Journal of Intelligence and CounterIntelligence 380.

[5] Robert Jervis, *Why Intelligence Fails: Lessons from the Iranian Revolution and the Iraq War* (Cornell University Press 2010); Richards J Heuer Jr, *Psychology of Intelligence Analysis* (2nd edn, Pherson Associates, LLC 2007); Uri Bar-Joseph and Rose McDermott, *Intelligence Success and Failure: The Human Factor* (Oxford University Press 2017); Bess J Puvathingal and Donald A Hantula, 'Revisiting the Psychology of Intelligence Analysis: From Rational Actors to Adaptive Thinkers' (2012) 67 American Psychologist 199, 202.

[6] National Research Council (US) (ed), *Intelligence Analysis for Tomorrow: Advances from the Behavioral and Social Sciences* (National Academies Press 2011) 34; Paul Slovic, Baruch Fischhoff and Sarah Lichtenstein, 'Facts versus Fears: Understanding Perceived Risk' in Daniel Kahneman, Paul Slovic and Amos Tversky (eds), *Judgment under Uncertainty* (1st edn, Cambridge University Press 1982).

Intelligence agencies' insular organisational culture and structural secrecy also render them particularly vulnerable to groupthink,[7] 'a mode of thinking that people engage in when they are deeply involved in a cohesive in-group, when the members' strivings for unanimity override their motivation to realistically appraise alternative courses of action'.[8] In-group mentalities hinder the expression of dissent and may lead to the exclusion of relevant information from consideration in analysis and decision-making processes. Groups also fall victim to an information-sharing bias, whereby group decisions are based on information that all members possess before discussion (shared information) rather than on information known to only one member (unshared information).[9] In the intelligence context, this means that 'key judgments for policymakers might disproportionately be based on a small subset of easily interpretable intelligence'.[10] In a community where secrecy, the need-to-know, the need to form judgments in ambiguous situations and time pressure are ever-present conditions of decision-making, the information-sharing bias thus further hinders the quality of analysts' predictions.[11]

Intelligence agencies are themselves bounded rational entities, but they are also self-interested entities. Agencies' funding, powers, and legitimacy are a direct function of their assessment of national security threats. Intelligence agencies possess an informational advantage over other governmental actors. They can use this advantage to mould the general public's perceptions of the threats and risks incurred, to influence the budget dedicated to national security concerns, and to request 'necessary' increases in their powers.[12] Such direct self-serving bias and conflict of interests preclude any claim to objectivity and neutrality.[13] Yet, administrations often take intelligence agencies'

---

[7] National Research Council (US) (n 6) 66–68; Oren Gross, 'Security vs. Liberty: On Emotions and Cognition' in David Jenkins, Amanda Jacobsen and Anders Henriksen (eds), *The Long Decade: How 9/11 Changed the Law* (Oxford University Press 2014) 58.

[8] Irving L Janis, *Groupthink: Psychological Studies of Policy Decisions and Fiascoes* (2nd edn, Houghton Mifflin 1982) 9.

[9] Garold Stasser and William Titus, 'Pooling of Unshared Information in Group Decision Making: Biased Information Sampling during Discussion' (1985) 48 Journal of Personality and Social Psychology 1467.

[10] Puvathingal and Hantula (n 5) 206.

[11] ibid 203–204, 206.

[12] Gross (n 7) 56–57.

[13] Ryan Alford, 'The Harbinger Theory of Terrorism and the Rule of Law: The Danger of "Balancing" Non-Derogable Rights against Security When Relying on Threat Assessments Produced by Self-Interested Intelligence Agencies' (2018) 22 The International Journal of Human Rights 1285.

threat assessments at face value. These elements highlight the fallibility of the threat assessments relied on by states' institutions and decision-makers.

Secondly, behavioural approaches allow us to better understand the responses adopted by intelligence and policy decision-makers. Decision-makers must often act on incomplete information while fearing future attacks and facing differing, sometimes contradictory, interests. The boundedness of their rationality leads even the most virtuous decision-makers to use heuristics when choosing a course of action.[14] The availability bias[15] and representativeness heuristics,[16] in particular base-rate[17] and gambler's fallacies,[18] may thus lead governments to not only fallaciously assess threats, but also to adopt extreme, stigmatising and discriminatory responses to past attacks and current threats.[19] Systemic and embedded institutional racist, sexist, and exceptionalist biases also greatly influence the assessment of, and responses to threats, yielding counterproductive results.[20]

In addition, domestic pressure often works against the adoption of internationally lawful and effective responses. The public's biases may indeed push decision-makers towards courses of action that satisfy their electorate, without however presenting any long-term benefit for the public or the state itself.[21] When fearing an attack, citizens expect their government to respond to the threat. Action bias predicts that the more unusual or drastic the response,

---

[14] Daniel Kahneman, Paul Slovic and Amos Tversky (eds), *Judgment under Uncertainty: Heuristics and Biases* (Cambridge University Press 1982).

[15] A cognitive bias whereby individuals assess the frequency of an event based upon how easily they can recall an instance of it. Individuals particularly tend to overestimate the likelihood of dramatic events attracting significant media coverage or triggering strong emotions. Kahneman, Slovic and Tversky (n 14) 164.

[16] A cognitive bias leading individuals to evaluate an event's probability by assessing how closely it relates to available data, ignoring the relevance of base rates in assessing probability. Kahneman, Slovic and Tversky (n 14) 163–164.

[17] When decisions are largely based on representativeness, other relevant information might not be sufficiently considered. The prior probability, or base-rate frequency of outcomes, describing the frequency of an event in the population or in the past, is one kind of such information. Kahneman, Slovic and Tversky (n 14) 153–154.

[18] Gambler's fallacy is present when small samples are deemed to be representative of the general context. In such cases, a person ignores the statistical independence of events. Kahneman, Slovic and Tversky (n 14) 7–8.

[19] Alexander Schulan, 'Behavioural Economics of Security' (2019) 4 European Journal for Security Research 273; Marc Sageman, 'The Implication of Terrorism's Extremely Low Base Rate' (2021) 33 Terrorism and Political Violence 302.

[20] E.g., Western intelligence agencies' assessment of the threat posed by al Qaeda before 9/11, and their responses to it both before and after.

[21] Bjørnskov and Voigt, 'When Does Terror Induce a State of Emergency?' (n 3).

the stronger its psychological reassuring effect on the population.[22] The risk of a violent attack from a terrorist organisation or a hostile state could well still be the same, but national security will have profited in the trade-off: the position of governmental institutions is now more secure and executive powers have increased. However, this does not mean that individuals' security has benefited in any way from this governmental exercise of power. Quite the opposite, for the benefit of such psychological reassurance, civil liberties may have been traded-off, the rule of law undermined, and security as a social good damaged.[23] Therefore, to respond to citizens' fear and/or to appear tough – both motives being irrelevant to the effective fight against a genuine national security threat – the government further threatens national security as a social good.[24]

From an external perspective, the rationality of this course of action is at best doubtful and could be explained by moral panics.[25] However, from the point of view of state leaders, this may well be a rational use of the public's fears.[26] Indeed, political leaders may consider that their interest in re-election, for instance, takes priority over the state's interest in dealing effectively with the threat. This is particularly likely following an attack, when outsiders are blamed and the crisis leads to heightened individual and group consciousness.[27] Since violent crises are consensus-generating events, in-group bias and group polarisation predict that when the measure adopted targets outsiders (or non-citizens), political leaders are likely to receive strong support from the electorate, while incurring few political costs.[28]

Representativeness heuristics also trigger problematic theories, such as the 'harbinger theory' identified by Robert Diab, according to which

> 9/11 was the harbinger of a new order of terror, in which further attacks in North America are likely to occur at some point in the near future, on a similar or greater scale as 9/11, possibly, but not necessarily, involving weapons of mass destruction

---

[22] Jeremy Waldron, *Torture, Terror, and Trade-Offs: Philosophy for the White House* (Oxford University Press 2010) 44.
[23] ibid 45.
[24] 'Human rights impact of policies and practices aimed at preventing and countering violent extremism', Report of the Special Rapporteur on the promotion and protection of human rights and fundamental freedoms while countering terrorism, Fionnuala Ní Aoláin, A/HRC/43/46, 21 February 2020.
[25] Gross (n 7) 52.
[26] Bjørnskov and Voigt, 'When Does Terror Induce a State of Emergency?' (n 3).
[27] Oren Gross and Fionnuala Ní Aoláin, *Law in Times of Crisis: Emergency Powers in Theory and Practice* (Cambridge University Press 2006) 220–227.
[28] ibid 220–227; Gross (n 7) 50.

... And on this basis, earlier assumptions about the absolute limits of state force against individuals have come to seem untenable or imprudent.[29]

The harbinger theory permanently erodes the rule of law by implying the necessity of trade-offs between individual freedoms and state power in the name of 'security'. What happens, however, is a trade-off between security as a social good (national security in a broad sense) and the security of governmental institutions (national security in a narrow sense), the sole beneficiary of this balancing exercise.

In addition, both leaders acting in their personal interest and those representing the state's may exhibit what Daniel Kahneman and Jonathan Renshon have called 'hawkish biases'.[30] According to Kahneman and Renshon, the biases uncovered by psychological research favour hawkish decisions in conflict situations, i.e., they favour suspicion, hostility, and aggression. The seven cognitive biases they examine[31] thus increase the probability that agents will act more 'hawkishly' than an objective observer would deem appropriate. In national security matters, which often take the form of (potential) conflict situations, decision-makers within the state would thus tend to react more aggressively than necessary, potentially triggering an escalation of threats and hostilities and bringing about counterproductive results.

Is it rational for decision-makers to favour the security of governmental institutions over security as a social good even if this strategy fails to respond adequately to the threat the nation faces? Objectively, no. Subjectively, however, decision-makers face domestic pressures (elections, parliamentary commissions, public opinion, protests, etc.) that frame the issue negatively, encouraging risk-seeking behaviour and preferences for appearing 'tough'.[32] Hindsight bias may likewise encourage tough responses to past attacks to avoid being blamed for failing to prevent future threats from materialising,[33]

---

[29] Robert Diab, *The Harbinger Theory. How the Post-9/11 Emergency Became Permanent and the Case for Reform* (Oxford University Press 2015) 99–100

[30] Daniel Kahneman and Jonathan Renshon, 'Hawkish Biases' in A Trevol Thrall and Jane Cramer (eds) *American Foreign Policy and the Politics of Fear: Threat Inflation since 9/11* (Routledge 2009) 79.

[31] Positive illusions; fundamental attribution error; illusion of transparency; endowment effect/loss aversion; risk seeking in losses; pseudo-certainty; and reactive devaluation.

[32] Amos Tversky and Daniel Kahneman, 'The Framing of Decisions and the Psychology of Choice' (1981) 211 Science 453.

[33] Hindsight bias refers to individuals' tendency to overestimate an event's likelihood after they observe its occurrence. As Oren Gross explains, in national security situations, 'the problem is that if people, in hindsight, believe that the risk was more foreseeable and still occurred, that might be interpreted to mean that not enough meas-

together with extreme measures to correct previous failures, resulting in a sort of 'accountability ping-pong'.[34] Leaders may also rationally consider that their personal or professional interest takes priority over the state's interest and utilise the public's biases to advance it. The answer is therefore more nuanced.

Behavioural approaches further help us understand the underlying interests and motives of states and their leaders on the international scene. In national security matters, altruistic and fairness considerations are invariably absent. Instead, states prioritise their own security over other goods and seem willing to sacrifice public goods and other states' security to protect their own.[35] This could well be explained by prospect theory (loss aversion).[36] Indeed, if states perceive attacks as a loss in their security and take their current or pre-attack status as the reference point, prospect theory predicts that they will be willing to take excessive risks to avoid future losses and will go to great lengths to protect their current security status. States would thus be expected to take an irredentist approach when feeling under threat or having suffered a 'loss' in national security, such as declaring a 'global war on terror'; sending troops into foreign states; and pursuing such war because its costs cannot be recovered (sunk costs fallacy),[37] even after it has long proven counterproductive. From this perspective, national security is about protecting the security of the state and its institutions, and about alleviating the electorate's fear. The national interest is the only interest that matters.

Further, peer pressure and institutional frameworks such as the UN Security Council and NATO have increased the focus on national security after

---

ures had been taken in order to prevent the harm from occurring in the first place'. Gross (n 7) 57.

[34] The term refers to reactive measures that overcorrect the latest politicised and sensationalised intelligence failure, thus paving the way for flipside errors. Philip E Tetlock and Barbara A Mellers, 'Intelligent Management of Intelligence Agencies: Beyond Accountability Ping-Pong' (2011) 66 American Psychologist 542.

[35] The numerous foreign interventions witnessed during the Cold War and since 9/11 are evidence of this tendency.

[36] Introduced by Kahneman and Tversky, prospect theory is a psychology-based utility theory that characterises decisions among risky alternatives with known probabilities. Prospect theory applies an S-shaped value function that assumes the value of zero at the reference point and is concave on the space of gains and convex on the space of losses. The S-shaped value function embeds loss aversion, according to which a gain generates a utility increase lower than the disutility caused by the same-sized loss. Daniel Kahneman and Amos Tversky, 'Prospect Theory: An Analysis of Decision under Risk' (1979) 47 Econometrica 263.

[37] The sunk costs fallacy is a mistake in reasoning whereby the sunk costs of an activity are considered when deciding whether to continue with the activity.

9/11 by prioritising international cooperation to face the terrorist threat.[38] Counterterrorism cooperation, for instance, is self-interested: states cooperate because their interests coincide and because they need other states' capabilities to face a transnational threat. The transnational nature of the modern terrorist threat means that, to fight it, states need to act at both domestic and international levels. Whether merged or separate, responses to domestic and globalised threats depend on public support, cooperation, and willing informants, i.e., citizens and other states' intelligence communities. No state, even the most skilled and technologically equipped, can by itself cover all world zones and all sorts of threats. Hence, even 'intelligence superpowers' like the United States are not self-sufficient in that respect, a fact that gives bargaining power and influence to its partners.

Through institutional frameworks, however, states are also subject to group biases. Research on groupthink shows that groups are vulnerable to several cognitive biases, which lead to in-group pressure towards conformity and cohesiveness, suboptimal performance, and a group-serving bias.[39] These biases are easily observed in the actions taken on the international scene in the wake of 9/11. Apart from the French opposition to the United States' intervention in Iraq in the UN Security Council,[40] no explicit opposition to the United States' 'global war on terror' could be witnessed from US allies. Rather, US allies supported most of its extra-legal operations,[41] and one can only assume that United States President George W Bush's framing of the choice as 'You're either with us or against us'[42] did not do much to encourage dissent and mitigate these group biases.

The framing of the terrorist threat as a 'global war' might also have reinforced elite decision-makers' hawkish biases. Finally, the complete lack of interstate accountability witnessed in intelligence matters, despite egregious violations of both interstate obligations and human rights norms, can be inter-

---

[38] See, UN Security Council Resolution 1373 (2001), and the invocation of the principle of collective self-defence under Article 5 of the North Atlantic Treaty on 2 October 2001, paving the way for the operation of the CIA-led rendition, detention, and interrogation programme.

[39] Janis (n 8) identified eight symptoms that characterise the phenomenon of groupthink. See Rose McDermott, *Political Psychology in International Relations* (The University of Michigan Press 2004) 249–260 for a summary and discussion of later research, and Puvathingal and Hantula (n 5) 203 for a discussion in relation to intelligence analysis.

[40] Address on Iraq, by Dominique de Villepin, French Minister of Foreign Affairs, at the UN Security Council. New York, 14 February 2003.

[41] See Chapter 3.

[42] Joint news conference with French President Jacques Chirac, 6 November 2001.

preted as evidence that states are unwilling to retaliate and sanction other states when security is at stake. The sanctioning dilemma is thus at its peak.

7.2.2 Regulatory Implications

These observations inform regulation in the international legal order. Whereas interstate forms of accountability are implausible in intelligence matters, other forms of accountability remain possible. In particular, mediated forms of accountability,[43] commonly triggered by individual complaints before human rights courts and bodies and by states' reporting obligations, have increased exponentially following revelations about the CIA-led and NSA-led programmes.[44] For the first time, intelligence activities became the subject of international litigation, and their legality was thoroughly assessed.

At the same time, we witnessed a momentum towards a heightened legalism of intelligence activities, resting on a series of interlocking changes[45] that increased demands for, and possibilities of accountability. The evolving nature of intelligence activities after the Cold War, now targeting individuals more directly, and the parallel 'humanisation' of international law thus led individuals to have legitimate expectations that their rights would be respected. Further, the increase in intelligence leaks and scandals triggered a renewed interest for intelligence activities and affected agencies' legitimacy. Finally, a new pervading legalism[46] in intelligence communities accompanied these communities' renewed understanding that compliance with international law is increasingly necessary to be perceived as legitimate and to benefit from citizens' and foreign services' cooperation.[47]

In recent years, therefore, there has been an increase in the likelihood that the intelligence community will be held to account by partner intelligence

---

[43] See Chapter 4.
[44] E.g., ECtHR, *Big Brother Watch and Others* v. *the United Kingdom* [GC] – Applications No 58170/13, 62322/14 and 24960/15, 25 May 2021; *Al-Nashiri* v. *Romania*, Application No. 33234/12, 31 May 2018; *Husayn (Abu Zubaydah)* v. *Poland*, Application No. 7511/13, 24 July 2014; *El-Masri* v. *The Former Yugoslav Republic of Macedonia*, Application No. 39639/09, 13 December 2012. UNCAT, *Agiza* v. *Sweden*, CAT/C/34/D/233/2003, 25 May 2005. CCPR, *Alzery* v. *Sweden*, Communication No. 1416/2005, CCPR/C/88/D/1416/2005, 10 November 2006. IACHR, *Khaled El-Masri* v. *United States*. Report 21/16. Petition 419-08. Report on Admissibility. OEA/Ser.L/V/II.157. Doc. 25. 15 April 2016.
[45] Ashley Deeks, 'Confronting and Adapting: Intelligence Agencies and International Law' (2016) 102 Virginia Law Review 599, 600–629.
[46] Margo Schlanger, 'Intelligence Legalism and the National Security Agency's Civil Liberties Gap' (2015) 6 Harv. Nat'l Sec. J. 112.
[47] Deeks (n 45) 600–629.

communities and citizens. This has been matched by a parallel increase in the likelihood that states will be held legally accountable for the acts of their intelligence community, both before human rights courts and bodies and before the international legal order as a whole. Such increases necessarily affect what states perceive to be their interest in national security matters. If exposure and accountability are increasingly likely, then this changes the costs and payoffs of pursuing a policy that would otherwise have remained secret. The result is that the likelihood of effective accountability, a legal factor, now represents the most important variable to explain and determine whether a state will comply with international law in its intelligence activities. I explain why in the following paragraphs.

The intelligence community's role is to protect national security and, in national security matters, states are self-interested. From this perspective, international law should not matter much for the intelligence community's choice of action: decision-making should be guided solely by the national interest. Yet, depending on how the state values its reputation, actions by other actors in the international legal order may affect what states perceive to be in their interest. States' willingness to cultivate a good reputation induces them to consider the impact of their actions on their reputation even when there might be benefits in acting otherwise.[48] States can have a reputation for various things, for instance complying with international law; respecting human rights; being a reliable treaty partner; siding with allies; but also being tough or ensuring complete secrecy. Their reputation is mainly a matter of how other states perceive them; whether they ascribe a particular behaviour to the actor or the situation; and how they evaluate the behaviour. Assessing the impact of reputation on state compliance can prove challenging,[49] especially since many biases and heuristics impact how a state is perceived by others.[50] Nevertheless, reputation remains an important factor to explain compliance with international law,[51] not least because the international legal order relies on conditional cooperation to function and being perceived as compliant enhances trust and brings political legitimation.[52] In addition, reputation is sometimes affected in very concrete and visible ways, such as when a state is prevented

---

[48] Andrew T Guzman, *How International Law Works: A Rational Choice Theory* (Oxford University Press 2008).

[49] See Rachel Brewster, 'Unpacking the State's Reputation' (2009) 50 Harvard International Law Journal 40.

[50] van Aaken (n 2) 479.

[51] Guzman (n 48).

[52] Ian Hurd, *How to Do Things with International Law* (Princeton University Press 2017).

from borrowing on international markets[53] or excluded from participating in international cooperative regimes or institutions.[54] In such cases, the costs of a negative reputation can be measured somewhat precisely.

For reputation to be affected, however, other actors must attribute the state's behaviour to dispositional rather than situational factors.[55] International courts and bodies produce information about non-compliant behaviour. They publicly expose such behaviour and shape the saliency, credibility, and framing of information for other actors in the international legal order.[56] In other words, (quasi-)judicial decisions produce information that facilitates effective reputational deterrence. They also indicate the type of behaviour that would have constituted a lawful response to the factual situation faced by the state. State accountability thus sets a normative benchmark. The judgment or decision authoritatively declares that, when facing situation x, states may not respond with y. If, in future instances, states still decide to face situations similar to x with response y, then other states are more likely to attribute this behaviour to dispositional rather than situational factors since y's unlawfulness and the existence of alternative courses of action were indicated before. State accountability thus has a dual role. It is first an informational device for states, allowing them to adjust their perception of other states by relying on the normative benchmark set by the court. Second, accountability constitutes a tool directly affecting the state's reputation through the persuasive quality of the judgments and decisions.

This dual role of state accountability means that the direct, reputational, and indirect sanctions imposed by competent accountability forums can increase the direct, reputational, and indirect costs of violations. When costs increase, it becomes less interesting for states to resort to extra-legal measures to respond to national security threats. The reputational threat induced by state accountability thus functions as a deterring factor. According to theories of deterrence, actors will generally be deterred from breaching the law when the legal penalty they would receive for a breach, multiplied by the likelihood of

---

[53] See the degrading situation of Argentina between 2007 and 2013 following its refusal to comply with arbitral awards mandating it to reimburse foreign investors. Daniel Peat, 'Perception and Process: Towards a Behavioural Theory of Compliance' (2022) 13 Journal of International Dispute Settlement 179.

[54] On outcasting in international law, see Anne van Aaken, 'Experimental Insights for International Legal Theory' (2019) 30 European Journal of International Law 1237, 1257–1259; Oona Hathaway and Scott J Shapiro, 'Outcasting: Enforcement in Domestic and International Law' [2011] Yale Law Journal 98.

[55] van Aaken (n 2) 477.

[56] Roy Shapira, *Law and Reputation: How the Legal System Shapes Behavior by Producing Information* (1st edn, Cambridge University Press 2020) 35.

swift detection and conviction, outweighs the gain.[57] The *perception* of the risk of accountability, more than the actual risk, is what deters actors from breaching the law.[58] Hence, how a state perceives the costs of accountability will determine the success of a deterrence strategy. In intelligence matters, this variable[59] is a function of the value that the state bestows upon relevant aspects of its reputation and (continued) cooperation with other states.

In intelligence matters, state accountability before competent human rights courts and bodies also has a trickle-down effect due to the necessity to cooperate with other states. Ashley Deeks conceptualised this as 'mechanisms of peer constraints' between intelligence communities.[60] Deeks describes the phenomenon whereby constraints on one state's intelligence community, whatever their nature or origin, also constrain peer intelligence communities because of the willingness or necessity of continued cooperation. Such a phenomenon can be observed through the effects of accountability for wrongful acts resulting from intelligence activities, at least in democratic states. Hence, a state facing a decision that its surveillance legislation breaches a human rights treaty will (ideally) alter such legislation. To avoid being held to account for its intelligence partners' acts, it should then require that the information it receives from other states respects similar standards; and that the information it shares with them be treated in accordance with the caveats imposed by its domestic legislation.[61] The standards imposed by the accountability forum will therefore 'trickle down' to the state's intelligence partners due to their willingness to keep the flow of information running. In addition, states subject to the jurisdiction of the same human rights body may preventively apply equivalent standards to their domestic regulation of surveillance, thereby triggering a similar trickle-down effect with their own intelligence partners. The

---

[57] Christine Parker and Vibeke Nielsen, 'Compliance: 14 Questions' in Peter Drahos (ed), *Regulatory Theory* (ANU Press 2017).
[58] ibid 228.
[59] The likelihood of effective accountability is measured in the model by adding together the state's positive reputation (R) and the costs of non-compliance (Cnc). See section 7.3.
[60] Ashley Deeks, 'Intelligence Services, Peer Constraints, and the Law' in Zachary K Goldman, Samuel J Rascoff and Jane Harman (eds), *Global Intelligence Oversight* (Oxford University Press 2016).
[61] CJEU, Case C-311/18 *Data Protection Commissioner* v. *Facebook Ireland Ltd and Maximilian Schrems* ('Schrems II'), Grand Chamber Judgment, 16 July 2020, para 105. But see ECtHR, *Big Brother Watch* (n 44), para 362; and *Centrum för rättvisa* v. *Sweden* [GC], Application No 35252/08, 25 May 2021, para 276: 'This does not necessarily mean that the receiving State must have comparable protection to that of the transferring State; nor does it necessarily require that an assurance is given prior to every transfer'.

need for cooperation therefore creates an accountability web, whereby states are encouraged to comply with the standards imposed on their intelligence partners by accountability forums that they may not even be subject to. In turn, a single decision may constrain multiple intelligence communities and have much broader effects than the single case forming the cause of action.

Intelligence decision-makers adopt responses to national security threats based on a rational choice approach, balancing the costs and benefits of potential strategies.[62] However, the recent instances of state accountability before human rights courts and bodies, coupled with the increased publicity of agencies' actions and individuals' expectations that their rights be respected,[63] have changed the costs, payoffs, and incentives. Analysis of these changes suggests that, if the goal is to effectively respond to national security threats (as opposed to, for instance, win an upcoming election), the increase of state accountability for extra-legal intelligence activities has made it more interesting – and thus *rational* – for states to comply with international law. Compliance is therefore in states' interest not only because it leads to more effective responses to national security threats but also, and crucially so for decision-makers, because of the enhanced risk of being held to account. Indeed, self-interest and reputational concerns impose that states account for the risk of accountability in their decision-making. By bringing intelligence activities back into the realm of the law, and by making them public and open to scrutiny, state accountability changes what states perceive to be in their interest. It acts both as a deterrent against extra-legal measures and as an incentive for states to comply with international law.

7.3 A COMPLIANCE-BASED MODEL OF EXECUTIVE INTELLIGENCE DECISION-MAKING

Because their rationality is bounded, intelligence decision-makers do not consider only objective costs and benefits when making decisions. In consequence, although decision-makers follow a rational choice approach, intel-

---

[62] As an example of this reasoning in practice, see the United Kingdom's balancing act regarding torture-tainted intelligence received from the United States during the war on terror: the unlikelihood (as assessed then) of any sanctions meant that MI5 'assessed that the legal and reputational risks were low and the intelligence it was receiving was highly valuable and therefore worth the risk'. Intelligence and Security Committee of Parliament, 'Detainee Mistreatment and Rendition: 2001–2010' (2018), para 129.

[63] This interaction effect is reflected in the model by the inclusion of the expectation of publicity (P) on the numerator line together with the likelihood of effective accountability (R + Cnc). See section 7.3.

ligence decision-making does not fit within a simple rational choice model. Such model therefore constitutes a poor explanatory tool for states' decisions. To represent executive decision-making in intelligence matters more accurately, I expand the rational choice model to account for the particularities of national security intelligence, behavioural insights, and recent developments in the international legal order.

The model I propose aims to account for the role and weight of the factors influencing states' decision-making in intelligence matters. It works as a *bounded* rational choice equation, integrating not only objective factors of risks and benefits, but also the state's subjective perception of the threat; decision-makers' personal interests; their perceptions of the state's values and identity; the weight they bestow upon these (positive) aspects of the state's reputation; and other domestic considerations (e.g., oversight, elections, public opinion). The decision-making model accounts for the dependencies of states in their responses to national security threats by factoring in the necessities of cooperation and the risk of alienating intelligence partners and sources. The model further assumes that the state will behave in a self-interested manner, meaning that the result of their decision-making process will reflect what they perceive to be in their best interest. In this sense, the model is not only a descriptive and explanatory tool, identifying the factors at play in decision-making, but it also possesses some predictive power. Indeed, although it is beyond the scope of this chapter to do so, the model can also be applied *ex ante* to determine whether it would be in a state's interest to go forward with a specific intelligence activity at a given date, thus producing a score of expected compliance for the future.

The model aims to represent executive decision-making at the state level, integrating behavioural insights within the representation of the last stage of decision-making within the state, here called 'executive decision-making'. The unit of analysis therefore becomes the state, although somewhat fictionally. Two main reasons justify this choice. First, the decision at stake concerns an intelligence activity which, if adopted, would engage the state's international responsibility. This means that regardless of the actual level of decision-making within the state, the wrongful act will be attributed to it under the law of state responsibility[64] and the state may be held to account for it. Second, this last level or stage of decision-making, regardless of whether the decision is in fact made at the highest possible level in the state apparatus, is the stage where all the biases and heuristics identified in section 7.2 coalesce. Biases in threat assessment, in the identification and framing of options to

---

[64] International Law Commission, Draft Articles on Responsibility of States for Internationally Wrongful Acts 2001 (Supplement No 10 (A/56/10), chpIVE1) 76.

respond to the threat, in the relationship between various domestic actors, and in interstate cooperation all add up and bundle together in the ultimate decision-making process by elite decision-makers.

The determination of the expectation of a given state's compliance (C) regarding an intelligence activity in breach of its international obligations is made according to an operation involving the following interrelated elements: the state's reputation (R [positive aspects] and R* [negative aspects]); the costs of compliance with international law (Cc); the costs of non-compliance with international law (Cnc); the benefits of non-compliance with international law (Bnc); and the foreseeable expectation of publicity of the activity (P). These elements are the result of a prior assessment of intelligence-specific factors, as explained in Table 7.1, and represent the considerations impacting a boundedly rational state's decision. The model is better represented by the following equation:

$$C = \frac{R + Cnc + P}{R^* + Cc + Bnc} \qquad (7.1)$$

In discursive form, the equation reads as follows: the *expectation of compliance* is equal to [*the state's positive reputation* plus *the costs of non-compliance* plus *the expectation of publicity*] divided by [*the state's negative reputation* plus *the costs of compliance* plus *the benefits of non-compliance*].

Using an equation allows for universal application of the model, to all states and all intelligence activities in breach of international law, by researchers and intelligence decision-makers alike. The scoring process required for the model is a qualitative exercise that does not purport to be perfectly objective. The model thus represents an attempt to quantify qualitative elements. This semi-quantitative method relies on a qualitative scale (see Appendix 7.1), defined for each element and factor (part of an element). The scale's sensitivity permits relative confidence in the result despite the possibility of small variations in the scores attributed to each factor by different users.

To use the model, one must score each factor from one to four assessing the criteria listed in Table 7.2 (a full scoring table with a scale is provided in Appendix 7.1) and run the equation on an intelligence activity in breach of international law. The result provides an indicative score of compliance (C). It represents the expectation that any given state behaving in what it believes to be its best interest will either conduct the activity in breach of international law or decide instead to comply with its international obligations. If the result (C) is inferior to 1, then it *is not* in the state's interest to comply with international law. Conversely, if C is superior to 1, it *is* in the state's interest to comply with international law. Section 7.4 provides an illustration of such functioning.

Table 7.1   Decision-making model

Element	Meaning	Factors and Formula	Scale[a]	Possible score
R	Positive Reputation	Human rights record and reputation × Quality of domestic oversight of intelligence activities	1–4 × 1–4	1–16
R*	Negative Reputation[b]	16 – R	NA	0–15
Cc	Costs of Compliance	Domestic costs × Intelligence losses	1–4 × 1–4	1–16
Cnc	Costs of Non-Compliance	Strength of accountability network[c] × Intelligence reputation and human rights reputation losses	1–4 × 1–4	1–16
Bnc	Benefits of Non-Compliance	Productivity of measure × Other intelligence and domestic gains	1–4 × 1–4	1–16
P	Expectation of publicity	Probability as assessed by decision-maker: null (1) – long-term (2) – medium-term (3) – short-term (4)	1–4	1–4

Notes: [a] For all factors, the scale goes from 1 (lowest) to 4 (highest). See Appendix 7.1 for additional details on the scoring process. [b] The state's 'negative reputation' constitutes the counterpart of the positive aspects of the state's reputation. The addition of positive and negative aspects should always be equal to 16. Negative aspects tend to reinforce the weight of extra-legal domestic considerations and are included in the denominator side of the formula, whereas positive aspects increase the weight given to considerations of international legality and figure in the numerator side of the formula. [c] 'Accountability network' refers here to all competent supra-national mechanisms and states capable of holding the state to account for a breach of its international obligations. It therefore represents the potential for transnational enforcement, not actual enforcement.

The equation's structure exemplifies the balancing of international legality against domestic considerations, representing the tension between international law requirements and perceptions of what the national interest requires. This balancing exercise is informed by the decision-makers' own interests and by the biases in the formulation and assessment of threats present at various stages of decision-making. Variables *R (positive reputation)* and *Cnc (costs of non-compliance)* taken together represent the likelihood of effective accountability, accounting for all possibilities of domestic and transnational enforcement of international legality. The higher the score for $(R + Cnc)$, the higher the likelihood that the state will be effectively held to account for a breach of its international obligations, directly or through collateral

Table 7.2 Factors

Factor	What is assessed[a]
Human Rights Record and Reputation	State's membership of human rights organisations; ratification of main treaties; engagement with procedures; persistence of systemic human rights issues; outward appearance of respect for human rights obligations
Quality of Domestic Oversight of Intelligence Activities	Existing domestic structure for oversight; actual powers and competences
Domestic Costs	Likely domestic backlash failing adoption of the unlawful measure under consideration
Intelligence Losses	Losses incurred if the state does not adopt the measure. E.g., disruption in existing intelligence-sharing framework
Strength of Accountability Network	Combined powers and competences of all competent accountability mechanisms (other states and international institutions)
Intelligence Reputation and Human Rights Losses	Likely harm to domestic and international reputation as a reliable intelligence partner if the unlawful measure is adopted
Productivity of Measure	Financial and human (personnel) costs of the measure compared to its intelligence benefits
Other Intelligence and Domestic Gains	Increased security (powers, missions, favourable opinion ratings, etc.) of governmental institutions
Expectation of Publicity	Probability, as assessed by decision-maker, that the measure will become public: never, or in the short, medium, or long term

Note: [a] See Appendix 7.1 for a full scoring table.

consequences. In contrast, domestic considerations are accounted for through variables $R*$ *(negative reputation)*, Cc *(costs of compliance – domestic costs)*, and Bnc *(benefits of non-compliance – other intelligence and domestic gains)*. The higher the score on the denominator line of the formula, the more likely it is that the state (as represented by the responsible decision-maker) will prefer to forego its international obligations in favour of domestic considerations. Finally, variable P *(expectation of publicity)* and, to a lesser extent, Cc *(costs of compliance – intelligence losses)* and Bnc *(benefits of non-compliance – productivity of measure)*, are activity-dependent variables that reinforce the likelihood of effective accountability (P) or the weight to be given to domestic considerations (Cc and Bnc).

7.4 HARNESSING THE MODEL: A COMPARATIVE CASE-STUDY

To demonstrate the model's functioning in concrete situations and illustrate the explanatory role of the likelihood of effective accountability, I conduct a comparative analysis using a 'most-similar cases' case selection method.[65] Known in social sciences as 'the comparative method', a most-similar system design is a standard case-selection principle for inference-oriented, controlled comparison in qualitative, small-N studies.[66] A most-similar research design requires that comparable cases be selected so as to hold non-key variables constant while isolating the explanatory power of the key independent variable with regard to the dependent variable (the phenomenon needing explanation). Here, the dependent variable is state compliance or non-compliance in intelligence matters. This method allows me to illustrate the explanatory power of the likelihood of effective accountability, as an independent variable, and to demonstrate the model's utility as a representation of intelligence decision-making.

For this purpose, I use a single unlawful intelligence activity as a common denominator: targeted assassination on foreign territory in the absence of a genuine armed conflict involving the state conducting the assassination. This commonly takes the form of a drone strike. The first reason for this choice is practical: targeted assassinations are a semi-public intelligence activity because they leave visible traces. Their authors can normally be identified relatively easily, even if the responsible state neither officially confirms nor denies its participation. The activity itself (the strike) constitutes a covert action, that is, a secret, state activity intended to influence political, economic, or military conditions abroad.[67]

Second, targeted assassinations on foreign territory are unequivocally an internationally wrongful act in the absence of a genuine armed conflict.[68] As lethal and territorially intrusive covert actions, peacetime targeted assassinations are in direct breach of the principles of non-intervention and territorial sovereignty.[69] They further constitute a gross violation of the victims' right to life under international human rights law (IHRL), independently of whether relevant human rights conventions apply *ratione loci*.[70] As explained by the

---

[65] John Gerring, 'Case Selection for Case-Study Analysis: Qualitative and Quantitative Techniques' in Janet M Box-Steffensmeier, Henry E Brady and David Collier (eds), *The Oxford Handbook of Political Methodology* (Oxford University Press 2008).

[66] Ran Hirschl, 'The Question of Case Selection in Comparative Constitutional Law' (2005) 53 The American Journal of Comparative Law 125, 133.

[67] See Chapter 1, section 1.2.1 for a definition of intelligence activities.

[68] Targeted assassinations are not necessarily lawful in times of armed conflict but, for the purposes of simplicity, situations of armed conflict have been excluded from this analysis.

[69] See Chapter 2, section 2.4.1.

[70] Human Rights Council, Report of the Special Rapporteur on extrajudicial, summary or arbitrary executions Agnès Callamard: targeted killings through armed

Table 7.3   *Case-study design*

State	Democracy	P5	Conducts targeted strikes	High national security threat	High-stake strike	Gain in intelligence	Pressure from electorate	Likelihood of effective accountability	Strike
France	YES	YES	YES	YES	YES	NO	YES	**HIGH**	**NO**
USA	YES	YES	YES	YES	YES	NO	YES	**LOW**	**YES**

former Special Rapporteur on extrajudicial, summary or arbitrary executions, Agnès Callamard, to be lawful, a drone strike must satisfy the legal requirements under all applicable international legal regimes, in this case *jus ad bellum* and IHRL.[71] A lawful targeted assassination on foreign territory in the absence of a genuine armed conflict is thus extremely unlikely.

For this 'most-similar cases' comparative analysis, France and the United States constitute matching cases. Both are considered democratic 'free' states according to Freedom House 2020 scores[72] (scoring respectively 90 and 86 out of 100) and are permanent members of the UN Security Council (P5). Both states are engaged in foreign military interventions abroad in the fight against terrorism; have been conducting targeted strikes in the Middle East as part of the anti-ISIS coalition; and have been facing acute national security (mostly terrorist) threats since 9/11. Looking at two high-profile strikes, each against the person considered by the relevant administration to pose the most acute threat to national security at the time, measure-dependent variables are again similar. There was no expected gain in intelligence; the electorate expected the administration to act on the threat, incurring costs if it did not and reaping domestic benefits if it did; and immediate publicity of the strike was inevitable. Both states are therefore similar in all relevant aspects but for the likelihood of effective accountability (the variable of interest). Yet, whereas the United States went ahead, France decided not to strike. These opposite outcomes constitute the dependent variable, the puzzle that the case-study seeks to explain.

---

drones and the case of Iranian General Quassem Soleimani, A/HRC/44/38, 29 June 2020, para 30.

[71] ibid.

[72] Notwithstanding the critiques of their methodology, Freedom House scores are useful to illustrate the difference between notions of domestic democracy, where France and the United States score similarly, and of respect for the international rule of law, where they score very differently. The disparity in scoring underlines the importance of taking as a main variable the potential for effective accountability rather than the state of democracy and public liberties.

Table 7.3 summarises the case-study's basic design, which will be further refined by applying the decision-making model to these two contemplated strikes.

This case-study serves a dual purpose. First, I seek to illustrate the potential of the model as a representation of executive decision-making in intelligence matters, showing how its various elements interact in reaching the state's decision to, in the present case, comply or strike. Second, I seek to show that the opposite outcomes in these two cases are due to a stark difference in the risk of being effectively held to account, represented by variable $(R + Cnc)$, other potential explanatory factors being similar for both states. In this way, I illustrate the explanatory and potential predictive power of this variable. In other words, the case-study constitutes a small-N test of the claim at the core of this chapter, namely, that the higher the result of $(R + Cnc)$, the higher the expectation of state compliance, all other factors being equal.

The two strikes under scrutiny are the following:

1. France – Non-adopted plan to strike Abdelhamid Abaaoud (Belgian-Moroccan citizen), in Raqqa, Syria, in late summer 2015 – Score $(R + Cnc)$: 14.
2. The United States of America – Assassination of Major General Qasem Soleimani (Iranian-Iraqi citizen), in Baghdad, Iraq, on 3 January 2020 – Score $(R + Cnc)$: 6.

7.4.1 France

In late summer 2015, French intelligence proposed that Abdelhamid Abaaoud, the Belgian-Moroccan Islamic State official linked to a failed attack on a French church and to the Thalys train attack in August 2015, be targeted for assassination.[73] Former French President François Hollande divulged this classified information during his mandate. Without explicitly naming Abaaoud, on 4 September 2015, Hollande told journalists Davet and Lhomme that he knew of a high-rise building in Raqqa, which housed 'a person who trains jihadists coming from abroad, either as fighters there, or to return to Europe and strike their home country. We think we know the place. And there's a Belgian-Moroccan who is running it'. Unbeknownst to the French, however, Abaaoud had already returned to Europe. In any event, '[w]e didn't strike the high-rise in Raqqa', Hollande told the journalists on 6 November 2015, 'there

---

[73] Pierre Alonso and Willy Le Devin, 'Comment la DGSE traquait Abaaoud de longue date' (*Libération*, 12 January 2017), https://www.liberation.fr/france/2017/01/12/comment-la-dgse-traquait-abaaoud-de-longue-date_1541034/ (accessed 9 February 2021).

are civilians around. We've made a rule for ourselves not to strike where there's a risk for the civilian population'.[74] Seven days later, Abaaoud led the attacks that killed 129 people in Paris and Saint-Denis. He was shot dead by French security forces on 18 November 2015.

France had been part of the US-led coalition bombarding ISIS targets in Iraq since September 2014. According to French and US figures from September 2015, France had carried out 215 of the nearly 4500 strikes there but limited its airstrikes to Iraqi territory. In the summer of 2015, therefore, France was not in an armed conflict with Syria. The strike under scrutiny would thus have constituted a violation of territorial sovereignty and an unlawful use of force. In the absence of a genuine armed conflict, the killing of civilians through an aerial strike could be qualified as a crime against humanity, and IHRL would be applicable. Besides, civilian casualties would likely have harmed France's reputation internationally and discredited the administration's counterterrorism strategy domestically. Hence, French intelligence correctly assessed that striking the building in Raqqa would be unlawful *and* that it would not be in its interest to strike. Applying the model at the estimated time of decision-making, September 2015, confirms this assessment:

> *R (positive reputation)*: France is a member of all relevant universal and regional human rights organisations but does not pride itself on a perfect compliance record, and systemic human rights issues persist in the country (human rights record and reputation: **3**). Its domestic system for the oversight of intelligence activities has historically been poorly endowed, but a law promulgated on 24 July 2015[75] gave legal status to intelligence activities and created a mixed (parliamentary and judicial) commission of oversight, the CNCTR.[76] However, the CNCTR started functioning on 3 October 2015, after the estimated date of decision-making, and gained some of its powers even later. Therefore, in September 2015, the domestic system of oversight was reliant on disparate legal provisions and a rather powerless oversight body: the CNCIS[77] (quality of domestic oversight of intelligence activities: **2**).
> *Cc (costs of compliance)*: Mid-2015, the French government was under intense political pressure to provide a strong response to the threat posed by ISIS and the high number of French 'foreign fighters' who had left to join its ranks. The acute terrorist threat and the expectation that security should be provided through all available means thus raised the costs of

---

[74] ibid, translated from French.
[75] LOI n° 2015-912 du 24 juillet 2015 relative au renseignement.
[76] Commission nationale de contrôle des techniques de renseignement.
[77] Commission nationale de contrôle des interceptions de sécurité.

compliance (domestic costs: **3**). No loss in intelligence could be expected from not going forward with the strike, as Abaaoud's assassination was not a precondition of maintaining any intelligence programme or cooperation (intelligence losses: **1**).

Cnc (costs of non-compliance): France's network of accountability mechanisms is strong owing to its acceptance of all optional mechanisms and its membership of the European Union, Council of Europe, and International Criminal Court (strength of accountability network: **4**). Were the measure adopted, several states would likely review the terms of intelligence sharing with France and attach human rights safeguards to the information they share to avoid being complicit in the (unlawful) killing of civilians. However, it is unlikely that they would stop all intelligence sharing in the counterterrorism context (intelligence and human rights reputation losses: **2**).

Bnc (benefits of non-compliance): By nature, assassination does not produce intelligence (productivity of measure: **1**). By going forward with the strike, the Hollande administration would show it is doing 'everything' to fight the terrorist threat, thus improving the security of governmental institutions. However, the killing of civilians would likely trigger an important domestic backlash, tempering these benefits (other intelligence and domestic gains: **2**).

P (expectation of publicity): Short-term publicity is inevitable (**4**).

Table 7.4 applies the model to France's contemplated strike on Abaaoud.

$$C = \frac{R + Cnc + P}{R^* + Cc + Bnc} = \frac{6+8+4}{10+3+2} = 1.2 \tag{7.2}$$

With a score of 1.2, France was expected to comply with international law, i.e., to renounce striking Abaaoud.

7.4.2 The United States of America

On 3 January 2020, a United States' drone strike near Baghdad International Airport targeted and killed Iranian major general Qasem Soleimani of the Islamic Revolutionary Guard Corps.[78] Soleimani was an Iranian-Iraqi citizen, commander of the Quds Force, and considered the second most powerful person in Iran. Nine others were killed alongside Soleimani. Among them

---

[78] For a factual summary see Jean Galbraith, 'U.S. Drone Strike in Iraq Kills Iranian Military Leader Qasem Soleimani' (2020) 114 American Journal of International Law 313.

Table 7.4   France

	Meaning	Factors	Score	Total
R	Positive Reputation	Human rights record and reputation	3	6
		×	×	
		Quality of domestic oversight of intelligence activities	2	
R*	Negative Reputation	16 – R	10	10
Cc	Costs of Compliance	Domestic costs	3	3
		×	×	
		Intelligence losses	1	
Cnc	Costs of Non-Compliance	Strength of accountability network	4	8
		×	×	
		Intelligence and human rights reputation losses	2	
Bnc	Benefits of Non-Compliance	Productivity of measure	1	2
		×	×	
		Other intelligence and domestic gains	2	
P	Expectation of publicity	Probability as assessed by decision-maker: null (1) – long-term (2) – medium-term (3) – short-term (4)	4	4

were five Iraqi nationals, including the leader and several members of Kata'ib Hezbollah, an Iraqi Shia paramilitary group supported by Iran.

The United States gave shifting and contradictory rationales for killing Soleimani. It first claimed that the strike aimed to stop an 'imminent attack',[79] but Secretary of State Mike Pompeo later corrected: 'We don't know precisely when and we don't know precisely where'.[80] Iran qualified the attack as an act of 'state terrorism' while Iraq affirmed that the attack undermined its national sovereignty, was a breach of its agreement with the United States, and constituted an act of aggression.[81] The Trump administration has not articulated any legal rationale for using force in Iraqi territory and against the five Iraqis, raising additional questions about the strike's legality under *jus*

---

[79] Statement by the Department of Defense, 2 January 2020, https:defense.gov/ Newsroom/releases/Release/Article/2049534/statement-by-the-department-of -defense/ (accessed 4 March 2021).

[80] Real Clear Politics, 'Pompeo: Attacks from Iran Were "Imminent" But "We Don't Know Precisely When"', 10 January 2020, https://www.realclearpolitics.com/ video/2020/01/10/pompeo_attacks_from_iran_were_imminent_but_we_dont_know _precisely_when.html (accessed 4 March 2021).

[81] This assessment is confirmed by Callamard (n 70), Annex, para 80. For a list of states' reactions to the strike, see 'Compilation of States' Reactions to U.S. and Iranian Uses of Force in Iraq in January 2020' (*Just Security*, 22 January 2020) https:// www.justsecurity.org/68173/compilation-of-states-reactions-to-u-s-and-iranian-uses -of-force-in-iraq-in-january-2020/ accessed 9 April 2020.

ad bellum. Further, the evolving legal rationales for targeting Soleimani raise serious questions about what role, if any, international law played in President Trump's decision.[82]

Indeed, according to the *Washington Post* of 4 January 2020, Trump approved the strike against Soleimani to avoid appearing weak amidst the ongoing Persian Gulf crisis.[83] Trump reportedly told associates after the strike that he was motivated to strike Soleimani for domestic political gain, particularly to sway Republican Senators to support him in his upcoming Senate impeachment trial.[84] *The New York Times* of 4 January 2020 thus reports that Trump had rejected the option to target Soleimani on 28 December 2019, but changed his mind after being angered by television news reports of 31 December showing the US embassy in Baghdad under attack by Iranian-backed protesters. By the evening of 2 January, Trump had finalised his decision to go for the most extreme option his advisers had provided him, which reportedly 'stunned' top Pentagon officials.[85] *The Times* also cites unnamed US officials as saying that the intelligence regarding Soleimani's alleged plot against the United States was 'thin' and that the Ayatollah had not approved any operation for Soleimani to carry out.[86]

The strike was unequivocally internationally wrongful on multiple grounds, among them the prohibition on the use of force (UN Charter, Article 2(4)), territorial sovereignty, the principle of non-intervention, and IHRL.[87] Applying the model however shows that, although the strike was not necessarily in the United States' interest, it was clearly in the interest of the Trump administration. Here, acting in his own and his administration's interest meant prioritising

---

[82] For a legal analysis of various legal arguments put forward, see Olivier Corten and others, 'L'exécution de Quassem Soleimani et Ses Suites: Aspects de Jus Contra Bellum et de Jus in Bello' (2020) 1 Revue Générale de Droit International Public 41.

[83] Missy Ryan and others, 'How Trump Decided to Kill a Top Iranian General', *Washington Post* (4 January 2020), https://www.washingtonpost.com/national-security/how-trump-decided-to-kill-a-top-iranian-general/2020/01/03/77ce3cc4-2e62-11ea-bcd4-24597950008f_story.html (accessed 4 March 2021).

[84] Michael Bender and others, 'Trump's New National Security Team Made Fast Work of Iran Strike', *Wall Street Journal* (10 January 2020), https://www.wsj.com/articles/trumps-new-national-security-team-made-fast-work-of-iran-strike-11578619195 (accessed 4 March 2021).

[85] Helene Cooper and others, 'As Tensions with Iran Escalated, Trump Opted for Most Extreme Measure', *The New York Times* (5 January 2020), https://www.nytimes.com/2020/01/04/us/politics/trump-suleimani.html (accessed 4 March 2021).

[86] ibid.

[87] Callamard (n 70) Annex.

domestic considerations to the detriment of international legality, geopolitical stability, and long-term national security.

R (positive reputation): The United States has ratified five of the 18 main universal human rights treaties and is a member of the OAS but without having ratified the Inter-American Convention on Human Rights. It considers itself bound by the IHRL corpus only to the extent that it corresponds to its constitutional rights, and only minimally engages with treaty bodies (human rights record and reputation: **2**). The existing domestic system for the oversight of intelligence activities, composed of various executive and legislative bodies, has important theoretical powers. However, it lacks formal independence, and its legitimacy is constantly being undermined by the executive branch and intelligence agencies, preventing effective oversight. The same effect is achieved in the judicial sphere by overreaching doctrines of state secrecy (quality of domestic oversight of intelligence activities: **2**).

Cc (costs of compliance): The Trump administration would likely have faced only a limited domestic backlash for not responding strongly to the Iranian-backed attacks on the US embassy in Baghdad. A less extreme measure would thus have sufficed to prevent it (domestic costs: **2**). The strike was not necessary to prevent any intelligence losses (intelligence losses: **1**).

Cnc (costs of non-compliance): The United States' accountability network is weak overall, owing to the United States' hegemonic position in the international legal order and to its lack of acceptance of any optional and individual complaint mechanism (strength of accountability network: **1**).[88] The Trump administration could reasonably expect that some states, especially in the Middle East, would review the terms of intelligence cooperation after the strike to avoid jeopardising their relations with Iran and to avoid being complicit in further unlawful actions of the type. It is also likely that some states would impose additional human rights safeguards on the intelligence they share with the United States. However, the United States' 'superpower' position in intelligence matters makes it unlikely that any state – even Iraq – would completely stop cooperating with the United States (intelligence and human rights reputation losses: **2**).

Bnc (benefits of non-compliance): By nature, targeted assassination does not produce any reliable intelligence (productivity of measure: **1**). However, the domestic benefits to be derived by the Trump administration were obvious – they constituted the very purpose of the strike – and the

---

[88] See Chapter 6, Table 6.1 for a detailed evaluation.

Table 7.5   The United States

	Meaning	Factors	Score	Total
R	Positive Reputation	Human rights record and reputation	2	4
		×	×	
		Quality of domestic oversight of intelligence activities	2	
R*	Negative Reputation	16 – R	12	12
Cc	Costs of Compliance	Domestic costs	2	2
		×	×	
		Intelligence losses	1	
Cnc	Costs of Non-Compliance	Strength of accountability network	1	2
		×	×	
		Intelligence and human rights reputation losses	2	
Bnc	Benefits of Non-Compliance	Productivity of measure	1	4
		×	×	
		Other intelligence and domestic gains	4	
P	Expectation of publicity	Probability as assessed by decision-maker: null (1) – long-term (2) – medium-term (3) – short-term (4)	4	4

strike itself was a powerful reassertion of US strength against Iran. This is despite the risks of further escalation and the danger imposed on US troops stationed in Iraq (other intelligence and domestic gains: **4**)

P (expectation of publicity): By nature, the strike was to be immediately public (expectation of publicity: **4**).

$$C = \frac{R + Cnc + P}{R^* + Cc + Bnc} = \frac{4 + 2 + 4}{12 + 2 + 4} = 0.55 \qquad (7.3)$$

With a score of 0.55, the United States was expected not to comply with international law, i.e., it was expected to strike.

7.4.3 Comparative Analysis

For a similar measure, contemplating a targeted strike against the person considered by the administration to pose the highest threat to their national security at the time, the United States obtains a score (0.55) opposite to that of France (1.2), with 1 being the threshold for expected compliance. France was expected to comply while the United States was expected to strike. The model helps explain why this is indeed what happened, and how this may have been foreseen had the model been applied pre-emptively on the dates of decision-making.

The first observation is that the strikes score similarly on all activity-specific factors. The difference in the final score (C) thus cannot be explained by the nature of the strikes considered. Further, if for simplicity purposes we code factors dichotomously as high (3 and 4) or low (1 and 2), both states get identical ratings (high or low) on all factors but four: *Human rights record and reputation (R)*; *Domestic costs (Cc)*; *Strength of accountability network (Cnc)*; and *Other intelligence and domestic gains (Bnc)*. These factors, pertaining to international costs and domestic costs and benefits, should therefore be considered relevant to explain the difference of outcome.

This finding highlights the complex interplay of international and domestic considerations. This is especially striking for the United States, which had, in absolute terms, equal losses and gains to make with the strike. However, the gains and losses were situated on different scales: international losses against domestic gains. Hence, prioritising domestic considerations led to the decision to strike. In contrast, France had a lot to lose internationally, and relatively less to gain domestically. The high risk of accountability thus acted as a pull towards compliance despite the high domestic costs associated with inaction.

The low score obtained by the United States on variable $(R + Cnc)$ is responsible for the Trump administration's (correct) determination that they had more to gain than lose in moving forward with the strike, i.e., the strike was in their interest. Intelligence officers' framing of options was designed to nudge President Trump towards their preferred, reasonable, course of action.[89] Yet, Trump's own interests and biases led him to pick the most extreme option (hence 'stunning' Pentagon officials). His perception of the strike's costs and benefits was altered by salient media reports, his fear to appear weak, and his upcoming impeachment trial. Trump's change of perception can be explained by representativeness heuristics and prospect theory (loss aversion). It also explains why the United States struck Soleimani on precisely 3 January 2020, when it could likely have done so on any other day. Behavioural insights thus prove extremely valuable to explain the strike and are duly accounted for in the model.

Domestic considerations – short-term benefits, especially in an election year – overshadowed other short- and long-term costs internationally. The United States' position in the Middle East had been irremediably altered, and it was impossible to reliably predict the importance of the risk of further escalation. Yet, it appears that the extremely low risk of effective accountability, coupled with the fact that the bulk of the costs would not be borne by the

---

[89] As explained by *The New York Times*, 'In the wars waged since the Sept. 11, 2001, attacks, Pentagon officials have often offered improbable options to presidents to make other possibilities appear more palatable.' Cooper and others (n 85).

Trump administration itself, but rather by foreign states in the short term (Iran and Iraq first) and the United States in the longer term, played in favour of prioritising shorter-term domestic considerations. The Trump administration thus correctly assessed that any harm to the United States' low human rights reputation would be dwarfed by the domestic and geopolitical gains made by the administration. This is where the main difference with the French case lies: the United States had very little to lose in terms of human rights reputation and international legal accountability to start with. This, in turn, multiplied the weight of domestic considerations in the decision-making process, as illustrated by $(R^* + Bnc)$ in the denominator line of the equation.

In contrast, despite the peculiar terrorist threat of 2015 and the resulting domestic pressure on the government, the one thing that prevented France from engaging in a similar (albeit imprecise) strike was the likelihood of effective accountability from supra-national mechanisms and intelligence partners: it could not risk killing civilians. France's respect for civilians' lives, as professed by President Hollande, represents the state's values (whether genuine or utilitarian) and its perception of its identity. The model accounts for these values and self-perceptions through the four factors constituting the likelihood of effective accountability $(R + Cnc)$. This variable further constitutes a protective feature for these values, ensuring that the factors' influence on decision-making will incentivise the state to abide by its values and help sustain its perceived self-identity.

Even though the target of the proposed strike, Abaaoud, turned out to be the mastermind of the attacks of 13 November 2015, abstaining from the strike still avoided serious harm to France's intelligence and human rights reputation. Mid-2015, French intelligence thus assessed that, despite important domestic and short-term costs, there was a long-term protective effect for France's national security in not engaging in gross violations of international law. The high likelihood of effective accountability acted as a pull towards compliance by altering what the state perceived to be in its interest. It bears mentioning that, had France moved forward with the strike, it would have been entirely unproductive since Abaaoud had already left Raqqa for Europe at that time. The strike would therefore have further harmed France's intelligence reputation. Remarkably, this was only avoided due to the high likelihood of effective accountability. One may nevertheless note that the French administration gave way to political pressure on 27 September 2015 with a first airstrike on Syrian territory, illustrating the difficulty of conciliating domestic and international considerations. Yet, this airstrike targeted an ISIS training camp and did not cause civilian victims, thereby striking a balance between France's counter-terrorism and reputational interests, and between international obligations, values, and domestic considerations.

This 'most-similar cases' comparative case-study first demonstrated the model's utility as a representation of executive decision-making in intelligence matters by accounting for relevant legal and extra-legal factors, including decision-makers' biases and heuristics. It further illustrated the explanatory function of the likelihood of effective accountability, represented by $(R + Cnc)$, regarding state compliance in intelligence matters. Indeed, the case-study confirmed that the opposite outcomes in the French and American cases were due to a difference in the likelihood of effective accountability. Provided the direct relationship between a state's score on $(R + Cnc)$ and compliance is confirmed in larger-N samples, this variable could also be used as a predictive tool for state compliance.

Finally, although their validity for other cases also needs to be empirically confirmed, the case-study raises additional observations regarding the interplay of international and domestic considerations. First, the higher the score on variable $(R + Cnc)$, the less weight is given to domestic considerations in decision-making. Conversely, a low score on variable $(R + Cnc)$ indicates that domestic considerations will likely be at the top of decision-makers' concerns, to the detriment of international law.[90] What constitutes rational behaviour for executive decision-makers in intelligence matters thus depends upon the potential for effective accountability $(R + Cnc)$ of each state, all other factors being equal.

7.5 CONCLUSIONS: ACHIEVING COMPLIANCE

Accurately understanding executive decision-making in intelligence matters is a crucial first step to regulate such activities effectively at the international level. The behavioural analysis and modelling efforts pursued in this chapter evidence the crucial role played by the international legal order in incentivising compliance, to the effect that the likelihood of effective accountability now constitutes the determining factor for states considering whether to comply with international law in their intelligence activities. This finding allows me to explain state behaviour (compliance and non-compliance) in intelligence matters.

This chapter's findings also hold significant strategic implications, allowing me to identify compliance-enhancing paths. Indeed, the decision-making model shows that increasing the likelihood of effective accountability increases

---

[90] Looking at the United States, this seems to be the case regardless of the absolute score attributed to domestic gains, and regardless of the relative score of domestic gains compared to international losses, but further empirical research is needed to confirm this assessment.

the probability of compliance and decreases the weight given to extra-legal and domestic considerations in decision-making, regardless of the intelligence activity and state considered. In addition, human rights courts and bodies have the capacity to increase the costs of non-compliance for states through the publicity of their decisions, the quality of their argumentation, and the internalisation and diffusion of their norms and standards. Hence, rather than focusing on the regulatory framework itself (international law), regulatory approaches aiming to enhance compliance should focus on improving accountability, targeting both the available supporting, rewarding, and sanctioning tools and the decision-making factors influenced by these tools. Regulatory interventions should thus focus on enhancing the powers of international accountability mechanisms and the quality of the domestic oversight of intelligence activities, and on strategic litigation before competent accountability mechanisms.

Since increased compliance is dependent upon a more systematic enforcement of state responsibility, the existence and use of varied forms of international legal accountability should constitute the focal point of regulatory approaches. As shown in section 7.2.2, the implementation of this strategy has partially begun: the increasingly active stance adopted by supra-national mechanisms of accountability, coupled with the increased publicity of intelligence activities, has led to several states being held accountable for their intelligence activities, and to several more changing their policies and practices in response.

This observation prompts two additional remarks regarding the achievement of compliance through effective accountability. First, although the theoretical strength of a state's network of accountability mechanisms represents the upper limit of what can be achieved in terms of actual and effective accountability,[91] this ceiling is an evolving one. This is because the expectations of other states evolve and what they consider appropriate or acceptable may change due to their own network of accountability mechanisms and the factors influencing their beliefs, preferences, and motives. Second, what the ceiling represents in terms of the risk of actual accountability is also changing because even seemingly innocuous or inconsequential mechanisms can become more active in holding states to account. Procedures that are similarly overlooked can also have unforeseen systemic effects on states' beliefs and preferences, and thus on their behaviour. This last observation joins with recent empirical research showing that engagement with the reporting procedures of treaty-monitoring bodies leads to improved human rights compliance through the pervasive

---

[91] See Chapter 6, section 6.7.

systemic learning and adaptation induced by the process.[92] The boundedness of states' rationality can therefore also be used to improve compliance and respect for the international rule of law.

These findings further underscore the importance of looking at the international legal order as a networked, nodal regulator, in which even self-reporting procedures and minimal engagement by states can activate stronger nodes, affect states' beliefs, increase the pressure applied by the network, and signal other states. Hence, action by the weaker nodes can have consequences for future compliance, especially in such an interdependent field as intelligence. The shift from realism to formalism observed since the end of the Cold War is now increasingly supported by actual enforcement of the formalist view, so that theory and practice are slowly becoming aligned.

Finally, to improve compliance despite the limits of accountability networks, one also needs to identify the social, contextual, and personal factors affecting not only accountability, but also compliance itself. In fact, if states comply there is no need for subsequent (coercive) enforcement at international level. Despite the crucial role of effective accountability in determining compliance, I have therefore also endeavoured to identify other relevant factors affecting compliance in this chapter. These factors encompass the first two layers of regulation under the heading of the likelihood of effective accountability, in addition to other empirically identified domestic, international, legal and extra-legal factors influencing state behaviour in intelligence matters. The following, concluding, chapter deals with the consequence of compliance, namely the effective protection of states' security. Such is, after all, the rationale for intelligence.

---

[92] Cosette D Creamer and Beth A Simmons, 'The Proof Is in the Process: Self-Reporting Under International Human Rights Treaties' (2020) 114 American Journal of International Law 1.

APPENDIX 7.1　　SCORING TABLE

In the decision-making model, all factors are attributed a score on a qualitative scale ranging from one to four. The choice of a unique scale from one to four allows the scorer to qualitatively score factors with sufficient precision while still obtaining comparable scores for all factors. To the extent possible, the formulation of the scale allows the external observer to put themselves in the shoes of the decision-maker state at the time of decision-making, whether this time is in the past, the present, or the future. Some of the criteria assessed are objective in that they rely on a factual assessment of openly available data, but others rely on the knowledge of the state and its expectations, and integrate the state's beliefs, preferences, and motives. However, a perfectly 'subjective external' assessment remains impossible, and this limitation, inherent to the model, is acknowledged.

Apart from the expectation of publicity, which acts as an activity-specific multiplier with regard to the likelihood of effective accountability, the initial score of each factor is then multiplied by the initial score of the other factor forming part of the element of the equation. This leads to each element (but for P; and R*, which is scored by comparison with R) having a numerical value between one and sixteen: 1 – 2 – 3 – 4 – 6 – 8 – 9 – 12 – 16. Factors and their scale are defined in the following table.

Table 7A.1 Scoring table

Factor	What is assessed	Scale
Human Rights Record and Reputation	The state's membership of human rights organisations; ratification of human rights treaties; outward appearance of respect for its human rights obligations and willingness to improve (e.g., implementation of judgments, engagement with treaty bodies' procedures, etc.).	1: null or clearly insufficient. 2: member of some human rights bodies and ratification of some of the main treaties but human rights are not at the forefront of government policies and many important systemic human rights issues remain in the country. 3: member of relevant human rights bodies and ratification of the main treaties; the state prides itself in participating in human rights improvement but a few significant human rights issues persist in the country. 4: member of all relevant human rights bodies; ratification of the main treaties; acceptance of individual complaint procedures; and the state prides itself in having a near-exemplary human rights record.
Quality of Domestic Oversight of Intelligence Activities	The state's existing domestic structures for oversight of its intelligence activities, the presence of a sufficiently independent democratic oversight body, and their actual powers, including *ex ante* authorisation of intrusive powers; complaints handling; access to information related to foreign intelligence cooperation; and sufficient resources.	1: null or clearly insufficient. 2: existing system of oversight but lacking most of the powers necessary for effective oversight (e.g., no access to classified documents). 3: existing system of oversight with some actual power but lacking several of the necessary qualities or competences. 4: existing and effective system of oversight that complies with most of the recognised standards and good practices.
Domestic Costs	The backlash likely to be faced by the current administration if they maintain the status quo and do not adopt the internationally wrongful measure under consideration.	1: the current administration will not face any domestic backlash if they do not adopt the measure. 2: the current administration will face some limited domestic backlash if they do not adopt the measure. 3: the current administration will face important domestic backlash if they do not adopt the measure. 4: the current administration will most likely be overthrown if they do not adopt the measure.

Factor	What is assessed	Scale
Intelligence Losses	The losses in intelligence if the state does not adopt the measure, either because cooperation with foreign partners will be hindered or because a domestic programme will be disrupted or interrupted, or both. The factor only covers losses in the sense that maintaining the status quo will lead to intelligence losses. The definition thus excludes from consideration the gains to be made by adopting the measure under scrutiny.	**1**: no losses in intelligence obtained domestically or through cooperation if the measure is not adopted. **2**: some limited intelligence losses (e.g., disruption of a small programme or diminution of the flow of intelligence sharing with another state) if the measure is not adopted. **3**: significant intelligence losses (e.g., interruption of a small programme or disruption of an important programme or of the flow of intelligence sharing) if the measure is not adopted. **4**: vital intelligence losses (e.g., interruption of intelligence cooperation or of a successful programme) if the measure is not adopted.

Factor	What is assessed	Scale
Strength of Accountability Network	The following factors (see Table 5.1) are assessed as weak, medium, or strong, leading to an overall evaluation of the strength of the network of accountability mechanisms comprised of all other states and competent supra-national courts and bodies: *Capacity to constrain and escalate:* Jurisdiction *ratione materiae*; Jurisdiction *ratione personae*; Investigatory powers; Powers to sanction non-cooperation; Capacity to order remedies; Capacity to sanction; Reputation of account-holder state (Standing in the international legal order; Relative power; Human rights record); Capacity of account-holder state to constrain compliance in practice (Interdependencies; Leverage tools). *Legitimacy:* Overall reputation; Participation of the state under scrutiny; Capacity to reward compliance or de-escalate; Independence (Budget and resources; Formal independence; Judicial independence; Relative power). *Accessibility and publicity:* Representation of public interest; Publicity of proceedings; Publicity of outcomes; Accessibility to non-state accountability holders (Information; Financial and geographical accessibility; Procedural accessibility).	**1**: the network of accountability mechanisms is weak all around. **2**: the network of accountability mechanisms is generally weak but possesses some stronger aspects. **3**: the network of accountability mechanisms is generally strong, with some weaker aspects. **4**: the network of accountability mechanisms is strong all around.

Factor	What is assessed	Scale
Intelligence Reputation and Human Rights Reputation Losses	The reputation of the state as an intelligence partner and domestically. Intelligence reputation losses are most likely to occur when other states or citizens deem it unwise to cooperate with the state because of human rights concerns and/or because the intelligence produced is deemed unreliable or unusable. A loss in intelligence reputation is therefore correlated with the state's human rights reputation, and is only compensated by access to new and otherwise inaccessible intelligence if this intelligence is considered reliable as well as usable, i.e., not tainted by human rights violations.	**1**: if the measure is adopted, this will have no effect on the state's reputation, whether for human rights or for intelligence: other states and citizens will maintain identical intelligence cooperation. **2**: if the measure is adopted, some states will likely review the terms of cooperation or impose additional human rights safeguards, and citizens' trust in the state will be harmed. **3**: if the measure is adopted, many states will likely review the terms of cooperation or impose additional human rights safeguards, and some states and most citizens will likely stop all intelligence cooperation. **4**: if the measure is adopted, the state will become an outcast in the international intelligence cooperation arena and citizens' trust will be entirely lost.
Productivity of the Measure	The costs-benefits analysis of the measure. This includes financial and human (intelligence personnel) costs for the state but excludes all other costs as they are part of the wider analysis, and some (like human rights) are not to be balanced against other considerations.	**1**: the measure will not produce reliable intelligence. **2**: the measure will produce some reliable intelligence but not enough to justify its human and financial costs. **3**: the measure will produce reliable intelligence, meeting the costs. **4**: the measure will produce reliable intelligence, with benefits surpassing the costs.

Factor	What is assessed	Scale
Other Intelligence and Domestic Gains	The international and domestic intelligence reputation gains that adopting the measure will ensure (e.g., access to a new source of intelligence will drive international cooperation); and other domestic benefits that the administration will derive from such adoption. These include an appearance of toughness; a decrease in domestic opposition; increased favourable opinion ratings; and increased executive powers and missions. These domestic benefits usually take the form of increased national security in the narrow sense of the term, meaning the security of governmental institutions, and are not correlated with a decrease in actual security threats against the state and its population.	**1**: the measure will not increase intelligence reputation or national security. **2**: the measure will limitedly increase intelligence reputation or national security. **3**: the measure will significantly increase intelligence reputation or national security. **4**: the measure will strongly increase the intelligence reputation of the state *and* its national security.
Expectation of Publicity	The probability, as assessed by the decision-maker, that the measure will become public, either due to its nature (e.g., legislation, measures involving individuals, or able to be witnessed) or through leaks; and the timeframe of such publicity.	**1**: null or quasi-null. **2**: long-term risk. **3**: medium-term risk. **4**: short-term risk.

8. Epilogue: comprehensive regulation in the twenty-first-century security landscape

8.1 INTRODUCTION

I opened this book with my personal experience growing up in the post-9/11 world. This is a world whereby the exceptional measures enacted in the heightened climate of fear of 9/11 became permanent: the 'new normal'. Far from being specific to a French child born in the mid-1990s, the new normal is universal. Indeed, the US-led war on terror quickly took a global turn; and a series of Chapter VII UN Security Council resolutions ensured the universal spread of counterterrorism measures and philosophy. As I explained in Chapter 1, the new normal is characterised by the liberty–security conundrum: the twenty-first-century security landscape is made up of fallacious compromises, balancing exercises, and trade-offs between purported security and individuals' fundamental rights and liberties. Yet, are we safer today than on 10 September 2001?

The first seven chapters of this book were dedicated to theorising the model of regulation of intelligence activities that emerged, mostly as a result of non-compliance with international law, in the post-9/11 security paradigm. In this final chapter, it is now time to address the normative claim I introduced at the outset of the book: compliance with international law in their intelligence activities serves states' national security. To do so, I first summarise the main findings and contributions of the book (section 8.2). Then, integrating my model of regulation within the twenty-first-century security landscape, I draw the lessons from the past twenty years of counterterrorism and security practices and assess the normative consequences for the effective protection of national security (section 8.3).

8.2 A COMPREHENSIVE MODEL OF REGULATION

Despite the immense practical implications of intelligence activities for individuals and states around the world, the regulation of intelligence activities under international law remains a greatly under-theorised topic. Most of the (limited) conversation on intelligence and international law indeed revolves around the question of international law's applicability to intelligence activities, ignoring further regulatory issues. In consequence, this book's most significant contribution is that it moves the conversation on intelligence along by focusing much of its analysis on questions of accountability and effectiveness. More specifically, this monograph is the first of its kind to offer a comprehensive framework of regulation, moving from legality to accountability and compliance. The interdisciplinary methodological approach I adopted provides a holistic picture of the regulation of intelligence activities in the international legal order by integrating the social science context with the legal analysis. This novel approach allows me to empirically diagnose where and how regulation is still lacking in effectiveness and to identify practical compliance-enhancing paths.[1] It further allows me to conclude that effective regulation serves states' national security, as I will explain in the next section.

In this book, I considered all intelligence activities and forms of cooperation, and illustrated my argument with an in-depth case-study of responsibility and accountability in the CIA-led global war on terror. The international legal framework governing intelligence activities, drafted in Chapter 2, bridges and furthers the existing scholarship on intelligence activities. However, whereas existing legal scholarship on intelligence stops at this point, the contributions of this book extend far beyond the doctrinal legal analysis. The integrated model of regulation I theorised thus allows us to understand how intelligence activities are currently regulated under international law. To summarise my argument, I return to the research questions I raised in Chapter 1.

The question addressed in Part I (Legality) was the following: *How does international law govern intelligence activities?* I demonstrated that international law comprehensively addresses intelligence activities, albeit indirectly. In Chapter 2, I identified the legal framework through which we can apprehend intelligence activities, according to their objectives, means, and methods. I distinguished three types of activities: first, intelligence activities inherently prohibited by international law due to their objectives, in direct contradiction with core principles of international law; second, intelligence activities explicitly allowed by international law, within strict parameters; third, intelligence activities regulated according to their means and methods only, i.e., their underlying conduct. My analysis further disproved claims as to the lack of interaction between international law and intelligence activities. In addition, I explained that this first layer of regulation (legality) also includes the automatic engagement of state responsibility for intelligence activities constituting

---

[1] See Chapter 7, section 7.5.

internationally wrongful acts. As the case-study in Chapter 3 showed, international law indeed applies to all sorts of intelligence activities and complicity therein. In intelligence matters, one can thus systematically apply the primary and secondary rules of international law to determine whether state responsibility for an internationally wrongful act is engaged.

In Part II (Accountability), I turned to the following question: *Under which conditions does international legal accountability become an effective tool to regulate intelligence activities?* To answer this question, I first provided a novel conceptualisation of state accountability, namely international legal accountability, in Chapter 4. I distinguished it from state responsibility and I integrated forms of accountability beyond the interstate forms provided in the ILC Articles on State Responsibility[2] (ASR) to account for the role played by non-state actors in holding states to account. The taxonomy of forms of accountability I offered is of general applicability and constitutes an original contribution to the law of state responsibility, which I characterised as the missing part of the ASR. Through the conceptualisation of international legal accountability, it became possible to conceive of the enforcement of state responsibility as a second layer of regulation of intelligence activities. If state responsibility does not exist only at the theoretical level but can also be made concrete through processes of accountability, then the international legal order has the potential to constrain states' intelligence activities meaningfully.

To understand how the international legal order might be an effective regulator, I theorised effective accountability in Chapter 5. To this end, I first proposed that the international legal order be conceived of as the regulator of states' actions. Conceptualised as a network of accountability mechanisms unique to each state, the international legal order obeys a networked, nodal mode of governance. I thus analysed international legal accountability as a form of responsive regulation. In other words, the international legal order regulates states' behaviour through supporting activities, rewards, and escalating sanctions. Then, combining behavioural insights and regulatory theory, I put forward a theory of effective accountability. Accountability is effective when it embeds the principles of networked, nodal responsive regulation and leads to state compliance with international law.

Indeed, as demonstrated through the case-study in Chapter 6, the mere possibility of accountability is often insufficient to achieve accountability in practice (also called actual accountability), and there is no guarantee that such accountability will be effective in inducing compliance. Still, for accountability to be effective, it first needs to happen in practice. Without the possibility

---

[2] International Law Commission, Draft Articles on Responsibility of States for Internationally Wrongful Acts 2001 (Supplement No 10 (A/56/10), chpIVE1) 76.

of actual accountability, neither accountability nor regulation will be effective. Evaluating the theoretical potential of networks of accountability mechanisms according to the framework I developed in Chapter 5 thus provides us with an outline of what might be achieved in practice. This also means that the theoretical potential of a network of accountability mechanisms represents the upper ceiling of what regulation can achieve. In consequence, regulation suffers from the limitations inherent to each state's accountability network. The road to actual (but not necessarily effective) accountability thus rests, first, on the evaluation of the potential of networks of accountability mechanisms (i.e., the international legal order as a regulator). It then rests on the assessment of accountability gaps through a comparison between the theoretical strength of the network and actual accountability; and on the identification of the factors behind any discrepancy. Knowing what can be done for actual accountability to match the potential of the accountability network brings us a step closer to a more systematic enforcement of international law and responsibility. However, achieving not only actual but also effective accountability necessitates taking into account extra-legal factors and integrating them into a third layer of regulation: compliance.

In Part III (Compliance), therefore, I addressed the last sub-question: *How does international law influence state behaviour in intelligence matters?* To apprehend international law as a means to regulate states' activities effectively (i.e., induce compliance) in the international legal order, I endeavoured to provide an empirically accurate description of state behaviour in intelligence matters and of the factors influencing it. Indeed, understanding a state's reasons for acting is key to regulating the state's behaviour effectively. In Chapter 7, I set out to identify the link between compliance and the likelihood of effective accountability, understood as the extent to which a state's behaviour is affected by the likelihood that it will be held legally accountable. In this sense, the likelihood of effective accountability embodies the potential of international law to influence state behaviour. I thus modelled state decision-making in intelligence matters, identifying the role and weight of various factors in decision-making. On the basis of this evidence-based description of the reasons underlying states' choices in intelligence matters, I was able to affirm that the likelihood of effective accountability, a legal factor, is what determines whether a state will comply. Taking compliance as the standard for assessing the effectiveness of regulation, the likelihood of effective accountability thus determines whether regulation is effective.

In addition, the decision-making model furthers our understanding of state behaviour and highlights available paths to enhance compliance with international law in intelligence matters. Rather than focusing on legality, regulatory approaches should target accountability and aim to improve the tools at the disposal of the international legal order so that each network of accountability mechanisms can match its theoretical potential. Increasing the likelihood of effective accountability is the most reliable way to influence state decision-making to, in turn, enhance compliance and ensure that regulation will be effective.

With these answers in mind, I now turn to answering the overarching question addressed by this book: *How are intelligence activities regulated under international law?* The regulation of intelligence activities in the international legal order functions through a clear legal framework governing intelligence activities (legality); the existence and theoretical strength of a network of mechanisms to enforce state responsibility (accountability); and the integration of these two layers into responsive regulation, taking into account extra-legal factors influencing states' decision-making in intelligence matters (compliance). Effective regulation through the three layers leads to effective accountability, which itself leads to state compliance.

In the final pages of this book, I address the normative claim I presented at the outset of the book, namely that state compliance with international law in their intelligence activities serves states' national security. Relying on the model of regulation and drawing the lessons from the past two decades of counterterrorism intelligence, I thus make explicit the link between compliance and national security.

8.3 PROTECTING NATIONAL SECURITY IN THE TWENTY-FIRST-CENTURY SECURITY LANDSCAPE

The maintenance of international peace and security constitutes the *raison d'être* of the modern international legal system, as Article 1(1) of the United Nations Charter exemplifies. Since the coming into force of the Charter in 1945, however, international security has been most often equated with national security. The end of the Cold War and the attacks of 9/11 triggered a shift in what states considered to be the main threat to their security. As terrorism overpowered other threats in national and international security forums, counterterrorism became the focus of international peace and security. Yet, if the enemy changed on 9/11, the narrow, state-centric approach to security was not discarded. Rather, following a brief liberal interlude in the 1990s, it was revived and reinforced. After 9/11, territorial integrity and the security of the homeland population thus resumed, trumping all other considerations. However, this narrow conception of international peace and security, based on realist assumptions about security as a zero-sum game, has so far not produced the (national nor international) security that states crave.

Today's security challenges are global ones – if not in nature, at least in their effects. The past decades of terrorism, wars, climate change, pandemics, migration, and other global challenges have taught us that quick fixes and simple solutions to complex security problems do not work. In addition, global challenges require responses that no state's national security apparatus can provide on its own. The world is so highly connected and interdependent that confining security to arbitrarily defined national borders is impossible: a state's security depends upon the effective tackling of conditions conducive to heightened security risks everywhere. International cooperation is thus required to address the main security challenges faced by states.

Yet, whereas international (intelligence) cooperation was reinforced in the fight against terrorism, responses to the terrorist threat were characterised by short-term aggressive national security moves against non-state actors or states suspected of sponsoring terrorist groups, and by derogations from human rights and rule of law principles. Instead of annihilating their common enemy, this approach led states to aggravate the conditions conducive to national security threats.[3] In other words, the terrorist threat was *reinforced* by counterterrorism measures.

In the current international order, states remain the main purveyors of security despite their preponderant role in fostering global insecurity. On the one hand, states constitute the main threat to human dignity and security. They thus lie at the root of threats to human, national, and international security. On the other hand, international law still endows states with the responsibility to provide security at all levels. States are responsible for securing the rights of individuals in their jurisdiction;[4] they may not endanger the security of other states and must endeavour to settle their disputes peacefully so as not to jeopardise international security;[5] and they are charged with maintaining international peace and security through international organisations and collective security mechanisms.[6] Hence, for states to provide security adequately, they need to believe that it is in their interest: there needs to be a national security case for respecting human rights and international law. Lessons from the past twenty years of counterterrorism provide exactly that.

---

[3] The UN Global Counter-Terrorism Strategy identifies the following conditions as conducive to the spread of terrorism: 'prolonged unresolved conflicts, dehumanization of victims of terrorism in all its forms and manifestations, lack of the rule of law and violations of human rights, ethnic, national and religious discrimination, political exclusion, socio-economic marginalization and lack of good governance'. Similar conditions can be considered conducive to national security threats more generally. UN General Assembly, Resolution A/RES/60/288 (2006) 'UN Global Counter-Terrorism Strategy and Plan of Action' 4.

[4] ICCPR, Article 2(1); ICESCR, Article 2; ECHR, Article 1; ACHR, Article 1(1).
[5] UN Charter, Article 2(3) and (4).
[6] ibid, Article 2(5) and (6).

Empirical research has repeatedly shown that human-rights- and rule-of-law-compliant behaviour in the face of security challenges yields the most effective results.[7] Conversely, drastic and authoritarian measures, especially if discriminatory or perceived as such, tend to reinforce the conditions conducive to national security threats[8] and alienate the moderate parts of the population.[9] In addition, there is a strong lock-in effect, with originally exceptional and emergency measures becoming permanent, if not codified into ordinary law.[10] Hindsight from the past two decades thus teaches us that Washington's use of torture and other extra-legal methods in its 'war on terror' greatly damaged its national security.[11] It incited extremism in the Middle East,[12] hindered cooperation with its allies,[13] exposed US officials to

---

[7] Seung-Whan Choi, 'Fighting Terrorism through the Rule of Law?' (2010) 54 Journal of Conflict Resolution 940; Laura Dugan and Erica Chenoweth, 'Moving Beyond Deterrence: The Effectiveness of Raising the Expected Utility of Abstaining from Terrorism in Israel' (2012) 77 American Sociological Review 597; Christian Bjørnskov and Stefan Voigt, 'When Does Terror Induce a State of Emergency? And What Are the Effects?' (2020) 64 Journal of Conflict Resolution 579; Tom Parker, *Avoiding the Terrorist Trap: Why Respect for Human Rights Is the Key to Defeating Terrorism* (WORLD SCIENTIFIC (EUROPE) 2019).

[8] See above footnote 3.

[9] Recent examples of counter-productive repressive national security strategies include: Nigeria's 2009 crackdown against Boko Haram, leading to its metamorphosis from a largely nonviolent dissident sect with some criminal characteristics into a violent and virulently anti-state movement, now the leading terrorist group in Africa; and Kenya's reaction to al-Shabaab, alienating the Somali and Muslim communities and now considered to constitute the main driver for recruitment.

[10] The lock-in effect can be due to a number of reasons, ranging from increased powers of the executive and intelligence agencies to the dynamics of competitive domestic politics. In France, for instance, this took the form of a codification into ordinary law of part of the powers normally exclusive to a declared 'state of emergency' under law No 55-385 of 3 April 1955 (LOI No 2017-1510 du 30 octobre 2017 renforçant la sécurité intérieure et la lutte contre le terrorisme).

[11] United States Senate Select Committee on Intelligence, *Torture Report: Committee Study of Central Intelligence Agency's Detention and Interrogation Program: Executive Summary* (2014); Douglas A Johnson, Alberto Mora and Averell Schmidt, 'The Strategic Costs of Torture' (2016) Foreign Affairs, https://www.foreignaffairs.com/articles/united-states/strategic-costs-torture (accessed 1 August 2020).

[12] Thérèse Postel, 'How Guantanamo Bay's Existence Helps Al-Qaeda Recruit More Terrorists' [2013] The Atlantic, https://www.theatlantic.com/international/archive/2013/04/how-guantanamo-bays-existence-helps-al-qaeda-recruit-more-terrorists/274956/ (accessed 9 December 2021).

[13] Anna-Katherine Staser McGill and David H Gray, 'Challenges to International Counterterrorism Intelligence Sharing' (2012) 3 Global Security Studies 76. See also Great Britain Intelligence and Security Committee, *Rendition* (2007) 47, https://irp.fas.org/world/uk/rendition.pdf

legal repercussions,[14] undermined its diplomacy,[15] and offered an opportune justification for other governments to commit human rights abuses.[16] The Taliban's return to power in Afghanistan in August 2021 constituted the final symbol of the war on terror's complete failure. States that cooperated with the US in its war on terror, received or relied on information collected or provided by the US, or partners using similar interrogation methods, were seen as condoning these methods and were thus tainted by association. As such, they were exposed to the same consequences, and their national security was damaged by their association with the taint of torture, foreign interventions, and gross human rights violations.[17] The strategic price paid by the US and its allies for what was an entirely unproductive policy is therefore completely disproportionate to the non-existent intelligence and security gains.[18]

Decades earlier, a similar point could have been made about France's use of torture in Algeria, which had the effect of turning the entire Algerian population into sworn enemies of France virtually overnight.[19] Contrary to the oft-advanced argument that torture led to French victory in the Battle of Algiers, informants succeeded far more than torturers did in gaining critical information.[20] Further, the point made by French torturers and apologists that

---

[14] See the in absentia conviction of 23 US agents in an Italian court for the role they played in the extraordinary rendition of Hassan Mustafa Osama Nasr from Milan to Cairo in 2003. Tribunale Ordinario di Milano, Sentenza No. 12428/09, 4 November 2009.

[15] Larry Butler, 'The Global War on Terror and Diplomatic Practice' [2021] The Foreign Service Journal 26.

[16] E.g., Fionnuala Ní Aoláin, 'Abusive "Counterterrorism" Crackdowns Choke Independent Civil Society in the Middle East', *Just Security* (25 August 2022), https://www.justsecurity.org/82813/abusive-counterterrorism-crackdowns-choke-independent-civil-society-in-the-middle-east/ (accessed 31 August 2022); Phelim Kine, 'How China Hijacked the War on Terror', *POLITICO* (9 September 2021), https://www.politico.com/news/2021/09/09/china-hijacked-war-on-terror-511032 (accessed 8 August 2022).

[17] This is recognised by the 2010 UK 'Consolidated Guidance to Intelligence Officers and Service Personnel on the Detention and Interviewing of Detainees Overseas, and on the Passing and Receipt of Intelligence Relating to Detainees', para 8. See Chapter 3 for an extensive analysis of the issues of state responsibility raised by such cooperation.

[18] It is striking (even slightly shocking to a European eye) that the first finding of the SSCI Study relates to the lack of effectiveness of the CIA-led rendition, detention, and interrogation programme. Yet, even more striking is the fact that throughout the 524-page executive summary, one cannot find a single example of actual intelligence gained through the programme.

[19] Tzvetan Todorov and Arthur Denner, 'Torture in the Algerian War' (2007) 24 South Central Review 18.

[20] Darius M Rejali, *Torture and Democracy* (Princeton University Press 2009) 522.

torture was the *only way* to win the war is obviously mistaken since France lost the war despite systematic torture and abuses. The logical conclusion should be that torture was not the way to win this war (or any other). The use of torture in the Battle of Algiers forced a politics of extremes, alienating those who may have cooperated with the French, and ultimately led to French defeat.[21] It also precipitated the end of the Fourth Republic and led to a profound democratic and political crisis. Yet, the lesson does not seem to have been learnt by its allies. Quite the opposite, French torturers were then invited to give training on their 'anti-subversive war' model to, inter alia, the CIA and Pinochet's secret police.[22]

Torture is one of many examples in support of taking into account the medium- and long-term consequences of intelligence activities when assessing their effectiveness – and thus when deciding on the conduct (i.e., internationally lawful or not) to adopt to protect national security. More than twenty years after 9/11 and the beginning of the 'global war on terror', there is now overwhelming evidence about the inverse relationship between respect for the rule of law and terrorist risk.[23] As a result, a future backlash against states' national security should normally constitute a strong incentive to comply with human rights law at home and abroad.[24] In addition, neuroscience teaches us that, if the lowest threshold of survival is hard to attain, human beings are genetically wired to do anything to survive, including using pre-emptive violence and committing seemingly immoral acts.[25] In contrast, models of sustainable

---

[21] Marnia Lazreg, *Torture and the Twilight of Empire: From Algiers to Baghdad* (Princeton University Press 2008).

[22] This has been particularly well documented by Marie-Monique Robin in her book *Escadrons de la mort, l'école française* (Editions La Découverte 2003) and in her eponymous documentary. The clear legacy of France's 'anti-subversive war' in Algeria with respect to the infamous Operation Condor is explicit, and French cooperation with the responsible Latin American dictatorships continued through the 1970s. Its influence on other counterterrorist operations, including the CIA-led programme, has also been evidenced by Robin in her book

[23] UN Global Counter-Terrorism Strategy (n 3), Pillar IV; Manfred Nowak and Anne Charbord (eds), *Using Human Rights to Counter Terrorism* (Edward Elgar Publishing 2018); Parker (n 7).

[24] For further exploration of this argument, see Sophie Duroy, 'The Regulation of Intelligence Cooperation under International Law: A Compliance-Based Theorization' in Arianna Vedaschi and Kim Lane Scheppele (eds), *9/11 and the Rise of Global Anti-Terrorism Law: How the UN Security Council Rules the World* (Cambridge University Press 2021).

[25] Nayef Al-Rodhan and Ioana-Maria Puscas, 'Global Security and Neurophilosophy: Understanding the Human Factor' in Robin Geiß and Nils Melzer (eds), *The Oxford Handbook of the International Law of Global Security* (Oxford University Press 2021) 125.

governance, based on human dignity, are the most reliable predictor of human nature at its best.[26] In consequence, for states to place the rule of law and human rights at the core of their intelligence and security policies is right not only in principle, but also from a pragmatic perspective.[27]

Similar observations apply to internationally wrongful intelligence activities targeting other states (rather than individuals). Such activities tend to aggravate the security dilemma[28] and trigger an escalation of further acts jeopardising all parties' security. As Arnold Wolfers explained as early as 1952, 'it should always be kept in mind that the ideal security policy is one which would lead to a distribution of values so satisfactory to all nations that the intention to attack and with it the problem of security would be minimized'.[29] In summary, whereas national security as a zero-sum game creates a vicious cycle, approaches to national security that comply with international law and human rights can create a virtuous cycle, with global effects.

Finally, as this book demonstrated, the likelihood of effective accountability is a determining factor in states' decision-making in the context of national security intelligence. Because intelligence activities are often considered to trump ethical and legal concerns due to the interests they seek to safeguard, this is a crucial finding in support of the national security case to respect human rights and international law. State accountability for intelligence activities in breach of international law became both a possibility and a reality in the aftermath of 9/11. This shift in international practice allowed me to theorise the model of regulation I have presented throughout this book. In this sense, international legal accountability constitutes the keystone of regulation.

The risk of effective accountability encourages states to implement effective domestic oversight of their intelligence activities. When they are effective, domestic mechanisms constitute the most efficient way to prevent and remedy internationally wrongful acts resulting from intelligence activities while avoiding public disclosures and the exposure of facts and intelligence techniques to third parties. The role of the international legal order as a regulator of states'

---

[26] ibid.

[27] The UN Charter, Article 55(c) already hinted at this: 'With a view to the creation of conditions of stability and well-being which are necessary for peaceful and friendly relations among nations based on respect for the principle of equal rights and self-determination of peoples, the United Nations shall promote: …c. universal respect for, and observance of, human rights and fundamental freedoms for all without distinction as to race, sex, language, or religion.'

[28] The security dilemma is a situation whereby 'the means by which a state tries to increase its security decrease the security of others'. Robert Jervis, 'Cooperation under the Security Dilemma' (1978) 30 World Politics 167, 169.

[29] Arnold Wolfers, 'National Security as an Ambiguous Symbol' (1952) 67 Political Science Quarterly 481, 498.

intelligence activities is thus inversely proportional to the effectiveness of domestic oversight mechanisms. This means that the regulation of intelligence activities under international law will be fully effective once there will no longer be a need for international legal accountability. The internalisation of international legal norms within domestic legal systems and oversight mechanisms will then suffice to ensure compliance.

In the meantime, the risk of effective accountability acts as a pull towards compliance because it changes the costs, payoffs, and incentives of engaging in extra-legal actions. Accountability processes publicise facts and open them to scrutiny, criticism, and backlash. In this way, state accountability acts both as a deterrent against extra-legal measures and as an incentive for compliant behaviour. In consequence, compliance with international law is increasingly in states' interest both because it constitutes the most effective response to national security threats, and because of the increased risk of accountability. The risk of state accountability thus deters counter-productive behaviour and encourages behaviour that benefits the state and serves its national security goals: compliance with international law. As a result, effective international legal accountability not only ensures compliance, it also secures adequate and effective responses to national security threats.

In conclusion, compliance with international law in their intelligence activities serves the national security interests of states. My hope is that the theoretical and empirical evidence presented in support of this claim throughout this book can contribute to changing the scholarly and political discourse on trade-offs between security and liberty, and between national security intelligence and international law. The integrated model of regulation that developed in response to post-9/11 intelligence activities should therefore not be seen as a hindrance to the achievement of national security, but rather as the means to this end. Only through a clear legal framework governing intelligence activities, an international legal order capable of enforcing state responsibility for violations of the legal framework, and responsive regulation making accountability effective will intelligence be able to fulfil its existential aim of protecting national security. The most reliable path to long-term national security is the effective regulation of intelligence activities under international law.

Index

Aamer, Shaker 241
Abaaoud, Abdelhamid 271–2, 279
Abdallah, Suleiman 205–7, 215
Abou Elkassim Britel 194
Abu Zubaydah 75, 76, 79, 204, 216–17, 219–22
accessibility of forums 182
action bias 11, 255–6
Afghanistan 80, 85–6, 87, 94, 186, 201–2, 204–5, 206, 231
African Charter on Human and Peoples' Rights (ACHPR) 214
African Commission on Human and Peoples' Rights (ACommHPR) 208, 210–14
African Court on Human and Peoples' Rights (ACtHPR) 208, 226
airspace 56–8
    Chicago Convention on International Civil Aviation 52, 54, 88, 92–3, 103, 105, 187
    war on terror, CIA-led 87, 88, 92–4, 95, 103–7, 233
Albania 106
Aldrich, RJ 19, 123
al-Alwi, Moath 192
Alzery, Mohammed 203
American Declaration of the Rights and Duties of Man 192, 193, 195
Ameziane, Djamel 192, 193–6
Amin, Mohammed Farik Bin 80
Andrew, C 42
Anti-Ballistic Missile Treaty 57
armed conflicts 46, 86, 91–2
    cyber intelligence 59–60
    definition 85
    espionage 33, 58–9
    non-international 68, 85–7
arms control treaties 34, 57–8
arrests 139, 207, 224–5, 230
    and state complicity 101–3

al-Asad, Mohammed 205, 206–7, 210–14, 215
assassination, targeted
    model of decision-making: comparative case study 268–80
Attash, Walid bin 80, 216–17
Australia 95
authoritarianism 9
Ayres, I 167

al-Baluchi, Ammar 80, 216–17
el-Banna, Jamil 224–5, 229–31
al-Barq, Samr 216–17
base-rate fallacy 255
Bashmilah, Mohamed Farag Ahmad 194
behavioural approach to compliance 250–53
    achieving compliance 280–82
    harnessing model: comparative case study 268–80
    intelligence decision-making 253–60
    model of executive decision-making 264–8
        comparative case study 268–80
    regulatory implications 260–64
behavioural economics 24, 182
Belgium 95
Bellaby, RW 12
bias(es) 25, 182, 251, 253, 255, 258, 261, 265–6, 278, 280
    action 11, 255–6
    availability 255
    direct self-serving 254
    in group 256, 259
    groupthink 254, 259
    hawkish 257, 259
    hindsight 257–8
    information-sharing 254
bilateral agreements 54

Statute of Forces Agreements
    (SOFAs) 75, 99
Bin Laden, O 20
Bin Lep, Mohammed Nazir 80
Black, C 105
Bosnia and Herzegovina 94
Bosnian Genocide 112
bounded rationality 158, 251, 252, 254,
    255, 264–5, 282
Bovens, M 133, 152
Braithwaite, J 167, 172, 175
Braithwaite, V 170–71
Brunneé, J 125–6, 133
Buchan, R 36, 38
Bush, GW 74, 75, 82, 89, 95, 259

Callamard, A 270
Cameron, I 138
Canada 95
Canaries 105
Castellanos-Jankiewicz, L 142
catharsis 152
Chestermann, S 34, 37, 57
Chicago Convention on International
    Civil Aviation 52, 54, 88, 92–3,
    103, 105, 187
China 208
cognitive psychology 24, 25, 182
Cold War 7, 34, 41, 45
    end of 6, 32, 34, 42–3
Committee against Torture (UNCAT)
    186, 193
    Djibouti 208, 214
    G.K. v. Switzerland 118
    Poland 222–3
    UK 236, 240–41, 243
    US 196–9, 203, 204
communication 171, 173
compliance 4, 22, 29, 39, 161–2
    behavioural approach 250–53
        achieving compliance 280–82
        harnessing model: comparative
            case study 268–80
        intelligence decision-making
            253–60
        model of executive
            decision-making 264–8
        regulatory implications 260–64
    capacity-building (enabling) 173
    courts: persuasive judgments 165

decision-making model 25–6
education 173
effective accountability
    as bridge between
        accountability and
        compliance 182–3
    evaluation framework 176,
        177–80
    and national security 4–5, 26, 29
    persuasion (engagement) 173
    procedural fairness 164–5, 172
    rewards 166, 176, 180
    social science and legal methods
        25–6
concluding observations of treaty bodies
    173, 196–9
conflict of interests 254
consent 51, 52, 65, 127–8, 161, 178, 186,
    208, 217, 226
    diplomatic premises 62
    legitimacy 162, 165
    as promise 162–3
    tacit 38
    war on terror, CIA-led 87, 92–3,
        101, 111
Constitutions 9
constructive knowledge 106, 107, 111,
    114, 116, 117, 207, 234
Convention on the Law of the Sea
    (UNCLOS) 52, 54
    airspace over exclusive economic
        zone 57
    high seas 55–6
Council of Europe 150, 217, 218, 237,
    273
covert action 18–21, 269
    'at home' 68
    cyber 50
    definition 18, 47–8
    formalism 35
        pragmatism and 38
    inherently prohibited 47–50
    wartime 58
Crawford, J 125
crimes against humanity 201, 202, 272
criminal law 80, 99–100, 104, 221, 243
    espionage 62
    torture 108, 110–11, 117
cultures, non-Western 42

customary international law 35, 38, 41, 69
    force, prohibition of use of 48
    non-intervention 48
    opinio juris 35–7, 41, 56, 60
    peremptory norms 104
    state practice 36, 56, 60
    state responsibility 22, 109, 118–19, 132, 143, 159, 168
    territorial sovereignty 54
    UNGA: Friendly Relations Declaration 46–7
cyber covert action
    non-intervention 50
cyber diplomatic and consular intelligence collection 61–2
cyber espionage 50, 53–4
    diplomatic or consular 62
    remote access 53
        non-intrusive 63–4
cyber infrastructure
    armed conflict 59–60
    diplomatic missions: obligations of receiving state 66
    electronic intrusion 54
        and territorial sovereignty 52, 53, 63
    privacy and data collection from foreign 67
    remote access non-intrusive 64–5

data collection, bulk 41
Deeks, A 37–8, 43–5, 263
definitions
    armed conflict 85
    covert action 18, 47–8
    enforced disappearance 89
    espionage 21
    intelligence activities 17–21
    intelligence community 21
    international legal accountability 133–4
    nodal governance 159–60
    regulation under international law 21–2
    torture 111
detention 15, 135, 139, 252–3
    extraterritorial jurisdiction: IHRL 85

war on terror, CIA-led 75, 76, 77–81, 85, 88–90, 92, 93–5
    international legal accountability 194–6, 199–200, 204, 205–8, 214, 215, 216–17, 219–22, 224–6, 230, 231, 235–6, 242
    proxy detention 77, 94, 98, 99, 119, 206, 208, 215
    state complicity 98–107, 115
deterrence 169–70, 173–5, 179, 251, 262–3
Diab, R 256–7
dialogue-based enforcement 173, 251
Diego Garcia 105, 232–3, 241, 242
dignity 12, 79
diplomatic assurances 240
    and refoulement 90
diplomatic and consular relations 52
    intelligence collection
        by receiving state 66
        underlying conduct, regulated by 61–3
    treaty law 34, 38, 54, 61–2, 66, 88, 92
disclosure 178–9
distributed denial of service (DDoS) 64–5
Djibouti 94
    international legal accountability in CIA war on terror 184–6, 244–5
        accountability network 208–10
        assessment of practice 210–16
        evaluation 210
        state responsibility 205–8
doctrinal legal methods 23
domestic courts 136–7, 235, 242, 243
domestic intelligence 65–8
domestic oversight 14, 15, 122, 134, 135–9, 144, 150, 200, 224, 237, 276
Dourad, Guled Hassan 205, 207–8
Drahos, P 167
drone strikes, lethal 41, 50, 139, 269, 270
Dubai 105
due process 88, 90, 196
    see also procedural fairness
duty to warn 67–8

effective accountability 154–5, 243–6, 261, 281
   as bridge between accountability and compliance 182–3
   evaluating accountability: framework 176
      capacity to constrain and escalate 177–80
      legitimacy 180–81
      publicity and accessibility 181–2
      international law and states' preferences, interests and motives 155–8
   model for decision-making 267–9, 270, 278–9, 280
   networked governance 159–61
      behavioural insights 161–6
   theory of 169–76
Egypt 80, 94, 105, 106, 203, 204
enforced disappearance 3, 15, 68, 82, 89–90, 91, 98, 107, 135, 206, 207, 217, 230
erga omnes
   accountability 130–32, 133, 143, 145
   obligations 125, 129, 130, 131–2, 133
espionage 32, 33, 34–7, 40, 41, 68–9
   armed conflict 33, 58–9
   criminal law 62
   cyber 50, 53–4
      diplomatic or consular 62
      remote access 53
      remote access non-intrusive 63–4
   definition 21
   diplomatic or consular 62, 63
Estonia 65
ethics 2–3, 12–13, 15, 32
Ethiopia 94
European Committee for the Prevention of Torture (ECPT) 100
European Convention on Human Rights (ECHR) 224, 237, 242
   art 3: torture 222
   art 5: liberty and security 102–3
   art 13: effective remedy 222

European Court of Human Rights (ECtHR) 219–22, 236, 237, 238, 243, 244
   burden-shifting analysis 213, 222
   immunities 243
   intelligence cooperation activities 204
   jurisdiction 84–5, 113–14, 243
   rendition, detention and torture 203, 212–13, 219–22, 223–4
   state complicity 99, 102–3
   surveillance 150
European Union 150, 180, 217, 218, 219, 273
   cooperation and development policies 173
evidence 149
   prohibition of torture-tainted 118, 149, 240
exclusive economic zone (EEZ)
   airspace over 56–7
explicitly allowed activities 55, 69
   reconnaissance 55–8
   wartime intelligence 58–60
expression, freedom of 91
extraordinary rendition 50, 74, 77–8, 88–9, 90, 92–5, 105
   international legal accountability 194, 196, 203, 205–8, 215, 216, 219–22, 224–5, 230, 232–3, 234, 235, 241
   stopover states 105–7, 232–3

fact-finding inquiries 152
fair trial
   war on terror, CIA-led 88, 91, 92, 98
fairness 156, 157, 169, 173, 174, 176, 252, 258
   procedural 161, 164–6, 168, 171, 172, 178, 180
   see also due process
Feinstein, D 71
Fikfak, V 165–6
fines 174
Fleck, D 34–5, 37, 50
force, prohibition of use of 46–7, 272, 275
   covert action 48
   territorial sovereignty 54
Forcese, C 38–9, 53, 138

formalism 14, 33, 34–7, 42, 43–5, 68, 282
  pragmatism and 37–40
framing 156, 158, 259, 262, 265–6
France 25–6, 208, 259
  model of decision-making: comparative case study 268–80
funding of accountability mechanisms 181
Furundzjia 112

The Gambia 94
  international legal accountability in CIA war on terror 184–6, 244–5
    accountability network 226–7
    assessment of practice 227–31
    evaluation 227
    state responsibility 224–6
gambler's fallacy 255
game theory 25
Geneva Conventions 86, 92
  Common art 1 110, 112, 115
Georgia 94
Germany 95
Global South 19
Grant, R 144
group polarisation 256
groupthink 254, 259
guilt 157, 161, 163

Hague Regulations 1899 and 1907 58
harbinger theory 256–7
al-Hawsawi, Mustafa 80, 192
Heuer, RJ 42
heuristics 25, 182, 251, 253, 255, 261, 265, 280
  representativeness 255, 256–7, 278
high seas 55–6
Hollande, F 271–3, 279
Hong Kong 94
Human Rights Committee (CCPR) 83, 114, 133, 186, 203
  Djibouti 208, 215
  General Comment No. 31 111
  General Comment No. 36 83
  Poland 222
  UK 236, 240, 241, 243
  US 196, 197–9, 203, 204
Hurd, I 161

immunities 54, 63, 65, 136, 145
incomplete contract 171, 172
independence of judges 181
Indonesia 80, 94
inherently prohibited activities 46–7, 69
  covert action 47–50
  territorially intrusive acts 50–54, 63
intelligence legalism 44–5, 260
Inter-American Commission on Human Rights (IACHR) 186, 191–6, 205
Inter-American Court of Human Rights (IACtHR) 191
International Civil Aviation Organization (ICAO) 187
International Committee of the Red Cross (ICRC) 75, 79, 92, 100, 208
International Court of Justice (ICJ) 131, 133, 146, 186–7, 187, 208, 236
  Bosnian Genocide 112
  diplomatic intelligence collection 61
  Monetary Gold 109, 112, 140, 143, 210, 243
  Nicaragua v. *US* 48
  Statute: art 38 21–2
  Timor-Leste v. *Australia* (Order of 3 March 2014) 66
International Covenant on Civil and Political Rights (ICCPR) 196, 198, 242
  art 7: torture 111, 203
International Criminal Court (ICC) 187, 208, 222–3, 226, 236, 273
  Afghanistan 201–2, 204–5
International Criminal Tribunal for the former Yugoslavia (ICTY)
  Furundzjia 112
  Tadic 85
international human rights law (IHRL) 7, 9–13, 14, 16, 38, 54, 269–70, 272, 275, 276
  beliefs about equality and fairness 157
  covert action 50
    'at home' 68
  diplomatic staff 63
  domestic intelligence 65, 67, 68
  drone strikes 269, 270

duty to warn 67–8
enforced disappearance *see separate entry*
exhaustion of domestic remedies 132
human targets 14, 41, 43, 50
   underlying conduct 50
   international legal accountability 122, 131–2, 133, 137, 138, 145–6, 147, 148, 149, 150, 152, 245
      compliance 173, 179
      damages 174–5
      independence 180
   jurisdiction 82–5
   negative interference by state 10
   networks of accountability mechanisms 159, 160, 164, 165–6
   obligation to protect 94, 100–101, 102, 103, 104, 105, 106, 115, 135, 207, 217, 233
   outcasting 164
   protect individuals 10, 127–8
   realist authors 41
   war on terror, CIA-led 82–5, 87, 88–91, 186, 191–6, 217
      state complicity 98, 100–104, 105, 106–19
   wartime intelligence 59
   see also individual rights, courts and treaty bodies
international humanitarian Law (IHL) 54, 186
   cyber intelligence 59–60
   distinction, principle of 60
   Geneva Conventions 86, 92
      Common art 1 110, 112, 115
   non-international armed conflict 68, 85–7
   war on terror, CIA-led 85–7, 91–2, 100, 107, 109–10, 112
   wartime intelligence 59–60
international intelligence cooperation 14, 15, 93–5, 107–19, 135–6, 204, 234–6
   intelligence sharing as internationally wrongful act 119
      demand for information 116–17
      executive use 118–19
      passive receipt 117–18
      provision 117
      sending agents to interrogate detainees abroad 113–15
   lawful and non-stigmatising practices 151
   practical limits if interstate accountability 144–5
   precautionary measures 138–9
   third-party (or operator control) rule 15, 137–8, 144
International Law Commission (ILC) 147
   Draft Articles on State Responsibility (ASR) *see under* state responsibility
international legal accountability 3–4, 15–16, 22, 27–8, 122–5, 153, 281
   basic elements 125–6
   definition 133–4
   effective accountability *see separate entry*
   forms 127–33
      erga omnes 130–32, 133
      interstate direct 130
      interstate mediated 130, 132, 140
      mediated 129, 130–31, 132
      method 129–33
      relationship 128
      standing 129
      surrogate 129, 131, 132–3
   for intelligence activities 134–5
      domestic oversight 135–9
      gaps and shared accountability 139–43
      harmful outcome 140–41
      mediated and surrogate forms 145–6
      practical limits of interstate accountability 143–5
   networked or nodal responsiveness 167–8
   objectives 146–7, 169
      enforcing international legality 147–8
      reliable intelligence 148–50
      truth, transparency and legitimacy 151–2

social science approaches to international law 23–5
standing 129, 145–6
war on terror *see* international legal accountability in CIA war on terror
international legal accountability in CIA war on terror 184–6, 243–6
  Djibouti *see under* Djibouti
  Poland *see under* Poland
  The Gambia *see under* The Gambia
  UK *see under* United Kingdom
  US *see under* United States
international legal order 3–4, 14, 24, 147, 154, 158
  conditional cooperation 157–8, 162
  networked governance 159–66
  preferences, interests and motives of states 155–8
  responsive regulation 167–9
international telecommunications law/regulations 54, 63
interrogation methods 67, 148
  war on terror, CIA-led 72–3, 74, 75–6, 77–80, 88–9, 95
    international legal accountability 194, 196, 206, 207, 208, 217, 230, 234
    state complicity 98
Iran 94
  Soleimani 273–7
Iraq 42, 85, 86, 87, 94, 186, 231, 272, 274, 277
al-Iraqi, Abd al-Hadi 80
Italy 94, 105

Japan 208
al-Jaza'iri, Abu Yasir 216–17
Johnson, LK 20
Jordan 94, 105, 106
jurisdiction
  ACommHPR 213
  aircraft: criminal 104, 105
  foreign military bases: criminal 99–100
  human rights treaties 82–5, 113–14, 115
  universal 178
jus ad bellum 270, 274–5

jus cogens/peremptory norms 82, 89, 93, 104, 107, 131
  Draft Articles on State Responsibility (ASR)
    art 40: peremptory norms 117, 142
    art 41: peremptory norms and secondary obligation 94, 107, 110, 112–13, 115, 117, 118–19, 142–3
justice
  procedural 164–5, 170
  restorative 173

Kahneman, D 257
Kasuku, J 19
Kenya 205
Keohane, R 144
Khadr, Omar 192
Khan, Majid 80
killings, extra-judicial 15, 135
knowledge 105, 109, 114, 117, 119
  CIA-led war on terror: public knowledge timeline 95
  constructive 106, 107, 111, 114, 116, 117, 207, 234

Lander, S 144
Lauritzen, P 13
Lauterpacht, H 39
law-in-context approach 25
legal positivism 23
legality 3, 22, 26–7, 68–9
  doctrinal legal methods 23
  explicitly allowed activities 55, 69
    reconnaissance 55–8
    wartime intelligence 58–60
  inherently prohibited activities 46–7, 69
    covert action 47–50
    territorially intrusive acts 50–54, 63
  paradigm shift 34, 42–5
  scholarly divide: realpolitik vs formalism 33, 68
    formalism and pragmatism 37–40
    formalist account 34–7
    realist account 40–42

underlying conduct 61, 69
    diplomatic and consular
        intelligence collection
        61–3
    domestic intelligence 65–8
    remote access non-intrusive
        cyber activities 63–5
legitimacy 170, 188–90, 254, 260
    consent and 162, 165
    effectiveness of regulation and loss
        of 175
    evaluating accountability:
        framework 178, 180–81
    independence 172, 180
    international courts and tribunals
        168
    perceived legitimacy of system 164
    political 161, 173, 175
    procedural fairness 171, 172, 178,
        180
    of the rule 162, 174
    truth, transparency and 151–2, 169
lex specialis 51, 55, 59
liberty and security of person 68, 88, 89,
    91, 98, 102, 104, 115
liberty–security conundrum 7, 9–13, 23,
    70
al-Libi, Ibn Sheikh 80
Libya 80
life, right to 68, 90, 91, 98, 104, 107,
    115, 235–6, 269
Lithuania 201, 204
lock-in effect 9
Locke, J 9
Lotus 34
Lubin, A 39–40

Macedonia 95, 203
El-Masri, Khaled 194, 203, 212–13
mediation 173
methods 22
    accountability: social science
        approaches to international
        law 23–5
    compliance: social science and legal
        25–6
    legality: doctrinal legal 23
Middle East 42, 270, 276, 278
military attachés 62

mistaken identity 139
model of decision-making 264–8
    comparative case study 268–80
Mohamed, Binyam 194
Mohammed, Khaled Sheikh 80, 216–17
Monetary Gold 109, 112, 140, 143, 210,
    243
Morocco 94, 105
multilateral agreements 54
Murphy, K 165

al-Nashiri, Abd al-Rahim 80, 204,
    216–17, 219–22
Nassar, Seitmarian 241, 242
national courts 136–7, 235, 242, 243
NATO (North Atlantic Treaty
    Organization) 74–5, 93, 99,
    103–4, 175, 180, 217–18, 219,
    237, 245, 258–9
Navarrete, I 36, 38
necessity 67, 73, 82
negotiation, integrative 173
networked governance 159–61
    behavioural insights 161–6
networked or nodal responsiveness
    167–8, 169
Ní Aoláin, F 184
Nicaragua v. *US* 48
nodal governance 159–61
nodal or networked responsiveness
    167–8, 169
non-governmental organisations (NGOs)
    167
non-intervention, principle of 34, 35, 38,
    46–7, 55, 269, 275
    covert action 48–50
    cyber 50
    diplomatic staff 63
    international dispute settlement
        communications 66
    non-intrusive remote action cyber
        activities 65
    territorially intrusive acts 50–51
    war on terror, CIA-led 92
non-refoulement 90, 91, 102, 108, 110,
    195, 206–7, 214, 217, 219, 226
non-state actors 6, 7, 13, 16, 43, 44, 45,
    68, 158
    accessibility of forums 182

international legal accountability 125, 126, 127–8, 129, 132, 145–6, 210
networked governance 165
responsive regulation 167
Northern Ireland 47
Nurjaman, Encep 80

Obama, B 195, 197, 198, 200
organised crime 11
Organization for Security and Co-operation in Europe (OSCE)
   field missions and training 173
Orwell, G 76
outcasting 163–4, 166, 169, 175, 176, 251
Outer Space Treaty 1967 55

pacta sunt servanda 161
Pakistan 94, 95
paradigm shift 34, 42–5
   'humanisation' of international law 45
   intelligence legalism 44–5
   powers of intelligence agencies 44
   public awareness 43–4
Pareto optimality 166
Pegasus scandal 11
perception of risk of accountability 263
peremptory norms/*jus cogens* 82, 89, 93, 104, 107, 131
   Draft Articles on State Responsibility (ASR)
      art 40: peremptory norms 117, 142
      art 41: peremptory norms and secondary obligation 94, 107, 110, 112–13, 115, 117, 118–19, 142–3
Permanent Court of International Justice (PCIJ)
   Lotus 34
Poland 105
   international legal accountability in CIA war on terror 184–6, 201, 203, 244
   accountability network 217–19
   assessment of practice 219–24
   evaluation 219

state responsibility 216–17
Pompeo, M 274
precautionary measures 138–9, 192, 193, 195
prisoner status of spies 58, 59
privacy/private and family life 11–12, 15, 65, 67, 68, 91, 107, 135
procedural fairness 161, 164–6, 168, 171, 172, 178, 180
   see also due process
proportionality 52, 60, 67
prospect theory (loss aversion) 258, 278
public goods 164, 176, 258
publicity 181–2

al Qaeda 42, 86

Radsan, AJ 40
rational-choice model 174–5, 250–51, 264–5
al-Rawi, Bisher 194, 224–6, 229–31
realism 6, 14, 33, 35–6, 38–42, 43, 68, 168, 282
reciprocity 6, 14, 32, 34, 43, 44, 45, 63, 166
reconnaissance 55–8
remedy, right to effective 90–91, 102, 108, 132, 235, 236, 243
rendition *see* extraordinary rendition
Renshon, J 257
reparation 90–91, 147, 148, 195, 230
representativeness heuristics 255, 256–7, 278
reputation 3–4, 123, 139, 144–5, 149, 152, 162, 166, 174, 175, 178, 179, 180, 188, 196, 198–9, 215–16, 234, 237, 243, 261–3, 264, 265, 266, 267, 268, 272, 273, 276, 278, 279
responsive regulation 167–9
restorative justice 173
rewards 166, 168, 169, 170, 172, 173, 176, 180, 251
Roach, K 139
Romania 105, 201, 204, 217
Rubenstein, J 146
rule of law 3, 7, 9, 11, 12, 30, 118, 122, 151, 218, 224, 230, 242, 256, 282
   harbinger theory 257

Russia 6

SALT I Agreement 57
sanctions 147, 161, 163–6, 167, 168–70, 171, 172, 251
    evaluating accountability: framework 177, 178, 179, 180
    pyramids of supports and 172–6
Schedler, A 123, 124, 151
Scheinin, M 83
Scott, L 18
sea
    Convention on the Law of the (UNCLOS) *see separate entry*
    passage rights of foreign vessels 131
secrecy 14, 15, 47, 122, 134, 136, 145, 152, 178, 237, 254
    need-to-know 138, 254
    plausible deniability 138
    war on terror, CIA-led 75, 77, 78, 89, 90, 94, 95, 107, 213, 215, 216, 218
self-determination 46–7
shame 147, 157, 161, 163, 164, 169
al-Shibh, Ramzi bin 80, 216–17
signalling 156, 161, 162, 168, 170, 173
Simsek, B 166
Slaughter, A-M 158
Snowden, E. 11–12
social science approaches to international law 23–5
social science and legal methods 25–6
Soleimani, Qasem 273–7, 278
sources of international law 21–2
    customary international law *see separate entry*
    UN Security Council (UNSC) Chp VII resolutions 8
South Africa 95
sovereign equality of states 66
sovereignty 35, 38, 46–7, 55, 269, 272
    airspace 56–8, 87, 88, 103
    cyber espionage 62
    cyber infrastructure 52, 53, 63
        governmental functions 64–5
    territorially intrusive acts 50–54, 63
    war on terror, CIA-led 87, 88, 92–3, 101

wartime 59
Soviet Union 32, 57
Spain 105
Sri Lanka 105
state responsibility 69, 123, 132, 168
    Draft Articles on State Responsibility (ASR) 15–16, 22, 83, 124, 128, 145, 147, 153, 159
        art 1: internationally wrongful acts 102
        art 15: composite act 141
        art 16: aid or assistance 81, 94, 101, 105, 106, 107, 109–10, 112, 113, 116, 117, 217, 233
        art 17: direction and control 98
        art 25: necessity 82
        art 33(2): non-state entities 125
        art 40: peremptory norms 117, 142
        art 41: peremptory norms and secondary obligation 94, 107, 110, 112–13, 115, 117, 118–19, 142–3
        art 42: injured states 129
        art 48: non-injured state 125, 129, 130
        Pt Three 22, 125, 130, 134, 143
stigma 147, 161, 255
sunk costs fallacy 258
support activities 168, 169, 170, 175, 251
    pyramids of supports and sanctions 172–6
surveillance 3, 11–12, 20, 41, 56, 67, 150, 252–3
    arms control treaties 34
    evidence from unlawful 149
Sweden 95, 203
Syria 94, 272, 279

Tadic 85
Tallinn Manual 2.0 59–60
    cyber espionage
        changes/deletes data: delivery of government function 63–4
        remote access cyber intelligence activities 53, 63–4

underlying conduct 53–4, 64
Tanzania 95
targeted assassination
    model of decision-making:
        comparative case study
        268–80
Tenet, G 76
territorial integrity 7, 38, 46–7, 51, 293
territorially intrusive acts 50–54, 63
    wartime 58
terrorism 7–11, 13–14, 15, 34, 42, 72, 135, 149, 259, 270
Thailand 75, 95
theology 42
third-party (or operator control) rule 15, 137–8, 144
Timor-Leste v. *Australia* (Order of 3 March 2014) 66
torture 3, 15, 131, 133, 135, 136, 139, 252–3
    Committee against (UNCAT) 186, 193
        Djibouti 208, 214
        G.K. v. *Switzerland* 118
        Poland 222–3
        UK 236, 240–41, 243
        US 196–9, 203, 204
    Convention against 106–8, 111–12, 114, 115, 117, 233, 236, 242
        art 3: refoulement 110, 214
        art 4: complicity 110–11, 115, 116, 117
        art 15: evidence in proceedings 118
    and cruel, inhumane and degrading treatment 67, 68, 78, 88–9, 91, 98, 111, 112, 205, 207, 231
    peremptory norm 82, 107, 112–13
    reliability of intelligence 75, 79–80, 148–50
    war on terror, CIA-led 71, 72–3, 75, 76–7, 78, 88–9, 91
        international legal
            accountability 194–5, 196–9, 201, 203–4, 205–8, 210, 217, 219–23, 230, 231, 234–6, 240–41
        state complicity 98, 100, 102, 104, 106–19
trading privileges 175
transboundary harm 64
transnational corporations 167
transparency 15, 44, 122, 136, 151–2, 218, 223, 241
Trump, D 274–9
trumped-up cases 139
trust 166, 171, 173
truth commissions 152, 195

Ukraine 6
UN Charter 103–4, 187
    art 2 46–7, 48, 66, 88, 275
UN General Assembly (UNGA) 133, 146
    Friendly Relations Declaration 35, 46–7, 49
    Resolution 36/103 47, 49
UN Human Rights Council (HRC) 186, 191, 199, 244
UN Security Council (UNSC) 237, 258–9
    Chp VII resolutions 7–9
        (1373) 8, 14, 135
UN special mandate holders 173, 186, 199–200, 215, 223, 230, 241–2, 243
UN Special Rapporteurs
    extrajudicial, summary or arbitrary executions 230
    human rights and counter-terrorism 184
undercover agents 52
underlying conduct, regulated by 61, 69
    diplomatic and consular intelligence collection 61–3
    domestic intelligence 65–8
    remote access non-intrusive cyber activities 63–5
United Arab Emirates (UAE) 95
United Kingdom 19, 86, 95, 105
    Intelligence and Security Committee 77–8, 224–5, 231, 232, 233, 234, 236, 241, 242
    international legal accountability
        in CIA war on terror 184–6, 230, 244, 245
        accountability network 236–8
        assessment of practice 240–43

evaluation 238
state responsibility 231–6
United States 19, 25–6, 57, 148, 217, 259
  9/11 attacks 6, 7, 13–14, 34, 42, 81–2
  Bin Laden, killing of 20
  covert action
    definition of 47
  habeas corpus 197
  international legal accountability in CIA war on terror 184–6, 230, 237, 244, 245
    accountability network 186–91
    assessment of practice 191–205
    evaluation 188–91
    state responsibility 186
  model of decision-making: comparative case study 268–80
  war on terror, CIA-led *see separate entry*
universal periodic review (UPR) 173, 199, 215, 223, 242, 243

van Aaken, A 155, 157, 163, 164, 166, 176
Venice Commission 103, 150
Vienna Convention on Consular Relations (VCCR) 62, 66, 88, 92
Vienna Convention on Diplomatic Relations (VCDR) 61–2, 66

war on terror, CIA-led 6, 14, 23, 25, 43, 69, 70–73, 119–20, 150, 259
  applicable legal framework 81–2
    human rights 82–5
    international humanitarian law 85–7
    interstate obligations 87–8
    rights and obligations affected 88–93
  factual and policy background 74–7
  international legal accountability in CIA war on terror *see separate entry*
  rights and obligations affected 88–93
    enforced disappearance 89–90, 91
    international humanitarian law 91–2
    interstate obligations 92–3
    liberty and security of person 88, 91
    non-refoulement 90, 91
    other human rights 91
    rights to remedy and reparation 90–91
    torture and cruel, inhumane and degrading treatment 88–9, 91
  secret detention and extraordinary rendition 77–81
    high-value detainees (HVDs) 78–9, 202, 208, 216–17
  state complicity 93–7
    cooperation in arrest, detention and transfer into CIA custody 101–3
    hosting CIA black sites 99–101
    intelligence sharing with CIA 107–19
    stop, refuel and fly through national airspace 103–7
    taking custody of CIA detainees (proxy detention) 98
warn, duty to 67–8
Warner, M 17, 21
wartime intelligence 58–60
World Health Organization (WHO)
  country cooperation strategy 173
World Trade Organization (WTO) 163
Wright, Q 58–9
Wyler, E 142